Liquidate: How Money is Dissolving the World

Alf Hornborg

Routledge
Taylor & Francis Group
LONDON AND NEW YORK

First published 2025
by Routledge
4 Park Square, Milton Park, Abingdon, Oxon OX14 4RN

and by Routledge
605 Third Avenue, New York, NY 10158

Routledge is an imprint of the Taylor & Francis Group, an informa business

British Library Cataloguing-in-Publication Data
A catalogue record for this book is available from the British Library

ISBN: 9781032679969 (hbk)
ISBN: 9781032702179 (pbk)
ISBN: 9781032702186 (ebk)

DOI: 10.4324/9781032702186

Typeset in Sabon
by codeMantra

Liquidate: How Money is Dissolving the World

li-quid-ate [*'lIkwIdeIt*] VERB
1. convert into cash 2. dissolve, destroy

Liquidate: How Money is Dissolving the World examines the emergence of money and its social and ecological repercussions. It views money as a new phenomenon in the evolution of life that has fundamentally transformed ecosystems and human social relations.

The appearance of coined money around 600 BCE coincided with the first abstract philosophies and religions. This book shows how changes in human–environmental relations have reflected changes in social relations generated by money. The detached modern view of nature mirrors the socially detached modern individual. However, the abandonment of animism has not diminished the human propensity for fetishism – the perception of artefacts such as money tokens as indexes of what they represent. Market prices obscure the asymmetric global resource transfers that make increasingly advanced technologies possible where there is enough money. Our fetishised understandings of money and technologies cannot deal with the escalating production of entropy underlying climate change. They also drive the dramatic reduction of biological and cultural diversity under globalisation. Given these problems, many people reassess premodern and indigenous societies in search of more sustainable ideas on how to organise exchange.

Liquidate: How Money is Dissolving the World will be of interest to scholars working in anthropology, sociology, economics, history, semiotics, comparative religions, and indigenous studies.

Alf Hornborg is an anthropologist and Professor Emeritus of Human Ecology at Lund University, Sweden.

In memory of David Graeber, the most creative and boundless of minds

Contents

Acknowledgements

For a book as wide ranging as this one, the perspectives and suggestions from colleagues in a variety of disciplines have been invaluable. I am indebted to several people who have agreed to comment on drafts of various chapters. All of them have improved the text, but the responsibility for any remaining shortcomings is mine alone. For extensive and incisive comments on selected chapters, I am particularly grateful to Kaj Århem, Keith Hart, Kalevi Kull, Desmond McNeill, Jason Nesbitt, Susan Paulson, and Darryl Wilkinson. I have also benefitted from chapter perusals by Stefan Arvidsson, Sigurd Bergmann, Brett Clark, Steve Gudeman, Yogi Hendlin, Anne-Christine Hornborg, Andrew Jorgenson, Mikael Kurkiala, Thomas Malm, Max Pieper, Ariel Salleh, and Frank Salomon.

At Routledge, I am indebted to Katherine Ong, who has supported my project from the start, and to Yuga Harini, whose editorial assistance has been exemplary.

The following chapters are in part based on articles published or in press elsewhere:

Chapter 1: *Biosemiotics*, published online July 19, 2023
Chapter 3: *De Gruyter Handbook of Degrowth* (2024), edited by Lauren Eastwood and Kai Heron
Chapter 4: *Contributions to Political Economy*
Chapter 5: *Ecological Economics* 214 (2023): 107997; *Technology & Philosophy*, published online February 9, 2024
Chapter 6: *Oxford Encyclopedia of Climate Science*, published May 22, 2024
Chapter 7: *Kritisk etnografi: Swedish Journal of Anthropology* 6(1): 23–31 (2023); *Globalizations* 21(5): 990–1008 (2024)
Chapter 10: *Sustainability Science*, published online April 18, 2024; *HAU: Journal of Ethnographic Theory* (2024)

Introduction

There is a growing apprehension that modern civilisation is heading towards disaster. Although inconceivable to most people, we are being pushed towards global collapse by an idea. It is the idea that everything can be exchanged for anything else. Money may seem innocent and is even widely celebrated as the greatest invention ever made by humankind, but in the space of a geological second it has come to threaten the entire biosphere. We have used money for less than 1% of human history. It is unique to our species – it is also uniquely transformative and uniquely destructive. This book traces the roots and ramifications of the idea of generalised commensurability.

The denunciation of money has been voiced so many times over the course of history that it may seem unnecessary to add anything to it. Ever since the first coins were minted in the Aegean area around 600 BCE, countless philosophers, theologians, and social theorists have deliberated on what money is and how it harms human relations to each other and to the world. This book is not an attempt to provide an overview of such deliberations. It is, rather, an effort to understand why money remains a mystery even for economists, and why current alarms about global disasters tend to circumambulate the role of money as the very driver of catastrophe. The argument is twofold. On the one hand, it aims to show that money indeed is the primary cause of the human predicament in the Anthropocene. On the other hand, it attempts to account for the ways in which it tends to escape our attention. If the social and ecological repercussions of money can be shown to be in the process of making the Earth uninhabitable, why does the denunciation of money seem trivial or even provoke ridicule? Why do innumerable reports documenting the alarming course of climate change and ecological degradation hardly ever mention money? These are complex issues that require us to shift between the perspectives of different disciplines. Given the interdisciplinary nature of the discussion, it is inevitable that some readers will find certain parts of it too elementary while other parts may be difficult to digest.

I realise that the topic of each chapter would deserve to be expanded into a separate book, but that would counteract my aim of bringing together perspectives on money from very different fields. The current fragmentation of

DOI: 10.4324/9781032702186-1

perspectives on the human predicament is central to our dilemma. It is well captured by Vaclav Smil:

> I tend to think about modern scientists as either the drillers of ever-deeper holes (now the dominant route to fame) or scanners of wide horizons (now a much-diminished group). Drilling the deepest possible hole and being an unsurpassed master of a tiny sliver of the sky visible from its bottom has never appealed to me. I have always preferred to scan as far and as wide as my limited capabilities have allowed me to do.[1]

I have been fortunate to work in the interdisciplinary field of human ecology, which in my view is the closest thing in Swedish academia to what in the United States is called 'four-field anthropology.' All the topics in this book, though diverse, should be accessible to a four-field anthropologist: semiotics, the history of civilisation, animism, fetishism, unequal exchange, the cultural construction of technology, ecological Marxism, climate justice, globalisation, loss of cultural diversity, ethnogenesis, the archaeology and ethnohistory of the prehispanic Andes, indigenous identities, phenomenology of place, experiments with local money.... Drawing on these diverse topics has required an embarrassingly long and heterogeneous bibliography. Hopefully it can serve as a guide to further reading. In this introduction, I shall briefly outline – chapter by chapter – the main course of the argument. It thus also serves as a general synopsis of the book.

*

To begin with, we must think of money in an evolutionary context. How can we account for its appearance, quite recently, in the history of our species? This is the topic of Chapter 1, which introduces Part I, dealing with the semiotics of money fetishism. The ability to think of different things as interchangeable abstractions is possible only for a human brain. The perspective of semiotics – the study of signs – helps us understand how humans and other living beings attach meanings to things in their environments. The exchange and interpretation of signs is fundamental to any ecosystem, as when an animal detects another animal or plant by recognising its scent, sound, or flavour. Evolution has equipped animals and plants with the capacity to emit and to interpret – that is, to communicate – such signs of their existence. This is arguably the very foundation of ecosystems. What makes humans special is that they have developed semiotic capacities that go beyond those of other animals.

The first and most obvious way in which human communication differs from that of other animals is their ability to use symbols. Symbols are signs that have meanings that a society or group of people agree on. The best example is language, but all cultural sign systems are based on symbols. A symbol – like a word, a gesture, or a prestigious artefact – signifies something that is recognised within a particular society or group, such as a concept, an emotion, or a social position. The symbol does not evoke what it refers to in any other way – for example by being similar to it – than through cultural agreement, so its features seem to have an arbitrary relation to what it means. This element of arbitrary cultural agreement makes it unique to humans, giving our species the ability to develop diverse ways of behaving and organising social relations that may strengthen feelings of common identity but are increasingly detached from processes of natural selection.

Money represents another step in this liberation from ecological constraints. Although emerging from symbolism, the modern money sign is not in itself a symbol, because there is no social agreement on what it should refer to; it can be given any meaning that its owner wishes. From an evolutionary perspective, money is thus a completely new kind of sign. This observation is an important point of departure for the rest of the book. It has momentous implications for the impacts of human social processes on the rest of the biosphere, for how we think about those impacts, and for how we imagine that they might be alleviated.

*

Chapter 2 traces the historical emergence of money and how it has shaped how we think about ourselves, the universe, and economic value. From the third millennium BCE, there are documented concerns in Mesopotamia with quantitative equivalences between weights in silver and wool, volumes of grain, surface areas of fields, and even human labour. Already 5,000 years ago, in other words, notions of 'value' were abstracted from the diverse material properties of different commodities. It is particularly significant that labour could be conceived as having an abstract exchange-value, reflected not only in the prices of slaves but also in wages based on workloads. Silver became a convenient measure of value in such economic transactions, initially as a unit of account and later as the substance of coins. Over the millennia, precious metals have continued to be treated as intrinsically valuable. In ancient Greece and Rome, silver was closely connected to warfare and slavery, as it was used to pay mercenaries in wars to capture slaves, some of whom ended up working in the silver mines. Money posed a philosophical conundrum to Aristotle, whose misgivings about its social repercussions reverberated through the centuries via St. Paul and Thomas Aquinas to Karl Marx.

As Richard Seaford has shown, the adoption of coined money in several parts of the world during what Karl Jaspers called the Axial Age (800–200 BCE) appears to have fundamentally transformed not only social relations but also how humans thought about their own selves in relation to the cosmos. This cognitive shift had profound existential and spiritual implications, as it reframed the role of abstractions in human life. It meant a break with the way people had previously thought of the world. People in pre- and non-modern societies tend to experience moral principles and forces as immanent in the things that surround them, a worldview traditionally referred to as 'animism.'

Abundant ethnographic evidence indicates that people in such societies are inclined to perceive the various components of their environment, including those that moderns would classify as inanimate, as sentient subjects with intentions and agencies that need to be reckoned with. The uncertainties of human life – from failures in hunting to being struck by disease – are attributed to refractory agencies in the environment that must be appeased through gifts and proper behaviour. The delicate deliberations that guide humans in navigating social life are extended to the non-human environment.

This understanding of the human condition was largely transformed in the commercial civilisations. The social and human–environmental relations that emerged in the Axial Age – and more decisively during the European Enlightenment – were conducive to a 'disenchantment' of the world in the sense that subjective agencies were relegated to a transcendent domain. This left the empirical world – reality accessible to the senses – devoid of moral sensibilities that might constrain human action. The expansion of money as a dominating force in social life thus coincided with a loss of concern about morally compelling forces in nature. It also seems to have been conducive to the emergence of philosophies and religions concerned with abstract notions of human transcendence. Chapter 2 begins to unravel how these concurrencies could be explained, but the relation between money and disenchantment is a theme to which we return throughout the book.

It may seem paradoxical or even offensive to denounce the artefact that many historians have celebrated as foundational to the progress of civilisation, but my point is not to rate these developments as unequivocally 'good' or 'bad.' It is, rather, to take stock of what we know about the trajectory of human society and where it appears to be taking us. Regardless of how highly we value the myriad achievements of human civilisation, its prospects of respecting the biophysical boundaries that constrain its existence in the early 21st century seem increasingly slim. If this alarming global predicament ultimately derives from our obsession with the idea of money, there are good reasons to subject that idea to closer scrutiny.

*

Animism – the tendency to attribute intentions and agency to nonhumans – appears to have been a part of the repertoire of our species for hundreds of thousands of years. In sharpening our attentiveness to unpredictable environments, it enhanced our capacity to adapt to a great variety of habitats around the globe. For post-Axial Europeans, however, such a blurring of distinctions between subjects and objects has been dismissed as a cognitive error – a mistaken projection of human subjectivity onto non-human things. When documented among indigenous, non-European peoples with whom they came into contact, many European colonisers condescendingly classified such perceptions as ignorance and superstition. A classic discussion of this divergence between European and non-European worldviews is Charles de Brosses' 1760 text on *fetishism*.

Chapter 3 explores the semiotics of fetishism. In the 18th century, the term was used ethnocentrically by Europeans to distinguish what they perceived as African magic and idolatry from European religion. It signified the delusions of people who worshipped their own creations. In psychiatry, the term fetishism has been used for sexual attachment to an inanimate object or a body part. In the history of religion, it has referred to faith in an amulet or idol that is perceived as the seat of a metaphysical being. As de Brosses emphasised, fetishes are not just taken to *represent* metaphysical beings but *are* such beings. Similarly, as Karl Marx incisively observed, objects that are contingent on social relations may be perceived as autonomously powerful or productive. Marx thus challenged Eurocentric condescension by claiming that modern money and commodities are also examples of fetishism. His classic definition of fetishism is that social relations between people are represented as relations between things.

Using the terms of semiotics, we can say that fetishism is founded on an indexical mode of reference. Indexes are signs that indicate the presence of what they refer to. Although a money token such as a banknote is ultimately just a piece of paper that *represents* economic value, that piece of paper *is* simultaneously the value that it represents. It is not simply a representation referring to something – in this case value – through social agreement, but an indexical sign signifying the actual identity of what it refers to. The difference between indexical and other modes of reference can have significant implications for how artefacts are handled. Unlike personal tally-sticks or gifts symbolising social relations, money invites both hoarding and theft.

There seems to be a pervasive tendency among human societies to transform representations into indexes. Objects that symbolise social relations or transcendental ideas tend to become identified with those relations and ideas. Like the famous shell valuables that were traded between islands in the *kula* trade of premodern Melanesia, money fetishism illustrates how our preoccupation with artefacts tends to deflect our attention from the social relations that they represent.

*

Marx's critical analyses of capital in 19th-century Britain reflected on how money had the power to dissolve traditional social relations and generate deep social injustices. He showed how the exchange of labour time for wages is mystified as reciprocal and fair, because money serves as a veil that hides unequal transfers between social groups. Similarly, we can now show, market prices mystify the unequal global trade of other biophysical resources such as embodied land, materials, and non-human energy. This is referred to as ecologically unequal exchange. Such asymmetric resource transfers are necessary for the growth of technological infrastructures in the nations, regions, and cities that can afford such growth. Although organised and mystified by the abstract language of money, capital accumulation is a material process that concentrates the products of embodied labour, land, materials, and energy in increasingly powerful technologies. Modern technologies are thus unthinkable without money. Chapter 4 introduces Part II, which focuses on how money organises flows of matter and energy. It explores how the veil of market prices obscures unequal global flows of biophysical resources.

The Marxian perspective has critically revealed the role of money in generating social inequalities and unsustainable rifts in social metabolism. It is nevertheless constrained by a 19th-century outlook on 'value': rather than seeing that the very idea of economic value is a notion defined by the artefact of money – that is, a measure of how much money a commodity will fetch – it maintains that money attempts to represent an objective but invisible quantity of value based on what Marx called 'socially necessary labour time.' The Marxist framework is also constrained by its view of technological progress as a development that will benefit all humankind, rather than a result of capital accumulation, exploitation, and economic inequalities. In both these ways, classic Marxist theory remains mired in 19th-century political economy. Its critique of the 'capitalist system' finally deflects our attention from the fundamental idea of general commensurability that is inscribed in money.

In the 19th century, abstract economic concepts of 'labour-power' and 'value' emerged in tandem with the conceptualisation, in physics, of 'energy.' Like money and value, the concept of energy is an abstraction that obscures the specific contexts that it transcends. It refers to natural forces that can be harnessed by different technologies, regardless of whether they derive from forests, waterfalls, winds, sunlight, or minerals. Much as labour-power is conceived as the animating force of society, energy is understood as the force animating nature. It is not a coincidence that labour and energy theories of value are very similar, claiming that there are objective values that derive from specific inputs in production. Marx's concept of labour-power is ambiguously placed at the boundary between economics and physics, sometimes explicitly equated with energy.

The modern translation of all elements of nature and society into abstract exchange-values works like a veil that makes us ignorant about the biophysical aspects of the world economy. Looking at the world through the lens of market prices, we tend not to see the material transfers and transformations that they organise. In hindsight, we are now aware of the extent to which the transition to fossil energy in colonial Britain was entwined with a systematic displacement of both workloads and environmental loads to its dependent peripheries. Slave labour and inexpensive plantation land overseas were essential to the accumulation of steam technology in the 19th-century cotton industry. However, unequal transfers of embodied labour and land were obscured and normalised by the economic idiom of market prices.

*

The implied connection between such asymmetric transfers and technological progress is another example of fetishism. Chapter 5 explores the conundrum of technological fetishism. The thought that the rising productivity of labour in industrial metropoles is accomplished at the *expense* of their peripheries is generally as unthinkable to Marxists as it is to mainstream economists. It has nonetheless been shown that industrialisation in mid-19th-century Britain involved a massive net appropriation of embodied human time and natural space from its overseas periphery. Yet, the phenomenon of technology is generally imagined as independent of its global context. Technical artefacts are thus as fetishised as other commodities, but the view that they are *autonomously* powerful or productive lingers on among mainstream economists and Marxists alike. The accumulation of technological infrastructure tends to be seen as an *extra-social* process in the sense that it is understood as representing the progressive and intrinsically innocent harnessing of natural forces. Our deeply ingrained habit to distinguish between nature and society keeps us from seeing how entangled they are in technology.

Technological progress is widely invoked as a magical wand that applies politically neutral engineering to nature. This Promethean myth is illustrated by the energy transition that occurred during the Industrial Revolution, in which the uneven advantages of ecologically unequal exchange and environmental load displacements were transmuted into the seemingly neutral concerns of economic rationality and engineering. Although both markets and machines are hybrid phenomena that span the conceptual divide between nature and society, our dualist worldview has classified economy as belonging to society and technology as pertaining to extra-social nature. Fields such as ecological economics are demonstrating that the economy necessarily also implicates nature, but our worldview is even more resistant to the converse fact that technology – in being contingent on global exchange rates – implicates *world society*. Because it is contingent on money, modern technology is an inherently distributed phenomenon, saving time and space for some at the expense of time and space lost by others.

Although most of us now acknowledge the adverse impacts of fossil energy technologies on climate and global ecology, there is a general trust in technological salvation beyond hydrocarbon-based modernity. It is assumed that various post-carbon technologies will replace fossil fuels without significantly constraining per capita energy use in the global North. Decarbonisation is understood as an engineering challenge detached from geopolitical asymmetries. However, transitions to low-carbon energy technologies and other forms of climate mitigation tend also to involve global environmental injustices of various kinds. A central challenge for transdisciplinary theory in the Anthropocene is to understand how such tendencies may be inherent in the technological systems that are promoted by the world market.

My main point in Chapter 5 is that the production and operation of technological artefacts are imbued with economic rationality. They should not be conceptualised as distinct from the global organisation of society. This distributive dimension of markets and technologies becomes apparent as we aim to abandon the fossil energy regime. We discover how our seemingly neutral concepts of energy and technology may obscure global processes of appropriation of human labour time and natural space. Such processes are as insidiously inscribed in low-carbon energy technologies as in the fossil-fuelled technologies that they are intended to replace. To see these pervasive injustices as inherent in technologies, we must acknowledge the social essence of technical artefacts. This in turn requires a deep transdisciplinarity that links physics, industrial ecology, the philosophy of technology, social theory, world trade, the history of ideas, and several other fields.

*

Our inability to see the globally *distributed* conditions of modern technological progress is particularly problematic as it afflicts our ways of dealing with global warming. This is discussed in Chapter 6. Since the late 1980s, critical theorists have increasingly addressed the relation between capitalism and environmental degradation, including climate change. Many environmentalists and ecosocialists have criticised classical Marxist theory for celebrating the intensification of technological productivity and ignoring environmental issues. Responding to such charges, 'ecological Marxists' such as Paul Burkett and John Bellamy Foster have been intent to show that the theoretical framework conceived by Marx and Engels is quite attuned to ecological concerns. In reviewing their classical texts, however, the eco-Marxists have unwittingly exposed some fundamental obstacles to an environmentally attuned Marxism. A central problem is the contradiction between a materialist or ecological theory of value and the Second Law of Thermodynamics, also known as the Entropy Law. Whether focusing on inputs of labour-power or energy, such theories of value neglect the dissipative character of any production process. While there is no way of deriving economic value from inputs of energy or labour in production, there is an inevitable correlation between rising value and increasing *entropy*, that is, physical disorder. Economic growth must accelerate the production of entropy, such as greenhouse gas emissions.

Climate change has become a prominent concern in eco-Marxist literature, but it raises doubts about classical Marxist views on technology and production. The problem with capitalism appears to be much more fundamental than who owns the means of production. The chapter argues that the Marxian critique of exploitative social relations and capital accumulation must ultimately confront money itself – and the industrial technologies that it makes possible. A genuinely materialist understanding of global warming since the Industrial Revolution would recognise the accumulation of fossil-fuelled technology in wealthier parts of the world-system as resulting from ecologically unequal exchange. Such asymmetric resource transfers, driven but also obscured by market prices, have simultaneously aggravated global inequalities and greenhouse gas emissions contributing to climate change.

*

Chapter 7 introduces Part III of the book, which deals with how money affects experience, social relations, and culture. It begins by considering the role of money in producing the social condition we refer to as 'modernity.' European sociologists in the 19th and early 20th centuries witnessed rapid changes in human social life as great numbers of people moved into cities. The increasing interaction with strangers promoted a detachment from familiar social contexts, a trust in abstract systems such as money, and a generalisation of sociability that is cognate to the market's generalisation of exchange. The general commensurability of goods and services that are exchanged on the market implies an abstract concept of economic value. To offer goods and services for sale is to conceptualise them as independent of specific contexts. Engagement in commercial exchange is thus conducive to abstract ways of thinking, that is, the elimination of specific details in order to apply more general concepts and perspectives.

It is often observed that the globalising and decontextualising logic of the market promotes homogenisation. The ongoing reduction of biological diversity is paralleled by similarly alarming reductions of cultural diversity. Chapter 7 explores these parallels. Money has rapidly transformed the operation of ecological and evolutionary processes. Whereas the general history of life on Earth has increased the diversity of species over the long term, repeatedly rebounding after five earlier periods of mass extinction, the ecological consequences of the modern world economy represent a sixth extinction event, drastically reducing biodiversity.

Parallel to the unprecedented rate of species extinction during the past few centuries, there has been a rapid loss of cultural diversity. This is most clearly documented in linguistics. There are formal analogies between biological speciation and the historical proliferation of languages as well as between the currently accelerated loss of both species and languages. In part, these parallels can be attributed to similar mechanisms. The modern inclination towards homogeneity is as evident in monocultures in agriculture and forestry as in the cultural hegemony of Hollywood, supermarkets, and fast-food restaurants, all of which can be traced to the logic of money. Diametrically opposed to such drives towards uniformity are biodiversity 'hot spots' with high numbers of endemic species, conspicuously often in areas with high cultural and linguistic diversity. This geographical correlation of biological and cultural diversity indicates that such areas have remained relatively unaffected by the homogenising impacts of money. It reflects the inclination of small, marginalised languages to encode locally specific ecological knowledge, as in ethnobiological classification systems.

In this sense, cultural diversification can be seen as related to the biological adaptation of populations of organisms to their specific environments. However, the tendencies towards diversification of species and languages are generally driven by quite different processes: whereas the former assumes an originally shared spectrum of genetic variation that is subjected to divergent selective processes, the latter frequently involves human groups actively accentuating their ethnolinguistic distinctness vis-à-vis each other. Rather than drawing assumptions about the drivers of diversification from biological models of speciation, linguists can build on anthropological perspectives recognising that cultural diversity reflects interaction rather than isolation. This is illustrated by an outline of the history of language use among indigenous peoples in Amazonia and the Andes. In both regions, the expansion of colonial and commercial interests has radically reduced the scope for maintaining indigenous ethnolinguistic identities. However, the cultural history of South America suggests that it is not impossible to combine the social integration of extensive geographical areas with continued ethnolinguistic diversity. This is exemplified by the Inca Empire, which actively maintained ethnic diversity within its boundaries. The issue pivots on the extent to which people are encouraged to cultivate two separate spheres of social life, provisionally called the 'local' and the 'global.' This should be an essential consideration in deliberations on how humankind might curb the logic through which cultural diversity is being dissolved. It would require that we acknowledge how economic processes tend to lead to social and ecological homogenisation and that we envisage possible ways of safeguarding and enhancing diversity. The maintenance of cultural diversity is feasible only if local contexts of identity- and meaning-creation are granted a certain measure of autonomy.

*

Chapter 8 takes a closer look at the Inca Empire, as it is the only major civilisation that has organised a vast territory and a massive population without the use of money. It represents a unique experiment in social organisation that provides insights on the conditions for, and the consequences of, a society without money. The reason for the absence of money was the suppression of entrepreneurial trade by the Inca elite, who monopolised the long-distance procurement of prestigious valuables through state-controlled specialists. Although inadvertent, a consequence of this policy was that local, kin-based communities (*ayllu*) were comparatively autonomous vis-à-vis the state. They were relatively protected from external exploitation, accumulation, and impoverishment and generally emphasised local egalitarianism, democracy, and social welfare. Their autonomy also promoted economic resilience and cultural diversity. Unlike the conditions in other premodern civilisations, Inca policy blocked the transformation of prestigious ornaments from emblems of rank into impersonal money objects. The Spanish invasion after 1532 introduced conceptions of the economic value of precious metals that were very different from traditional Andean cosmologies. This shift again illustrates how symbols are transformed into indexes, which is a common denominator of different kinds of fetishism.

The indigenous people encountered by the Spaniards in the Central Andes were animists, attributing agency to what the Europeans considered lifeless things. For theorists of the Axial Age, they were clearly pre- or non-Axial. Given Seaford's proposal that there is a connection between Axiality and money, it is significant that the Andeans did not use money. Animism can be seen as an expectation of balanced reciprocity between humans and nature. It has been suggested that animism is an extension of social relations to nature. The introduction of money tends to change social expectations from balanced to 'negative reciprocity.' If human–environmental relations reflect social relations, a society using money can thus be expected to generate experiences of nature that are very different from those of animists. Chapter 8 concludes by suggesting that this may be a way of accounting for the relations between money, Axiality, modernity, and disenchantment. With the Spanish conquest began the historical process through which the fetishism of money increasingly eclipsed indigenous animism.

*

Closely related to issues of cultural diversity and non-modernity is the concept of 'indigenousness' or 'indigeneity.' Indigenous people are thought of as the antithesis of modern people – and indigenousness as diametrically opposed to modernity. Beyond the complex modern politics surrounding indigenous identities, the concept refers not to biological ancestry but to cultural worldviews, particularly as they relate to social and human–environmental relations, sustainability, and money. Parallel to the colonial and commercial expansion of Europe over the past few centuries runs the history of indigenous, non-European others who continue to represent alternative and more sustainable ways of organising human societies. Chapter 9 examines the distinction between modern and indigenous, and its relation to money. A common denominator of the many observations on the ecological sensibilities of indigenous people appears to be their *embeddedness*: their rejection of abstraction and the decontextualising forces of money. Another way of expressing this is their commitment to a specific *place*.

The debate on 'the ecological Indian' that engaged many historians and anthropologists over three decades – most intensely from the late 1970s to the late 2000s – reflects a genuine concern about alternative ways of organising human–environmental relations. This concern continues to pervade social and environmental debate. Many environmentalists praise indigenous peoples as guardians of 'traditional ecological knowledge,' which might help us become more sustainable. A more profound aspect of what is being referred to as indigenous ecological wisdom, however, is the inclination to maintain a close attachment to place. Such attachment is conducive to the kind of *relational* ontologies that Edward Tylor disparaged as animism.

*

Given that the idea and artefact of money can be shown to be a source of so many aspects of the current predicament of humanity, we may seriously consider whether it might be feasible to mitigate some of these problems by modifying its design. At the risk of being dismissed as a 'social engineer,' I present such a utopian thought experiment in Chapter 10. Rather than expecting social movements such as the climate movement or the labour movement to circumvent globalisation and push national politicians to rectify the ills of capitalism, as if the responsible agent were an abstract 'system' to be overturned, we need to understand the extent to which human behaviour is shaped by the everyday artefacts through which we live our lives. This insight should prompt us to reconceptualise politics as largely a matter of how our artefacts are designed. It should also lead us to see that the destructive obsession of the world economy with growth is ultimately not generated by how mainstream economists think, but by the artefact – all-purpose money – that *shapes* how they think.

A corollary of the fact that we can trace so much of our ecological, social, cultural, and existential predicament to the fetishised artefact of general-purpose money should be that many of our problems could, in principle, be alleviated by deliberately constraining its dissolvent logic. Instead of systematically dismantling constraints on generalised commensurability, as is the aspiration of mainstream neoliberal economics, a policy for greater sustainability and global justice would rather acknowledge and reinforce *distinctions* between different kinds of values. Such distinctions were pervasive in the many premodern economies that anthropologists call 'multicentric.' Applied to the modern context, it might mean recognising the incommensurability of local resources for subsistence, on the one hand, and products of advanced research and engineering – such as medical and information technologies – on the other hand. Rather than blurring the boundary between them by making them interchangeable on the world market, a nation could in principle decide to establish separate spheres of exchange for the two types of values, each with its own currency. By issuing a special-purpose, complementary currency that can only be used to purchase goods and services produced within a specified radius from the point of purchase – and distributing it to all the nation's inhabitants as a universal basic income – such a reform would encourage a compartmentalisation of 'local' versus 'global' transactions. It could be expected to radically reduce long-distance transports, greenhouse gas emissions, and economic vulnerability, while enhancing economic, ecological, and cultural diversity as well as local resilience and cooperation. In many ways, it would lead in the same direction as advocated by the burgeoning movement for *degrowth*. Indeed, it is difficult to see how degrowth could be achieved without redesigning money.

In thus concluding the book with a utopian vision of how money could be transformed, this final chapter suggests a way of thinking about how humankind might transcend the impasse of the Anthropocene. If the expansion of the world market can be reassessed as nothing short of a semiotic self-destruction of the biosphere, human efforts to redesign money to promote sustainability could be understood as the biosphere – through the agency of humans – aiming to rectify an evolutionary detour and taking control over its own future.

Note

1 Smil 2022: 9.

Part I

The semiotics of money fetishism

1 The empty sign

Money is a sign – a vehicle of communication. Like other kinds of signs, it organises relations. Some kinds of signs have been essential to the interaction of animals and plants since the beginnings of ecosystems. The signs known as *indexes* refer to things or beings to which they are directly connected, like the song of a bird or the scent of animal tracks. The signs we call *icons* are in some way similar to that which they refer to, like the patterning of an animal mimicking another species or making it indistinguishable from its background. Indexes and icons have been part of ecological and evolutionary processes for hundreds of millions of years. A mere few hundred thousand years ago, humans developed the capacity to use a third kind of sign: the *symbol*. The meaning of a symbol hinges on a general agreement in a group or society. In other words, its reference to something is based not on connection or similarity but *convention*. The human capacity for symbolic communication is best illustrated by language, but it is fundamental to all cultural phenomena. These are the three basic kinds of signs recognised in the field of semiotics since it was founded by the American philosopher Charles Sanders Peirce.

Merlin Donald suggests that the first two major transition periods in hominid cognitive evolution – the emergence of human species over two million years ago and that of *Homo sapiens* in the past 300,000 or 400,000 years – roughly correspond to the stages he calls 'Mimetic' and 'Mythic.'[1] In semiotic terms, the two stages represent cumulative advances in communication based on iconic and symbolic modes of reference, respectively.[2] Examples of mimetic action include body-language, gesturing, imitation, pantomimes, reduplication of prior events, and rehearsing and refining one's skills. Mimetic behaviour is fundamental to ritual and theatrical activities, cultural conformism, various forms of art and crafts, and many other aspects of social life. Central to what Donald calls the mythic stage is the emergence of language and narrative thought, which presuppose the use of symbols.

For most of human existence, symbolism has been an asset for our species, promoting its capacity to adapt to a variety of habitats around the planet. A few millennia ago, however, the early civilisations of Mesopotamia began using a sign that was neither index, icon, nor symbol.

DOI: 10.4324/9781032702186-3

This new kind of sign is money.[3] Money initially took the form of weights of precious metals, grains, or other materials that were used as measures of exchange-value, but around the sixth century BCE the first stamped coins appeared in the Aegean area, China, and India. The novelty of money tokens is that they can be given any meaning that their owners wish.

The past few millennia of human history are very much the history of money. Its essence is the idea of exchange-value: an imagined, abstract equivalence between two or more unlike things. As we shall see in the next chapter, the propensity to abstract – to conceive of general categories that are detached from the tangible details of specific contexts – has propelled the emergence of new religions, philosophies, and ultimately sciences. It has been fundamental to the global history of civilisations, trade, technologies, production, and environmental change. The alarming predicament of the Anthropocene prompts us to critically reconsider the various repercussions of abstraction for human cognition, worldviews, social identities, economic processes, and ecological systems.

Signs of life

The argument in this chapter is based on the general conviction, shared by the fields of bio- and ecosemiotics,[4] that living systems are no less constituted by flows of signs and meanings than by flows of matter and energy. But first we must acknowledge that biomass at any scale, from the organism to the biosphere, must comply with the Law of Entropy. It must ingest greater quantities of high-order matter-energy than it discharges – and subsist on dissipating the difference. This also applies to what I have called the 'technomass' of human society.[5] The global technomass continuously produces vast and increasing volumes of disorder, to the detriment of the atmosphere, the oceans, and the diversity of non-human life. Unlike the metabolic processes of organisms, the disorder generated by the technomass degrades the conditions for life and reduces biodiversity. In order to grasp these destructive material trajectories, we must reconsider the semiotic agency of the human species.

There is widespread agreement that signs occur only in living systems, which means that Peirce's controversial suggestion that 'the universe may be composed exclusively of signs' was exaggerated.[6] Deliberations on the operation and properties of signs can be traced back to the identification of medical symptoms in ancient Greece. Distinctions between 'natural' signs and communicative signs (most centrally words) go back at least to St. Augustine around AD 400. Over the centuries, it was acknowledged that words tend to be arbitrary signs whose meanings derive from conventions. Focusing on linguistic signs, Ferdinand de Saussure proposed that all signifiers have arbitrary relations to their signifieds. Peirce established a general typology of signs based on how a signifier relates to its signified, whether through contiguity (index), similarity (icon), or convention (symbol). Whereas linguistic signs are generally symbolic and arbitrary human constructions, indexical and iconic signs occur throughout all living systems. Peirce's framework thus extends beyond human language to all communicative processes.

Although apparently unaware of Peirce's work, the Estonian zoologist Jakob von Uexküll developed a semiotic approach to ecology, realising that the interaction of organisms in an ecosystem is contingent on their subjective perceptions of their environments.[7] Uexküll called an organism's subjective world its *Umwelt*. The Danish biochemist Jesper Hoffmeyer applied Peirce's semiotic framework to biological processes even at the level of cells.[8] Whether concerned with linguistic, ecological, or biochemical processes, all these contributions refer to communicative relations in living systems. As Sebeok reminds us, '[i]t is important to realize that only living things and their inanimate extensions undergo semiosis, which thereby becomes uplifted as a necessary, if not sufficient, criterial attribute of life.'[9] Sebeok writes:

> When it comes to questions of phylogeny, I have always contended that the emergence of life on earth, some 3.5 billions of years ago, was tantamount to the advent of semiosis. The life science and the sign science thus mutually imply one another.[10]

The identification of semiotic phenomena with animateness – and the concomitant distinction between living and non-living matter – is crucial. The neglect of this distinction explains some of the confusing assertions of so-called Actor-Network Theory (ANT).[11] Bruno Latour has blurred the boundary between living and non-living 'actants' by equating signification with agency:

> Signification is a property of all agents, in that they never cease to have agency; this is equally true of [Tolstoy's Marshal] Kutuzov, the Mississippi, the CRF [corticotropin releasing factor] receptor, and the gravity through which bodies 'comprehend' and mutually 'influence' one another. [...] In other words, existence and signification are synonyms. *As long as they are acting, agents signify*.[12]

What Latour is really saying is the converse: 'As long as they are signifying, they are agents.' This is a distortion of semiotics, suggesting that to signify is to act and that every conceivable entity in the universe – living or non-living – thus can have agency simply by existing. But merely to be perceived – or even to exert the physical power of the Mississippi or the gravitational pull of astronomical bodies – are not examples of agency comparable to the purposive activities of living beings, because being perceivable or having physical forces are merely properties of matter. In contrast to the notion of agency promoted by ANT, semioticians following Hoffmeyer have defined agency as 'the ability of an organism to act in order to fulfill needs.'[13] Unlike rivers, planets, volcanoes, or hurricanes, organisms have needs and purposes honed by natural selection, and natural selection presupposes a genetic code to work on. Genetic codes, nervous systems, and consciousness are all part of the 'code duality' of living systems.[14] In cybernetic approaches to cognition, too, the recursive relation between inner representation and external environment defines the 'autopoiesis' of living systems.[15] The anthropologist Eduardo Kohn has criticised Latour and other post-humanists for not acknowledging the difference between 'selves and objects,' observing that only the former use signs to 'represent the world in some way or another.'[16] Similarly, in response to Stanley Salthe's suggestion that even tornadoes involve rudimentary semiosis, Hoffmeyer objects that they do not exhibit 'the kind of digital analog translational dynamics which characterize all kinds of life.'[17]

This is not to deny that it is difficult to identify the exact threshold between animate and inanimate. Like Hoffmeyer, Sebeok asserts that '[s]igns, inclusive of indexes, occur at their most primitive on the single-cell level, as physical or chemical entities...'[18] At the level of organisms, semiosis is indistinguishable from perception. What happens when an organism perceives some feature of its environment is usefully expressed by Gregory Bateson in terms of 'a difference that makes a difference [to somebody].'[19] The term information should be reserved for the relation between a perceiving subject and whatever it perceives. It is not a quantity that is located in the objective world.[20] A contrast or 'difference' in the environment is requisite to perception. According to semioticians, it is only when a contrast or difference in the environment is interpreted by the organism as signifying something, perhaps prompting a response, that it becomes information. As Hoffmeyer suggests, '[a] sign is not the same thing as a piece of information, but [...] only becomes "information" through an act of interpretation.'[21] He continues:

> In biology [...] information is not the kind of non-contextual concept it is in information theory. Biology mostly operates on an instructionist conception of information, and in the end this conception makes the transport metaphor of information – the flow or passing of information – quite illegitimate.[22]

The perceived 'difference' in an organism's environment can derive from three distinct sources: the inanimate environment; some inadvertent signs of another organism; or purposeful communication between organisms.[23] All three kinds of semiosis presuppose an interpreting subject, but only the last requires two interacting subjects deliberately exchanging signs. The question is, at which point is it reasonable to assert that biochemical processes at the cellular level are examples of semiosis, that is, involve an interpretant?

Hoffmeyer's efforts to reveal semiotic processes at the biochemical level raise questions about the applicability of Peirce's triadic model (sign – object – interpretant) to the interaction of molecules.[24] In his pursuit of connections between the objective and the subjective aspects of existence, Hoffmeyer has explored the boundary zone between molecular processes and sentience. He argues that '[b]io-molecules are (nearly) always carriers of signs [...] and their function in the organism cannot be understood simply through an analysis of their chemistry.'[25] In explaining and applying Bateson's distinction between analogic and digital coding, Hoffmeyer asserts that genetic codes are based on symbolic signs: 'Digital codes are [...] necessarily based on symbolic signs (in the Peircean sign taxonomy), whereas analogic codes are based on icons and/or indexes.'[26] Observing that genetic codes are digital, he proposes that the molecular processes through which DNA is replicated involve symbolic reference:

> [The] invention of symbolic reference is in no way uniquely human. The potential of symbolic reference has been exploited by the life process as long as it has been based on the replicative sign systems of DNA and RNA molecules.[27]

As we shall see, this is difficult to reconcile with Hoffmeyer's own concessions about the uniquely human capacity for symbolic reference and with the predominant anthropological definition of symbolism. To alleviate the contradiction, Hoffmeyer distinguishes between 'endosomatic' and 'exosomatic' symbolic reference,[28] but the very idea of endosomatic symbolism, to most anthropologists and the human sciences in general, remains a contradiction in terms. He argues that the semiotic process in which a gene participates is 'neither based on similarity nor on immediate physical causality, but on a conventional (or historically appearing), regular connection...'[29] In excluding two of Peirce's three modes of reference (iconic and indexical), Hoffmeyer is compelled to conclude that genetic replication is based on symbols. As this conclusion seems incompatible with Peirce's own conception of the symbol, the impasse can only be resolved in one of three ways: by reconsidering either the premise that genetic replication is an instance of semiosis, or the denial that it is based on indexical or iconic reference, or the assumption that there are only these three semiotic alternatives.

The pairing of molecules in DNA is indeed at the very threshold between inert and animate matter, but even if it is to be understood as a rudimentary form of semiosis, it cannot serve as an example of symbolic reference. While convincingly demonstrating how semiosis can emerge from inert matter, Hoffmeyer's contribution should be understood as illuminating the transition to life and sentience rather than imputing embryonically communicative properties to molecules. To trace continuities between non-living and living matter is not tantamount to demonstrating that features of the latter are immanent in the former.

Although qualified by Sebeok, Peirce has asserted that a sign 'is either an *icon*, an *index*, or a *symbol*.'[30] It is widely held that indexical and iconic signs are logically and chronologically antecedent to symbols, and many scholars in the humanities are convinced that only humans regularly use symbols, most prominently illustrated by language. Hoffmeyer observes that 'simple iconic and indexical forms of semiosis are widespread in nature, whereas symbolic reference is a much more restricted kind of semiosis which may perhaps be the privilege of a few big brained animals.'[31] At one point, he suggests that the capacity for symbolic reference is unique to humans, and he appears to agree with the neurobiologist Terrence Deacon that, under natural conditions, only humans are able to communicate by means of symbols.[32] Deacon has proposed that the emergence of the capacity for symbolism and language can be traced in the evolution of the human brain, as evident in the fossil record.[33] Although he does not equate symbolism and language, Sebeok similarly concludes that the growth of brain volume in early hominids reflects the expansion of linguistic competence.[34] The evolution of the human species has pivoted on its semiotic and communicative capacities, which have had momentous repercussions throughout the biosphere. As Elizabeth Kolbert reflects,

> [w]ith the capacity to represent the world in signs and symbols comes the capacity to change it, which, as it happens, is also the capacity to destroy it. A tiny set of genetic variations divides us from the Neanderthals, but that has made all the difference.[35]

Drawing on Peirce, Deacon argues that the relationship between the different kinds of signs (that is, modes of reference) is hierarchical, so that 'indexical reference depends upon iconic reference, and symbolic reference depends upon indexical reference.'[36] He asserts that '[s]ymbolic relationships are composed of indexical relationships between sets of indices and indexical relationships are composed of iconic relationships between sets of icons.'[37]

This Peircean way of thinking about the relations among the three kinds of signs seems unnecessarily complex. If indexical signs relate to their referents through contiguity and association, examples should include the scent, sounds, or tracks of an animal as well as the aroma or flavour of a plant. It is difficult to see why such indexical signification, which must have been elementary foundations of ecological relations since the dawn of life, should require 'iconic relationships between sets of icons.'[38] If iconic signs, on the other hand, relate to their referents through similarity, ecologically relevant examples should include the camouflage patterning of various species, selected for as a means of *avoiding* signification/perception by predators, as well as mimicry, which may deter potential predators by falsely signifying disagreeable properties that the organism does not possess.

The symbolic species

The most controversial of the three modes of reference is the symbol. Deacon suggests that in order for symbolic reference to be possible, indexical associations between signs and referents must be abandoned in favour of associations between the signs themselves, which is the essence of language and cultural imagination.[39] While anthropologists following Leslie White tend to hold that symbols are peculiar to humans,[40] Sebeok asserts that none of the three kinds of signs is 'criterial of, or unique to, humans.'[41] He proposes, for instance, that when honey-bees conduct their 'dancing' movements (to communicate the location of a food source) on a vertical surface, as opposed to a horizontal, the signification is symbolic rather than indexical.[42] Citing the biologist Francois Jacob, Sebeok asserts that the capacity of organisms to form symbolic concepts 'obtains far down in phylogenesis,' and declares that 'animals undoubtedly do have symbols.'[43] However, none of the examples provided by Jacob or Sebeok illustrate symbolism in the anthropological sense. Jacob notes that '[e]ven a rodent can learn to distinguish a triangle from a square or a circle and to associate shape with its quest for food,'[44] but such learning merely illustrates what B.F. Skinner called 'operant conditioning,' the capacity to indexically associate a geometrical shape with food. Indeed, Sebeok in passing suggests that the 'conditioned reflex' of a Pavlovian dog associating the sound of a metronome with food qualifies as an 'arbitrarily paired symbol.'[45] Sebeok's other examples include arbitrary 'tail work' in dogs, cats, horses, and primates as well as the arbitrary nature of a gift offered by certain male insects to females prior to copulation.[46] Again, the arbitrary relationship between signifier and signified does not suffice to identify symbolism, as neither mammalian tail posture nor insect mating behaviour are signs arrived at through social agreement.

The disagreements concerning the occurrence of symbolism thus appear to derive from the ambiguous ways in which it is defined. On the one hand, following Saussure, the symbol is often defined in terms of an 'arbitrary' relationship between sign and referent. On the other hand, the criterion provided by Peirce is that the relationship is exclusively 'conventional.' While seemingly equivalent, as both can be opposed to modes of reference based on contiguity or similarity, the two criteria are not completely congruent. It is possible to argue, for instance, that a particular signifier relates to its signified neither through contiguity nor similarity, although its use cannot be said to derive from a convention. The ambiguous relation between the two ways of defining symbols is illustrated by Hoffmeyer's claim that the coupling of molecules in DNA is 'arbitrary or based on a historically established "convention."'[47] A digital code, he writes, is based 'in part on discontinuities between its constituent signs, in part on an arbitrary (conventional, generally historical or customary) relation between the sign and the signified.'[48] A convention is understood by anthropologists as a cultural phenomenon based on social custom or agreement. The essence of symbolic codes such as languages is that they are socially negotiated. When 'convention' is more loosely defined as habitual behaviour or even biochemical regularities, regardless of whether the regularity or habit has been formed through social agreement, many kinds of repetitive animal behaviour and even biochemical processes could be classified as symbolic. We have seen how this has led Sebeok to propose that insects are capable of symbolic behaviour. Sebeok's application of Peirce's framework is not entirely consistent, however: at one point, he reminds us that a symbol, in Peirce's view, rests on 'intellectual operations.'[49] Neither Hoffmeyer's identification of symbolic signs in DNA molecules nor Sebeok's claim that insects use symbols thus seems compatible with Peirce's original conception. Followers of Hoffmeyer have defined 'symbol' as 'a sign that refers to its object by virtue of a general (rule- or law-based) habit, or by virtue of a convention,'[50] but if 'habit' can mean any regular or repetitive juxtaposition of two physical, chemical, or biological elements, the momentous significance of symbolic reference – as elaborated, for instance, by Deacon – is completely lost.

To be compatible with Peirce's original definition and with general usage of the term 'symbol' in the humanities – as a sign the meaning of which is based on social agreement – the concept of symbolic reference should be restricted to cultural and linguistic phenomena. To concede that the symbol is a 'higher' and more complex mode of reference than the index and icon is difficult to reconcile with the claim that it occurs among insects and molecules. To the extent that Sebeok and Hoffmeyer have identified sign processes among insects or molecules that cannot be classified as involving either indexical or iconic reference, it would seem more productive to propose some additional category of sign, rather than to adopt the concept of symbol and give it a new and controversial definition. As Deacon has observed, symbolic reference has immeasurably widened the scope for semiotic creativity. In making it possible for humans to create representations that have no empirical referents, it is the foundation for language, abstract thought, and fantasy.[51] The recent addition of symbolism to the global 'semiosphere'[52] has had tremendous repercussions for all life on Earth. It accounts for the emergence of culture out of nature (the biosphere) through transformations in its modes of semiosis. Contrary to suggestions that the distinction between nature and culture is merely an idiosyncrasy of modern Westerners,[53] the dividing line can be analytically identified as separating those processes that are completely unaffected by symbols, on the one hand, from those that are to some extent contingent on them, on the other hand. This means that, prior to the emergence of symbolism a few hundred thousand years ago, there was only nature; it also means that very little of the current biosphere has escaped the influence of culture.

The semiotics of money

The most convulsive product of the human imagination is undoubtedly money. Yet, although a very peculiar kind of sign with cataclysmic global consequences, money is rarely recognised as a semiotic phenomenon. There is, for instance, hardly a mention of money in Sebeok's classic introduction to semiotics[54] or in Hoffmeyer's wide-ranging deliberations on the role of signs in living systems.[55] Given the current predicament of the Earth System, we urgently need to focus our attention on money and recognise it as a species of sign over which its human creators have lost control, and the destructive semiotic logic of which is permeating the entire biosphere.

As semioticians generally recognise, the evolution of life has generated a hierarchy of increasingly complex modes of reference currently culminating in symbolism and language. If Sebeok's and Hoffmeyer's discoveries of arbitrary sign use at the 'lower' end of this semiotic hierarchy might suggest adding a category to Peirce's typology, modern money arguably qualifies as a new and unique form of sign at the opposite end. Money is obviously a sign, but it does not fit into any of the three categories established by Peirce, as it does not refer to a specific commodity either through similarity, contiguity, or convention.[56] Market transactions *momentarily* involve the reference of money to commodities, but there is no persistent connection between a sum of money and a particular commodity or service. The essential property of all-purpose money is rather its capacity to adopt almost any meaning that its owner attributes to it. In this sense, it is a sign devoid of a referent. Yet, it is perceived as pure value and universally coveted. The perception of money tokens as embodiments of supreme value is a cultural and thus semiotic phenomenon.

Money is not a symbol referring to something through social agreement, but an index signifying the actual identity of what it refers to: 'value.' Economic value is an abstract idea emerging from and reinforced by the artefact of money. Any theory of value ultimately derives from habits of thought that are engendered by the artefact of money. Instead of reiterating the customary idea that money is a representation of value, we must invert the relation between signifier and signified and conclude that the very *concept* of value refers to money. To gain reflexive distance to the phenomenon of money we must be prepared to defamiliarise the notion of value and ask what the sign 'value' stands for. As we shall see, it is as deliberately vague and uncommitted as the word 'freedom,' which might well serve as its synonym.[57] It shares with symbols a contingency on social convention, but rather than specifying a particular reference, the convention it embodies is the delegation to individuals of the licence to let their money refer to whatever they wish.

The unprecedented dissociation of money from gold, materiality, and production has had formidable reverberations in the sphere of culture theory since the early 1970s, inspiring Jean Baudrillard's deliberations on the postmodern 'autonomy of the signifier' and the 'political economy of the sign.'[58] Two hundred years prior to this recent detachment from matter, the generalised commensurability promoted by all-purpose money had generated a colonial world-system that coalesced into the Industrial Revolution at its core. In integrating a global system of highly asymmetric transfers of material resources, money brought huge volumes of embodied labour, land, energy, and materials to late 18th-century Britain, converging in technologies for harnessing fossil energy that in turn reinforced accumulation. The generalised pursuit of money drove new and accelerating global resource flows, abetted by the new technologies. Central to this seemingly inexorable logic of resource dissipation is the inevitable correlation between monetary value and physical disorder. Economic production processes simultaneously increase exchange-values and entropy.[59] Such is the algorithm which drives the metabolism of the modern technomass, the waste products of which are saturating the atmosphere and the biosphere. This kind of waste is not just a semiotic, cultural category, as the anthropologist Mary Douglas proposed.[60] It is an incontrovertibly material phenomenon that reorganises the conditions of life on Earth. However, it is ultimately a product of semiotic processes – the emergence of a new kind of sign with momentous consequences for the ecological systems into which it is introduced. As a sign system generated by life but threatening to destroy the conditions of life, all-purpose money is clearly a biosemiotic phenomenon that deserves urgent attention.

Karl Marx recognised the infatuation with money as a species of *fetishism*. Although both money and fetishism are topics that have generated voluminous discussions elsewhere, remarkably few semioticians have applied their conceptual tools to illuminating them. A semiotic analysis of fetishism can succinctly capture the conundrum that has preoccupied generations of culture theorists since Charles de Brosses in 1760 deliberated on the professed difference between African magic and European religion.[61] Sebeok devotes a chapter in his book *Signs* to 'Fetish Signs,' but considers the phenomenon almost exclusively in the sense that it has been used in clinical psychiatry: as sexual attachment to an inanimate object or body part.[62] In psychiatry, fetishism has been approached as a disorder or 'deviation' whereby the fetishised object is detached from its original context, often in the form of synecdoche (a part substituting for the whole), and indexically associated with sexual gratification. There is brief mention by Sebeok of the semiotics of commodity fetishism as evoked by Marxist approaches to political economy,[63] but the semiotics of money appear not to have advanced much beyond Georg Simmel's classic *The Philosophy of Money*.[64] There have been sporadic attempts to apply semiotic perspectives on money, but they tend to be entangled in deliberations on particular aspects of economic history,[65] framing the specific politics of money in semiotic terms rather than approaching the appearance of money as a general, evolutionary event with repercussions cascading through the semio-/biosphere. Much as fetishism in both the history of religion and psychiatry has been diagnosed in terms of category mistakes, Marx's notions of money fetishism and commodity fetishism were similarly intended to denote semiotic errors.

As Uexküll realised, the flows of matter and energy in ecological systems have always been contingent on flows of signs. The environmental histories of ecosystems can be narrated in terms of the semiotic flows that have organised them over time.[66] It is possible to show how different kinds of signs produce different ecological consequences. Up until the arrival of humans, ecosystems and the biosphere had only experienced the organising potential of indexical and iconic signs. Jointly, these two modes of reference had generated an increasingly complex biological diversity. The proliferation of new species and ecological niches was an essentially semiotic process, reflecting the evolutionary emergence of new varieties of perception and communication based on indexical and iconic reference. The constitution of pre-human ecosystems was exclusively founded on the exchange of sensory signs, including auditory, olfactory, visual, and tactile signals between and within species. The arrival of humans introduced symbolic reference and language, emergent new forms of perception and communication that contributed to the transformation of many ecosystems. Symbols did not replace the operation of the other two modes of reference but added to and in some ways transcended them. Linguistic communication permeated ecosystems through cultural schemas such as ethnobiological classification systems, animistic metaphorisations of human–environmental relations, and food taboos. Finally, money and money-based economic signals, while ultimately products of symbolic imagination, overtook language in terms of transformative potential. Whereas human–environmental relations mediated by sensory and linguistic communication in some instances have been shown to enhance biological diversity,[67] economic sign systems everywhere tend to pose a threat to biodiversity. From an evolutionary perspective, the emergence of new forms of semiosis has thus reached a point where it no longer increases diversity but undermines it.[68]

It can be argued that the capacity for symbolism is complicit in the destruction inflicted on the biosphere by money, because without symbolic signs there would be no money. Nevertheless, we must acknowledge that humans have engaged each other and their environments through symbolism for hundreds of thousands of years without posing a threat to the biosphere. What triggered the Anthropocene was not symbolism but general-purpose money.

Money is not in itself a symbol but presupposes symbolic reference much as symbols presuppose indexical reference. It qualifies as a new species of sign based on its exceedingly open mode of reference. It does not refer to any object by convention but owes its specific properties precisely to the absence of such conventions. The message conveyed by the money sign is an imputation of maximum *freedom* to the recipient: the freedom to interpret the message in any conceivable way, which means converting it into whatever resources or services its owner desires. Related to this semiotic novelty is another peculiar feature of modern money: it is a sign system with only one character. Unlike digital codes such as DNA molecules, alphabets, or musical scores, the money system has a single digit. It thus cannot compose and convey instructions or any other form of meaningful messages. The money sign is unique in lacking both a referent and a code. It is an emergent phenomenon in the semiosphere that has fundamentally transformed the logic of communication in living systems. The challenge for an ecosemiotic approach to money is twofold: to understand how such a sign has emerged in the evolution of the biosphere, and to account for its impacts on ecology and diversity.

Hoffmeyer has suggested that the evolution of life on Earth has entailed a growth in what he calls 'semiotic freedom,' defined as 'the depth of meaning an individual or a species is capable of communicating.'[69] He chose to use the word 'freedom' to indicate that semiosis has become less and less determined by the constraints of natural law, which does support my contention that the replication of DNA molecules is too constrained by the laws of chemistry to qualify as a symbolic process. Over the course of evolution, Hoffmeyer shows, the sign has increasingly detached itself from its signified. He indicates that this split is the ultimate source of mind/matter dualism.[70] Indeed, the influence of symbolism is what justifies the analytical distinction between 'social' and 'natural' aspects of phenomena. We have seen how the emergence of symbolic reference and human culture illustrates the dissociation of sign from signified. The money sign is clearly a further step in the same direction. Symbolic thought and language have endowed humans with the freedom to construct their own imaginary worlds, but these have generally been collectively embraced through cultural conventions. If deployed by individuals in a completely idiosyncratic – that is, asocial – manner, symbolic reference may be perceived by the remainder of society either as divine inspiration or insanity. The uniqueness of the money sign is that it explicitly and deliberately detaches itself from the constraints of convention, encouraging individuals to interpret it as freely and idiosyncratically as they wish. In practice, of course, many factors influence people to spend their money in certain conventional ways, but *in principle* they are free to follow their own idiosyncrasies. Viewed as an aggregate global phenomenon, the only regularity that we can expect in monetary flows is that their expansion correlates with accelerating entropy.

It is often acknowledged that centuries of globalisation have reduced both cultural/linguistic and biological diversity.[71] As Claus Emmeche observes, '[w]hat looks like increased "semiotic freedom" so to speak, becomes in fact increased uniformity and a standardization of nature.'[72] In listing eight 'key principles of ecosemiotics,' Timo Maran and Kalevi Kull declare (as Principle 4) that '[h]uman symbolic semiosis (with its capacity of de-contextualization) and environmental degradation are deeply related.'[73] Having traced the emergence of the money sign to the human capacity for symbolic reference, we turn now to how it is connected to globalisation, decontextualisation, and loss of diversity.

Fundamental to all semiotic inquiry is the insight that meaning is contingent on *context*. Over billions of years of evolution, semiosis has driven diversification and speciation by calibrating the genetic codes of organisms with their specific ecological contexts. However, the past six centuries of human history have been characterised by the diametrically opposite logic, closely tied to the ramifications of money: evolutionary success has been geared to being *independent* of context. In various ways, this tendency preoccupied the major social theorists of modernity in the 19th century, whose reflections were succinctly synthesised in Anthony Giddens' concept of 'disembedding.'[74] Drawing on Simmel and other theorists of money, Giddens demonstrates the central role of money in generating the social conditions of modernity.[75] Karl Polanyi, too, focused on the fundamental transformation of society brought about in 19th-century Britain by all-purpose money and the 'disembedded' market.[76] Whether we refer to its systemic repercussions as 'capitalism,' 'modernisation,' or 'globalisation,' the logic of money has pivoted on decontextualisation. Commodity fetishism, cosmopolitan personalities, and universalising knowledge production all have this in common: they presuppose and encourage the capacity of exchange-values, people, and concepts to detach themselves from the particular and the local. Whereas premodern semiosis tended to enhance embeddedness in local contexts, modernity and globalisation have favoured mobility, interchangeability, and abstraction. In the idiom of political economy, this is to observe that 'exchange-values' have become hegemonic at the expense of 'use-values.' As Baudrillard has shown, use-values are semiotically determined.[77] Exchange-values, in contrast, are quantitative and prone to digitalisation.[78]

The expansion of money and the global market has transformed the selective pressures shaping the formation of both social and ecological systems. Chances of survival are no longer primarily about calibration within ecological or local contexts but may increasingly be a matter of transcendence or emancipation from the specific. The logic of selection in the modern, globalised world benefits both cultural and biological generalists. As I shall argue in Chapter 7, the organisms, objects, and thoughts that are most likely to spread are those that are least dependent on context. This drift towards decontextualisation is ultimately a corollary of what must be seen as a new mode of reference in the history of life: a (money) sign that liberates interpretants to imagine its referent as they fancy, almost without constraints. The uniqueness of the money sign is that it does not communicate any indication of what it might refer to, whether through contiguity, similarity, or convention. This level of semiotic freedom appears to represent a threshold where its repercussions no longer generate increasing diversity but rather the opposite: accelerating entropy. It is the point at which freedom from constraints shades into chaos. Paradoxically, the sign that most historians and not least economists celebrate as the epitome of human progress is simultaneously the root of the global ecological crisis that threatens us, along with innumerable other species, with extinction. At this point in history, further progress must mean acknowledging the semiotic basis of the Anthropocene predicament and assuming control over our own semiosis. As Per Aage Brandt observes, '[w]e may have to discuss the possibility of "sustainable symbolization" and, thus, of the sustainability of money as such.'[79] He pertinently asks, 'Can money be changed into something less pervasive and destructive?'[80]

A semiotic perspective on money might focus on how it relates to context, difference, and entropy. It is a sign, invented by humans, that neglects all contexts, recognises no differences, and conveys no other message than to reward activities that inevitably increase entropy. Its logic reverses the evolution of complexity and diversity throughout the planetary biosphere. Ironically, the thrust of this evolutionary process has for several billion years been a struggle *against* entropy by generating ever more complex layers of 'difference that make a difference.' The challenge confronting humankind is whether to allow money fetishism to mindlessly continue to dismantle such differences, diversity, and complexity, or to assume responsibility for the sign that was to serve us but has become our master. Can money be *redesigned?* We shall explore this question in Chapter 10; suffice it to say here that the dissolvent logic of money might be curbed by recognising more than one currency and distinguishing between them as referring to separate spheres of value, separate functions, and separate scales of geographical reach. It would mean inscribing difference and sensitivity to context in the sign system through which we engage each other and the remainder of the semiosphere. In investing intentions in the design of our currently vacuous monetary signs, it would signify a crucial advance in semiotic agency. It would finally comply with Roy Rappaport's profound insight:

> If evolution, human and otherwise, is to continue humanity must think not merely *of* the world but on *behalf* of the world of which it is a very special part, and to which, therefore, it has enormous responsibilities. … Humanity, in this view, is not only a species among species. It is the only way the world has to think about itself.[81]

Notes

1 Donald 2012.
2 Jung 2012: 83.
3 Donald (2012: 64–71) identifies developments during the so-called Axial Age (800–200 BCE) – to be discussed in the next chapter – as significant parts of what he calls the 'Theoretic' stage in human cognitive evolution, in which external representational technologies are developed, including currencies, writing, mathematics, and records of trade.
4 Nöth 1998; Kull 1998; Hornborg 2001b; Hoffmeyer 2005; Emmeche *et al.* 2002; Maran and Kull 2014; Maran 2020.
5 Hornborg 2001b.
6 Sebeok 1994: 14.
7 Uexküll [1940] 1982.
8 Hoffmeyer 2005.
9 Sebeok 1994: 6.
10 Sebeok 1994: 114.
11 Latour 2005.
12 Latour 2017: 69–70, emphasis in original.
13 Emmeche *et al.* 2002: 26.
14 Hoffmeyer 1996.
15 Maturana and Varela 1987.
16 Kohn 2013: 7, 9.
17 Hoffmeyer 1998: 465–466.
18 Sebeok 1994: 68–69.
19 Bateson 1972: 423–440.
20 Gare 2020.
21 Hoffmeyer 2005: 421.
22 Hoffmeyer 2005: 428.

23 Sebeok 1994: 78–79.
24 Hoffmeyer 1996, 1998.
25 Hoffmeyer 2005: 421.
26 Hoffmeyer 2005: 102, my translation.
27 Hoffmeyer 2005: 332–333, my translation.
28 Hoffmeyer 2005: 333.
29 Hoffmeyer 2005: 333, my translation.
30 Peirce cited in Sebeok 1994: 68.
31 Hoffmeyer 2005: 424.
32 Hoffmeyer 2005: 20, 329.
33 Deacon 1997.
34 Sebeok 1994: 124.
35 Kolbert 2014: 258.
36 Deacon 1997: 74.
37 Deacon 1997: 75.
38 There is disagreement among semioticians about whether the logical sequence should be icon-index-symbol or index-icon-symbol; Ding 2016; Kull 2019.
39 Deacon 1997: 69–101.
40 White 1940. Some anthropologists are not as unequivocal on this point, as when Philippe Descola (2013: 184) writes that some animals can produce a 'limited symbolic system.'
41 Sebeok 1994: 20.
42 Sebeok 1994: 33.
43 Sebeok 1994: 36.
44 Jacob 1974: 319.
45 Sebeok 1994: 121.
46 Sebeok 1994: 36.
47 Hoffmeyer 2005: 106, n 63, my translation.
48 Hoffmeyer 2005: 110, my translation.
49 Sebeok 1994: 65.
50 Emmeche *et al.* 2002: 30.
51 Hoffmeyer 2005: 335.
52 Hoffmeyer 1996.
53 Latour 1993; Descola 2013. Descola's (2013: 85) explicit 'rejection of dualism' is valid only as the observation that a nature/culture divide is not universally recognized in the worldviews that he reviews; it does not invalidate the *analytical* distinction between those aspects of reality that do not presuppose human society and symbolism, on the one hand, and those that do, on the other. To identify the repercussions of symbolic modes of reference – for example, in human bodies, landscapes, and climate change – is an incontrovertible, empirical matter, not a matter of cultural worldview. It is not more of an ethnocentric projection than the distinction between 'interiority' and 'physicality' (Descola 2013: 116) that organizes Descola's typology of ontologies.
54 Sebeok 1994.
55 Hoffmeyer 1996.
56 Hornborg 1999, 2016: 39.
57 This relation between money (value) and freedom is fundamental to Simmel's ([1900] 1990) insights in *The Philosophy of Money*.
58 Baudrillard [1972] 1981, [1976] 1993.
59 Georgescu-Roegen 1971.
60 Douglas 1966.
61 Morris and Leonard 2017; see Chapter 3.
62 Sebeok 1994: 93–104.

63 Sebeok 1994: 95.
64 Simmel [1900] 1990.
65 For instance, Brandt 2017; Oakley 2023.
66 Hornborg 2001b.
67 See, for instance, Balée 1994.
68 Eriksen 2021, 2023.
69 Hoffmeyer 2005: 222, 434; Emmeche *et al.* 2002: 23.
70 Hoffmeyer 1996.
71 Emmeche 2001; Maran and Kull 2014: 47; Eriksen 2021, 2023; see Chapter 7.
72 Emmeche 2001: 249.
73 Maran and Kull 2014: 45.
74 Giddens 1990.
75 Giddens 1990: 22–26.
76 Polanyi [1944] 1957.
77 Baudrillard [1972] 1981; Sahlins 1976.
78 The use-value/exchange-value distinction thus evokes Bateson's and Hoffmeyer's observations on the duality of analog versus digital codes.
79 Brandt 2017: 156.
80 Brandt 2017: 160.
81 Rappaport 1994: 165–166.

2 Money and civilisation

In considering the phenomenon of money, we must distinguish between money as an idea and money as an object, collectively recognised as a physical measure of exchange-value. Money in the latter sense did not appear until around 600 BCE, in what is now Turkey. Although ideas of money appeared in human societies much earlier, the oldest archaeological indications we have are from ancient Mesopotamia. By 3000 BCE, the city of Uruk in Sumer was engaged in large-scale production and export of woollen cloth in exchange for copper and other metals, wood, and other resources.[1] Like later strategies of accumulation, the textile industry of Sumer generated expanding trade with its hinterlands and more distant regions, concentrating increasing volumes of resources and workers in urban centres. Metals – most importantly silver – provided abstract measures of value with which to quantify and establish equivalences between goods and services. Judging from cuneiform accounts, during the third millennium BCE silver became an almost universal measure of value in Mesopotamia. The early centuries of the Bronze Age in the Near East saw the emergence of concepts of equivalence based on weights in silver. Such equivalences established exchange-values (that is, prices) of weights of wool, land rent, volumes of grain, slaves, various kinds of labour (remunerated in rations of grain or wool), and precious imports such as lapis lazuli and gold.[2] At the end of the third millennium BCE, for instance, a silver *shekel* (ca. 8.33 g) was equivalent to 180 grains of barley.[3] Widely shared systems of weighing suggest intensive trade contacts ranging from the Aegean to the Indus and a need for exact comparisons of metals.[4] The international exchange of metal also extended into Bronze Age Europe, where convergent weight standards indicate trade with Mesopotamian merchants, no doubt via eastern Mediterranean intermediaries.[5]

Prior to the appearance of the first coinage around 600 BCE, money or exchange-value was an abstract idea – a measure of account – but it referred to a concrete substance (silver). With precious metal coinage, money became a concrete *embodiment* of that idea. Idea and substance were no longer separable. Previously, a lump of silver would not be mistaken for an idea, but coinage generated an ambiguity about the character of money that has been a prominent theme through more than two and a half millennia of human history.

DOI: 10.4324/9781032702186-4

Phrased in terms of semiotics, the conundrum has been whether the coin is a symbol or an index of exchange-value? The coin unites idea and substance, incarnating an abstract concept in a physical object in much the same way as an idol of worship, or a fetish. Ingeniously illustrated in Keith Hart's discussion of 'heads or tails – two sides of the coin,'[6] the fact that a coin is simultaneously a token and a commodity has shaped the intertwined trajectories of economic discourse and economic history. Whereas so-called credit theories of money emphasise the politically constructed foundations of its exchange-value, commodity theories stress its economic value (originally as bullion) on the market. The tension between these two perspectives on money has also been expressed as the opposition between chartalism (from Latin *charta* = token) and metallism, and between Keynesianism and monetarism.[7] After the final abandonment of the gold standard in 1971, and with the subsequent dominance of electronic money, the idea and the substance of money have again been separated. The ambiguity about whether to focus on the political backing of money tokens or on the market value of their substance has evaporated. A commodity theory of money is currently difficult to defend. The ambiguity that was introduced around 600 BCE thus lasted approximately 2,600 years.

It may not be a coincidence that what Karl Jaspers called the Axial Age began about the same time as the appearance of coinage.[8] The 'two sides of the coin' paradigmatically expressed the relation between form and substance, which has preoccupied philosophers ever since. This duality can also be phrased in terms of the relation between symbolic and indexical reference, transcendence and immanence, or abstract and concrete. As money tokens made from precious metals simultaneously have immanent and transcendent qualities, they are consummate fetishes. In this chapter, we outline the role of money in the history of civilisation, including its significance for what is being referred to as Axiality. In Chapter 3, we will examine the phenomenon of fetishism. As we shall see in Chapter 4, money fetishism deflects our attention from the material substance of the commodities traded on the world market, leaving abstract exchange-value as the exclusive concern of economics.

A brief early history of money

In the early second millennium BCE, silver and tin were used as units of account in the long-distance caravan trade between the city-state of Assur in Assyria and Kanesh (Kültepe) in Anatolia (modern Turkey). The Assyrian merchants brought tin and lapis lazuli imported from what is now Afghanistan and more distant parts of Asia, as well as precious textiles manufactured in Babylonia. Some of the tin may have been derived from as far away as the borders of China. Tin was in high demand for bronze production, not least in the eastern Mediterranean. In exchange for these valuables, the Assyrians received silver and gold from Anatolia. Their incentives largely derived from the fact that tin could be exchanged for silver in Anatolia at the rate of 7:1, while in Assur the average rate was only 15:1.[9] To profit from such discrepancies in market values is called arbitrage. The Babylonian textiles were also used by the merchants to pay taxes in Anatolia.[10]

It has been observed that many non-modern valuables or proto-currencies – such as precious metals, beads, shells, feathers, furs, jewellery, and textiles – were used as adornments for human bodies.[11] Clothing and adornment are universally signs of social identity. Early forms of money thus appear to have served as semiotic markers of qualitative social difference and specificity, whereas modern money signifies quantity and standardised equivalence. This semiotic transformation is clearly related to the transition from symbolic to indexical reference that we identified in the previous chapter. Clothing and adornments of various kinds are symbols of social status or personal qualities, pervasively signifying the wearer's rights and obligations vis-à-vis others, but modern money is an impersonal index of abstract exchange-value that can be infinitely quantified and accumulated regardless of the owner's social relations. The pervasive exchange of textiles as embodiments of value in non-modern societies often suggests a rudimentary form of money, but the material properties of cloth precluded their adoption as a liquid medium of exchange.[12] Precious metals conveniently combined the functions of all-purpose money as a durable and stable store of wealth, a quantifiable and divisible measure of value (unit of account), a trustworthy means of payment, and a portable medium of exchange. Already 5,000 years ago, the concern with abstract equivalences and proper rates of exchange (prices) in ancient Mesopotamia was reified into a concept of value (a unit of account) based on weight of silver, which increasingly would come to be coveted as an intrinsically valuable material, but it was not yet money in the sense of coinage – that is, standardised pieces of metal representing official exchange-values backed by a king or emperor.

Archaeological discoveries show that Eurasia in the second millennium BCE was integrated by extensive networks of long-distance exchange reaching from Cornwall to the frontiers of China. Much of this trade was stimulated by the demand for bronze and the tin and copper required to produce it. Deposits of tin were rare and remote from markets, as illustrated by the mines in Cornwall and Kazakhstan. It is remarkable to consider how such vast trade relations were able to connect these far-flung societies into what arguably was a 'world-system'[13] before there was any coined money. The bronze-using kingdoms and empires of the eastern Mediterranean and Near East (Minoans/Mycenaeans, Hittites, Egyptians, Mitanni, Babylonians) were tightly bound together by trade and royal intermarriage. This extensive interconnectedness, which clearly evokes contemporary patterns of globalization, made Bronze Age societies vulnerable to a 'perfect storm' of calamities leading to economic collapse around 1180 BCE.[14] The strategic importance of tin, and the dependence of local elites on imports of prestige goods made from bronze, represented significant risks. The 1300 BCE shipwreck off Uluburun, Turkey, illustrates the intensive trade that connected substantial parts of the Bronze Age world. Probably bound for the Aegean, the cargo of the sunken ship included almost a ton of tin and ten tons of copper – 'enough raw metal to outfit an army of three hundred men with bronze swords, shields, helmets, and armor'[15] – as well as a ton of resin from Canaan, ebony logs from Nubia, raw glass from Mesopotamia, scarabs from Egypt, gold jewellery, ivory from hippopotamus, an elephant tusk, and many other valuable things.[16] Such was the intensity of trade more than six centuries before the introduction of coinage.

The use of irregular lumps of silver in commercial transactions was widespread in the eastern Mediterranean during the first half of the first millennium BCE. As metallurgy progressed, the kingdom of Lydia and the neighbouring region of Ionia (in what is now Turkey) developed the use of unstamped lumps of electrum (a natural amalgam of gold and silver) into the first gold and silver coins.[17] By the late seventh century BCE, these coins had become more regular in form, purity, and weight, as officially guaranteed by the stamp of the ruler. The idea of coinage was quickly adopted in Greece and beyond. As Glyn Davies observes,

> [T]o most people most of the time, money has simply meant coins. In the western world for two thousand years since coinage was invented, the relationship between bullion and coinage has been the foundation of private and public finance.[18]

Coins made from precious metals became particularly significant to rulers, who used them to pay wages to mercenaries. Beyond the rations of grain or wool that had been distributed in ancient Mesopotamia, salaried soldiers are the earliest unequivocal instances of wage labour. The soldiers were employed in wars of conquest that captured more bullion for the royal or imperial mints as well as captives, some of whom were enslaved to work in mines, yielding self-reinforcing processes of accumulation. Geoffrey Ingham refers to this pattern as a 'military-coinage complex.'[19] As armies moved across the landscapes of the ancient world, the money spent by soldiers – for instance, on food, drink, and prostitution – entered wider spheres of circulation, contributing to a general commercialisation of social life. Much of this money returned to the issuer through taxation of the conquered populations. For some proponents of a chartalist or credit theory of money, this issuing of tokens through which political elites extract goods and services while guaranteeing their own continued access to them (through taxation), is the very point of money.[20] Such systems appear to have developed out of the exchange of precious metals and other valuables between local elites. In keeping track of debts, obligations, and compensations, elite gift exchange served to maintain balanced social relations between communities. As such relations grew increasingly asymmetric, money became a tool for powerful groups – early states – to extract resources from politically dominated populations.

> [B]ullion exchange between elites circulated to create and clear social debts, and then city-state authorities co-opted traditional bullion gift-giving

> and literally remade it into financial money with which to mobilize resources.[21]

Thus, from a chartalist perspective, 'social, government, and private monies are parallel frameworks of accounting used to keep track of debits and credits in different realms of value.'[22]

Technological improvements enabled the Greeks to exploit the richly silver-bearing ores of Laurion (near Athens), Macedonia, and some Aegean islands. At their most intensive exploitation, the silver mines of Laurion may have employed around 30,000 slaves.[23] Money could also purchase civilian wage labour in ancient Greece, at the rate of two *obols* (equivalent to one-third of a *drachma,* variably representing between three and six grams of silver) for a day's labour.[24] Athenian coins, particularly the four-*drachma* piece (stamped with an owl on one side and the goddess Athena on the other), were the most widely trusted standard for almost 600 years, until the Laurion mines were exhausted in 25 BCE. The Greek island of Delos in the late third century BCE became a major commercial centre, trading a wide range of goods from various parts of the world, including timber, slaves, and valuables from as far away as China. Delos became increasingly dominated by Roman merchants and was strengthened by the rise of Rome, as when Rome destroyed its rivals Carthage and Corinth. Delos was thus a significant historical link between the commercial spheres of Greece and Rome.

The rapid military expansion of the Macedonian Empire under Philip II and Alexander the Great in the fourth century BCE was propelled by the self-reinforcing conversion of bullion into armies and conquests into more bullion.[25] In Alexander's army, cavalry soldiers were paid two *drachma* per day, infantry one *drachma*, and ordinary mercenaries two-thirds of a *drachma* (twice the wage of a civilian labourer).[26] At its full extent, the total daily cost for his army would have been around 120,000 *drachma*, which approximates half a ton of silver per day. Yet, its conquests of bullion and slaves continuously surpassed its costs, with major treasures appropriated from Susa (Persia), Damascus (Syria), Alexandria (Egypt), and many other centres. The emperors of Macedonia followed the Lydian kings in stamping their own portraits on the coins they issued, symbolically usurping the sovereignty of Greek divinities such as Zeus and Heracles. After having defeated the last Macedonian emperor in 197 BCE, the Roman general Flaminius emulated their pretensions by minting gold coins with his own image.[27] The personal connection between rulers and coinage subsequently became entrenched among Roman emperors.

Like Macedonia, the Roman Empire required huge volumes of metal coinage to maintain its expanding armies. During its expansions in the third to first centuries BCE, the investments paid off in terms of booty, slaves, mines, and tribute appropriated from Carthage, Sidon, Greece, Macedonia, Spain, and other conquests. As the expansion came to an end, however, Rome struggled for centuries with fiscal shortages, inflation, and severe debasement of coinage. By AD 270, Glyn Davies remarks, 'the so-called "silver" denarius [contained] only about 4 per cent silver.'[28] He continues:

> In the short space of four decades (244-84) … Rome had endured no less than fifty-seven emperors. The state was in a complete mess, administratively, economically and financially.[29]

The conscientious efforts of emperor Diocletian (284–305) notwithstanding, the economic problems continued. Diocletian's 'Edict of Prices' in 301 was a detailed attempt to control the prices of most goods as well as the rates for services and salaries ranging from agricultural workers to various ranks of civil service and army officers. Nevertheless, a mere 34 years after the edict, the price of wheat had increased 63 times.[30] The first Christian emperor Constantine (306–337) was able to augment the imperial treasury through new conquests, taxes, and confiscation of the wealth accumulated in pagan temples throughout the empire. Yet, inflation and the debasement of silver currency continued. Whereas Diocletian's edict had declared that a pound of gold was worth 50,000 denarii, six years later (in 307) it was worth 100,000 denarii, and in 324 as much as 300,000 denarii.[31] Such runaway divergences between the nominal value of money and its material purchasing-power have recurrently vexed and confused political leaders over the course of history. They illustrate the practical consequences of the perpetual ambiguity about the nature of money.

The two sides of the coin

As we have seen, the establishment of coinage introduced recurrent divergences between the nominal value of money tokens and their actual purchasing-power. Prior to that, precious metals were commodities that held exchange-value in proportion to weight. When bullion was minted into coins, there appeared the possibility of discrepancies between the commercial value of their material substance and the official value attributed to them by the issuing authorities. The former is the exchange-value negotiated through market transactions, the latter the formal value defined in terms of what the money can ideally be exchanged for, as purportedly guaranteed by the political leadership. Both are of course social constructions, as all attributions of value ultimately derive from human perceptions, but the tension between them reflects the problematic calibration of market and state, as the authorities attempt to control and stabilise continuously changing economic forces. Viewed as a commodity, the value of a coin is that of its material substance; viewed at 'face value,' it is worth what the authorities proclaim that it is worth. The relation between the two kinds of assessment is often represented as a dispute between two incompatible theories of money: the commodity theory and the claim (or credit) theory.[32] The commodity theory sees money primarily as a *medium of exchange*, based on its putatively inherent value (such as gold); the credit theory sees money primarily as a *unit of account*, based on its nominal claim to purchasing-power. Robert Rosenswig posits a fundamental disagreement between an orthodox economic view of money as primarily a medium of exchange, on the one hand, and a heterodox understanding of money as a unit of account imposed by people in power, on the other.[33] Whether a 'social accounting system (i.e., special-purpose money or primitive money)' or 'financial' money, he argues, its primary function is to keep track of debts and credits.[34] The polarisation of emphases on different functions of money tends to neglect their co-occurrence and historical fluctuations in their relative significance. It also leads to unnecessary contradictions, as when Ingham asserts that Marx's labour theory of value committed him and his successors to 'a version of the commodity theory of money, with all its attendant errors.'[35]

A conundrum of money is that it is *a measure of value that itself changes in value*. This is the case whether we embrace a commodity or credit theory of money. A philosopher in the 16th century could ponder the fact that the price of a silver ingot might change for the same reasons as that of cloth.[36] As Pierre Vilar ruminates on the history of metal money, '[e]verything depends on it, and it is dependent on nothing: in any case it is a strange quality for money which is an object, a metal.'[37] Similarly mystified was Daniel Defoe when in 1710 he contemplated the phenomenon of credit: 'I should say that it is the essential Shadow of Something that it is Not.'[38]

One aspect of the dispute between credit theorists and commodity theorists reflects the relation between different social scales – between money as a domestic issue within a political jurisdiction, on the one hand, and as an internationally coveted material, on the other. Money in the former sense has developed as a means of extracting labour and resources within a politically controlled territory, whereas money in the second sense has served as a standard of value in trade beyond political boundaries. Both entail systems of accounting, but they differ in terms of who or what guarantees consistent standards of measurement. This is well illustrated by John Locke's argument in the 1690s for a universal standard of silver coinage for Britain's trade with foreigners, as 'our coin, as theirs is to us, [is] but meer bullion, valued only by its weight.'[39] Locke's opponents advocated minting that was geared to a nominal unit of account, as a matter of domestic governance; in a sense, his own concern was also – if unwittingly – the establishment of social agreement, but at the international level.[40] Although invoking the 'intrinsic' value of silver bullion, Locke's image of money was no less founded on a social construction than that of the nominalists, even if less obviously. Ole Bjerg draws a similar conclusion about the gold standard that was abandoned by the United States in 1971, observing that 'the gold standard of the US dollar was instituted by fiat, that is, by a declaration from the state.'[41] As these examples illustrate, there is no such thing as intrinsic value, as both money of account and commodity money are socially negotiated exchange-values.

After the final abandonment of the gold standard by Richard Nixon in 1971, the adherence to a commodity theory of money does seem atavistic. In historical hindsight, however, the two antagonistic theories illuminate a fundamental ambiguity about money that has preoccupied authorities, philosophers, and economists from Aristotle to Nixon. This ambiguity has led to a polarisation of two opposing theories of money – each claiming to be universally applicable – but is ultimately a reflection of the inherent duality of money itself.[42] It has generated historical oscillations between emphases on either the commodity or the credit aspect of money.[43] In terms of semiotics, it arguably boils down to whether money is approached as symbol or index. Credit theories view money as symbolic in the sense that its purchasing-power is essentially a social agreement, while commodity theories view it as indexical in the sense that its purchasing-power derives from its intrinsic properties.

As we saw, long before the emergence of coinage, credit in ancient Mesopotamia was calculated in monetary metrics of value that functioned as units of account but were founded on weights of silver. Whether the clay tablets recording such debts could themselves serve as money (in the sense of a means of payment to a third party) is contested, but to the extent that all the later money tokens like coins and banknotes are understood as *promises to pay* (IOUs), as implied by credit theories of money,[44] the concept of transferable debt is not as specific to capitalism as is sometimes held.[45] Citing Mitchell Innes' assertion that '[c]redit and credit alone is money,' Ingham affirms that

> the issuer's mark did not necessarily guarantee a metallic standard, but simply that the issuer would accept the token in payment of a tax debt. (That is to say, the money was issued as a token of indebtedness.) Coins were, like all forms of money, credit instruments that represented abstract value or purchasing power.[46]

In the same vein, Ingham cites G.F. Knapp's insistence that 'money is the measure and not the thing measured,'[47] which in semiotic terms is to say that money is a representation rather than an index of value.[48] Similarly, John Maynard Keynes argued that it sufficed for the state to define the weights and grades of silver (for instance, *shekels*) that served as money of account in ancient Babylonia, with no coinage required.[49] However, given that the foundation of the ancient Mesopotamian unit of account was the commodity of silver, it seems as erroneous to here completely dismiss the relevance of a commodity theory of money as it would be to adhere to it after the abandonment of the gold standard. The two competing theories highlight the ambiguity of money mainly during the 2,600 years from the first coinage up until 1971; prior to coinage, a commodity theory of money could be relevant to the very conceptualisation of credit, but after 1971, it is no longer of any use. In other words, the appositeness of the two theories overlaps – and the tension between them is valid – primarily during those 2,600 years.

From the fall of Rome to Adam Smith

If the advent of the 'military-coinage complex' in the sixth century BCE represented the integration of bullion-based money of account and means of payment (in the form of coins), the fall of Rome in the fifth century AD marked the delinking of these two functions of money.[50] For several reasons, coined money virtually disappeared. As the fiscal resources of Rome dwindled, so did the number of its soldiers as well as the intensity of trade and production in the territories of the former empire. In Medieval Europe, most goods and services were paid for in kind – for example, corn, dried fish, or horses – but the sum was expressed with reference to some metal currency that served as money of account.[51] Although minting was resumed in the late Middle Ages, it was fragmented by the great number of jurisdictions. To maintain some coherence, Charlemagne (768–814) established an abstract money of account stipulating that a pound of silver cost 20 shillings or 240 pence (denarii). The delinking of means of payment and measures of value 'fostered a consciousness of money as dematerialized or "imaginary,"' in which people counted in pounds, shillings, and pence regardless of the deterioration of coinage.[52] Eight centuries after Charlemagne, the silver content of pound coins was only 3% of the ratio he had decreed, but its purchasing-power, relative to other coins, was unchanged. This delinking, Ingham writes, 'firmly re-established the abstract monetary calculation that had been practised in ancient Babylon.'[53]

The retreat of coinage from the fifth to the 12th century was accompanied by the Church condemnation of the desire for money as diametrically opposed to Christian virtues. Several citations from the Bible served to underscore this doctrine.[54] Greed – the 'love of money' – was condemned as a capital sin. Beginning in the late 11th century, however, the crusades again entailed an accelerating use of money. Like the mercenaries of the 'military-coinage complex,' the Christian crusaders needed easily transportable wealth to support them during long journeys through foreign territories. In the 13th century, there was intense ecclesiastical debate about what the Church called 'usury' – the lending of money at interest. Citing biblical texts, the Church prohibited lending at interest between Christians because it was a form of avarice and a *theft of time* (the time between loan and repayment), which ultimately belonged to God.[55] Thomas Aquinas and others argued that usury was a sin against justice, a virtue often invoked at this time. Aquinas followed Aristotle in arguing that usury was also a sin against nature, as money *does not reproduce itself*. In the late Middle Ages, the rejection of usury and mercantile profit was consistent with the relatively high value placed on manual work, compared with the early Middle Ages.

Paradoxically, however, the revalorisation of work and the increase of wage labour and money in the 13th century led to a gradual rehabilitation of lending at interest.[56] Wealthy merchant families in the north Italian city-states of Florence, Venice, Genoa, Pisa, and Verona established vast trade connections throughout Europe, Asia, and Africa and offered financial services, based on bills of exchange, that were unrestrained by Church doctrine. In serving as paper money, the bills of exchange accelerated commerce and liberated money from the constraints of particular currencies and bullion reserves. Although several Italian banking families suffered bankruptcy when the English king Edward III defaulted on his loans in 1343, their financial practices survived and to Fernand Braudel marked the beginnings of modern capitalism. It was funding from Genoa that financed Columbus' voyage to Hispaniola in 1492, inaugurating the European conquest and pillage of the Americas that was foundational to the emergence of the modern world-system.[57] The original transition from a medieval to a 'capitalist' economy in Europe has been variously identified between the 12th (Braudel) and the 18th (Polanyi) centuries, but Jacques Le Goff – focusing on the large transfers of precious metals from the Americas, the formation of a single market, and the establishment of a stock exchange – opts for the 16th and early 17th centuries.[58]

Silver from Spanish America was fundamental to the integration of a world economy. In the three centuries between 1500 and 1800, the 150,000 tons of silver that were derived from Mexico and Peru comprised around 80% of world production.[59] A major source of demand was China, which abandoned the paper currency that had been in use since the 12th century and in the 1570s adopted new legislation obliging people to pay taxes in silver. In the mid-16th century, the ratio of the value of gold to that of silver was around 1:11–12 in Europe but 1:6 in China. With the value of silver almost twice as high in China as in Europe, European merchants made huge profits from arbitrage. In the 18th century, around a third of the production of Mexican silver ended up in China.[60]

Le Goff argues that the medieval economy in Europe was basically a gift economy. He observes that, although in the late 14th and 15th centuries 'it may have ceased to be accursed and infernal, money remained suspect throughout the Middle Ages.'[61] Based on events such as the fall of Constantinople in 1453 and the end of the Wars of the Roses in 1485, Glyn Davies nevertheless posits the mid- to late 15th century as the dividing line between medieval and modern. As paper money eventually displaced silver and gold, he writes, releasing money from 'its metallic chains and anchors,' the 'apparently complete victory of the abstract over the concrete, the triumph of fiction over truth, provides the main theme and interest of the story of the five centuries from Columbus to Keynes.'[62] In the early 18th century, Bernard de Mandeville's *Fable of the Bees* (1714) finally completed the inversion of medieval morals by proposing that private vices generate public benefits, which inspired Adam Smith's central assumption in *The Wealth of Nations* (1776) that self-interest is conducive to the common good.[63] This has remained the creed of mainstream economics for 250 years.

It is far beyond the ambition of this book to try to survey the vast discourse on economics since Adam Smith, but I hope to illuminate – from several different perspectives – the phenomenon of money that serves as the underexamined foundation of that discourse. Only a minority of economists have asked questions about the semiotic nature and cultural origins of money. As Bjerg laments, '[t]he most curious thing about the contemporary philosophy of money is that it does not exist.'[64] Rather than become entangled in the arcane deliberations on the *management* of money that frame the practices and policies that preoccupy most modern economists, my aim is to gain a reflexive distance to the very idea and artefact of money: where does this idea of universal commensurability derive from, what makes it so unique as a mode of communication, and how has it transformed the societies and ecosystems in which it occurs? In the remainder of this chapter, we shall explore the relation between the development of money and the kind of social condition that we habitually refer to as 'civilisation.'

Money in the Axial Age and beyond

Given that the first appearance of coined money in ancient Greece coincided with a radical transformation of thought and philosophy, Richard Seaford has proposed that the former was conducive to the latter.[65] The fact that coinage and abstract philosophy emerged almost simultaneously in both Greece and India in the sixth century BCE – in the period that Karl Jaspers in 1949 called the 'Axial Age' – has inspired Seaford to extend his thesis into a more general proposition on the relation between money and thought.[66] The proposal is intriguing for several reasons. Seaford's argument is empirically rich and theoretically persuasive; it accounts for what might otherwise be thought of merely as remarkable historical coincidences; it suggests profound connections between money and religion; and – although probably beyond what Seaford had intended – it provides new insights on the divide between 'civilised' and 'non-civilised.' Few would deny that the phenomenon of money is inextricably interwoven with the history of civilisation and ultimately of modernity, but it is rarely acknowledged that, conversely, it may be the *absence* of money that defines what are currently celebrated as 'indigenous' people. As we shall see in Chapter 9, indigenous people are frequently extolled as the wise, egalitarian, and ecologically mindful counterpoint of modern civilisation. If there is some justification for this conception, there are reasons to reflect on the effects of money on 'Axial' people, their societies, and their environments.

Jaspers recognised that, in the period around 500 BCE (between 800 and 200 BCE), occurred 'the most deepcut dividing line in history.'[67] In what is now China, India, Iran, Palestine, and Greece, there independently appeared a number of radically new philosophers in the sense of individuals relying on the clarity of their own reason and insights.

> In this age were born the fundamental categories within which we still think today, and the beginnings of the world religions, by which human beings still live, were created.[68]

Although the theological and teleological framing of his argument may deter many modern readers, Jaspers' observations on the simultaneity of the birth of philosophy in at least three separate civilisations are indisputable. He mentions that, already in 1856, the German philosopher Ernst von Lasaulx noted that '[i]t cannot possibly be an accident' that, in the sixth century BCE, foundational religious reformers appeared in Persia (Zarathustra), India (Gautama Buddha), China (Confucius), Israel (the prophets), and Greece (the first philosophers).[69]

Jaspers' efforts to explain this convergence in terms of the spiritual awakening of humankind is not entirely persuasive, not least as his eulogy of Axial civilisation increasingly jars with its disastrous record of exploitation, imperialist warfare, and environmental degradation. If the trajectory of modern civilisation is to be understood as deriving from the kind of human enlightenment that appeared in the Axial Age, as many have argued, it is difficult to embrace it with unreserved enthusiasm. The benevolent tenets of world religions emerged in tandem with unprecedented plunder and violence, largely spurred by the pursuit of gold and silver. By the end of the Middle Ages, Christian doctrines had become compatible with the ruthless behaviour of European merchants and conquerors in their destruction of entire civilisations and the enslavement of millions. As Graeber points out, '[a]ny number of civilizations have probably been in a position to wreak havoc on the scale that the European powers did in the sixteenth and seventeenth centuries,'[70] but most did not, and we need to examine the specific incentives that propelled the violent European expansion. Before we do so, however, we shall return to Seaford's argument on the cultural context of monetisation in ancient Greece.

What was unprecedented about Greek coinage, writes Seaford, was that a piece of precious metal was stamped with a sign that granted it greater exchange-value than it would have as mere bullion. This 'fiduciary' or conventional value was established by the issuing authority and acknowledged within its jurisdiction. Greek city-states like Miletus in Ionia were the first thoroughly monetised societies in history. The confidence that their populations held in the abstract value of their coins appears to have been conditioned by communal rituals of sacrificial distribution of meat involving iron spits, from which the names of their coins (*obol* and *drachma*) were derived. This connection between money and ritual is significant, as coins – in being possible to transform into anything at all – initially appear to have been experienced as having metaphysical properties. Seaford emphasises the ritual roots of commercial exchange in ancient Greece by observing that 'the act of purchase is ritualised, with communally agreed symbols, actions or words embodying the abstraction of transferred ownership.'[71]

The originally divine nature of coinage is illustrated by the images of deities that were stamped on Athenian coins and by the use of the same phrase for acknowledging gods or coinage.[72] The abstract concept of universal exchange-value, embodied and reified in concrete objects of daily use, was a momentous cultural innovation that Seaford argues was conducive to abstract thought in other spheres of life:

> Early in the Greek experience of money we find the idea that money is everything. The idea that to be transformed into something (or everything) is to *be* that thing (or everything) is common in presocratic philosophy.[73]

In attributing metaphysical properties to tangible artefacts, coinage had affinities with ritual and worship, yet the quantifiability and homogeneity of money rendered it distinctly different from the uniqueness of talismans.[74] Seaford shows that the new concern with money was pervasive in ancient Greek society. He concludes that, although we have by now 'thoroughly internalized the metaphysics of money' that preoccupied the Greek philosophers, we find it

> hard to shake off a lingering sense of arbitrariness, of there being something indefinably unsatisfying – despite its inevitability and the massive progress it has achieved – about the individualist reification of money and the injustice and alienation thereby produced.[75]

The connection between the origins of coinage and abstract philosophy that Seaford traces in Greece appears also to be identifiable in the Gangetic basin in India in the fifth century BCE. It is quite possible that the idea of coinage spread from Greece to India, but the technical differences between how coins were made in the two areas suggests that it was not simply a matter of emulation.[76] Seaford argues that the new philosophies reflected the way in which the invisible essence of the coin served as a model for the invisible essence of the human individual.[77] He concludes that the first three societies to be monetised (Greece, India, China) were also the first three to produce, at about the same time, 'the idea of a fundamental cosmic principle...that is impersonal, abstract, all-pervasive, imperceptible and interiorised.'[78]

As Seaford himself notes, the voluminous research on the Axial Age presented in a major conference volume from 2012 more or less ignores the influences of monetisation on philosophical thought.[79] Already in the preface to his 2004 book, he anticipates that the traditional academic division of labour will result in a 'subconscious policing of the boundaries,' precluding the consideration of social processes in accounting for developments in philosophy.[80] In contrast to this reticence, David Graeber has enthusiastically incorporated Seaford's thesis in his ambitious effort to write a global history of money.[81] Graeber traces a long-term historical alternation between periods dominated by money of account ('credit money') and periods preoccupied with precious metals and 'commodity money.' Prior to the Axial Age, he observes, the agrarian empires in the fourth to second millennia BCE recognised virtual credit money in calculating transactions, debts, and obligations. By and large, recurrent cancellations of debt restrained the excessive occurrence of debt servitude and slavery. When the first coinage appears almost simultaneously in Greece, India, and China in the sixth century BCE, Graeber follows Seaford in noticing that this is precisely the time when the first major philosophers and religious leaders emerge in these areas. Focusing on intellectual developments, beginning with Zoroaster (or Zarathustra) in Persia, Jaspers had specified the Axial Age as lasting from 800 to 200 BCE. To include the birth of all major world religions, however, Graeber extends the Axial Age to 600 AD. This 'long' Axial Age (800 BCE–600 AD) 'saw the birth not only of all the world's major philosophical tendencies but also all of today's major world religions: Zoroastrianism, Prophetic Judaism, Buddhism, Jainism, Hinduism, Confucianism, Taoism, Christianity, and Islam.'[82] This period, as we have seen, was characterised by what Graeber (in an explicit modification of Ingham's term) calls a 'military-coinage-slavery complex.' Much of the precious metals that had been stored in temples and palaces were widely plundered by conquering armies and converted into coins with which to pay mercenary soldiers. The fact that war captives were frequently used as slaves in mines to extract more bullion for the mints[83] prompts Graeber to remark that '[o]ne can see how this process might feed upon itself.'[84] The spread of impersonal commerce, 'born of war,' he argues, was accompanied by a calculating, materialist ethos that saw the pursuit of profit as the ultimate human concern, but that also provoked opposition from movements and philosophers advocating altruism and charity. From this perspective, the Axial Age philosophers and religions were reacting to the excesses of the 'military-coinage-slavery complex.'[85] Graeber proposes that all the major world religions 'arose amidst intense arguments about the role of money and the market in human life, and particularly about what these institutions meant for fundamental questions of what human beings owed to one another.'[86] In his view, the expansion of the market was thus what spurred the development of Axial religions endorsing generosity and denouncing materialism and greed.[87] This interpretation complements Seaford's focus on how the preoccupation of Axial philosophy with abstraction appears to have been inspired by the abstract exchange-value of money – a conception evoking a transcendent level of reality where everything is convertible into anything else.

In Graeber's narrative, the Middle Ages exemplify the oscillation between commodity money and credit money. Not just in Europe, but over much of Eurasia, the end of the 'long' Axial Age in 600 AD saw the virtual disappearance of coinage and slavery and a marked decrease in warfare. Throughout the Middle Ages, the religions founded in the Axial Age – in reaction to the violence, materialism, and repression of the 'military-coinage-slavery complex' – dominated social relations and generally diminished usury and bondage. Not until around 1450 and the centuries thereafter was there a widespread revival of materialism and profit-seeking, as the capitalist empires of Europe resorted to military conquest, plunder, and slavery in their pursuit of precious metals and other valuable commodities from Africa, Asia, and the Americas. Graeber traces this rapaciousness to the logic of 'the careful financier, whose entire operations are organized around producing steady, mathematical, inexorable growth of income, [which] lies at the very heart of what we now call "capitalism."'[88]

Unpacking the concept of 'capitalism,' of course, we find the idea and artefact of money. Rather than simply denouncing the totality of social relations in which we are entangled, we can identify this extraordinary artefact as the source and *generator* of such social relations. Indeed, in recognising that the essence of capitalism is that the logic of money is granted *autonomy* – and politics, religion, law, and military power turned into its subservient accomplices – Graeber indirectly does identify the artefact of money itself as the culprit. David McNally similarly introduces his world history of war, slavery, finance, and empire by observing that 'money has been a technology of power.'[89] Citing John Locke, he incisively notes that money, in purchasing labour, extends the bodily powers of its owner to the bodies of labouring others.[90]

In 1717, the kind of metallist arguments advocated by Locke succeeded in establishing a gold standard for British currency, which was maintained as a materialist foundation of the British Empire for almost 200 years. The gold standard served as a check on financial speculation and bolstered the predominant view that, as Graeber puts it, '[t]here had to be some solid, material foundation to all this [finance], or the entire system would go insane.'[91] After a series of collapsing financial 'bubbles' in Britain in the late 17th and early 18th centuries, there was general awareness that an economy without such material anchors risked being as illusory and volatile as magic. Graeber notes that, to this day, there is a widespread suspicion that

> bankers are creating something out of nothing. They are not only frauds and magicians. They are evil, because they're playing God.[92]

The fetish unravelled

The 2008 financial crisis confirmed such suspicions. According to Graeber, it 'was exactly what it seemed to be: a scam, an incredibly sophisticated Ponzi scheme designed to collapse in the full knowledge that the perpetrators would be able to force the victims to bail them out.'[93] As it made evident, the new financial instruments that have proliferated in the age of 'financialisation,' although marketed as means of reducing the risks associated with volatile money, have instead increased instability.

In Graeber's account, the 'Age of the Great Capitalist Empires' ended in 1971, with the final abandonment of the gold standard and the introduction of electronic money. Rather than being anchored in gold, the world economy from now on relied on 'floating' exchange-rates. As Jack Weatherford notes, after 1971

> [t]he dollar rests on the power of the government and the faith of the people who use it – faith that it will be able to buy something tomorrow,

> faith that the U.S. government will continue to exist and to accept dollars in payment of taxes...and faith that other people will continue to believe in it. Aside from that faith, nothing backs up the dollar.[94]

Bank-created American dollars became what McNally calls 'global fiat money'[95] and replaced gold as the ultimate store of value in the world. This has granted the US a very privileged position in the global economic order. Graeber proposes that the vast sums of money that are spent in Asia to buy American treasury bonds – and thus cover the US deficit and keep the nation from going bankrupt – may be seen as 'tribute' rather than 'loans.'[96] McNally concludes that 'IOUs thus finance America's deficits with the rest of the world while subsequently returning to sustain its public debt (Treasury bills and bonds).'[97]

While the period of financialisation after 1971 has unquestionably meant a revival of credit money, the significance of this shift in terms of the parameters discussed by Graeber – the relative reduction of military violence, materialism, and repression – is not immediately evident. This is a topic to which we shall return in Chapter 4, as we consider the character of exploitative relations in the modern world economy. At this point, it will suffice to note the continuities between Graeber's account of history as an alternation between periods of excessive repression and liberation, on the one hand, and his and David Wengrow's perspective in *The Dawn of Everything*, which similarly posits a recurrent historical dialectic between hierarchy and relative equality.[98]

McNally observes that, with financialisation,

> the shift to a floating regime for world money was a system-altering transformation, and it continues to pose significant theoretical challenges for critical political economy, not least because the complete de-linking of world money from a fixed commodity is without precedent. ... All critical and radical theory is obliged to come to terms with this metamorphosis.[99]

In an attack on poststructuralism and social constructionism, McNally deplores how, following the abandonment of the gold standard in 1971, '[r]ather than epitomizing something else, national currency is said to reflect nothing more than itself, leading us into a monetary house of mirrors.'[100] His outrage at Derrida's understanding of 'value as monetary sign'[101] is predictable, given his Marxist conviction that value is objectively determined by socially necessary labour time, but, as we shall see in Chapter 3, Marx's pioneering application of the concept of fetishism to political economy does invite the kind of semiotic and constructionist perspectives that were developed by Derrida and Baudrillard. Although McNally may be justified in raging at the postmodern excesses of Derrida, financialisation has indeed accentuated this relative semiotic autonomy of money vis-à-vis labour and other material resources. The semiotic confusion regarding 'floating' money underscores the fundamental problems of money as such, particularly for theorists accustomed to thinking that it refers to some objective signified. The perplexed acknowledgement that it is a collective fantasy that does not really signify anything is a recurrent observation. Stuart Corbridge and Nigel Thrift, for instance, concede that they have no choice but to place their 'faith first in gold and silver, then in paper monies, and now in electronic representations of these paper tokens of "real" value.'[102] Bill Maurer similarly refers to the contentious history of moneys 'from specie to specie marked with the stamp of the sovereign to specie-backed paper to notional ledger-ticks, electronic or otherwise.'[103] Bjerg explores the complex interaction between monetary transactions and imagined values that comprise financial markets in contemporary capitalism, observing that the very functioning of money relies on its illusory character.[104] The notion of 'value' – that which money purportedly measures – must necessarily be elusive, given that *it is itself a measure of how much money it will fetch*. This circularity indeed evokes a house of mirrors. Bjerg suggests that 'it is the very elusiveness of value that generates financial trading.'[105] The only approximations of 'real' values for a financial trader are the future assessments of other traders. Ignorance and conjectures are fundamental to the functioning of money. Referring to Slavoj Zizek, Bjerg concludes that '[m]oney works not because we know how it works and how it comes into being, but rather *because we do not know* how it works and how it comes into being.'[106]

Repercussions of Axiality

A significant implication of Seaford's and Graeber's observations on the Axial Age is that the form or design of human artefacts may have momentous consequences for human thought and social relations. This is not a matter of determinism, as there is no suggestion of a simple causality through which the economy is reflected in ideas. Nor is it a claim that artefacts have 'agency,' as proposed by Actor-Network Theorists,[107] only that they may have implications for the agency of humans. Coinage is the material manifestation of an *idea* (money) that had engaged human minds for three millennia prior to the first mints in Lydia. When this idea was given material form as an object of exchange, it not only inspired renewed reflection on the phenomenon of abstract exchange-value but also generated new incentives and social strategies – the 'military-coinage-slavery complex' of the Axial Age. In the Middle Ages, as Graeber observes, the simultaneous decline of warfare, coinage, and slavery confirms their interconnectedness. After the 15th century, all three are again strengthened. To be sure, coins and other tokens of money are social constructions in the sense that they are artefacts that are attributed with exchange-value, but they can clearly have very material repercussions, both social and ecological. The question we must consider is whether monetisation – the adoption of coinage as a medium of social interaction – significantly tends to transform humans and their social relations. An obvious way of exploring this issue is to compare monetised and non-monetised people.[108]

When Jaspers coined the concept of the Axial Age, he referred to the 'axis' of world history that distinguished between what had preceded it and what came after.[109] Consistent with this conception is the frequent use of expressions such as 'pre-Axial' and 'post-Axial.' Given the momentous character of what transpired in the Axial Age – indeed, the extent to which it was foundational for what we call civilisation – its influence could be seen as the dividing line between 'civilised' and 'non-civilised.' The latter category is clearly problematic, considering how it has long been used derogatively by representatives of urban civilisations as synonymous with 'barbarian' or 'savage.' However, now that we have been witnessing a significant reassessment and upgrading of indigenous peoples throughout the world, it should be possible to discuss the essence of this polarity without risking insulting anybody. This is precisely what Marshall Sahlins has done in his posthumously published book *The New Science of the Enchanted Universe*, with the subtitle *An Anthropology of Most of Humanity*.[110] The Axial Age, says Sahlins, initiated a global cultural transformation that is still unfolding. Its essence is the shift from an understanding of divinity as immanently present in the world to the idea that the divine belongs to a transcendent level of reality.[111] Until their worldview is transformed by 'Axial ideologies' such as Christianity, most people experience the world as inhabited by a great number of 'spirits,' that is, nonhuman 'metapersons' with 'the essential attributes of persons, a core of the same mental, temperamental, and volitional capacities.'[112] In other words, a pre-Axial world is an immense cosmic society composed of various kinds of inevitably anthropomorphic beings who must be appeased in order for success or even health to be guaranteed. Navigating in such a world is like navigating in a vastly extended network of intersubjective social relations requiring sensitivity and diplomacy. Immanentism thus necessarily implies a *relational* understanding of the world. It was to account for such 'pre-Axial' ontologies that Edward Tylor in 1871 proposed the concept of animism.[113]

A post-Axial world, in contrast, is bereft of spirits and subjecthood, as echoed in Max Weber's observations on the 'disenchantment' of modernity. Indeed, Sahlins suggests that the early modern period and Enlightenment can be thought of as a 'Second Axial Age,' in which abstract categories such as 'religion,' 'politics,' 'science,' and 'economy' further reinforced the dichotomy between the material and the spiritual – or natural and supernatural – that had been introduced in the Axial Age. Transcendentalism – the relegation of divinity to another world – created a schism between the subjective and the objective, rendering human activities in the residual, disenchanted world impersonal and detached from relational concerns. Yet, in the end,

> we share the same existential predicament as those who solve the problem by knowing the world as so many powerful others of their kind, with whom they might negotiate their fate. People are not the authors of

> their life and death, the forces of their propagation, growth and decline, their illness and their health, the plants and animals upon which they subsist, the weather upon which their prosperity depends.[114]

Sahlins mobilises a vast range of ethnographic and historical documentation of non-modern, non-Western cultures to illustrate how what he calls 'immanentist' societies tend to manage the predicament of human finitude by hypostatising or *subjectivising* as 'metapersons' the various unpredictable forces that control human lives. He emphasises that his contrast between transcendentalism and immanentism is not concerned with how matters 'really are' but with how immanentist (pre- or non-Axial) societies can be understood in their own terms, without condescendingly disfiguring them as deluded by mistaken 'beliefs.' This genuinely anthropological approach not only entertains the *possibility* that our own image of objective reality may be as culturally constructed as theirs, but it also encourages us to reassess the various implications – existential, social, and ecological – of the relational ontologies that have been embraced by 'most of humanity' before they were marginalised or extinguished by the heirs of the Axial Age. This should be a significant consideration in the 21st century, as we take stock of the existential, social, and ecological trajectory of modern civilisation.

The observation that indigenous, non-Western societies encountered by European travellers often attribute personhood and agency to what Westerners would classify as inanimate objects has been made countless times over the past three centuries. While such assertions were long classified by Europeans as erroneous superstition – for instance, by Charles de Brosses in his book *The Cult of the Fetish Gods* (1760) – in recent decades anthropologists have increasingly argued that they may be valid statements about the worlds in which they are uttered. The so-called 'ontological turn' has advocated a radically relativist approach that recognises a multiplicity of worlds.[115] Other anthropologists have simply refrained from such assessments, focusing only on documentation. Regardless of ontological positioning, this humbler attitude towards 'the native's point of view' is undoubtedly more conducive to serious ethnographic research. As demonstrated by Sahlins' rich synthesis, the ethnographic record can throw new light on the history and variety of human thought. Sahlins nowhere claims that inanimate objects – even in their cultural contexts – *are* sentient agents, as some proponents of the ontological turn occasionally do, only that we need to fully respect such assertions if we are to understand the premises on which people are acting.

An intriguing part of Sahlins' argument, previously explored in his and Graeber's book *On Kings*, is that the relegation of metaphysical agency to a transcendent realm is matched by a transfer of hierarchical relations in the opposite direction, from gods to humans. Rather than being projections of political authority structures onto celestial divinities, he proposes, the pervasive cosmic hierarchies that were acknowledged by egalitarian societies around the world have predated and served as models for worldly stratification. 'Human political power,' says Sahlins, 'is necessarily and quintessentially hubris, the appropriation of divinity.'[116] The pantheons of hierarchically organised divinities venerated by non-Axial peoples were personifications of forces that conditioned their existence but whose power could be usurped by humans. Referring *inter alia* to Kaj Århem's ethnography of the Katu in Vietnam, Sahlins finds confirmation for his observation that 'the cosmic polity has the lineaments of a state,' and thus that 'the state is prefigured in cosmology before it is known in society.'[117] Tribal societies did not derive their gods from ancient civilisations, it was rather vice versa: hierarchical cosmologies predated civilisation. Sahlins concludes that 'kingship came from heaven to earth, not the gods from earth to heaven. The human polity appropriated the cosmic polity.'[118] This conclusion inverts the long-established consensus that concepts of celestial power reflect political hierarchies in human societies.[119]

A closer analysis of such spiritual hierarchies suggests that their metaphysical relations of authority may be conceived in terms of levels of abstraction, so that higher rank corresponds to concepts of type or essence whereas lower rank denotes empirical instances.[120] This would account, for instance, for the innumerable reports of spiritual 'masters' or 'keepers' of game animals recognised in hunting societies throughout the world. Referring to Louis Dumont's *Homo Hierarchicus*, Sahlins writes that hierarchy 'is built into the human way of thinking the world; it is ontological, insofar as the elements of the world are classed or categorized.'[121] In comparing the cosmologies of modern Inuit with those of Sumerians in 3,000 BCE, he finds that 'the two immanentist systems are fundamentally alike.'[122] In ancient Mesopotamia, 'the god is the class of which particular beings are instances,' and pieces of flint and reeds had a 'species-character,' a 'greater self' that was venerated for its power.[123] This observation should have important implications for our understanding of the Axial transition from immanentist to transcendentalist modes of thought. It suggests that the recognition of abstract categories in pre-Axial societies may have had hierarchical, spiritual implications that were to become formative of both transcendental religions and political stratification.

Money, animism, and fetishism

In his discussion of the Axial Age and its repercussions through history, Sahlins never connects its inclination towards transcendental abstractions to the phenomenon of money or coinage. Yet, the nature of his long-standing commitment to economic anthropology suggests that he would largely have agreed with Seaford's and Graeber's proposals. Thus, for example, Graeber and Wengrow refer to Sahlins when they observe that

> indigenous societies incorporated into the global economy, from Bolivia to Taiwan, almost invariably frame their own traditions, as Marshall Sahlins puts it, by opposition to the white man's 'living in the way of money.'[124]

Given that the category 'indigenous societies' must be understood as largely cognate with immanentist societies, this generalisation again suggests a connection between money and transcendentalism. An additional way of accounting for this connection, which we shall return to in Chapters 8 and 9, is to equate immanentism with animism, and adopt Philippe Descola's original definition of animism as an extension of social relations to include nature.[125] In the terminology of Sahlins' classic book *Stone Age economics*, such an understanding of animism would imply the extension of social relations of 'balanced reciprocity' to the natural world.[126] Money, however, would transform social relations from balanced to 'negative reciprocity,' encouraging avarice, accumulation, and the antithesis of sociability. To the extent that human–environmental relations are modelled after social relations, as in Descola's early definition of animism, it follows that commercial societies can be expected to generate alienation vis-à-vis the natural environment. This would be a concise way of understanding the relation between money, modernity, and disenchantment.

At the same time, however, the relation between money and animism presents a paradox. What fundamentally distinguishes immanentist from transcendentalist societies is arguably their proclivity to attribute divine agency to plants, animals, and inanimate objects – what ever since de Brosses has been referred to as *fetishism*. Indeed, money is an instance of the immanentist approach that underlies animism, yet its transformation of social reciprocity has been conducive to the abandonment of animism. It codified immanentism into the operation of the economy while banishing it from human–environmental relations.

It is intriguing to consider what the introduction of coinage would mean in an immanentist society that is thoroughly accustomed to the attribution of agency to inanimate objects. While it is reasonable to imagine, as Friedrich Engels and Marc Shell have done, that the first Greek coin may have been perceived as an amulet with the magical capacity to 'transform itself into any desirable or desired object,'[127] the revolutionary significance of this moment in history should have been that money (inevitably) became *mundane*. Soon after its introduction, coined money would have been reduced to a rather trivial aspect of everyday social life.[128] It thus posed the paradox of an intrinsically powerful object that could be fully controlled, a manifestation of abstraction that was entirely secular. In contrast to the myriad metapersons with whom immanentist societies have always had to reckon, here was finally a metaphysically potent object (or materialised agency) that could be managed, rather than requiring propitiation based on conjectures about its invisible desires.[129] Money trivialised the physical cosmos that it came to rule in part because it was itself trivial. It stimulated the transition to transcendentalism while simultaneously representing a survival of immanentism, as an object perceived as so immanently powerful that it eclipsed the previously ubiquitous object agency of pre-Axial worlds.

In constituting an object unassailably endowed with invisible powers, money signified the everyday *realisation* of fetishism. Indeed, fetishism is arguably more prominent and potent in the lives of modern people than in those of the peoples that de Brosses referred to as 'savages.' The uniqueness of money is that, in inherently representing boundless abstraction, it *combines* transcendentalism and immanentism. It is intrinsically empowered to be transformed into anything at all. Its 'fetish-character,' as identified by Marx, can be analytically accounted for in terms of its indexical mode of reference: its properties are *immanent* in money tokens. However, in invoking infinite abstraction, those properties are pre-eminently transcendental. In being universally convertible, the ancient Greeks imagined, money *is* everything. Like the Holy Grail, abstract wealth is 'invisible, intangible, but at the same time of infinite, inexhaustible value, containing everything...'[130] Money is everything, and yet – particularly in the current age of digital money – *nothing*. As Graeber concludes, 'money has no essence. It's not "really" anything....'[131] To unravel the peculiarity of money, we must separately consider these two aspects, which at first glance seem diametrically opposed: the concept of universal commensurability and the phenomenon of fetishism. In this chapter, we have traced the emergence of the former. In the next, we shall look closer at the semiotics of fetishism.

Notes

1 Scott 2017: 159.
2 Warburton 2018: 57, 62–65, 74. Contrary to a labour theory of value, the exchange-value of a precious artifact did not reflect the craftsmanship (labour) embodied in it, only its material substance (weight); Warburton 2018: 71–72.
3 Warburton 2018: 60. Ingham (2004: 94) gives the figure 240 grains (a *gur* = about 1.2 hectolitres) of barley. A *gur* of barley was initially estimated as the amount needed to feed a worker and his family for a month; Rosenswig 2024: 238.
4 Wilkinson 2018: 41.
5 Rosenswig 2023: 80. Initially restricted to trade in metals conducted by long-distance merchants, balances facilitated the emergence of money systems based on bullion; Green *et al.* 2024: 107, 132–139. By the mid-1st millennium BC, rulers began to exploit the economic ideology of bullion currency by issuing bimetal coinage – 'at once commodity in theory but fiat in practice'; Green *et al.* 2024: 147.
6 Hart 1986.
7 Yet other designations of the former include fiduciary, or fiat, money; Green *et al.* 2024: 138.
8 Seaford 2004.
9 Barjamovic 2018: 123.
10 Wilkinson 2018: 31–32.
11 Graeber 2001: 92; Wilkinson 2018. After the Romans withdrew from Britain in the early fifth century, Roman coins in Britain were transformed into ceremonial and prestigious valuables, and copies in the form of coin-like, stamped metal disks (bracteates) 'were made with a loop for suspension as jewelry or to be sewn into clothing'; Rosenswig 2023: 78. Referring to Tokovinine, Rosenswig (2024: 246) also mentions 'bundled tally sticks worn in the headdresses of some royal [Maya] figures as wealth displayed in a manner analogous to wearing shell and greenstone bead currencies sown into clothing.'

12 Wilkinson 2018: 35. John Murra (1962: 721) writes that, 'in the Andean area, the artifact of greatest prestige and thus the most useful in power relations was cloth.' However, it never assumed the function of money; see Chapter 8.
13 Frank 1993.
14 Cline 2014.
15 Cline 2014: 75.
16 Cline 2014: 77.
17 Davies 2002: 62–63.
18 Davies 2002: 65.
19 Ingham 2004: 99. Although a confirmed chartalist, Ingham thus acknowledges the great social transformations generated by the introduction of gold and silver coinage.
20 Rosenswig 2024. Adam Green and co-authors write that '[c]urrency issuers, such as the king or government, spend tokens in exchange for labor services or goods they require and simultaneously create a demand for these tokens by insisting that all citizens/vassals/subjects pay tax in the same token currency'; Green *et al.* 2024: 122.
21 Rosenswig 2023: 74.
22 Rosenswig 2023: 75. As Rosenswig (2024: 263) observes, how 'prestigious objects transitioned from media of social accounting, keeping track of on-going social relationships, to serving as financial money of taxation is an important issue of origins.'
23 Davies 2002: 70.
24 Davies 2002: 75–76. In ancient Greece, wage labour was widely regarded as comparable to enslavement; McNally 2020: 70–71.
25 It is ironic that Alexander, a pioneer of the 'military-coinage complex,' as a youth may have been tutored by none other than Aristotle, whose critique of money reverberates through history; Davies 2002: 81. Aristotle's doubts about the limitless pursuit of money through the exchange of commodities reflects ongoing social transformations in Greece in the fourth century BCE; Aristotle 1995: 24–30 (I:9–10).
26 Davies 2002: 82.
27 Davies 2002: 87.
28 Davies 2002: 98.
29 Davies 2002: 100.
30 Davies 2002: 103.
31 Davies 2002: 108.
32 Hart 1986; Ingham 2004: 6; Rosenswig 2023.
33 Rosenswig 2023, 2024.
34 Rosenswig 2023: 72. Applying Graeber's (2011) concept of 'social currencies' as means of accounting, Rosenswig shows how a given system of physical tokens can shift from a currency of social accounting to financial money (as when Iroquois wampum was repurposed by 17th-century European colonists; cf. Davies 2002: 39–42) and vice versa (as when Roman coins in Britain became a social currency after the Romans withdrew). Challenging the position of Nicola Ialongo and co-authors, he argues that hoards of bronze in the European Bronze Age (2300–800 BCE) represented assets for social/symbolic accounting rather than financial money.
35 Ingham 2004: 61. Paradoxically, given Rosenswig's (2023: 73) classification, this would put Marx in the orthodox camp. Marx's position on money was ambiguous. His assertion that paper money 'can never be anything but a symbol [of gold] ... could support the idea that Marx's monetary theory is mainly "metallicist"'; de Brunhoff [1973] 2015: 36–37. On the one hand, 'the physical

material used...is the crucial factor [as regards money's function as a standard of value]'; on the other hand, 'when it functions as a medium of circulation ... its material is irrelevant and its quantity becomes the crucial factor'; Marx cited by de Brunhoff [1973] 2015: 37.

36 Vilar 1976: 10–11. According to Vilar (1976: 26), the ratio of the values of gold and silver in 2700 BCE was 9:1, in 1800 BCE 6:1, and in 600 BCE 12:1.

37 Vilar 1976: 13.

38 Defoe cited in Ingham 2004: 41.

39 Locke cited in Desan 2014: 353.

40 McNally (2020: 143–144) observes that Locke's argument 'pivoted on the need for all economic transactions and contracts to be underpinned by a stable measure of value.'

41 Bjerg 2014: 159.

42 Hart 1986. Some scholars maintain that the distinction between commodity and credit theories of money reflects an ideological polarisation between orthodox and heterodox economists; Rosenswig 2023.

43 Graeber 2011.

44 'If money is just a yardstick,' Graeber asks, 'what then does it measure? The answer was simple: debt. A coin is, effectively, an IOU'; Graeber 2011: 46. Debts are social relations that can be objectified into alienable *things* such as medieval promissory notes, various kinds of credit instruments, coins, modern banknotes, and electronic money; Green *et al.* 2024: 120, 123.

45 Cf. Ingham 2004: 38–39, 46, 97, 108; Ferguson 2008: 28–29; Graeber 2011: 269.

46 Ingham 2004: 46.

47 Ingham 2004: 48.

48 As we shall see in Chapter 3, however, the fetish-character of money problematises the conventional view that money is a representation of value, as 'value' is in turn defined in terms of the quantity of money that something represents.

49 Ingham 2004: 51.

50 Ingham 2004: 109.

51 Vilar 1976: 33.

52 Ingham 2004: 110.

53 Ingham 2004: 110

54 Le Goff 2012: 3–4.

55 Le Goff 2012: 63.

56 Le Goff 2012: 68–72.

57 Wallerstein 1974.

58 Le Goff 2012: 142–150.

59 Marichal 2006, citing Dennis Flynn and Arturo Giráldez.

60 Marichal 2006: 40–42.

61 LeGoff 2012: 150.

62 Davies 2002: 174–175.

63 Dumont 1977. In terms of the history of ideas about morality, Mandeville's argument made it impossible to discriminate between good and evil, because 'what was considered to be the root of all evil, namely the love of money, was also the root of all that was good, namely the bargaining, market principle of Adam Smith'; Macfarlane 1985: 72–73. The triumph of capitalism thus subtly eliminated the very concept of evil, which had been 'encapsulated in St. Paul's warning that "The love of money is the root of all evil" (1 Timothy 6:10)'; Macfarlane 1985: 71.

64 Bjerg 2014: 81. 'Ironically,' he continues, 'the publication of Simmel's *Philosophy of Money* in 1900 marked the end rather than the beginning of the philosophical study of money.'

65 Seaford 2004. The connection between abstract exchange-value and Greek philosophy had previously been developed by A. Sohn-Rethel in the volume *Intellectual and Manual Labour* (1978). For a synopsis of the argument on 'Money, Philosophy, and the Violence of Abstraction,' see McNally 2020: 54–59. Georg Simmel ([1900] 1990: 152) similarly sensed a connection between money and '[t]he growth of intellectual abilities and of abstract thought.' Like Marx, he recognised that money generates abstract ways of thinking and acting, that is, modernity itself; Corbridge and Thrift 1994: 20–21.
66 Seaford 2020.
67 Jaspers [1949] 2021: 9.
68 Jaspers [1949] 2021: 10.
69 Jaspers [1949] 2021:16.
70 Graeber 2011: 314.
71 Seaford 2020: 286.
72 Seaford 2004: 142–143.
73 Seaford 2004: 259.
74 Seaford 2004: 149, 171.
75 Seaford 2004: 317.
76 Seaford 2020: 30–31, 319.
77 Seaford 2020: 260, 268.
78 Seaford 2020: 321.
79 Seaford 2020: 8, reference to Bellah and Joas 2012.
80 Seaford 2004: xi.
81 Graeber 2011.
82 Graeber 2011: 224.
83 David McNally (2020: 39) even proposes that money and slaves were in a sense equivalent.
84 Graeber 2011: 230.
85 Graeber 2011: 238–249.
86 Graeber 2011: 80.
87 This understanding of the Axial Age is reminiscent of Karl Polanyi's thesis on the dialectic between market and society in *The Great Transformation* (1944).
88 Graeber 2011: 318–319.
89 McNally 2020: 1.
90 McNally 2020: 148.
91 Graeber 2011: 342.
92 Graeber 2011: 344.
93 Graeber 2011: 373.
94 Weatherford 1997: 180.
95 McNally 2020: 218.
96 Graeber 2011: 371.
97 McNally 2020: 224.
98 Graeber and Wengrow 2021.
99 McNally 2020: 218–219.
100 McNally 2020: 219.
101 McNally 2020: 219.
102 Corbridge and Thrift 1994: 21.
103 Maurer 2006: 27.
104 Bjerg 2014: 84.
105 Bjerg 2014: 21.
106 Bjerg 2014: 151; emphasis in original.
107 Latour 2005.
108 This is an approach to which we shall return in Chapters 8 and 9.

109 Joas 2012: 10.
110 Sahlins 2022.
111 In semiotic terms, a fundamental feature of the Axial Age has been described as 'the transcendence of the signified over signification'; Jung 2012: 79.
112 Sahlins 2022: 2.
113 Tylor 1871.
114 Sahlins 2022: 14.
115 Latour 2010; Law 2015.
116 Sahlins 2022: 175.
117 Århem 2016; Sahlins 2022: 127.
118 Sahlins 2022: 173.
119 A typical expression of this assumption is Michael Taussig's (1980: 175) framing of Father Joseph de Acosta's 16th-century account of how indigenous people in the Andes were to be taught to honour the Christian God rather than the sun: Acosta mentions a Spanish captain who convinced a native chief that 'the sun is but a servant to the most high lord,' thus writing 'the master-servant relationship into nature.'
120 Sahlins 2022: 130.
121 Sahlins 2022: 131; Dumont [1966] 1972.
122 Sahlins 2022: 148.
123 Sahlins 2022: 154.
124 Graeber and Wengrow 2021: 58; Sahlins 1999: 414.
125 Descola 1994. In a more recent book, Descola (2013: 107, 123–124, 250) abandons references to 'nature' and 'society' in discussing ontologies that do not recognise this distinction.
126 Sahlins 1972: 191–195.
127 Graeber 2001: 101, citing Marc Shell.
128 McNally 2020: 16.
129 Taussig's (1980: 126–127) account of how rural people in Colombia ritually baptise banknotes illustrates how money might be perceived before it becomes an everyday triviality.
130 Graeber 2011: 296, referring to Marc Shell.
131 Graeber 2011: 372.

3 The semiotics of fetishism

Perceived as an index of exchange-value, the money token is the perfect fetish. When Marx adopted the concept of 'fetishism' to expose the illusions of European political economy, he inaugurated an enduring discourse contemplating the cultural dimensions of capitalism. Ever since de Brosses, Europeans had used the term for what they perceived as a confused veneration among non-European peoples of animals, plants, or objects *in themselves*, rather than a reverence for the transcendent forces or principles that they might represent. Fetishism was understood as the logical category mistake of hypostasis: a preoccupation with concrete surface phenomena rather than the power or structure that generates them. De Brosses' treatise in 1760 had identified the philosophical chasm between transcendental, monotheistic religion, on the one hand, and pagan cults of immanent divinities, on the other hand. His deep contempt for the latter served to buttress the prevalent Eurocentric worldview, according to which the thoughts and practices of peoples on other continents were ignorant, immature, and foolish. By Marx's time, it had become the common view in Europe that fetishism was a crude and primitive form of religion. Marx's proposal that 19th-century European economists were fetishists was thus a jarringly effective critique.

The original fetishism

The many centuries of European deliberations on idolatry and magic were fraught with controversies and contradictions because these concerns highlighted what were to be regarded as proper ways of relating to objects. This was a topic that implicated cultural encounters – and the gradual and uneven historical shifts – between immanentist and transcendentalist understandings of metaphysical agency. William Pietz has shown how European references to West African *feitiços* in the 15th, 16th, and 17th centuries must be understood against the shifting background of Christian theology, but that Christian categories could not grasp the particular phenomenon that so confounded the European merchants.[1] *Feitiços* (or *fetissos*) could be used as 'charms worn to protect against disease and misfortune, as objects of pious

DOI: 10.4324/9781032702186-5

offering, as oracles, as idols, as good luck tokens in fishing and in war, as well as oath-vehicles.'[2]

> [T]he paradigmatic image tended to be that of some inanimate material object: a wooden figure, a leather amulet, a gold necklace, a stone, a bone, a feather – by implication any material object at all, however useless or trivial.[3]

Although classified by Europeans as 'witchcraft,' the idea of the fetish originated in 'a mercantile intercultural space' created by trade relations between the mutually incomprehensible cultures of West Africa and Christian Europe, but proper to neither.[4] Early Christian theorists like Tertullian (c. 155–220 AD) and Augustine (354–430 AD) had established that the fabrication of 'artificial' (that is, fraudulent) sacramental objects based on external semblances (*simulacra*) was to be classed as idolatry.[5] For Catholics, the worship of material objects remains ambiguous, as illustrated by cults of relics and saints. In Catholic ritual, the Eucharist uniquely illustrates how objects manufactured by humans can – through consecration – be endowed with spiritual substance. Although denied by the doctrine of transubstantiation, Catholicism thus arguably retains a residue of immanentism, repudiated in the 16th century by the Protestant Reformation, arguably consummating what Sahlins called the 'Second Axial Age.'[6] In the 17th century, the Protestant Dutch who replaced the Portuguese on the Gold and Slave Coasts explicitly equated African fetishes and Catholic sacramental objects.[7] As Rosalind Morris notes, while Protestant commentators were prone to remark on fetishes, Catholic writers tended to speak of idols.[8] Catholics rejected idolatry but remained ambiguous about object agency as such, while Protestants – in dismissing all immanence – were unconditional harbingers of Enlightenment.

Another possible ambiguity regarding Catholic Church doctrine on *feitiços* can be identified in the divergence between Augustine's theology and the Roman emperor Constantine's *Theodosian Code* from 438, which absolves practices of 'remedies' – which, although based on superstition, were fundamentally benevolent – from being classed as criminal sacrilege.[9] Such ambiguities reveal a measure of uncertainty about the efficacy of what Augustine had dismissed as superstition. As Pietz observes, medieval Christian culture had no problems accepting that material objects could embody exceptional powers, whether as legitimate sacramental objects or the instruments of demonic spirits, later dismissed by the Enlightenment.[10] In 16th- and 17th-century accounts of merchant adventurers in West Africa, however, he traces the emergence of a new conception of material objects in terms of objective, technological and commercial use-values that were 'real' in a cross-cultural sense and impervious to the 'delusions of people lacking "reason."'[11] 'Reason' was established as the opposite of superstition: it was the capacity to see the material world as determined by impersonal laws of causality rather than personal intentions. For 17th-century European merchants, 'material objects came to be identified as proper to economic *as opposed* to religious activity.'[12] In the eyes of these Europeans, the Africans they encountered through trade had an 'irrational propensity to personify material (and especially European technological) objects, thereby revealing a false understanding of natural causality.'[13] For them, the Africans' inclination to personify technological objects and to perceive them as products of supernatural powers was evidence of the same primitive ignorance that made them unable to assess the proper value of commodities, such as the gold they naïvely traded for trinkets.

What the 17th-century European disavowal of fetishism dismissed as primitive superstition is now being reevaluated by modern anthropologists referring to animism, immanentism, or object agency.[14] Philosophers of Axiality and transcendentalism are being challenged by the radical relativism of neomaterialism, posthumanism, and the ontological turn. To illustrate how 18th-century Europeans would denounce any indication of immanentism, it is illuminating to explore de Brosses' text from 1760. The central point that he wanted to make is that the worship of animals, plants, and objects among non-Europeans (Africans, in particular) – as in ancient Egypt – should not be interpreted allegorically, as proposed by some theologians, but as direct and literal.[15] One of his justifications for concluding that it is 'the animal taken by itself' rather than an 'arbitrarily chosen emblem' that is worshipped is his conjecture about the presumably strained relation between hypothetical worshippers of cats and rats: 'for then there would be no matter for discord, with all of these types referring back to the same object, like different words of several languages when they signify the same thing.'[16] Although at times including in fetishism the worship of 'things endowed with a divine virtue: oracles, amulets, and protective talismans,'[17] he asserts that (fetishistic) 'worship devoted to certain natural works is essentially different from that which idolatry (as it is commonly called) devoted to works of art representing other objects, to which the adoration was really addressed.'[18] This phrasing suggests that de Brosses thought of fetishism as primarily a cult of living animals and plants, while the worship of inanimate artefacts is generally allegorical. As Pietz has shown, however, the very word 'fetish' ultimately derives (through Portuguese *feitiço*, 'magic' or 'witchcraft') from the Latin adjective *facticius*, denoting 'manufactured.' Fetishes should be distinguished from idols based on their embodied material power versus their 'iconic resemblance to some immaterial model or entity.'[19] For medieval Portuguese, the idol was a false god or spirit, whereas the *feitiço* was 'typically some fabricated object to be worn about the body' as part of a practice aimed at tangible effects.[20]

> Neither fully personal gods, nor fully impersonal charms or amulets, Fetissos were, simultaneously, quasi-personal powers and material objects that were capable of being influenced both through acts of worship, such as making food offerings, and through manipulations of material substances.[21]

Yet, recurrent phrases like 'idolatry and witchcraft' in Portuguese accounts from West Africa indicate that the two categories were not easily distinguished.[22] However, Pietz writes that 'the greater descriptive accuracy of *feitiço* over *idolo* for characterizing the sacramental objects of African religion led in time to the classification of African religion as *feiticaria* rather than *idolatria*.'[23]

The semiotics of fetishism

The very wide application of the concept of fetishism within the history of religion, political economy, psychiatry, philosophy, and aesthetics confirms that it refers to a particular phenomenon that has preoccupied Western thinkers for several centuries. Rather than dismiss the concept as obsolete and condescending, as many have done,[24] we might ask how its significance to Westerners reflects their own concerns, and whether there is, after all, a common denominator in its several applications that can be succinctly defined. In a general sense, it refers to a seemingly unwarranted human infatuation with an object. In a highly diverse list of examples of what might qualify as fetishes, Pietz includes flags, monuments, landmarks, talismans, sacramental objects, earrings, tattoos, cities, and nations.[25] As indicated by this list, the topic seems potentially as infinite as the propensity of humans to charge their artefacts and environments with special significance. Indeed, the discourse on various forms of fetishism is truly vast, and the list of possible ethnographic or historical cases of such human–object relations seems unlimited.[26] However, an analytically more focused approach would ask in what sense the concept of fetishism evokes a particular *kind* of human–object relations. What did de Brosses, Marx, and Freud have in mind when they applied the concept to primitive religion, ideological mystification, and sexual deviation? In all three cases, what these post-Enlightenment thinkers found extraordinary was the perception among certain people that an object – an amulet, a banknote, or a shoe – had *immanent* power. To the people concerned, these artefacts had an agency of their own that affected their persons. All three thinkers felt compelled to expose these varieties of fetishism by revealing more encompassing relations – theological,[27] economic, or psychological – that accounted for the myopic infatuation with objects. In semiotic terms, the objects had come to serve as *indexical* signs of what they referred to – divinity, economic value, or sexual desire.[28] A succinct definition of fetishism might be that it involves the transformation of non-indexical (for instance, symbolic) into indexical reference. In the Saussurian idiom adopted by Jean Baudrillard, it can be expressed as an identity between signifier and signified, or as the 'autonomy of the signifier.'

The concern with relations between humans and objects necessarily implicates the role of materiality. Pietz argues that the discourse on fetishism reflects the emergence of a 'theoretical materialism' that is incompatible with traditional philosophy.[29] Referring to Pietz's observations on the 'irreducible materiality' of the fetish, Patricia Spyer notes that the perspective of social constructionism 'begs the question of how and why certain things exercise the immense powers they do over persons and collectivities.'[30] It explains away, she continues, 'the extraordinary power that with fetishism is precisely the problem.' Yet, to replace constructionism with a 'new materialism' is insufficient, because it tends to displace agency to the object itself, rather than account for the dialectic between human attributions and signified objects.[31] Neomaterialism thus serves as a confirmation of fetishism. If, as Michael Taussig observes, '[t]he fetish absorbs into itself that which it represents, erasing all traces of the represented,'[32] this is clearly not the result of an agency originating in the object, but a consequence of how the object is perceived. Although, as will be evident in Chapter 4, I wholeheartedly agree with the neomaterialists that the material dimension of social processes is systematically ignored in most social theory, this omission is not rectified by attributing autonomous agency to – that is, fetishising – matter.[33]

The post-Enlightenment preoccupation with fetishes, curios, and rarities as displaced and *decontextualised* objects, which was foundational to many modern museum collections, appears to reflect the logic of the globalising market.[34] Peter Pels suggests that the decontextualised object, prone to be understood as having a power of its own, renders the tenets of social constructionism inapplicable. He criticises constructionism for treating 'the social as nothing but a human product' and seeing 'the materiality of social life as just an empty carrier or representation of human intention and artifice,' arguing that the fetish 'militates against this idealism and suggests a counterbalancing materiality.'[35] In revisiting de Brosses' and Pietz's opposition between the idol (as *representation* of a false spirit) and the fetish (as material *presence*), Pels suggests that the fetish challenges the post-Enlightenment discourse on representation, the Saussurian distinction between signifier and signified, and the very concept of the sign. The discourse on representation, he argues, is idealist in so far as the signifier is understood as material and the signified a mental category. However, although this may be a valid conclusion from much Saussurian semiotics (or semiology, as Saussure called the field), it is not a necessary implication of Peirce's model of the sign. Rather than a material signifier standing for a conceptual signified, it is equally plausible for a conceptual signifier to stand for a material signified. Moreover, the concept of indexicality or indexical mode of reference well covers the peculiarity of the fetish, understood as a sign that refers only to itself. Contrary to Pels' conclusion, the phenomenon of fetishism thus gives us no reason to reject the concerns of semiotics.

Marxian fetishism

Whereas most of the examples of 'fetishes' mentioned by de Brosses refer to living animals or plants, Pietz has shown that the *feitiços* encountered by Europeans in West Africa were generally artefacts. They were often fabricated tokens of oaths and social agreements, which they can thus be said to have symbolised, but were prone to be perceived as indexes – fearfully empowered agents – rather than mere symbols. In such situations, Graeber suggests, 'objects really do, in a sense, bring into being what they represent.'[36] When people take oaths and 'call on an object to strike them dead if they fail to live up to those obligations, that object does not thereby acquire the power to do so,' but it is undeniably endowed with the power to organise social relations.[37] Graeber follows Marcel Mauss in suggesting that such subject/object reversals are an integral part of how society is constituted. To thus understand fetishism as the attribution to objects of the power to organise society necessarily implies that such objects are perceived as intrinsically empowered. In modern societies, the closest thing to *feitiços* would be contracts, legal texts, and – of course – money. As Graeber observes, this phenomenon – humans making things which they then treat as if those things had power over them – is precisely what Marx had in mind when he used the concept of fetishism.[38] 'Like African fetishists, the argument goes, we end up making things and then treating them like gods.'[39] Marx recognised that, in capitalism, objects are regularly understood as having an agency that ultimately derives from that of humans: 'capital grows, money is always fleeing one market and seeking out another, pork bellies doing this, the annuities market doing that.'[40] From a Marxist perspective, as money represents the value of labour, and labourers work to get money, money is also 'a representation that brings into being what it represents.'[41] Graeber notes that the logic of fetishism – whether identified in magic, power relations, or the economy – is ultimately the paradox of something that exists 'only if other people think it does.'[42]

For Marx, the analogy between fetishism as a religious phenomenon and what he referred to as 'the fetish-character of the commodity'[43] is encapsulated in his observation that social relations between humans in both cases assume the form of relations between things. Thus, in Marx's view, the surplus value generated by labour erroneously appears to be the product of capital. This is most evident in the concept of interest-bearing capital, expressed in the formula M-M[1], which mystifies the social relations between capitalists and workers by attributing to money the capacity to propagate itself *by itself*. In Marx's own words, '[i]nterest-bearing capital is the consummate *automatic fetish*....'[44] Marx realised that the embodiment of abstract exchange-value in the concrete form of money was the very source of economic fetishism:

> In money the unfettered dominion of the estranged thing *over* man becomes manifest. The rule of the person over the person now becomes the universal rule of the *thing* over the *person*, the product over the producer.[45]

Agreeing with Adam Smith that property derives from labour, Marx criticised as fetishism the mercantilists' view that wealth consists in money and precious metals.[46] In *Grundrisse*, he observes that each individual

> must produce a general product – *exchange value*, or, the latter isolated for itself and individualized, *money*. ... [E]xchange value is a generality,

> in which all individuality and peculiarity are negated and extinguished. ... In exchange value, the social connection between persons is transformed into a social relation between things...[47]

Desmond McNeill asserts that the concept of fetishism is of central importance to Marx's theory of value, yet Marx's use of the term as an approximation of *mystification* – the attribution to things of characteristics which are 'not in fact inherent to them' – does not necessarily imply a theory of value at all.[48] McNeill believes that the concept of commodity fetishism cannot be appreciated 'without being very sympathetic towards Marx's labour theory of value – at least in its qualitative aspect,'[49] but this conclusion is unwarranted. The appositeness of Marx's invocation of fetishism is indisputable, but the fact that commodities are perceived as autonomous objects dissociated from the various inputs in their production is a valid observation regardless of our approach to value. Commodities are alienated from inputs not only of human labour but also of materials and nonhuman energy, which are equally essential. Whereas McNeill refers to Marx's remark that, '[f]rom the moment that men in any way work for one another, their labour assumes a social form,'[50] it is just as true to observe that all other biophysical inputs in production, embodied in commodities traded on the market, assume a social form. Money and commodities do transform social relations of exchange between people into relations between things, but this does not in itself confirm a theory of value exclusively focused on labour.

The omission of embodied materials and nonhuman energy – which are as unequally traded as embodied labour – is similarly questionable in McNally's '*de-fetishizing* criticism' of accounts of monetary and financial history that neglect the exploitation of labouring bodies.[51] McNally rejects the mercantilist devotion to precious metals as 'fetishistic' because it 'confuses the thing (precious metal) with the activity – labor – that brings it into being,' and thus 'mistakes a *result* for a cause,'[52] but as the phenomenon of 'financialisation' amply illustrates, it would be misleading to propose that money (whether metal, paper, or electronic) exclusively derives from labour. As we have seen, the phenomenon of fetishism is more complex than a confusion of 'cause' and 'result.'

The material, the social, and the perceptual

This questioning of the labour theory of value – the conviction that labour is the only input in production that generates surplus value – is importantly connected to the argument that will be pursued in Chapter 5, focusing on the fetishism of technology. Marx viewed technological progress – the ever-advancing forces of production – as capital accumulation spurred by competition between industrialists. In his view, machinery is congealed, past (or 'dead') labour, invested in the service of advances in engineering, while the requisite natural resources are understood as 'spontaneously provided by nature.'[53]

From a conventional Marxist perspective, the spectacular 'Industrial Revolution' in Britain can thus be accounted for as a product of British labour, British engineering, and British resources. As we shall see in the next chapter, however, such a view is no longer tenable. The machinery employed by early British capitalists embodied massive inputs of labour and resources from throughout the British Empire. The Industrial Revolution in Britain was globally constituted, but the lens of money prices obscured the asymmetric resource flows that made it possible. Again, the concept of fetishism can serve to contextualise the seemingly autonomous materiality of a human artefact. What I have recurrently referred to as 'machine fetishism' denotes our inclination to think of technical artefacts as detached from the global social relations through which they are constituted.[54] In succinctly capturing the essence of the Marxian concept of fetishism, Michael Taussig's account is clearly applicable to technical artefacts:

> If we 'thingify' parts of a living system, ignore the context of which they are a part, and then observe that the things move, so to speak, it logically follows that the things may well be regarded or spoken of as though they were alive with their own autonomous powers.[55]

Machines clearly illustrate how relations between people are perceived as relations between things. This illusion became particularly prominent during the Industrial Revolution in colonial Britain but remains hegemonic today. To expose machine fetishism as ideology is to challenge not only mainstream but also heterodox economics, because both are equally mired in the binary worldview in which material nature is axiomatically external to society and social theory. However, if Marx's concept of capital accumulation is extended to denote the asymmetric *material* flows that are congealed in technology, which means acknowledging that a distinction between the social and the material can only be made *analytically*, the ontological implications are deeply unsettling. The illusion that capital is productive 'in itself'[56] serves to mystify not only the exploitation of industrial labour but also the appropriation of embodied labour, land, materials, and nonhuman energy from throughout the world.[57] When a Marxist theorist observes that '[c]apital appears to be inherently, or autonomously productive; but it is not,'[58] such a post-dualist framing of capitalist fetishism must – counterintuitively – parochialise the myopic trust in technology and 'productive forces' that have bedazzled mainstream and Marxist economists alike. Technological increases in productivity in wealthier parts of the world regularly occur at the *expense* of labour and resources in other parts.

To propose that the work accomplished by a machine is in some sense illusory is indeed counterintuitive and must be qualified. In a physical sense, of course, it is not illusory, but in a social sense it *is*, because the work thought to be conducted by the machine is really a transmutation of labour and resources appropriated from elsewhere. The efficacy of the machine is contingent on terms of trade. The technological fetish differs from the original *feitiço* in that its power is not restricted to belief-based social phenomena like causing illness or underscoring authority but can include the *physical* power to transform the material world. In hindsight, this was the essence of the Industrial Revolution. In extending its agency beyond the social into the natural, the machine fetish was immune to deconstruction from the start, but this finally only reflects the ontological dichotomy of nature and society in Enlightenment thought – and the imagined unassailability of physical nature – rather than absolving the machine from fetishism. The power of the machine is not intrinsic to that object but concentrated in it by drawing resources from a global social field of appropriation.

To accept the machine as an example of fetishism means accepting that 'the social' is infused with 'the material,' because the material flows that pervade the social phenomenon of trade are essential to machine technology. But to decisively unsettle our entrenched habit of strictly distinguishing the material from the social, we need to elucidate how, in the machine, the material is also imbued with the social. A suitable point of departure might be McNeill's deliberations on the relation between the two. He resolutely asserts that '[m]aterial reality is independent of the beliefs of persons, social reality is not.'[59] Further on, he repeats that social phenomena 'owe their existence to the beliefs and actions of persons,' whereas '[m]aterial reality does not.'[60] However, given that the feasibility of a given technology is contingent on the market prices of inputs in its production and outputs of its operation, and that market prices – and the trust in money and monetary value as such – are ultimately contingent on beliefs, McNeill's seemingly incontestable assertions *do not apply to machines*. If machinery is capital, in the sense that they share the same conditions of existence, it dissolves McNeill's distinction between social and material phenomena. McNeill acknowledges that it would be 'impossible to describe any economic phenomenon in terms which did not refer to the beliefs of the society in which the phenomenon is manifested,'[61] but he does not recognise the extent to which technologies, although material, in turn may rely on such economic phenomena.

The seemingly impermeable conceptual boundary between physical nature and human society remains a formidable obstacle to grasping the human predicament in the Anthropocene. A crucial element in the argument that this boundary is not as impermeable as it seems is that it is *money that makes it permeable*. Given that the institutionalisation of money and market prices – ultimately based on beliefs – is fundamental to global social metabolism (in determining the ratios at which embodied labour and other biophysical resources are exchanged on the world market), the phenomenon of modern technology represents a sphere of reality where the social and the material intersect. This is why both money and technology continue to elude full comprehension in terms of being definitively positioned in the dualist worldview. To be able to assume responsibility for its technologies, humankind must be prepared to acknowledge the extent to which the global economy fuses arbitrary social arrangements and material conditions.

Pondering Marx's observation that the social relations of labour assume the form of value, McNeill asks himself if it is 'possible wholly to separate the perception from the social phenomenon perceived?'[62] Further on, he continues to deliberate on this topic:

> What is the relationship between the phenomenon of capitalism and the categories used to describe it? To what extent is the reality separable from the categories? How far do the categories themselves not merely reinforce but even create this reality?[63]

McNeill finally arrives at the fundamentally anthropological insight that '[t]he categories through which we perceive the economic system are themselves part of that system.'[64] Clearly, social phenomena are *contingent* on perceptions. However, given our deep-rooted – and in other respects valid – ontological distinction between the perceptual and the material, we tend to resist the acknowledgement that technologies, while material, are social phenomena.

The fetishisation of value

Having observed that the trust in money as a measure of value is ultimately a matter of belief, we also need to consider McNeill's discussion of Marxian value theory. Like Aristotle more than two millennia earlier, Marx was perplexed by the problem of commensurability. What is it that makes different kinds of things comparable on the market? Marx was discontent with Aristotle's reference to money: for him, the fact that all commodities could be exchanged for money was not an explanation but the phenomenon to be explained.[65] Using analogies referring to geometrical and physical properties, Marx concludes that 'the exchange values of commodities must be reduced to a common element, of which they represent a greater or a lesser quantity.'[66] He finds that the only conceivable common substance of commodities is 'simple, homogeneous, abstract general labour.'[67] However, unlike physically intrinsic properties like weight, Marx notes, exchange-value is a social property that is always relative to that of other commodities. McNeill rightly finds it problematic that Marx, while arguing that value is a relative, social phenomenon, uses 'analogies of an entirely natural, asocial kind in order to try and understand or explain the concept.'[68] He suggests that it was to avoid the idealism of Hegel that Marx chose a material model for conceptualising value, which in McNeill's view is inappropriate.[69] In attempting to straddle the issue, Marx's concept of abstract labour – 'socially necessary labour time' – is a hybrid between relative and intrinsic properties. It proposes that the value of a commodity is simultaneously relative to that of other commodities and inherent in the history of its production. When Marx refers to value as 'the immanent measure of commodities in exchange,' McNeill proposes that it would be more accurate to say that money is the measure of value.[70] In McNeill's view, Marx would have been more consistent if he had said that money is the measure and value that which is measured. His proposal presupposes that value is defined in the objective and intrinsic sense that Marx's labour theory of value suggests. It would indicate that money is to value like area to space, temperature to heat, and weight to gravity, where that which is measured is 'ontologically prior' to the measure.[71] But this reveals the limitation of the analogy, because it is in fact perfectly valid to suggest that money is ontologically prior to value.[72] Heat, gravity, and space are physical phenomena, but value is a social phenomenon. Thermometers, scales, and rulers do not create physical reality, but socially constructed phenomena can be *produced by our modes of measuring them.*[73] In applying analogies from natural science, Marx neglected the pioneering insight on social phenomena that was fundamental to much of his own thinking and rightly lauded by McNeill: that human categories are constitutive of economic systems. This is what justifies Marx's use of the concept of fetishism. As Graeber observes, money is a representation that brings into being what it represents. To say that money is a representation of value, as is commonly proclaimed by Marxists,[74] is to understand money as the signifier and value as the signified, but it would be more valid to invert the relation, recognising that the concept of value signifies the amount of money that a commodity can fetch on the market. Marx's concept of money fetishism is no less incisive when stripped of the labour theory of value – on the contrary, it is then that its true magic can be fathomed. McNeill writes that a central question in his book has been

> [w]hat is the ontological status of value; what is it that renders something valuable – transmuting it from an object to a commodity? And here the concept of the fetish is a useful analogy; for a fetish is, in a sense, 'real'; it has real effects, not because of its material but its social qualities: the shared beliefs and practices of society.[75]

This constructionist strain in Marx's thinking suggests that the logical answer to McNeill's question indeed is money. Money fetishism defines value. There is no need for a labour theory of value.

Instead of analogies to value derived from physical nature, McNeill proposes that Marx ought to have used the analogy of language and meaning. He finds it unfortunate that 'Marx tended to favour mechanical, material analogies – based in a nineteenth century, almost Newtonian world view.'[76] McNeill's aim is rather 'to show how semiotics can contribute to an understanding of value and the commodity, and hence of Marxian economics.'[77] Drawing on the Saussurian tradition, he argues that value in both economics and linguistics combines two kinds of relations: a relation of signification (between signifier and signified) and a relation between signifiers.[78] McNeill proposes that, in the Marxian terminology, exchange-value is to be understood as signifier and use-value as signified. It is valid to observe that a commodity's exchange-value is determined in relation to that of all other commodities (that is, other signifiers), but to equate use-value and signified raises problematic questions about Marxian value theory that McNeill does not acknowledge. Central to Marx's theory of value is that exchange-value signifies a quantity of socially necessary labour time, not a qualitative use-value. While McNeill recognises some of the limits of his analogy between economics and language – particularly the incapacity of language to quantify – he appears not to note how his equation of use-value and signified jars with the labour theory of value. Yet, his reasoning about how values are social constructs – 'they exist by virtue of meaning' rather than being 'simply concerned with material things' – is thoroughly justified, indicating why Marx's 'metaphors based on the material world are necessarily limiting.'[79] This is persuasively demonstrated in a chapter referring to some thinkers – from Veblen to Baudrillard – who have focused on the symbolic and cultural (as opposed to material) dimension of use-value and consumption.[80] The chapter ends with a critical comment on Marx's emphasis on production rather than consumption – and on his understanding of needs and use-values as material rather than social – but does not pursue the profoundly problematic implications that this should have for Marxist theory.

The fetishisation of nature

An important aim in McNeill's book is to show how Marxist theory can be applied to modern environmental issues. Six of the eight endorsements in the beginning of the book praise its application of Marx's framework to how capitalism shapes the relations between humans and their natural environment. Yet, after mentioning some recent debates in ecological Marxism, McNeill draws the disappointing conclusion that '[t]he main way in which Marx's theory of value connects with nature is through the concept of rent.'[81] Ground-rent is the sum of money paid by capitalist entrepreneurs to landowners for the right to exploit a piece of land. The discourse on rent is inextricably entangled with the idea that nature can be assigned a price, which McNeill himself rightly criticises.[82] His valid conclusion that rent theory is the main relevance of Marxian value theory for environmental issues is to concede that it does not have much to say on the topic. McNeill notes that several writers have found that Marxian value theory tends to be abandoned when environmental issues are addressed.[83]

Attempts to complement the Marxian labour theory of value with environmental considerations can be traced from James O'Connor to Jason W. Moore,[84] but the ensuing debates have demonstrated that the contradiction is not easily straddled. An illuminating exchange on the topic is the discussion between Giorgos Kallis and Erik Swyngedouw – *Do Bees Produce Value?* – which McNeill mentions.[85] Kallis asks Swyngedouw to explain why Marxian value theory privileges human labour, among all the inputs in production, as the only source of the kind of Value (with a capital V) that can be appropriated (as surplus value) by capitalists. Swyngedouw responds by providing a standard presentation of the Marxist framework. It is logically coherent, and there are some points of agreement – for instance, that natural resources are 'undervalued' – but Kallis remains unconvinced. He questions why Marxists reckon with the natural environment only in terms of 'rent' or 'productivity increase,' but not as a source of Value, and he believes that Marxist theory fetishises 'productivity' when it is treated as external to value creation. At a more general level, Kallis objects that the 'proof' that 'socially necessary labour time' (SNLT) is the only thing that two different commodities have in common ultimately rests on an unprovable assertion:

> This is how I understand Marx's LTV [labour theory of value]. It starts from an unprovable but reasonable assertion that this is what value is under capitalism and then on the basis of this premise builds a whole edifice, which gives a pretty compelling explanation of how capitalism works. ... But [the] usefulness of a theory should not be confused for reality.[86]

At this point, Swyngedouw appears to retreat, conceding that several Marxists have 'abandoned the LTV but argue that the analysis of capitalism as proposed by Marx is largely valid even if one rejects the LTV.' He dismisses Kallis' claim that Marx's labour theory of value is based merely on assertions, but his concession that the Marxist analysis of capitalism is not inextricably founded on it is significant.

A recurrent notion in Marxian critiques of capitalism is that labour and natural resources are 'undervalued' or 'underpaid,' but such a way of phrasing exploitation inserts the same conceptual error as committed by mainstream economists when they assert that market prices 'externalize costs.' The implicit assumption shared by both orthodox and heterodox economists appears to be that labour and natural resources have objectively 'correct' monetary values that market prices may fail to cover. The notion of objective values, whether based on socially necessary labour time or the value of ecosystem services, thus assumes that everything – including nature – can be evaluated in monetary terms. This follows logically from the view that money is a representation of value, rather than *vice versa*. It illustrates how the fetishised artefact of all-purpose money has not only become the measure of all things but also has infiltrated and organised the way we think about biophysical processes.[87] The length to which this fetishism will go is epitomised in the widespread complaint among Marxist, ecological, and environmental economists that capitalism does *not* properly value nature.[88] The implicit assumption again seems to be that money *can* measure the value of nature. This delusory notion finally also unravels the Marxian conviction that money is an approximate representation of value, defined in terms of 'socially necessary labour time.' What does it mean for a Marxist to say that 'it is the equilibrium price that comes closest to approximating value'?[89] In what sense can a sum of money paid on a global market be understood as a valid measure of the value of a given quantity of human time? Whose time, spent doing what, when, and where? Why should it be possible to approximate its correct value in terms of money?

The fetishisation of productivity

Besides environmental issues, a topic to which McNeill devotes a separate chapter is financialisation, that is, the increasing derivation of profits from financial income rather than from trade and production. A traditional Marxist approach would define financialisation as deriving from interest-bearing capital. In Marx's view, interest is 'part of the profit (which, in its turn, is itself nothing but surplus-value, unpaid labour....'[90] However, the ascendancy of financialisation has rendered the labour theory of value increasingly dubious. McNeill mentions the rising importance of capital accumulation from financial instruments such as derivatives based on housing mortgages and futures markets for agricultural products.[91] The material agency of money in financialisation invalidates Marx's distinction between 'real' and 'fictitious' capital.[92] McNeill reviews the argument of Brett Christophers that financial capital is as productive of value as labour, suggesting a complete revision of Marxian value theory.[93] Financialisation underscores the conclusion in the previous section that money may be 'ontologically prior' to value. Money begets more money as a result of its own fetishised inertia – there is no need to search for a more 'real' source of value than the idea of value itself. Whereas a conventional Marxist approach would regard financialisation as an extreme fetishisation of the exploitation of labour (that is, as an excessive mystification of 'real' social relations), Christophers' observation goes beyond the division into real versus illusory, as the illusions are part of the fabric of capitalist society and contribute to generating its inequalities. We could add that the attribution of agency to pork bellies and markets for annuities which Graeber ridicules[94] is finally no more fetishistic than Marxian references to the agency of 'capital' itself.[95] The critique of money fetishism is thus itself fetishised. The fetishisation of an abstract 'capitalist economic system' is evident, for instance, in Paul Sweezy's claim that capitalism has an 'obsession with capital accumulation,' 'never standing still,' 'adopting' and 'discarding' methods of production, 'opening up new territories,' 'subjecting' weak societies to its purposes, 'riding roughshod' over its own beneficiaries, and 'perceiving' the natural environment as a means to profit-making.[96] Such anthropomorphic projections of immoral intentions onto an 'economic system' deflect our attention from the idea and artefact of money, which ultimately *incites* people to behave in such unethical ways.

Graeber's brilliant history of debt[97] was largely induced by the global financial crisis that began in September 2008 and abundantly illustrated what the excessive fetishism of financialisation could have in store for some of the participants in the money game. Graeber's indignation is evident:

> For years, everyone had been hearing of a whole host of new, ultra-sophisticated financial innovations: credit and commodity derivatives, collateralized mortgage obligation derivatives, hybrid securities, debt swaps, and so on. These new derivative markets were so incredibly sophisticated... ... The message was transparent: leave these things to the professionals. You couldn't possibly get your minds around this. ... Then, when the rubble had stopped bouncing, it turned out that many if not most of [these new forms of securitization] had been nothing more than very elaborate scams.[98]

How does the fetishised idea of value organise the material world? How do we account for the fact that Marxist theory, while ultimately concerned with the logic of money, is so focused on tangible processes of production and 'productive forces'? To unravel this paradox of historical materialism, we must revisit Marx's understanding of industrial technology and the pervasive but misleading distinction between the material and the social. As we have seen, Marx appears to have consistently believed in an ultimate divide between material objects and social relations, distinguishing between machinery and the *use* of machinery.[99] McNeill quotes Marx and Engels' assertion that a machine for spinning cotton 'becomes *capital* only in certain relations,'[100] but my point is that the new machines developed during and since the Industrial Revolution are capital – that is, part of capitalist social relations – to begin with. Their physical existence is contingent on asymmetric global resource transfers. The Industrial Revolution was the point in history when new technologies could be developed only because of the discrepant prices of labour and other resources within the colonial and capitalist world-system. The turn to steam technology in British cotton factories was inextricably connected to the Atlantic slave trade, inexpensive slave labour in the cotton plantations, and inexpensive American land. While Europeans could not detect such a difference between premodern machines and steam engines, the discontinuity signified *the point at which human ingenuity did not suffice to account for technological progress*. From now on, advanced technologies were inherently contingent on environmental and workload displacement through the world market. Industrial machines *are* capital in their very constitution.

McNeill interprets Marx's position as implying that 'an emphasis on the social as opposed to the material necessarily also involves an emphasis on relations as opposed to entities.'[101] But this opposition is questionable, as objects perceived as 'entities' on closer scrutiny generally also prove to consist of relations. This is as evident in the field of ecology as in the study of the global economy: no unit of study can be accounted for except by reference to the wider context of relations. From this perspective, the fact that capital 'appears to be inherently, or autonomously productive, but it is not'[102] implicates not only the local relation between worker and capitalist but also the global relations of exchange that have made industrial machinery possible. The machine is a material object but simultaneously represents a (global) social relation. The asymmetric exchange relations embodied in machines are socially constructed in the sense that market prices (that is, exchange rates) reflect the subjective 'willingness to pay' of market actors. Industrial technology thus invalidates McNeill's assertion, echoing Marx's assumption, that material reality is independent of the beliefs of persons, whereas social reality is not.[103] Machinery dissolves the conventional distinction between the material and the social. It also reveals the inadequacy of a 'materialism' that conceptualises the substance of social exchange in terms of 'value.'[104]

The theory of ecologically unequal exchange has disturbing implications for our understanding of modern technology, which must problematise the Marxist understanding of the relation between the material and the social, as reflected in the distinction between technical 'productive forces' and social 'relations of production.' The productive forces of industrial Britain were not simply products of engineering knowledge applied to nature but of asymmetric, global social relations. The capitalist drive for increased productivity through technological innovation that was celebrated by Marx and Schumpeter is ultimately a way of displacing work and environmental loads to low-wage sectors of the world economy. The heightened productivity of the British worker was thus accomplished at the expense of people and environments in Britain's colonial periphery. The relations of production had become global, but Marx's interpretation of the social processes of mid-19th-century Britain remained conceptually confined to the factory. He concluded that the rationality of mechanisation is 'limited by the requirement that less labour must be expended in producing the machinery than is displaced by the employment of that machinery,'[105] but appears not to have let his celebration of technology be marred by considering that a machine might well embody more labour than it displaces, due to wage disparities between different sectors of the global economy – in other words, that low-wage labour in extraction may subsidise the operation of industrial machinery.

As the conceptual divide between material objects and social relations continues to govern our thoughts 250 years after the onset of the Industrial Revolution, we must determine precisely in what sense modern technology deludes us. Great intellectual energy has been invested in attempting to dissolve the boundary between the material and the social aspects of technology, most famously by the so-called 'material turn' or 'new materialism' championed by Bruno Latour and the proponents of Actor-Network Theory. The phenomenon of modern technology clearly dissolves the boundary between the material and the social in a more fundamental way than generally imagined by proponents of the new materialism. To Marx, as to most of his contemporaries, dissolving that boundary was simply unfeasible. The operation of the steam engine to him ultimately signified a 'natural' (extra-social) phenomenon rather than a social relation – a relation between things rather than a relation between people. In Chapter 5, we shall explore some of the modern consequences of such technological fetishism.

At this point, we can observe that the original *feitiço* and the machine share two features that jointly justify their common classification as species of fetishism: (1) they are both based on illusions and mystifications of social reality and (2) they are both means of subjugating and exerting power over others. In the former case, their power can be neutralised by subjective means, as when dismissed by 'enlightenment' as superstition. Technological superiority, however, cannot be thus neutralised, as millenarian attempts at indigenous resistance (for instance, the Lakota Ghost Dancers) have bitterly experienced. Although ultimately founded on the subjective perceptions of market agents, technological power remains inaccessible to deconstruction, because it is *one step removed* from the perceptual. In the passage from market conditions to engineering, the contingency of the latter on the former is lost from view, and the power of the machine appears invincible. In the next two chapters, we shall examine how this invincibility is devised.

Notes

1 Pietz 1985, 1987, 1988.
2 Pietz 1987: 43.
3 Pietz 1988: 109.
4 Pietz 1987: 24.
5 Pietz 1987: 27. The epistemology of resemblance and analogy underlying much of the thought dismissed as 'magical' illustrates the significance of what Peirce called iconic modes of reference.
6 Although Max Weber did not refer to the Axial Age, he classified Catholic practices as remnants of or relapses into magic. Hans Joas (2012: 20) interprets Weber's concept of 'disenchantment' as denoting 'demagicisation.'
7 Pietz 1987: 39.
8 Morris 2017: 146. Morris (2017: 311) even suggests that the 'new materialisms' and 'Object-Oriented Ontologies,' which have emerged in the wake of Bruno Latour's defence of what de Brosses and his followers dismissed as fetishism, represent 'the late vengeance of the Catholic missionaries and sailors who did not speak of fetishes.'
9 Pietz 1987: 32.
10 Pietz 1987: 35.
11 Pietz 1987: 36.
12 Pietz 1987: 40; italics in original.
13 Pietz 1987: 23.
14 Descola 2013; Sahlins 2022; Latour 2010.
15 As Daniel Leonard (2017) explains, de Brosses' text is largely a polemic aimed at 'figurism,' the inclination to understand such worship as distorted traces of more transcendental tenets. De Brosses' ambition is to identify the specific character of fetishism as a distinct form of primitive religion once prevalent throughout the world, rather than to engage in speculative figurism, which occurs 'whenever the forces of "civilization" wish to remake the past in their own image'; Leonard 2017: 15.
16 De Brosses [1760] 2017: 72.
17 De Brosses [1760] 2017: 46, 111.

18 De Brosses [1760] 2017: 61. De Brosses ([1760] 2017: 121) writes that 'the worship of animals seems to be markedly older in Egypt than that of idols.'
19 Pietz 1985: 7.
20 Pietz 1985: 10; Pietz 1987: 36.
21 Pietz 1987: 40.
22 Pietz 1987: 31, 37.
23 Pietz 1987: 37.
24 For instance, Latour 2010. 'To accuse something of being a fetish,' says Latour (2004: 243), 'is the ultimate gratuitous, disrespectful, insane, and barbarous gesture.' As Pietz (2021: 266) has recently observed, '[n]owadays the theory of fetishism is discredited as a colonial phantasm, and most people would agree with the anthropologist Marcel Mauss that the notion "represents nothing but an immense misunderstanding between two civilizations, the African and the European."'
25 Pietz 1985: 14.
26 For overviews, see Apter and Pietz 1993; Spyer 1998b; Iacono 2016; Morris 2017.
27 For de Brosses, the more encompassing relations of the fetish were theological, whereas Pietz (1987: 23) emphasises 'the dependence of the fetish for its meaning and value on a particular order of social relations, which it in turn reenforces.'
28 Sebeok 1994: 101. Given this semiotic perspective on fetishism, a central controversy underlying the Reformation was whether the sacraments of the Eucharist are to be understood as symbols or indices.
29 Pietz 1985: 6.
30 Pietz 1985: 7; Spyer 1998a: 5.
31 Latour 2010; Bennett 2010.
32 Taussig 1992: 138.
33 Hornborg 2021; Boysen and Lundsfryd Rasmussen 2023.
34 Pels 1998: 109–113.
35 Pels 1998: 112.
36 Graeber 2001: 251.
37 Graeber 2001: 251.
38 Graeber 2007: 137.
39 Graeber 2007: 140.
40 Graeber 2007: 140. Bjerg (2014: 31) similarly observes that people tend to speak about 'the Market' as an independent entity, although '[i]t could be argued that the market as such does not exist.' This tendency may be part of a wider pattern than is recognised by Marxian political economy. Sahlins (2022: 71–72) notes that the modern attribution of personhood and agency to inanimate entities is pervasive, extending to universities, corporations, currencies, political parties, town councils, nations, and much more.
41 Graeber 2007: 141.
42 Graeber 2007: 143. Graeber adds that, in a more general way, this is also the paradox of creativity. The perception that our creations have power over us is not an illusion – it is simply true that 'we tend to become the slaves of our own creations.'
43 Morris 2017: 188.
44 Marx cited in McNeill 2020: 68.
45 Marx cited in McNeill 2020: 28.
46 McNeill 2020: 30–31. In this restricted sense, Marx challenged a commodity theory of money, but as Ingham (2004: 61) has argued, his labour theory of value is conducive to a commodity approach to money. Marx at times followed Ricardo in proposing that the value of gold and silver is determined by the quantity of labour time that they embody, but he also aspired to account for artificially scarce but

'valueless' money as an 'instrument of circulation, completely detached from its metallic substance'; de Brunhoff [1973] 2015: 24, 26, 33–37. Suzanne de Brunhoff ([1973] 2015: 35) concedes that 'the analysis of paper money is not entirely clear in *Capital*.'

47 Marx [1939] 1973: 157.
48 McNeill 2020: 36, 40.
49 McNeill 2020: 75.
50 McNeill 2020: 45.
51 McNally 2020: 2, 135; emphasis in original.
52 McNally 2020: 122; emphasis in original. McNally (2020: 183) also classifies as 'fetishism of precious metals' the American mistrust of paper currency in the 18th century.
53 Marx [1876] 1976: 284.
54 See, for instance, Hornborg 1992, 2001a, 2023.
55 Taussig 1980: 36.
56 As Morris (2017: 190) observes, the phrase 'in-itself' is the very mark of fetishism.
57 The perspective of 'ecologically unequal exchange' (Dorninger *et al.* 2021) would contest McNeill's (2020: 202) assertions that 'all inputs into production can be expressed in terms of labour' and that 'exploitation occurs [only] in production, not in exchange.'
58 McNeill 2020: 70.
59 McNeill 2020: 117.
60 McNeill 2020: 121.
61 McNeill 2020: 122.
62 McNeill 2020: 54.
63 McNeill 2020: 115–116.
64 McNeill 2020: 122.
65 McNeill 2020: 218–221.
66 Marx [1876] 1976: 127.
67 Marx cited in McNeill 2020: 132.
68 McNeill 2020: 138.
69 This indeed helps to explain how an abstract idea – value – became reified into the foundation of historical materialism.
70 McNeill 2020: 136.
71 McNeill 2020: 137.
72 The concept of value can be traced to 14th-century English as referring to 'the monetary worth of something' (Merriam-Webster.com Dictionary 2021). Historically, the very idea of value is thus defined in relation to the artefact of money. In his early deliberations on money fetishism, Marx suggested that goods have value 'only insofar as they represent money, that is to say only insofar as they are bearers of exchange value'; Iacono 2016: 106. He understood this condition as the result of an inversion of a presumably 'original' relation, in which money represented the value of goods, rather than goods representing money. Prior to developing his labour theory of value, Marx asserted that 'the actual value of things…is their *exchange value*, and the exchange value resides in money… Money, therefore, is the *true* value of things…'; Marx cited in Iacono 2016: 107, emphases in original.
73 It is ironic that McNeill (2020: 187) explicitly deplores Marx's use of metaphors based on the material world, whereas value 'must be understood as a social phenomenon,' but without reflecting on the fallacy of positing that the phenomenon of value must be ontologically prior to its measurement in money.
74 See, for instance, David Harvey's (2018: 51–71) book chapter 'Money as the Representation of Value.'

75 McNeill 2020: 248.
76 McNeill 2020: 142.
77 McNeill 2020: 175.
78 McNeill 2020: 184.
79 McNeill 2020: 187.
80 McNeill 2020: 225–243.
81 McNeill 2020: 269.
82 McNeill 2020: 260–261.
83 McNeill 2020: 251–252.
84 O'Connor 1998; Moore 2015. For an overview of Marxist efforts to address environmental issues, see Chapter 6.
85 Kallis and Swyngedouw 2018; McNeill 2020: 257.
86 Kallis and Swyngedouw 2018: 49.
87 It is noteworthy that several meticulous Marxist theorists have observed that Marx's deliberations on capital are essentially concerned with the societal consequences of money. Heinrich (2014) affirms that 'value cannot exist without money,' Moseley (2016) writes that 'Marx's theory is a monetary theory from beginning to end,' and Bellofiore (2018) notes that Marx's value theory uniquely 'introduces money in the very initial deduction of value.'
88 See, for instance, Huber 2017.
89 Harvey 2018: 63.
90 Marx cited by McNeill 2020: 281.
91 McNeill 2020: 279.
92 McNeill 2020: 284–294.
93 McNeill 2020: 301, 308.
94 Graeber 2007: 140.
95 An example of such attribution of agency to capital is Marx's account of how merchant's capital becomes 'the servant of industrial capital, and *carries out*... functions' in relation to it; Marx cited in McNeill 2020: 282, emphasis added.
96 Sweezy cited by Magdoff and Foster 2011: 37.
97 Graeber 2011.
98 Graeber 2011: 15.
99 McNeill 2020: 33, 47.
100 McNeill 2020: 47, emphasis in original.
101 McNeill 2020: 48.
102 McNeill 2020: 70.
103 McNeill 2020: 117, 121–122.
104 McNeill's account of Marxist theory, for instance, is completely detached from the material substance – the embodied tons, joules, hectares, and labour hours – of production and exchange.
105 Marx [1867] 1976: 515.

Part II

Money, materiality, and entropy

4 Beyond the veil of market prices

In tracing the origins and uses of money through history, we noted that the European conquest and colonisation of the Americas in the 16th and 17th centuries were largely driven by the fetishised demand for bullion, which was perceived as the index of exchange-value throughout Eurasia. The doctrine of mercantilism was fundamentally concerned with the national accumulation of bullion and dominated European colonialism until the late 18th century, when arguments for free trade heralded the turn to economic liberalism. Already when Adam Smith in 1776 published his volume *The Wealth of Nations*, however, the concept of 'free trade' served as a mystification of exploitation. The obsession with abstract exchange-values, hypostatised as money, obscured the flows of real, material resources that were embodied in – that is, had been used in producing – the traded commodities. This means that market exchange was an ideal social arrangement for organising systematically asymmetric transfers of embodied biophysical resources, including labour time, without making the asymmetries apparent to the participants in the exchange. A prime example is the import of plantation produce to Great Britain in the 1770s, which represented significantly greater volumes of embodied land and labour than were embodied in the industrial exports for which they were exchanged.[1] Similar observations can be made, for instance, regarding the British import of bar iron from Sweden, which on average in the 1760s represented the annual growth of over one million hectares of forest and almost 14,000 person-year-equivalents of labour.[2] The divergent assessments of international trade based on monetary or biophysical metrics, respectively, can illuminate the contradiction between perspectives that variously describe urban centres of economic growth as 'value-adding machines' or 'parasites' living off their hinterlands.[3]

In attributing a monetary value to all things – and making their price a primary aspect of their definition – the phenomenon of money has enveloped the world in a veil of quantitative abstractions that obscures its metabolic materiality. In this chapter, we shall focus on the asymmetric global flows of embodied resources – the ecologically unequal exchange – that make modern technologies possible. We have referred to the mainstream invisibility of this reliance on unequal exchange as 'machine fetishism,' observing that

DOI: 10.4324/9781032702186-7

machines, in being both material and social, disrupt the customary distinction between nature and society in modern thought. Modern technologies are thus as paradoxical a phenomenon as the money that makes them possible. In organising and obscuring social transfers of biophysical resources, money blurs the boundary between the social and the natural. Enabled by money, modern technologies represent the interpenetration of social organisation and the laws of physics. Because it ultimately rests on human perceptions and beliefs, money – through technology – thus challenges Enlightenment convictions by making it possible to mix the subjective and the objective.

The concept of fetishism is widely used in the sense of mystification, denoting situations where something is being obscured. As Bonno Thoden van Velzen has observed, 'fetishes tend to *conceal* rather than to elucidate.'[4] In what follows we shall consider what it is that the fetishism of money and machines conceals. Karl Marx established the heterodox conviction that monetary measures such as wages and prices obscure more essential transfers between market actors. In this chapter we shall consider how such non-monetary transfers are conceptualised in heterodox economics and argue that a genuinely materialist perspective should focus on their physical aspects. In conceiving exploitation in terms of 'value,' which can only be imagined as measurable in money, Marxian economists paradoxically remain confined to the hegemonic worldview of mainstream economics. The value of labour is defined in relation to the market price of its product. Marxist analyses of transfers of 'surplus value' aim to calculate the monetary worth of 'underpaid' or 'unpaid' labour, contending that this discrepancy between the cost and the productivity of labour should be understood as the share of the product price that is claimed by the capitalist. The ontological foundation of Marxian value theory is thus monetary valuation. This is clearly also the case in Arghiri Emmanuel's analysis of 'unequal exchange' in international trade, in which he refers to disparities in wage levels between different countries as the explanation of asymmetric transfers of value between nations.[5] However, the understanding of unequal exchange between nations exclusively in terms of transfers of labour value has raised questions about asymmetric flows of other kinds of resources such as energy and materials. The growing attention to global patterns of ecologically unequal exchange raises questions about the limits of this discourse.[6] The ontological foundation of ecologically unequal exchange (EUE) can hardly be monetary valuation. The acknowledgement of asymmetric transfers of non-human energy, materials, and embodied land must imply a shift towards a genuinely materialist account of global social metabolism.

The pervasive aspiration to translate multidimensional commodity flows into a single metric has inspired attempts to quantify EUE in terms of a monetary 'drain' from the global South.[7] Although this is indeed a case of massive 'cost-shifting,'[8] a materialist approach to EUE cannot be confined to highlighting the monetary dimension of world trade. References to environmental 'costs' give the illusory impression that ecological degradation can be assessed in monetary terms. Similarly misleading is the intimation that the main implication of EUE research is that the global North saves money by shifting costs to the global South. The asymmetric transfers of embodied energy, materials, land, and labour to centres of accumulation do not just represent a systematic cost-shifting by these centres but are *physically* constitutive of their productive infrastructures. In augmenting their output of market commodities, these technological infrastructures generate increasing quantities of exchange-values (that is, money) in such areas, which in turn expand their claims on the resources of other areas. They also generate accelerating degradation throughout the biosphere. An exclusive focus on flows of monetary values fails to reckon with the causal interpenetration of money and materiality. Mainstream economists' preoccupation with money and profits represents *one* perspective on what drives world society, while a map tracing the asymmetric flows of material resources provides another. They are two different perspectives on the same global foundations of economic expansion, or capital accumulation. The former deals with ideas and social arrangements, the latter with their peculiarly invisible material rationale. If our civilisation is to have a future, we must learn to see beyond our ideas.

To grasp processes of ecological deterioration and climate change, we urgently need to recognise the interaction of economy and material metabolism. Rather than conceptualise such physical processes as 'market failures' and 'externalities' that are redeemable in monetary terms, we must acknowledge the limits of mainstream economics and embrace the transdisciplinary insight that money cannot compensate for entropy. The asymmetric transfers revealed by studies of EUE should be conceptualised as unequal flows not of economic values but of embodied biophysical resources measured in joules, tons, hectares, and labour time.

The acknowledgement of EUE thus has more far-reaching ontological implications than is generally recognised, even by researchers dedicated to documenting its occurrence. Rather than being content with accounting for economic and environmental inequalities and injustices generated by systematic cost-shifting, research on EUE suggests a radical ontological shift from neoclassical to ecological economics and to the insights of environmental sociology.[9] Instead of understanding world trade and economic development in terms of flows and accumulation of money capital, the EUE perspective focuses on the material features of *social metabolism*. In this view, 'capital accumulation' is a literally material phenomenon: it denotes the (typically urban) concentration of metals, oil, cement, timber, agricultural crops, workers, and other physical resources that are required for the reproduction of an advanced technological infrastructure. Such concentration of material resources is clearly the flip side of an accumulation of money – which is, essentially, the capacity to make claims on other people's labour and resources – but the focus is shifted to what this material process ultimately signifies, if, for a moment, analytically isolated from the flows of money. Beyond the immediate acknowledgement of abysmal gaps between incomes, consumption levels, and ecological footprints in different parts of the world, a materialist approach should recognise that what Marx observed about commodity fetishism is equally valid for technological artefacts. In other words, the technical objects that are amassed in the global North are no less fetishised than other commodities, in the sense that they obscure the global social relations of exchange to which they owe their existence. Technological fetishism is a subcategory of commodity fetishism. The implications of this perspective are devastating for conventional accounts of technological development. It means, for instance, that the celebrated breakthroughs of the Industrial Revolution in 18th-century Great Britain should be reassessed in relation to the asymmetric flows of embodied labour and other resources that at the time constituted the capitalist world-system – and, of course, that the technological dominance of powerful nations today is similarly founded on unequal exchange.

Although it raises bewildering questions about what kinds of technologies are morally defensible, and about how world trade could possibly be regulated to avoid EUE, the ontological shift towards a consideration of global social metabolism may be more readily accepted today than a few decades ago. The context of potentially disastrous climate change and ecological devastation has made many of us less committed to a faith in the progress of modern civilisation than were previous generations. The seemingly inexorable rise in greenhouse gas emissions is difficult to handle for neoclassical economics but completely predictable from the perspective of ecological economics: in accordance with the Second Law of Thermodynamics, the CO_2 emissions represent entropy generated by the metabolism of the global, fossil-fuelled infrastructure. As Nicholas Georgescu-Roegen observed more than 50 years ago, the expanded production of economic exchange-values promoted by neoclassical economics must correlate with an expanded production of entropy.[10] A corollary of this observation is that the aggregated outputs and waste of an industrial infrastructure 'will have greater entropy than the total entropy of the less valuable inputs.'[11] This regularity applies also to the social metabolism of the global North, taken as a whole: its products and emissions represent more entropy than its inputs. The general pattern documented in EUE research can thus be phrased in terms of thermodynamics: the resources embodied in imports to the global North represent less entropy than the exports for which they are exchanged.

The emergence of the EUE approach

The identification and conceptualisation of EUE belongs within the wider tradition of political ecology, a genre in the environmental social sciences emphasising interdisciplinary studies of how social power and natural environment are intertwined. Political ecology initially emerged in the 1970s and 1980s among anthropologists and geographers who were dissatisfied with the functionalist assumptions of the school of cultural ecology. In the 1960s, cultural ecology had focused on case studies of traditional subsistence practices in local communities as adaptations to the non-human environment. Pioneers of political ecology such as the anthropologist Eric Wolf and geographers Harold Brookfield and Piers Blaikie rejected functionalism and instead emphasised the role of power inequalities and global political economy in shaping human–environmental relations. They emphasised that the local resource flows studied by cultural ecology were connected to the asymmetric metabolic flows of the world-system. However, they did not at the time have access to the requisite data or methodologies to substantiate such claims.

The concept of 'ecologically unequal exchange' represents the convergence of two separate strands of research from across the divide between social and natural sciences.[12] In the social sciences, Emmanuel's identification of unequal exchange was embedded in the theoretical framework of the Marxist labour theory of value. It was thus presented as an asymmetric transfer of labour value from low- to high-wage countries. At roughly the same time, natural scientists were beginning to focus attention on the uneven flows of natural resources such as raw materials and energy through modern economies.[13] The systems ecologist Howard T. Odum presented a model for understanding social and economic processes in terms of flows of embodied energy. He coined the notion of 'emergy' as shorthand for 'embodied energy,' but later redefined it as 'energy memory' and explicitly claimed that it was a measure of economic value.[14]

Using the analytical framework of world-system analysis,[15] the sociologist Stephen Bunker applied the concept of unequal exchange to asymmetric flows of energy, but presented his intervention as a modification of classical Marxist theory by approaching energy as an underpaid 'natural value' complementary to labour values.[16] A few years later, Stephen Lonergan observed that theories of unequal exchange based on labour and energy theories of value are analytically very similar.[17] In both frameworks, inequalities are conceptualised as deviations of market prices from 'real' values, whether conceived in terms of embodied labour or embodied energy. Howard Odum and Jan E. Arding pioneered the quantification of such assessments by proposing that the export of shrimp from Ecuador to the US represented a measurably unequal exchange of embodied energy between the two countries.[18] Odum's methodology for assessing such inequalities in international trade focused on the amount of 'emergy' that, on average, was purchased per dollar exchanged between two countries.[19]

An important but generally neglected consideration in the conceptualisation of EUE is the logically inverse relation between productive potential and economic value, as revealed by Georgescu-Roegen's foundational observation that production processes generating an increase in utility (economic value) simultaneously imply a dissipation of energy and matter, that is, an increase in entropy. Rather than suggest a derivation of economic exchange-value from some biophysical input such as labour or energy, as in Marxist and other heterodox value theory, we need to understand the physical *consequences* of the production of value, namely, that the market exchange of finished industrial products for fuels and raw materials will inexorably reward the dissipation of natural resources in core areas of the world-system with economic access to more resources to dissipate. In other words, economic growth means that the more resources the core has dissipated today, the more new resources it will be able to dissipate tomorrow. Moreover, the core tends to use the periphery not only as a source of resources but also as a sink for its entropy in the form of pollution and waste.[20]

The EUE approach, broadly defined, has inspired a variety of quantitative approaches. Mathis Wackernagel and William Rees showed that consumption patterns in wealthier countries imply a quantifiable appropriation of embodied, ecologically productive land ('ecological footprints') from other countries.[21] Applying the ecological footprint measure, Andrew Jorgenson and James Rice have empirically identified EUE by tracing how wealthier nations appropriate environmental space from less wealthy ones, for instance, through deforestation.[22] Marina Fischer-Kowalski and Helmut Haberl have developed methods for translating statistics on international trade into flows of embodied matter and energy,[23] which have been foundational to studies in industrial ecology and global resource use[24] as well as to estimates of the 'physical trade balances' (PTB) of nations.[25] As predicted by EUE theory, the PTB tends to be positive for most European nations[26] but negative, for example, for most nations in South America.[27]

Andrew Jorgenson and Brett Clark have edited a special issue of the *International Journal of Comparative Sociology* devoted to the theme *Ecologically Unequal Exchange in Comparative Perspective*.[28] The eight articles in this special issue cover a wide range of global environmental inequalities generated by international trade, including the geographically skewed impacts of specific types of energy use, biodiversity loss, climate change, and other biophysical consequences of economic processes. Particularly noteworthy here is the inclusion among EUE phenomena of climate change,[29] which highlights the urgency of – and the relevance of EUE theory for – grasping the biophysical features of global social metabolism. The concept of 'carbon footprint' illuminates how greenhouse gas emissions are embodied in commodities and transferred through international trade.[30] The impact of trade on biodiversity loss has similarly been explored in terms of the 'biodiversity footprints' of nations.[31] A special issue of the *Journal of Political Ecology* was devoted to various concepts and methodologies emerging from or relevant to the EUE approach, including calculations of environmental load displacement, physical trade balances, embodied Human Appropriation of Net Primary Production (eHANPP), Life Cycle Analysis (LCA), and ecological debt.[32]

Another approach to identifying the occurrence of EUE is to calculate unequal flows of both embodied labour time and natural space in international trade. Studies of Britain's overseas trade in 1850 reveal how the British cotton textile industry at that time relied on asymmetric transfers of embodied labour time and embodied ecological space appropriated from its former colonies in North America.[33] By estimating the quantity of labour hours and hectares of land required to produce two volumes of commodities that at a given point in time are equivalent in terms of exchange-value, it is possible to assess whether the exchange of those commodities at that time would have entailed an asymmetric exchange of embodied labour or land. This method for calculating EUE, referred to as 'time-space appropriation,' has been applied to other societies and historical contexts.[34] It provides a methodological bridge between quantitative ecological economics and historical research emphasising the roles of asymmetric resource flows in world history.

Drawing on databases on international flows of raw material equivalents and embodied energy,[35] embodied land,[36] and embodied labour,[37] it has been possible to show that established core regions of the world-system (United States, Europe, and Japan) in 2007 were net importers of all these kinds of biophysical resources, empirically confirming the theory of EUE.[38] A more comprehensive study has identified the same pattern as applying to the trade between high- and low-income nations in the world between 1990 and 2015.[39]

EUE theory necessarily crosses conventional boundaries between social and natural sciences, drawing on perspectives as widely separated as history and thermodynamics. Drawing, as we have seen, on a range of methodologies based on non-monetary metrics, it focuses on *asymmetric transfers of embodied biophysical resources and risks obscured by the apparent reciprocity of monetary transactions*. It seeks to reveal what is concealed under the veil of market prices.

The global interaction of money and materiality in the history of technology

To posit the occurrence of EUE in international trade is not in itself a normative or moral statement, but a conclusion based on empirical methods for assessing the biophysical substance of commodity flows. It means demonstrating that trade perceived by mainstream economists as balanced (in monetary terms) may be highly asymmetric in terms of the transfer of embodied biophysical resources. A central challenge is to account for the invisibility of EUE in mainstream interpretations of development in the history of economic thought. Whereas earlier economic schools had been concerned with the physical substance of trade, such as its demands on land (the Physiocrats), labour (classical political economy), and materials (the mercantilists), such concerns were largely abandoned in modern theories of international trade. In focusing exclusively on monetary values and market dynamics, neoclassical economics discarded even the possibility of identifying physical asymmetries in exchange. It is significant, for instance, that Paul Krugman and Robin Wells' monumental volume *Economics*, featuring a 27-page, four-column index, does not even mention 'unequal exchange.'[40] The conceptual and structural conditions of this shift of perspective should no doubt be understood in relation to the turn to fossil energy, which was conducive to a cornucopian image of unlimited economic growth. But rather than viewing growth as based on a Promethean understanding of technological progress, an EUE perspective implies that growth and technological advance may be based on global social processes with some features of a zero-sum game. The theoretical implications of understanding modern technological systems as global social phenomena have generally not contaminated mainstream conceptions of technologies as innocent manifestations of enlightenment, detachable from the social contexts in which they have emerged.

The history of human energy use is generally presented as a progression in engineering knowledge based on a succession of discoveries and inventions.[41] This is undoubtedly a necessary condition for technological progress, but not a *sufficient* one. A conclusion from EUE research is that the global social aspects of energy transitions may be no less significant than technical knowledge. The concept of 'technological progress' is conventionally viewed as a matter of local ingenuity, while the global patterns of distribution to which it is often connected are generally ignored. The turn to fossil energy in early industrial Britain, for instance, tends to be attributed exclusively to the invention of the steam engine, rather than to the economic incentives to engage in various strategies of environmental load displacement and EUE that it made possible. The intensified exports of textiles and other products from Britain in the 19th century granted the country access to vast amounts of land, labour, and materials in its periphery. This embeddedness of steam technology in the structure of the world-system can serve as a point of departure for examining more recent technologies in terms of their dependence on global processes of EUE. The use of fossil energy has alleviated pressures on European environments for over two centuries, regardless of where the fossil fuels are extracted. Moreover, the global North's net imports of fossil energy can also be seen as an environmental load displacement to extractive areas in the Middle East, Africa, and South America. The contemporary vision in Europe and elsewhere of a post-carbon economy has grown out of the twin threats of climate change and peak oil, but it represents a difficult impasse for the mainstream worldview that was consolidated in the 19th century. To replace the dependence of modern society on concentrated subterranean energy deposits, representing hundreds of millions of years of solar radiation, with reliance on the capacity to harvest *current* flows of such radiation through renewable energy technologies, remains an elusive challenge for engineering. It also presents a difficult challenge for the conventional economic worldview, conditioned by fossil energy, which holds that land is a substitutable resource.

The anthropologist Maurice Godelier argued that, even in the most severely stratified societies, unequal exchange tends to be represented as reciprocity, that is, as a fair exchange.[42] Economic anthropology has shown that humans all over the world are concerned with reciprocity. The Maori native who in 1909 gave us the classic account of the 'spirit of the gift' exemplifies the widespread conviction that human exchange ought to be reasonably balanced.[43] To systematically appropriate other people's labour or resources is generally perceived as morally unacceptable. Yet the history of civilisation is the story of increasingly more sophisticated ways of doing precisely this: that is, appropriating other people's labour and resources, *and developing worldviews to justify it*. Such cultural rationalisation of inequalities is not to be understood as a malicious intention to conceal injustices, but as largely subconscious processes that are opaque to the participants themselves. The very fact that so much cultural effort is invested in obscuring the arbitrariness of inequalities suggests that significant asymmetries in human societies need to be morally justified. Coercion was not enough to maintain slavery or serfdom – these material systems of appropriation also required their supporting worldviews, such as racism and medieval theology, respectively. EUE research suggests that mainstream economics similarly, if inadvertently, has the effect of rationalising global inequalities today.

The global prerequisites for the Industrial Revolution – illustrated by how the expansion of steam power arguably implicated slavery – suggests that the new system of appropriation which in the late 18th century began generating the abysmal inequalities we see today is the very symbiosis between money and globalised technology. Some technologies are clearly tantamount to a displacement, by means of unequal exchange rates on the market, of work and environmental burdens to groups with less purchasing-power. What is locally feasible is thus contingent on the rates at which embodied labour and other biophysical resources can be imported from elsewhere. This symbiosis of money and technology underlies, for instance, the capacity of contemporary financial transactions to propel physical production processes based on unconventional fossil fuels extracted in North America from tar sands or through fracking, regardless of their very low 'Energy Return On energy Investment (EROI).' Another example is the claim that photovoltaic energy – although also low-EROI and subsidised by fossil fuels[44] – is becoming economically competitive with fossil fuels, an assertion that is in part based on the reduction of labour costs derived from shifting production of solar panels to Asia. The investigation of such relations between market conditions and technological progress can only be pursued by considering trade as flows of biophysical resources, rather than merely as flows of exchange-values.

A central implication of the EUE perspective is that the fossil-fuel economy was neither created nor is being upheld by humankind in general, and that intra-species inequalities are part and parcel of contemporary history and cannot be ignored in attempts to understand it.[45] As we have seen, it is arguable that the technological breakthrough represented by James Watt's steam engine might not have occurred nor proven so widely useful if there had not been great global demand for inexpensive cotton cloth among West African slave traders and American slave owners. Slavery, slave plantations, and the triangular trade between Europe, Africa, and America were the foundation for the Industrial Revolution in several ways: by creating demand for its products, by providing cheap labour for harvesting its raw materials, and even by offering the plantation as a template for the organisation of industrial production. Most importantly, the Industrial Revolution was contingent on market prices determined by processes in the 18th-century world-system, a conclusion that coincides with Andre Gunder Frank's reconceptualisation of technological development as 'a *world economic process*, which took place in and because of the structure of the world economy/system itself.'[46] Robert Marks has succinctly summarised this global perspective on early British industrialisation:

> The ability of one part of the world – in this case western European, led by Britain – to escape from the limitations of the biological old regime by tapping stored sources of energy (coal and then oil) was contingent and came about as a result of a global conjuncture.[47]

Technological progress, in this view, is not merely a matter of innocent breakthroughs in engineering, but of devising new and profitable systems for displacing work and environmental pressures to other populations and geographical areas.

Rethinking 'free trade' and 'comparative advantage'

To thus rethink the history of technology necessarily also means rethinking global environmental history.[48] The geographies of extraction and accumulation are determined by the trajectories of the world-system. To the extent that transformations of ecosystems and landscapes in the past and present can be understood as imprints of global processes of EUE, this requires renewed efforts at integrating environmental history and social theory. After Britain repealed its protectionist Corn Laws in 1846, the increasing imports of grain to England reflected lower production costs, including land rents and wages, in Prussia and North America, compared to those of England. The modern outsourcing of many kinds of production to China follows the same logic. To assert that the relatively low wages and land rents of 19th-century Prussia and 21st-century China offer these countries a 'comparative advantage' in world trade could be regarded as a euphemism for other countries taking advantage of their relative poverty and relatively lax environmental legislation. Since the days of Ricardo, the language of free trade has promoted the displacement of both work and environmental loads to less affluent sectors of the world-system. It continues to justify patterns of world trade that result in deepening inequalities and some of the most important sources of greenhouse gas emissions, such as industrial agriculture, deforestation, intensified export production, and global transports of bulk goods.

The 19th-century British shift to fossil fuels as a source of mechanical energy fundamentally transformed the conditions of economic rationality. It relaxed the ancient imperative to extract energy – firewood, charcoal, and fodder for draft animals – from the surface of the landscape and generally reduced the significance attributed to land as a factor of production. Ricardo concluded that the three factors of production – land, labour, and capital – were substitutable, so that, for example, a British shortage of land could be compensated by an abundance of capital. This observation was based on the experience of the Industrial Revolution, but it did not raise any significant concerns regarding the global implications of locally substituting capital for land. As the repeal of the Corn Laws illustrated, however, the appropriation, through trade, of the products of other nations' land, is tantamount to environmental load displacement. The 'ecological relief' which fossil fuels and imports of grain, timber, cotton, sugar, and other colonial produce granted to Britain represented a geographical space several times the total land area of Great Britain.[49] While historical research shows that fossil fuels and imports of embodied land converged in making European expansion possible, it does not pursue the implications of the fact that the use of fossil fuels in the export production of industrial products was what made the expanding imports of embodied land possible. From this perspective, industrialisation can be rethought as a strategy for appropriating, through the profits derived from exports, access to eco-productive space elsewhere in the world-system. Calculations of ecological footprints and other measures of environmental load displacement confirm that similar strategies have continued to be fundamental to economic growth and technological progress in core countries for over 200 years. Viewed in this light, 'capital' is land and labour appropriated *elsewhere*.

The growing emphasis on commerce and accumulation since the early modern period reflects the increasing significance of money in the European merchant states of the time. In contrast to the largely agrarian societies of medieval Europe, the Genoese, Dutch, and British trading empires thrived primarily through the accumulation of money profits. Whereas agrarian societies were predominantly focused on harvesting solar energy through crops, livestock, and the labour of humans and draft animals, mercantile societies shifted focus to the management of money. Although modern concepts of energy did not appear until the mid-19th century, humans have no doubt always been intuitively aware of the vital significance of the sun and what we now refer to as photosynthesis. The growing preoccupation with money did not represent a liberation from the dependence on these vital flows of energy, but a new strategy for gaining access to them through expanding purchasing-power. The money accumulating in Europe provided access to vast solar-derived resources on other continents, including farmland, forests, livestock, game, fish, and not least human labour. Money can thus be viewed as a kind of fictive energy, in the sense that it is imagined as a vital flow that nourishes society.

At first sight, definitions of unequal exchange based on 'underpaid values' may seem indistinguishable from the identification of asymmetric resource flows outlined above, but the difference is important. It is untenable to posit the existence of material *values* that are not recognised by the market actors who negotiate exchange rates. Economic values are determined by humans based on their preferences and assets. The material resources that are asymmetrically exchanged on the market should be conceptualised precisely as material resources, rather than as values. Regardless of whether it derives from human labour, draft animals, or fossil fuels, energy is not a value. Notions of underpaid material use values and 'natural values' confuse the physical and the economic. The inclination of some ecological economists to equate energy and value has been as misleading as the Marxian distinction between them has been ambiguous and contradictory. The struggles of Marxian and ecological economics to conceptualise how market exchange orchestrates asymmetric material transfers is based on legitimate intuitions about the causal entanglement of money and energy, but the assertion that labour-power and other forms of energy represent 'underpaid values' is analytically flawed. The significance of asymmetric transfers of material resources is not that they represent underpaid values, but that they contribute to the physical expansion of productive infrastructure at the receiving end. The accumulation of such technological infrastructure may yield an expanding output of economic value, but this is not equivalent to saying that the resources that are embodied in the infrastructure have an objective value that exceeds their price.

Although Marx understood the machines of his time as devices for exploitation, much of his writing suggests that he believed that they could be extricated from capitalism and made to serve the proletariat. This is a paradox, because it means that the social theorist who taught us to understand how artefacts in capitalist society tend to be fetishised – that is, to represent social relations as if they were relations between things – was himself suffering from the illusion of 'machine fetishism.' Both mainstream and heterodox conceptions of technology tend to relegate the responsibility for its various political and ecological consequences to its misuse by corporations and politicians. There is a widespread belief that 'technology as such' would not have to implicate injustices, and that this purified conception of technology can be extricated from political contexts where it is used to generate social injustices and ecological degradation. This belief in a decontextualised, transcendent, and emancipatory science of engineering has been fundamental not only to mainstream historiography but also to classical Marxist visions of social progress.

Up until the Industrial Revolution, the periphery of the colonial world-system was a source of embodied land and labour for the European core. The Industrial Revolution transformed the character of world trade and the organisation of European society. The shift to subterranean, inorganic energy sources alleviated much of the pressure on European land for firewood, charcoal, and horse-fodder, but industrial Britain remained dependent on its colonies and former colonies for land, labour, and increasingly also materials. Land in the periphery continued to be used to provision the core with food energy such as sugar and materials such as cotton, and both kinds of production required vast inputs of labour. The substitution of subterranean for organic energy was understood as a stage in an inevitable progress towards more advanced technologies representing a liberation of labour as well as an emancipation from land. Steam technology was perceived as a breakthrough in engineering, regardless of the world market prices of cotton, African slaves, and American land. It was understood as the product of European ingenuity, rather than as entwined with global processes of EUE and accumulation. Ricardo's perception of capital and new technology as substituting for labour and land represents a local outlook, rather than a global view of social metabolism.

This perception of technological progress continues to frame deliberations on energy transitions in the modern world. From the start, the reliance on fossil fuels has been accompanied by concerns regarding their finiteness and their detrimental environmental consequences, which has stimulated a succession of visions of more sustainable energy technologies: hydroelectric, nuclear, biofuels, wind, photovoltaic, and so on. After over a century of such technological visions and development, however, around 85% of global energy use continues to be fossil, and the use of fossil energy shows no signs of diminishing.[50] Considering the thoroughly globalised supply chains that characterise the modern world economy, this means that 85% of the energy used to produce and maintain the infrastructure for both nuclear and renewable energy technologies is fossil.[51] The close connection between energy use and economic growth is well established. Although concerns regarding climate change are alarming, and despite seemingly momentous declarations such as at COP 21 in Paris in December 2015, there is little indication that the global political establishment, by and large, is seriously committed to abandoning fossil fuels. This constitutes an impasse not only in terms of the aggravating contradiction between economic growth and sustainability but also in terms of our theoretical understanding of technological progress. The acknowledgement of EUE can help us widen our concept of technology to include not only the requisite achievements of engineering but also its dependence on global exchange rates, such as the prices of fuels, rare minerals, labour, and land. Under which market circumstances, for instance, is it feasible to propel European cars with sugarcane ethanol from Brazil or batteries based on cobalt mined in West Africa? These are the kinds of questions we shall pursue in the next chapter. A fundamental implication of EUE research is that globalised technologies are thoroughly *social* phenomena in the sense that their feasibility is ultimately contingent on discrepancies in the relative prices of labour and land in different parts of the world. Their underlying rationale is the strategic displacement of workloads and environmental loads to less privileged groups in global society.

Notes

1 Hornborg 2013.
2 Warlenius 2016.
3 Green *et al.* 2024: 6.
4 Thoden van Velzen 1990: 78.

5 Emmanuel 1972.
6 Dorninger *et al.* 2021.
7 Hickel *et al.* 2022.
8 Kapp 1950.
9 Givens *et al.* 2019.
10 Georgescu-Roegen 1971.
11 Kåberger and Månsson 2001: 174.
12 Hornborg 1998; Givens *et al.* 2019.
13 Ayres and Kneese 1969; Odum 1971.
14 Odum 1988.
15 Wallerstein 1974–1989.
16 Bunker 1985.
17 Lonergan 1988.
18 Odum and Arding 1991.
19 Odum 1996.
20 Muradian *et al.* 2002; for an overview, see Givens *et al.* 2019.
21 Wackernagel and Rees 1996; see also York *et al.* 2003.
22 Jorgenson 2003; Jorgenson and Rice 2007; Rice 2007.
23 Fischer-Kowalski and Haberl 1997.
24 Schandl *et al.* 2016; Krausmann *et al.* 2017.
25 Pérez Rincón 2006.
26 Lenzen *et al.* 2012a, 2013; Infante-Amate and Krausmann 2019; Magalhães *et al.* 2019.
27 Samaniego, Vallejo and Martinez-Alier 2017. These empirical findings confirm Eduardo Galeano's (1973) indignant narrative in his pioneering book 'Open Veins of Latin America.'
28 Jorgenson and Clark 2009.
29 Roberts and Parks 2009; Jorgenson 2012.
30 Peters *et al.* 2011.
31 Lenzen *et al.* 2012b.
32 Hornborg and Martinez-Alier 2016.
33 Hornborg 2013.
34 Singh and Ramanujam 2010; Bogadóttir 2016; Warlenius 2016.
35 Lenzen *et al.* 2012a, 2013.
36 Yu *et al.* 2013.
37 Simas *et al.* 2014.
38 Dorninger and Hornborg 2015.
39 Dorninger *et al.* 2021.
40 Krugman and Wells 2018.
41 For instance, Smil 2017.
42 Godelier 1986.
43 Mauss 1925.
44 Prieto and Hall 2013.
45 Malm and Hornborg 2014.
46 Frank 1998: 204; emphasis in original.
47 Marks 2015: 210.
48 Hornborg, McNeill and Martinez-Alier 2007.
49 Pomeranz 2000; Hornborg 2013.
50 York and Bell 2019; Smil 2022.
51 Prieto and Hall 2013.

5 Technology as fetish

Consider the word 'liquidate.' Codified in our subconscious is the understanding that to turn something into money is equivalent to destroying it, melting all that is solid into liquid – or air, to use Marx's and Engels' expression in *The Communist Manifesto*.[1] If we grant the logic of money free reins, what kind of society will be the result, and what kind of human–environmental relations? Zygmunt Bauman exposed the peculiar social condition that he called liquid modernity, in which identities and relations have become increasingly fluid, uncertain, and prone to shift. The metaphor of liquidation also captures the interface of economics and physics, evoking how money converts material resources like minerals, soils, and forests into fungible flows to feed the expanding physical infrastructure of capital. The apparent solidity of this infrastructure – what we are accustomed to thinking of as *technology* – is thus illusory: its material forms are but congealed resource flows orchestrated by flows of money. The globalised rhizomes of technological infrastructure are *socionatural* webs spun by our species throughout the biosphere of which it is a part. Money is the essential lubricant of this global machine.

Towards a global, material, and distributive perspective on technology

To shift perspective on modern technology in this way – from an index of historical progress to a measure of ongoing appropriation – is to grant proper significance to its dependence on physical resource transfers. The accumulation of global 'technomass' is comparable to biological phenomena like the growth of biomass sustained by the extension of roots, rhizomes, or tentacles: that is, processes of extraction, transfer, and storage of biophysical resources. In this respect, the technomass perspective at first sight has much in common with the kinds of worldviews that have been labelled 'neo-materialism,' 'the new materiality,' and 'the material turn' in social theory. Indeed, it is more genuinely materialist even than historical materialism. It identifies a glaring omission in conventional narratives of human social development that claim to account for technological advance exclusively

DOI: 10.4324/9781032702186-8

in terms of ingenious blueprints, that is, breakthroughs in engineering. Yet, the technomass perspective crucially emphasises the role of money – a semiotic phenomenon – in reproducing those asymmetric material flows, which, unlike biological growth, are inextricably entwined with severe social injustices. The material turn tends not to concern itself with either the semiotics of money or global injustices. It can thus serve as a corrective to mainstream accounts only in a very restricted sense.

Whereas conventional perspectives on technological progress focus on national achievements, engineering knowledge, and historical development, the Anthropocene predicament should prompt us to reconceptualise modern technology from a global, material, and distributive perspective. The former approach has dominated the modern worldview since it was established in 18th-century Britain, reflecting the experience of the first nation to industrialise. A global *sociometabolic* perspective does not 'deny' any of the three aspects that are emphasised in the traditional view: that dense technological infrastructure will accumulate in restricted geographical spaces, that it requires engineering, and that it tends to advance in a cumulative and progressive manner. These are all predictable historical experiences of industrialisation. However, in all three respects, these experiences are insufficient to explain it, because (1) the accumulation of infrastructure in the wealthiest nations is contingent on resource transfers from all over the world; (2) these material flows are as indispensable for technological development as engineering; and (3) the asymmetric global flows of embodied labour and other resources generate a polarised world society of more versus less 'developed' populations. A global, material, and distributive perspective sees technological infrastructure as a network of conduits for transferring human and non-human energy and materials from peripheral to core sectors of the world-system. The global technomass can be likened to a supra-organic biomass whose rhizomes or tentacles continuously disembed and dislodge such biophysical resources to be siphoned off to centres of accumulation.[2] Human history entails the integration of previously autonomous sociometabolic systems into an increasingly global social metabolism. These metabolic processes are enabled by processes of monetisation and conceptual abstraction, whereby categories such as 'value,' 'price,' 'work,' 'energy,' and 'electricity' serve to recast previously contextualised resources into disembedded, fungible commodities that are accessible for extraction. To apply a rather dramatic metaphor, the conceptual reframing[3] or reconfiguration of the world in such terms can be compared to the processes through which a predator's gastric acids dissolve its prey for digestion.[4]

Given the conventional image of technology as a neutral realisation of engineering knowledge, mainstream economists should find it hard to come up with a *theoretical* reason why technical artefacts such as electrical cars or household robots could not, in principle, be equally available to all the eight billion humans in the world. Should the obstacles really be phrased in terms of 'failed development' or perhaps 'market failure'? The fact that this Promethean fantasy is so incompatible with global social reality reflects the inadequacy of its underlying understanding of the phenomenon of modern technology. In not recognising the inextricable interfusion of machines and money, such techno-optimism is professed by both right- and left-wing ecomodernists in current debates on sustainability. It is also reflected in the frequently repeated assertion that the introduction of fossil energy was revolutionary in demanding very little space, which neglects the vast expanses of colonial plantation land that were required to accumulate the *money* that was invested in the British steam engines. While coal mines and oil wells may be almost punctiform, the machines for *harnessing* fossil energy represent capital accumulation that enables their owners to draw on resources from vast expanses of land throughout the world.

When people are confronted with the fact that green, sustainable technologies in the global North may depend on inputs of low-wage labour (including its ecological footprint) and environmentally damaging resource extraction in the South, the standard reaction is to propose that the requisite minerals should instead be mined in the North. According to such visions, this would make the technologies both sustainable and fair. But they ignore the extent to which the feasibility of the technologies may be *contingent* on global wage gaps. What such visions make evident is the conceptual boundary we tend to draw between technologies as solid, physical forms and the social relations of exchange and asymmetric flows of embodied resources of which they are constituted. To an extent we are not prepared to acknowledge, modern technologies are contingent on the market prices of requisite inputs of labour and resources. Yet, such constraints generally do not affect our concept of technology but are instead expressed in the fetishised language of market prices and financial crises.

The relation between technology and trade is widely understood as random and unpredictable, rather than comprehensible in terms of some structural regularity. This can be exemplified by some comments offered in passing by Kenneth Pomeranz and Steven Topik in their lucid review of the emergence of the modern world economy:

> Slave-planted cotton in the United States is probably the outstanding example of technological progress in one place leading to the extension of drudgery and misery elsewhere, but there are others. When the McCormick reaper conquered the American Midwest…the demand for twine boomed, too, and much of it came from the Yucatán where conditions of near-slavery were introduced in order to grow cheap henequen. … The labor that the reaper-binder saved in the Midwest was expended in the tropics. The consequences are often unpredictable and even contradictory when the butterfly of world trade begins to beat its wings.[5]

Although perhaps unpredictable in its specifics, my point is that, in a *general* sense, the propensity of technological systems to displace work or environmental loads is quite predictable. Pomeranz and Topik at one point cite Marx's observation that, '[w]ithout slavery, no cotton; without cotton, no modern industry.'[6] In Marx's time, it was nevertheless out of the question to seriously propose that the very existence of industrial technology was entwined with – even contingent on – slavery. In the 21st century, such proposals on the ontological entanglements of technology, trade, and global injustices are not only conceptually possible to make but also increasingly reasonable to consider.

Periods of major crises in history tend to lead to a rethinking of concepts that have previously been taken for granted. The Anthropocene is such a period. In what follows, I shall give some examples of the kinds of reasons we have for reconceptualising our concept of 'technology.' We begin by reconsidering the seemingly self-evident phrase 'energy technology.'

Unpacking the black box of 'energy technology'

For several decades now, there has been a pervasive awareness that modern society is unsustainable.[7] The world economy is growing ever more unequal, while the lifestyles of more affluent nations, to which the rest aspire, are ecologically destructive and even in principle impossible to universalise. The lifestyles associated with modern affluence have long been contingent on fossil energy. The predominant response to this impasse is to express faith in technological progress. Most politicians, researchers, and people in general appear to believe that a global shift of technologies can lead to a sustainable and more equal world. A central focus of this vision is the transition from technologies based on the combustion of fossil fuels to others harnessing non-carbon sources of energy. This shift would mean abandoning the energy sources that have been crucial to the feasibility of modern society since the turn to steam technology in early 19th-century Britain. The implications of such a shift are often underestimated. As Vaclav Smil reminds us,

> we are a fossil-fueled civilization whose technical and scientific advances, quality of life, and prosperity rest on the combustion of huge quantities of fossil carbon, and we cannot simply walk away from this critical determinant of our fortunes in a few decades, never mind years.[8]

Yet, the call for decarbonisation is generally not associated with a call to radically transform modern society. It is assumed that a society's energy technology can be replaced without major implications for the organisation of society, much as a defective component of a machine can be replaced with a faultless one. At the most general level, it is this assumption about the ultimately *extra-social* character of technology that must be challenged.

This is not to deny, of course, that there have been numerous and often theoretically sophisticated efforts to transcend the distinction between the social and the material. Since the 1960s, many researchers from several disciplines have explored the relations between technologies and their social contexts. This ambition, frequently subsumed under the label of 'Science and Technology Studies (STS),' has been shared by fields devoted to the history, sociology, anthropology, and philosophy of technology. The discourse that can be classified as belonging to the STS tradition is vast and diverse, spanning several conceptual frameworks, professional associations, academic programs, and peer-reviewed journals. Significantly, however, most STS scholars derive from the social sciences and humanities, showing very little or no interest in the physical resource requirements of the technologies that they investigate. Even less have they considered the extent to which technologies rely on the asymmetric global flows, orchestrated by the world market, through which these resources are procured. Yet, it is arguably at this global level that the relations between material artefacts and their social contexts most urgently need to be theorised. Six decades of STS have not problematised the virtually complete academic separation of the *global* 'social' (understood as the capitalist world-system) and the *genuinely* 'material' (understood in terms of physical resource theory). At stake, it seems, are prevalent understandings of 'society' and 'materiality.'

Some recent efforts to span the divide notwithstanding, the materiality of technical artefacts tends to implicitly relegate them to an extra-social realm of physical nature.[9] Energy technologies and transitions are understood as having various kinds of social consequences that can be documented through empirical research but are not in themselves recognised as social phenomena. Resorting to hybrid concepts such as 'socio-technical,' 'socio-material,' or 'socio-ecological' systems does not suffice to eradicate this conceptual division. Although transitions to low-carbon technologies have pervasively been associated with social disempowerment and impoverishment,[10] such social repercussions are treated as contingent circumstances that do not implicate the technologies as such. The massive amount of empirical research on energy transitions may thus be obscuring the proverbial forest for the trees. The academic divisions separating engineering sciences from social sciences exacerbate the fragmentation of our understanding of energy transitions.

Accounts of the relation between technology and social theory have opposed social constructionism[11] and neo-materialism,[12] understanding the latter's focus on materiality as a way to grant agency to objects such as artefacts.[13] For Bruno Latour, the modern boundary between matter and society has defined the division of labour between the natural and the social sciences.[14] In other words, matter has been equated with nature, as distinct from society. To fundamentally challenge the conventional distinction between the material and the social, however, we must recognise that the materiality of our artefacts is *itself socially constituted*. Rather than simply upgrade the role of materiality in society, as if it implied an 'agency' equal to the purposive action of living organisms, we must understand the very stuff of technologies as products of social exchange. Artefacts do not just have social consequences stemming from their material properties – they *owe their existence and material properties to social processes.* The phenomenon of modern technology thus dissolves the boundary between the material and the social in a more profound way than generally imagined by neo-materialists such as Latour.

I hope to show that there are some recurrent patterns that justify theoretical conclusions on energy technologies and transitions that transcend conventional distinctions between relations and objects, economy and technology, and ultimately between society and nature. In our efforts to theorise energy justice, we must be prepared to ask if non-living artefacts can be endowed, even inadvertently, with an implicit agenda.[15] While such a reconsideration of customary categories can be bewildering, the predicament of the Anthropocene demands nothing less.

The social rationale of technological systems: a historical perspective

To make the argument on energy technologies clearer, we shall first reiterate the point made in the previous chapter on the historical adoption of fossil-fuelled technologies. Historians of technology frequently follow David Landes' classical view that the turn to fossil energy in late 18th-century Britain was an essentially local triumph of ingenuity and a paradigmatic case of technological progress.[16] In hindsight, we are now able to conclude that the technological developments in Britain at that time were fundamentally contingent on its position as the centre of a colonial empire. As we saw in Chapter 4, the spectacular expansion of its cotton textile industry largely relied on markets based on the Atlantic slave trade and American plantation owners who needed inexpensive clothing for their slaves. Moreover, it was slave labour that provided the British textile factories with inexpensive raw cotton. Analysed in terms of global flows of embodied labour and land, organised and obscured by flows of money, the mid-19th-century British trade in cotton textiles entailed highly asymmetric transfers of biophysical resources from the peripheries to the core of the capitalist world-system. This was the context that prompted and enabled the adoption of fossil-fuelled technology. From the very start, what seemed a local breakthrough was a localised manifestation of what were clearly global processes.

The Industrial Revolution represents a quintessential energy transition. The shift from organic energy to coal had momentous implications. Conventional narratives emphasise how steam technology was able to replace human and animal labour with machines, and how it alleviated the country's land constraints by deriving energy from subterranean sources rather than horizontal surfaces such as fields, pastures, and forests.[17] Contemporary British reflections on the Industrial Revolution generally understood it as a product of national ingenuity, entrepreneurship, and natural resource endowments.[18] Engineering and technological progress were perceived as the revelation of possibilities inherent in nature. This understanding was shared even by the most vehement critics of industrial capitalism, including Marx, who thought of the progress of the 'productive forces' as nature's gift to capital.

As the Industrial Revolution illustrates, the joint operation of world trade and technology must be recognised as a mode of global social organisation. Trade and machinery are not separate phenomena but inextricably connected. Because all the material components of technologies are transmuted into monetary exchange-values, the aggregate economic rationality of market actors inexorably generates pervasive material regularities such as the displacement of resource demands to low-cost areas. As 'rational' market actors will generally be looking for the best deals, this will inexorably expand the demand for commodities produced with as low-wage labour and low concerns for the environment as possible. The technological systems favoured by the market will thus have this implicit logic inscribed in them.

It therefore seems feasible to propose that market-promoted technologies may have an inherent momentum that generates displacements of work and environmental loads to social groups with less purchasing-power. To identify such a social momentum or inclination in a technology is quite in line with several foundational observations on how humans may 'delegate' power-serving functions to artefacts.[19] It is also consistent with claims about the tendency of fossil-fuelled technologies to aggravate power inequalities, displace CO_2 emissions to the global periphery, and in other ways materialise the polarising logic of capitalist society.[20] While mainstream accounts of world trade and technological progress celebrate the benevolent agency of the market's 'invisible hand,' analyses drawing on the heterodox perspectives of political ecology and global environmental justice thus tend to invert the signs. As a recent survey of 332 case studies shows, even the efforts around the world to shift to low-carbon energy technologies are strongly inclined to exacerbate disempowerment, impoverishment, private accumulation, and ecological degradation.[21] As Benjamin Sovacool notes, while low-carbon energy sources are often presented as more equitable and just than fossil energy, his survey indicates that this is far from the truth:

> [C]limate mitigation creates a fulcrum for elitism, discrimination and the consolidation of wealth. Every form of climate mitigation is linked to at least one process of enclosure, exclusion, encroachment, and entrenchment, and many are linked repeatedly and persistently. Almost one-third (28.3%) of cases in the corpus are linked to *all four* processes, suggesting that climate mitigation efforts consistently exclude others, concentrate assets, and harm communities. The implication here may be that while issues of inequality and exclusion are extrinsic to a given technology, they are intrinsic to the current regime of low-carbon energy.[22]

Should we account for these tendencies as simply incidental or as somehow inherent in climate mitigation efforts? The pattern seems clear enough to justify a theory of energy justice that goes beyond statistical analyses of empirical research results, but how shall we understand the suggestion that technologies should be absolved from blame and the corollary distinction between low-carbon technologies and 'regimes of low-carbon energy'? Must we reconsider whether technological systems really should be exonerated as intrinsically innocent? Historical materialists and neo-materialists alike – not to mention mainstream historians and philosophers of technology – continue to be hesitant about attributing some form of inherent directionality to technological systems. It remains counter to modern common sense to impute insidious designs to inanimate artefacts, yet we may have to acknowledge that the harnessing of non-human energy, no less than slavery, is a *social* arrangement: a strategy for displacing work and environmental burdens onto disempowered others. The theoretical challenge is to account for the apparent occurrence of such *propensities* in technological systems. Given the quite material consequences of global market logic, it is reasonable to propose that the world economy is the medium through which social asymmetries are inscribed in technologies. This basic observation should be fundamental to any attempt to theorise the relation between the social and the material, including the purported 'agency' of technical artefacts.

Looking back at the Industrial Revolution, it is not difficult to understand the transition to fossil energy as having a total social rationale that was invisible to contemporary observers. We can now see that the growth of technological infrastructure in Britain and other core nations in the 19th century was tantamount to an expanding appropriation of (human) time and (natural) space from their peripheries. It may be more difficult to accept, however, that such asymmetric transfers of embodied labour, land, energy, and materials through ecologically unequal exchange – measured not in the fictive reciprocity of money prices but in physical metrics of labour time, hectares, joules, and tons – remain pervasive in the modern world.[23] A corollary of these asymmetric material transfers is the accumulation of technological infrastructure in core areas. The symbiosis of world trade and modern technology, in other words, continues to accomplish a continuous appropriation and redistribution of time and space. While they may seem to be distinct phenomena, studied by separate disciplines, trade and technology together constitute a social strategy for displacing resource constraints to other parts of the world-system. The implicit tendency towards ecologically unequal exchange, promoted by the global market, automatically translates into a technological rationality that favours the displacement of work and environmental loads to low-cost countries. It no longer seems justifiable to exonerate the technology 'itself' if its very feasibility hinges on prices that are conducive to such asymmetries. Rather than representing the politically neutral progress of humankind, the affluent lifestyles and social conditions of modernity must be recognised as the privilege of a global minority, accomplished at the expense of the rest of the world.

To understand why our customary celebration of the Industrial Revolution is so antithetical to this decidedly less flattering narrative, we must consider how it has been framed in terms of the new conceptual abstractions that emerged historically in tandem with the technological changes. Of pivotal importance is that we rethink the concept of energy. The conceptualisation of energy in physics was closely linked to the development of economic theory.[24] Its identification of forces in nature capable of 'doing work' appeared in tandem with the abstract conceptualisation of human 'labour-power' and economic value.[25] Through the lens of energy, the universe was conceived as a gigantic machine. Features of the natural environment such as minerals, forests, waterfalls, wind, and sunlight all became reducible to abstract power. The discovery of energy and steam technology was an unprecedented success story, but the promotors of the Industrial Revolution were unlikely to see how the large-scale harnessing of steam power was dependent on the relative world market prices of African labour, American land, raw cotton, cotton textiles, iron ore, and coal. Having been abstracted into quantifiable exchange-values, the fungibility of all these resources on the market obscured the causal connections between trade and the conditions for technological progress. Thus, as economy and technology were assigned to opposite sides of the society/nature divide, the social essence of technology became invisible. Given the structure of our modern worldview, it appears literally unthinkable that the seemingly innocent concepts of 'energy' and 'technology' in themselves would be complicit in a systematic displacement of resource demands from more to less affluent parts of world society. Yet, this may be a conclusion towards which the predicament of the Anthropocene is inexorably pushing us.

The industrial revolution as a transformation of the relations between energy and space

Graphically illuminated by the concept of 'ecological footprint,' it has become commonplace to view *consumption* as an index of the appropriation of ecological space. However, such insights have generally not affected our conceptions of *technology*. Advanced technologies, although they may be economically accessible only to a privileged minority, are not understood as inherently associated with consumer affluence. On the contrary, technology is often viewed as a means of increasing efficiency and reducing the ecological footprint.[26] It appears that the physical form of a technological artefact is primarily perceived as the embodiment of a revelatory *idea*, rather than a material entity contingent on metabolic processes. Conceptualised as an innovative idea, a new technology is unlikely to be scrutinised as an insidious socio-metabolic strategy for displacing resource requirements to others.

Over the past decade, a great number of critical examinations of the distributive dimensions of ostensibly sustainable and climate-friendly technologies have been presented,[27] but they rarely lead to a reconceptualisation of modern technology as a *generically* distributive phenomenon. A recurrent critique is that the new technologies merely displace, rather than solve, problems of unsustainability. Although the philosophy of technology[28] is a well-established field with a venerable historical tradition going back to Jacques Ellul, Martin Heidegger, Lewis Mumford, and Karl Marx, it currently devotes virtually no attention to the asymmetric resource flows and global environmental injustices that are often requisite to modern technological systems. Neither the school concerned with 'the social construction of technology'[29] nor the neo-materialists promulgating Actor-Network Theory[30] address such global flows and asymmetries.

Beyond the deliberations of philosophy and sociology, technology is conventionally understood simply as human ingenuity applied to the revelation of nature, inherently untainted by social inequalities and displacement strategies. Technology tends to be viewed as the progressive pursuit of ever higher levels of efficiency and rationality, rather than representing the use of nature to organise the material inequalities of societies. The extent to which local gains in efficiency occur at the expense of other populations appears not to concern most contemporary thought on technology. Although in innumerable ways they illuminate how the designs of technologies are shaped by the societies in which they are built, even sociologists and philosophers of technology tend to ignore how, through the asymmetric resource flows which make them possible, technologies generate and aggravate social inequalities. The assumption seems to be that the technicalities of engineering and design are somehow detached from the concerns of environmental justice. Discourses on 'metabolic rifts'[31] and 'ecologically unequal exchange'[32] are apparently considered irrelevant to the operation of technological systems. As opposed to this insulation of technological politics from the distributive materiality of global social metabolism, we should acknowledge that the former is imbued with the latter and that theories aspiring to grasp technology as a total social phenomenon must necessarily be transdisciplinary, integrating perspectives from both social and natural sciences.

To rethink technology in terms of the appropriation of space requires that we transgress several discursive boundaries, not only between the philosophy of technology and environmental justice but also the boundary that separates social theory, on the one hand, from the empirical quantification of physical resource flows conducted within the field of industrial ecology, on the other hand. Social scientists articulating the perspectives of political ecology and environmental justice are rarely oriented in the burgeoning, quantitative research which provides these theories with abundant empirical confirmation. Conversely, researchers working with material flow analysis and industrial ecology rarely connect their results to the voluminous theoretical discourse on political ecology and environmental justice. The two types of research frequently converge in their understanding of the ecological asymmetries of world trade, and both accounts – analytical explanation and empirical documentation – are crucial components of a counter-narrative to the mainstream celebration of the global market. The relative lack of connection between them appears to derive not from disagreement but from the conventional separation of social versus natural science, theoretical conceptualisation versus empirical quantification, and ethical positioning versus objectivism.

To give but one example of such fragmentation, Thomas Wiedmann and Manfred Lenzen's invaluable review of quantitative research on the destructive ecological and social footprints of international trade[33] represents an incontrovertible confirmation of the arguments on neocolonialism and environmental load displacements asserted by theorists of political ecology, environmental justice, and ecological Marxism. Nevertheless, few of the latter theorists refer to this body of research, nor do Wiedmann and Lenzen refer to contributions from such theory. In other words, although these two academic fields fully confirm each other's understandings of the world economy, there is very little communication between them. Furthermore, neither of these convergent fields interacts with – or perceives itself as relevant to – the philosophy of technology.

In economics, after the demise of Physiocracy, the 19th-century abandonment of ecological space as a relevant parameter can be understood as part of a general abandonment of concerns about the material substance of traded commodities in favour of the neoclassical preoccupation with abstract monetary metrics, consumer preferences, and market equilibrium. Neither businessmen nor economists had any reason to publicly reflect on the fact that the capital that Britain accumulated, and that could substitute for its relative lack of land, itself relied on the appropriation of embodied land from overseas. The annual output of a single British textile factory required very little British space – basically the area occupied by the factory itself – but relied on vast expanses of cotton plantations on other continents. The shift from domestic wool to imported cotton as the main raw material for the British textile industry thus represented a massive environmental load displacement from Britain to its global periphery.[34] At the height of its imperial power, Britain appropriated the produce of a land area several times greater than its total national territory. This was not only a result of coercion, as when fossil-fuelled technologies were applied to military control,[35] but also of the operation of the allegedly neutral principles of market equilibrium endorsed by the economists.

While a frequently mentioned rationale of the Industrial Revolution was the capacity to save space, it can be viewed as ultimately a strategy to gain access to increasing expanses of space elsewhere. Through global markets for mass-produced textiles, fossil energy gave Britain economic access to the produce of land and labour on other continents, and through new transport technologies such as railways and steamships, it physically conveyed the flows of commodities and raw materials that constituted Britain's imperial metabolism. In other words, a technology conventionally represented as saving space radically increased the ecological footprints of its beneficiaries.

These relations between energy, technology, movement, space, and time can be visualised with the aid of the conceptual framework of so-called 'time geography,' developed by the geographer Torsten Hägerstrand.[36] The transport technologies propelled by fossil energy gave British capital access to increasing expanses of geographical space by increasing velocity, that is by *reducing the amount of time required to traverse a given space*. This signified an inversion of the pre-industrial condition, in which it was access to eco-productive space that provided transport energy such as horse fodder. In pre-fossil times, in other words, a person's ecological footprint constrained his or her use of energy, whereas in modernity the use of fossil energy instead expands the size of a person's footprint. The central relevance of movement and mobility for the relation between energy and space is highlighted by the recent aspiration to maintain modern mobility beyond the use of fossil energy.[37] Although the material modalities of social polarisation differ between fossil-fuelled and electric vehicles, the logical connection between velocity and inequality identified by Ivan Illich half a century ago persists to this day:

> As societies put price tags on time, equity and vehicular speed correlate inversely. ... Beyond a certain velocity, passengers become consumers of other people's time, and accelerating vehicles become the means for effecting a net transfer of life-time.[38]

Indeed, the mining of cobalt in the Democratic Republic of the Congo, much of it for use in electric vehicles in the global North, at times suggests 'a modern form of slavery.'[39]

A consequence of consigning technology to an extra-social, 'natural' domain is that it is not recognised as social strategy. Nature, as distinct from society, cannot be criticised. Regardless of how insidious the social repercussions of a technology may be, they tend to be perceived as incidental and inadvertent rather than intrinsic to the logic of the technology. In our modern worldview, physical artefacts cannot have purposes and are thus immune to critique. Although philosophers of technology have demonstrated how political agency is regularly delegated to technical artefacts, the designs of technologies tend to be conceptually distinguished from their social consequences. This divide between material metabolism and social organisation has been a pervasive obstacle to acknowledging the role of fossil-fuelled technologies in furthering the interests of Euro-American imperialism. In the next section, I shall argue that it may also constrain our understanding of the global, social rationale of low-carbon transitions. This is not to indicate a resistance against such transitions, but a corollary to a general reconceptualisation of 'energy technologies.'

Spatial implications of a shift to renewable energy

The use of steam technology in 19th-century Britain converted coal and cotton fibres into great quantities of exchange-values in the form of cotton manufactures, which were in turn converted into the appropriation of labour and land in the cotton plantations. From a global, socio-metabolic perspective, it is thus pertinent to consider if the deliberations of engineers on the technical aspects of harnessing fossil energy can be rethought as a transmutation and political neutralisation of what were ultimately means of appropriating labour and land from other areas. The human toil and ecological impoverishment of the cotton plantations were not counted as part of the deliberate machinations of British textile manufacturers, and yet they were indispensable prerequisites for the expansion of steam technology. There is thus a sense in which engineering can be viewed as a fetishised preoccupation with the design of artefacts 'as such,' as if they had no connection to the displacements of work and environmental loads to which they were conducive.

What implications should this perspective on energy technologies have for our understanding of a transition to renewable energy? If the Industrial Revolution represented the historical inauguration of the age of fossil energy, a shift to renewable energy is tantamount to ending it. In some respects, this should logically entail a reversal of the socio-metabolic logic that has propelled global social processes for the past 200 years. Most importantly, if the transition to fossil energy meant an emancipation from land, and a shift to renewable energy instead implies greater land requirements, we need to develop transdisciplinary theory to understand how energy and space are related under specific technological regimes. If fossil energy for two centuries has been fundamental to the logic of capitalism, industrial production, and world trade, what do visions of a post-carbon society imply for the biophysical and spatial organisation of the world economy? Moreover, if the emancipation from land constraints in 19th-century Britain was the foundation of modern economics, what modifications would an acknowledgement of land requirements imply for post-fossil economic theory?

The limited extent to which mainstream thought acknowledges the social and distributive aspects of technological systems is currently being revealed by the unanticipated difficulties that nations are having in implementing their proposals for transitions to renewable energy.[40] Based on the conception of technological progress that was established in the 19th century, deliberations on the feasibility of harnessing low-carbon sources of energy have been conducted without proper consideration of how such technologies presuppose relatively low market prices of the labour, land, energy, and materials required to assemble them. Although sceptics have observed, for instance, that a large-scale shift to biofuels would compete with food production and reduce biodiversity, and that technologies for photovoltaic power would require vast quantities of materials,[41] space,[42] and embodied energy[43] – yielding a disturbingly low EROI[44] – such objections have not generally discouraged technological visions of a post-carbon modernity. However, there are reasons to doubt that the envisaged technologies for harnessing renewable energy will be able to replace the fossil energy currently covering almost 90% of the energy demands of global human society, particularly as the per capita energy requirements of a growing world population are projected to rise sharply in the coming decades.[45] When translated into the quantities of materials and space required to substitute for current levels of fossil energy use, technologies for harnessing renewable energy sources would demand substantial proportions of the Earth's land surface, leaving a deficit of land for food production, forestry, natural biodiversity, and other concerns.

The necessity of a shift away from fossil energy is obvious to most people accepting its role as a major contributor to climate change. Even if its emissions of greenhouse gases could be dealt with through carbon capture and storage, or if its climate impacts could be alleviated through geoengineering, the problem remains that stocks of fossil fuels are limited and increasingly costly to extract. The predicament is compounded by the fact that technologies for renewable energy require considerably more space and materials per unit of harnessed energy than fossil fuels, while at the same time we shall need to reduce our ecological footprints as well as our per capita consumption of materials.[46] In addition to these physical constraints, we need to consider how such technologies could be economically feasible for most of the world's population, given that the great discrepancies in per capita purchasing-power are making access to low-carbon energy technologies the prerogative of affluent nations.

Vaclav Smil's demonstration of the 'power densities' of different energy technologies provides a useful point of departure for summarising my argument on the tacit and neglected social rationale of energy technologies.[47] Smil defines power density as W/m^2, that is, watts (or joules per second) per square metre. He notes that mainstream modern economics shows very little interest in space or land but convincingly demonstrates that the rate of energy flow per unit of surface area should in fact be our essential concern. However, his calculations of power density reckon only with the spatial extent of the technological infrastructures under consideration, not with their footprints beyond the technological artefacts themselves. To thus calculate a technology's power density without reckoning with its spatial requirements beyond the surface area occupied by the technology itself illustrates what I have called 'machine fetishism.' It is tantamount to conceptually isolating the local, physical operation of the technology from the global, social resource flows that make it possible. If sustainability and justice are concerns defined in global terms, it must be considered fetishistic to envisage the adoption of new technologies within a given nation without reckoning with their global requirements and repercussions.

Common to the fetishism of money, commodities, and machines is the perception of artefacts as autonomous vis-à-vis the social relations of exchange on which they are contingent. Machine fetishism, however, has ontological implications that go beyond the conventional understanding of Marx's concept of commodity fetishism. In both cases, the inputs of labour time and natural space embodied in human artefacts are invisible and mystified, but machine fetishism has become foundational to Marxist theory in the form of a 'Promethean' trust in the progress of the productive forces. In this respect, classical Marxism subscribes to the illusion of machine fetishism that was so essential to the historical experience of 19th-century Britons. When David Harvey explains how Marx was able to expose the 'fetishism of technology,' he refers to the illusion of capitalists that machines are autonomous sources of productivity[48] but shows that Marx identified the true and obscured source of productivity as living labour in the factory, rather than the labour and other resources that had been embodied in the production of the machine in distant mines, plantations, and other sites of extraction. While Harvey is correct in understanding modern technology as 'a distinctive sphere of action' specific to industrial capitalism, its defining feature is not primarily that engineers 'scientifically dissect nature in order to exercise control,'[49] but that its efficacy is contingent on asymmetric global transfers of resources.

The most radical critics of industrial capitalism failed to perceive that the operation of machine technology – its abstract potential to conduct work – is not simply a function of 'natural' forces, as if it could be achieved without globally asymmetric resource flows. The physical power of the machine is not attributable to the machine itself, in isolation, but contingent on the social relations of exchange of which it is an expression. The mainstream distinction between economy and technology – detaching the former from nature and the latter from global society – is reproduced in the Marxian distinction between 'relations of production' and 'productive forces.' The new technologies that emerged in Britain in the late 18th and early 19th centuries were indeed manifestations of capital accumulation, but rather than intrinsically neutral revelations of nature that could be excised from capitalism and transferred to a post-capitalist mode of production, they embodied a severely unequal world economy. The accumulated capital that made them possible signified a vast ecological footprint. Rather than conceiving of capital, land, and labour as distinct factors of production, I proposed in the previous chapter, we must reconsider capital as representing land and labour appropriated *elsewhere*. This applies not merely to historical processes in the 19th century but continues to be a fundamental condition of technological development to this day.

Smil aptly concludes that energy studies have 'accomplished a remarkable feat by largely ignoring space as a key organizing determinant of modern systems supplying fuels and electricity.'[50] This is a very valid conclusion, but I would like to complement it with the observation that they have also ignored the *total global economic space* upon which energy technologies rely for their very existence. The discourse on post-fossil energy justice urgently needs to be extended to encompass systematic considerations of ecologically unequal exchange – the global displacements and asymmetric resource transfers that are implicitly requisite to our seemingly virtuous investments in low-carbon energy technologies.

We have seen that it is an extensively documented fact that transitions to low-carbon energy technologies and other forms of climate mitigation tend to involve disempowerment and environmental injustices of various kinds.

The argument here is that such tendencies are inherent in the social rationale of technological systems promoted by the logic of the world market. Our tendency to focus on technologies 'in themselves,' as if they could be detached from the global social metabolism from which they emerge, is symptomatic of machine fetishism. Rather than merely investigate the social and ecological repercussions of technological systems, viewing them as unintended consequences, the focus of energy justice research should be to discover the tacit, distributive functions that are inscribed in the technologies to begin with. While not as likely to yield the kind of 'solutions' that politicians and market actors are demanding, such research should enhance our ability to comprehend the confounding predicament of the Anthropocene.

The global context of digital technologies and 'artificial intelligence'

The distributed character of modern technologies is well illustrated by the simple device known as a 'dumbwaiter.' It is a kind of elevator originally associated with Thomas Jefferson, who wished to host dinners without the presence of his servants. Its rationale was not primarily to reduce work but to make it invisible. From a global perspective, as we have seen, it is possible to see both the turn to fossil energy (the Industrial Revolution) and the efforts to abandon it (the transition to renewables) as imbued with the same logic. The universal commensurability of labour inputs and resources exchanged on the world market – that is, the idea embodied in money – continues to encourage opaque displacement strategies.

This most certainly also applies to technologies based on 'Artificial Intelligence' (AI). The aim of AI is to create machines that quite literally are taught the requisite cognitive skills to emulate and even surpass human intelligence. Whereas the widespread scepticism against AI has largely focused on the social and ethical consequences of making humans redundant, and dystopian scenarios of AI that harm human beings, there are increasing concerns about what has been characterised as 'AI (or data) colonialism.'[51] Not only have AI technologies been shown to be much more resource-intensive and environmentally damaging than most people assume,[52] but they are also based on severe exploitation of low-wage labour.[53] Mystifyingly referred to as 'the cloud,' the expanding global infrastructure for data processing and storage is no less material and exploitative than other technological systems since the Industrial Revolution.

To operate in a socially acceptable manner, 'intelligent' machines, like children, must be socialised. As all parents know, this requires a lot of work teaching them to categorise and evaluate the myriad phenomena of social life. Like a fully socialised child, an intelligent machine thus embodies great quantities of human labour. What to parents is a matter of teaching children to attach words and normative judgements to things and various other kinds of phenomena, for engineers in the AI business is known as 'data-labelling.'

Machine learning is founded on the tagging, or annotation, of massive amounts of data in texts, sounds, images, or videos. For predictable reasons, this 'ghost work'[54] underlying AI technology is outsourced to the least expensive labour in countries such as the Philippines, Venezuela, and Kenya. Much as Georg Borgström's concept of 'ghost acreages' referred to invisible, embodied land, the concept of ghost work refers to invisible, embodied labour. Both exemplify how the abstraction of inputs in production is conducive to mystification. As so often before in history, the experience of a miraculous new technology that seems to make human labour superfluous is an illusion, because it ultimately represents the *displacement* of workloads onto less privileged social groups. Much of the work seemingly conducted by the new machines is really conducted by invisible labourers in the global South. The magical displacements of workloads and environmental loads, contributing to ever deeper global gaps, tend to pass under the radar of mainstream economists because they are obscured by the veil of money and by our entrenched ontological divide between the social and the material.

In this chapter, we have considered three examples of technological systems – early industrial steam power, recent transitions to renewable energy sources, and artificial intelligence – that all have been shown to be conducive to 'machine fetishism,' obscuring their essential reliance on asymmetric global transfers of embodied labour and other resources. The question that we must ask is if such concerns about mystified inequalities in these three instances of technological advance are coincidental, or if they exemplify a pattern that should prompt us to reconceptualise the very ontology of modern technology? Common to all three cases are global displacements of workloads and environmental loads, involving extensive injustices and disempowerments. If these cases do add up to a significant pattern, why is it that we have not seen it? It appears that our dualist ontological blinders have obscured the *socionatural* character of technology, preventing us from grasping the entanglement of global social relations with the materiality of the Earth. As we have seen, this entanglement is both organised and obscured by the idea of money. Money is an agreement pertaining to the organisation of social relations, while technology deludingly appears to pertain merely to the organisation of matter and energy. In being contingent on money, the phenomenon of modern technology must defy the society/nature divide. Like the various other sign systems that have been constitutive of ecological systems from the very beginning, money transcends the distinction between the subjective and the objective, reorganising perceptions as well as flows of matter and energy. Technology is a product of this reorganisation. Given the severe inequalities of world society, we should not be surprised to find that the global technomass itself is a manifestation – and money the means – of intraspecific parasitism. As Latour observed, with his characteristically enigmatic prose, 'science is indeed politics pursued by other means, means that are powerful only because they remain radically other.'[55]

Notes

1 The phrase was also used by Marshall Berman as the title of his book *All That Is Solid Melts into Air* (1982), subtitled *The Experience of Modernity*.
2 Although devoid of social theory, and at times appearing to attribute autonomous agency to the technomass, attempts have been made to estimate the physical volume and metabolic requirements of what P.K. Haff (2013) and others call the global 'technosphere,' which are clearly at a scale rivalling those of the lithosphere, atmosphere, hydrosphere, and biosphere; see Zalasiewicz *et al.* 2017.
3 This reframing was famously identified by Martin Heidegger ([1954] 1977) in his concept of 'enframing' (*Gestell*).
4 The metaphorical understanding of money as a universal solvent is well established, as when Bill Maurer (2006: 24) casually refers to 'the Simmelian money-as-acid hypothesis.' To this observation I have added the metaphor of a *gastric* acid, emphasizing that solubility is requisite to appropriation.
5 Pomeranz and Topik 1999: 113, 140.
6 Pomeranz and Topik 1999: 223.
7 For a succinct overview of the global predicament of modernity, see Murphy *et al.* 2021.
8 Smil 2022: 5.
9 Latour 1993.
10 Sovacool 2021a.
11 The foundational text is Bijker *et al.* 1987.
12 Latour 2005.
13 Matthewman 2011: 19.
14 Matthewman 2011: 109.
15 This is not to suggest, however, that artefacts have 'agency' beyond the implementation of asymmetries inscribed in them – through the market – by the global social order.
16 Landes 1969.
17 Sieferle [1982] 2001; Wrigley 1988.
18 Adas 1989; Berg 1980.
19 Winner 1980; Johnson 1988.
20 Huber 2008; Malm 2016; Roos 2023.
21 Sovacool 2021a.
22 Sovacool 2021a: 13; emphasis in original.
23 Dorninger *et al.* 2021; Hickel *et al.* 2022.
24 Illich [1983] 2013; Mirowski 1989; Rabinbach 1990; Daggett 2019.
25 Even Marx´s labour theory of value was modelled on the First Law of Thermodynamics (the law of the conservation of energy). For Marx, Caffentzis (2013: 149–150) observes, '[n]o machine can create new value nor transfer more value to its product than it loses. This law parallels the laws of conservation of force and energy found in the classical theory of machines and in the theory of heat engines.'
26 An extreme example of this argument is Asafu-Adjaye *et al.* 2015.
27 Huesemann and Huesemann 2011; Bonds and Downey 2012; Zehner 2012; Rogers 2010; Andersen 2013; Franquesa 2018; Dunlap 2019; Mulvaney 2019; Sovacool 2014; Roos 2023.
28 Ihde 1993; Mitcham 1994; Scharff and Dusek 2014.
29 Bijker *et al.* 1987.
30 Latour 2005.
31 Foster *et al.* 2010.
32 Jorgenson and Clark 2009; Hornborg and Martinez-Alier 2016; Frey *et al.* 2019; see Chapter 4.
33 Wiedmann and Lenzen 2018.

34 Wilkinson 1973; Pomeranz 2000.
35 Headrick 1981.
36 See Gren 2009.
37 Sovacool 2017.
38 Illich [1973] 2013: 84–85.
39 Sovacool 2021b.
40 Smil 2016.
41 Georgescu-Roegen 1993.
42 Smil 2015.
43 Hall and Klitgaard 2011.
44 Prieto and Hall 2013.
45 Smil (2022: 183) notes, for instance, that 'the global impact of the recent turn toward decarbonizing electricity generation – by installing solar PV panels and wind turbines – has been completely negated by the rapid rise of greenhouse gas emissions in China and elsewhere in Asia.'
46 Schandl *et al.* 2016.
47 Smil 2015.
48 Harvey 2018: 109.
49 Harvey 2018: 118.
50 Smil 2015: 254.
51 Gray and Suri 2019; Couldry and Mejias 2019; Hao 2022.
52 Crawford 2022; De Vries 2023.
53 Gray and Suri 2019; Lohmann 2020; Crawford 2022. Moreover, AI technologies enable corporations to exploit the *users* of these technologies by mining the internet for information on various aspects of their lives; Zuboff 2019; Couldry and Mejias 2019. Finally, in facilitating increasingly persuasive 'confidence tricks,' AI tends to undermine the abstract social *trust* that is fundamental to modernity. In provoking a generalised *distrust* of technologies for telecommunication, the development of AI thus appears to have caught up with the social foundations of modernity.
54 Gray and Suri 2019.
55 Latour 1993: 111.

6 Money, entropy, and climate change

Many of the key concerns of this book – money fetishism, social injustices, unequal exchange, and the significance of mechanisation – can be traced to Karl Marx's radical rethinking of human history. Over the past half century, however, many followers of Marx's worldview have found some parts of it difficult to reconcile with rising worries about environmental degradation and climate change. My aim in this chapter is to critically review a selection of Marxist literature applying radical philosophical and social-science perspectives on climate change. Given the predominance of natural-science research on climate, this inevitably means addressing the role of 'nature' in radical social theory. As the topic of climate change in the Anthropocene has only become prominent in recent decades, the overview stretches no further back than the 1980s. Although the focus is on perspectives emerging from Marxist philosophy and social theory, the chapter occasionally also refers to foundational contributions from other discourses such as feminist theory, ecological economics, and the environmental movement. It will be argued that the recent formation of an 'ecological Marxism' represents an attempt to resume Marx's and Engels' struggles to liberate their materialist analysis of the human predicament from the constraints of idealist political economy and its reification of the notion of value. I hope to show that these efforts have not always been completely successful.

In spanning the conceptual divide between nature and society, the phenomenon of global warming should lead us to decisively shed the veil of mainstream economics and prompt us to recognise the metabolic materiality of world society. Given that the emissions of greenhouse gases resulting in climate change can be explained in terms of thermodynamics – as *entropy* – the global economy generating those emissions must be reconceptualised as a material process. The recognition of the imperative to reconceptualise the economy as material has haunted Marxism and other heterodox approaches to economics since the mid-19th century, yet its far-reaching implications continue to pose conceptual hurdles for the most radical of theorists. For this reason, we shall particularly examine recent efforts to integrate thermodynamics and social theory. Given the focus on Marxist theory, much of the discussion will address how heterodox theorists conceptualise the relations

DOI: 10.4324/9781032702186-9

between energy/entropy, value, and money. This theoretical puzzle is pivotal to our comprehension of ecological degradation in general but has become acutely significant as we acknowledge the potentially disastrous trajectory of anthropogenic climate change.

As extensively documented by environmental historians, observations on how the activities of humans are transforming their natural environment – including climate – have been made for several millennia.[1] Up until the end of the 20th century, however, such observations were generally confined to restricted localities or regions subjected to tangible degradation such as deforestation, overharvesting of game or fish, or unsustainable agriculture. As the insight that greenhouse gas emissions caused by humans are altering global climate became increasingly established in the final decades of the 20th century, it presented a new challenge to the predominant modern worldview. More strikingly than other forms of anthropogenic environmental change, global warming has problematised the traditional Western distinction between nature and society. Over the past four decades, it has provoked intensive academic discussions about how to deal analytically with the conundrum of a global environment that is interfused with the metabolism of world society. These deliberations have been particularly important to fields and movements that articulate radical critiques of the environmental consequences of the modern world economy, such as ecological Marxism, ecofeminism, and the environmental movement. In different and sometimes contradictory ways, they have struggled to radically reconceptualise the relation between humans and their natural environment. As such efforts predate the late 20th-century concerns about climate change, a brief background is in order.

Nature in Marxist theory

In her book *The Death of Nature* (1980), the environmental historian Carolyn Merchant made a foundational contribution to ecofeminism by proposing that ideas about human mastery over nature since the 17th century have been entwined with patriarchal ideas about men's mastery over women.[2] She suggests that modern developments in science and technology have been founded on a hierarchical and exploitative approach to the relation between humans and non-human nature that has replaced more holistic, premodern worldviews, alienating humans from an environment increasingly degraded by their activities. This conceptual split between thinking human subjects and subordinate natural objects, often referred to as Cartesian dualism, has been criticised since it was first articulated by the philosopher René Descartes (1596–1650) and, following Merchant, particularly by ecofeminists. For Val Plumwood, the 'objectification' of nature is closely associated with its commodification under capitalism.[3] The understanding of modern environmental crises as products of an alienating split between humans and nature – and the corresponding vision of a 're-enchanted' and more integrated mode of being – is shared also by significant parts of the environmental movement, such as the 'deep ecology' of Arne Naess[4] and the relational environmentalism of Neil Evernden.[5] Rarely, however, do prominent ecofeminists like Merchant and Plumwood or environmental philosophers like Naess and Evernden acknowledge the fact that elaborate critiques of the human objectification and domination of nature can be traced to the Frankfurt School of Marxism known as Critical Theory.[6]

The ideas of Georg Lukács provide an important if ambiguous point of departure for much of the discussion on the role of nature in Marxist theory. In contrast to the approach of Friedrich Engels, who understood Marxist philosophy as applicable to both society and nature, Lukács argued that it is only relevant to the human sphere of history and society. While Engels thought of natural science as a model for the study of society, thus abandoning the otherwise critical attitude to mainstream knowledge production with which he and Marx approached political economy, the Frankfurt School instead criticised science and technology as capitalist instruments of domination and violation of nature. This stance represented a break with the celebration of technological progress in classical Marxism. Although the Critical Theorists posit a dualism of nature versus society, their observations on the social character of knowledge production simultaneously invite arguments on the sociality of what we know as 'nature.' The philosopher Steven Vogel observes that the tradition of Marxism deriving from the Frankfurt School continues to struggle with the tension between its commitment to an objective, materialist view of nature and its critique of the very notion of objective knowledge.[7] Classical Marxist materialism meant grounding social theory on natural science, but Lukács rejects the possibility of immediate knowledge of nature. This impasse of Critical Theory has thus inspired two divergent kinds of critiques of science and technology: either that they fail to respect the ontological otherness of an objective, extra-social nature, or that they obscure – through reification – the extent to which their conceptions of nature are social constructions. While the former critique, prominent in Horkheimer and Adorno, is fundamental to much environmentalist thought and to most proponents of ecological Marxism, Vogel endorses the latter, constructionist position that is pervasive in Western Marxism and traceable to Lukács: that nature and society are indistinguishable, because the environment is largely the product of social processes. In proposing a 'critical theory of nature,' Vogel advocates a deconstruction of this social framing of nature, 'a deconstruction oriented by the hope that humans could take responsibility for the world they inhabit instead of believing that world to be determined by external forces they are unable to control.'[8]

These ambiguities about the role of nature in Marxist theory have spawned voluminous discussions long before global warming became a prominent topic of environmental debate. Since the early 1990s, the burgeoning literature on ecological Marxism has increasingly addressed the relation between capitalism and environmental degradation. In part, this 'greening' of Marxism has been a response to recurrent challenges from ecosocialists, ecofeminists, and the environmental movement. As the environmentalist Bill McKibben writes, it 'is not at all *that* radical to talk about who is going to own the factories, at least compared with the question of whether there are going to *be* factories.'[9] In the same vein, Ariel Salleh deplores that

> Marx's ideological position on technology overlooks the environmental dialectic of the machine's existence. The ecosystem is ravaged as its resources are mined, smelted, turned by other workers, transported, assembled, operated, repaired, and finally dumped.[10]

Eco-Marxist theorists have been pressed to demonstrate the relevance of their conceptual framework for environmental issues. It has been important for them to reject critiques of productivism provoked by Marx's 'Promethean' praise of the historical advance of the productive forces. For those Marxists to whom Prometheanism ought to be confined to ecomodernist think-tanks like the Breakthrough Institute, which famously anticipates a 'good Anthropocene,'[11] this has been an essential requirement for merging 'red' and 'green' sentiments into a radical ecology movement.

Over the past two decades, the ecological turn in Marxist theory has led to an expansive discussion of capitalism and climate. Much of the discussion has been tantalising in the way it reveals the conceptual difficulties modern people tend to experience in attempting to think holistically about phenomena that span the divide between society and nature. These difficulties are evident in the kinds of impasses demonstrated by various participants in the debate, whether keeping social exchange relations and the material properties of artefacts rigorously separated or denying any analytical distinction between the social and the material. Beyond simply ignoring nature (like mainstream economics), it is clearly as misleading to consider nature entirely a social construction as it is to reduce social processes to physics. The challenge, not only for Marxists but also for all people concerned about global warming and other sustainability issues, is to find a balanced view of the interpenetration of social and natural factors, recognising that the distinction between them pivots on the human use of *symbols*, which exist nowhere but in human societies. The permeation of the biosphere by biochemical consequences of human activity must be classified as a social factor, as it would not exist without the symbolic systems – cultural patterns of communication, consumption, economy, and technology – that propel human societies. But although justifying the analytical identification of the social, in the sense of anthropogenic or 'human' (versus non-human) phenomena, this distinction should not preclude the awareness that humans are a part of the material processes of physical nature, rather than a Cartesian outsider struggling to gain mastery over it. While metabolically fused with nature, human social processes are distinguishable from those of the pre-human biosphere by their derivation from symbolic communication.

The escalating urgency of climate change and its challenge to Marxism

Writing in the aftermath of an unprecedented American drought in 1988, Bill McKibben in his book *The End of Nature* (1989) was one of the first to recognise the unsettling ontological and existential implications of anthropogenic climate change. 'By changing the weather,' he claims, 'we make every spot on earth man-made and artificial.'[12] While we have been used to the idea that 'there is a world of man and a world of nature,' climate change means that 'now there is nothing that isn't us.'[13] Because it is no longer a separate category beyond our control, McKibben argues, late 20th-century nature cannot inspire reverence or mystique. He thus expresses the existential quandary of what was to be called the Anthropocene, which continues to pose a conceptual dilemma for theorists of human–environmental relations. It should be noted, however, that it is our *awareness* of these circumstances that changes our experience of nature, not the physical fact that nature and society are interfused. For example, the so-called Little Ice Age in the 16th and 17th centuries may have resulted from mass depopulation of the Americas, leading to extensive reforestation and carbon uptake of abandoned, previously cultivated landscapes,[14] yet nobody at the time perceived the severe winters in Europe as produced by social processes in the world-system. Even the interfusion of nature and society thus compels us to distinguish between objective processes and subjective perceptions.

This does not mean having to *choose* between approaching nature as objective reality *or* cultural construction, but to acknowledge both aspects and their continuous interaction. In contrast to many anti-dualist ecological theorists in ecofeminism and posthumanism, the philosopher Kate Soper adopts a critical realist position that rejects the kind of constructionist arguments that completely deny the extra-discursive reality of nature.[15] While conceding that any distinction between the 'reality' and the cultural representation of nature is itself conceptual, she finds it unjustified to conclude that no ontological distinction should be made 'between the ideas we have of nature and that which the ideas are about,' in other words, 'between that which is and that which is not an effect of culture.'[16] Writing at a time when constructionism posed more of a challenge to environmental science than it does today, Soper incisively reminds us that 'it is not the discourse of "global warming"...that has created the conditions of which it speaks.'[17]

In the late 1980s, McKibben suggested that the greenhouse effect might be regarded as '*the* important political issue.'[18] Indeed, by the early 1990s, global warming had gained a sufficiently prominent position in public discourse to pervade U.S. Vice President Al Gore's bestselling book *Earth in the Balance* (1992), published in the same year as the Earth Summit – the United Nations Conference on Environment and Development (UNCED) – in Rio de Janeiro. The Kyoto Protocol was signed in 1997. Gore's influential film and book *An Inconvenient Truth* (2006) earned him a share of the Nobel

Peace Prize in 2007. Events such as these helped to establish global awareness of climate change. At the turn of the millennium, however, the challenge it posed to ecological Marxism had yet to be realised.

One of the first concerted efforts to merge Marxist political economy and ecological issues is the collection *Is Capitalism Sustainable?*, edited by the economist Martin O'Connor.[19] The title, according to the editor, encapsulates 'the sorts of questions that are on everybody's lips since the Rio de Janeiro conference in 1992.'[20] Only one of the book's 13 Chapters – 'Ecological Economics and Ecosocialism' by the economic historian Joan Martinez-Alier – mentions climate change. Martinez-Alier, who specifically refers to 'the scare in the United States in the summer of 1988'[21] as a significant moment in the history of climate change research, observes that the economists' concept of 'externalities' is useless in aspiring to assign economic values to environmental degradation. In what 30 years later comes across as a striking understatement, he cautions that 'the valuation of the greenhouse effect is embedded in uncertainties and distributional conflicts.'[22]

1988 was the year when carbon dioxide-induced global warming was 'discovered,' spurred by the warm summer in the United States and by the establishment of the Intergovernmental Panel on Climate Change (IPCC) and the United Nations' Environment Programme (UNEP).[23] 1988 was also the year when James O'Connor, another contributor to Martin O'Connor's collection, founded the eco-Marxist journal *Capitalism, Nature, Socialism*. He introduces the new journal by suggesting that 'there may exist a contradiction of capitalism which leads to an "ecological" theory of crisis and social transformation.'[24] Ten years later, he published a collection of articles titled *Natural Causes: Essays in Ecological Marxism*, in which he argues that the contradiction between humans and nature is '*the* basic contradiction of world capitalism at the end of the 20th century.'[25] He briefly refers to the 'warming of the atmosphere' as an example of how capitalist accumulation is destroying its 'own conditions,'[26] illustrating 'The Second Contradiction of Capitalism.' O'Connor mentions in passing that the composition of the atmosphere is the result of human impacts on nature,[27] that general interest in the greenhouse effect is growing each year,[28] and that global warming is one of the most important threats to the natural world,[29] but such observations do not lead him to theorise the relation between capitalism and climate change beyond the general recognition that there is a contradiction between capital and nature. The marginal role of climate change in O'Connor's framework is evident from the fact that the book's index has no entries for 'climate,' 'carbon,' 'global warming,' or 'greenhouse effect.' At the end of the 20th century, global warming had not yet begun to occupy centre stage in ecological Marxism.

It was not until Joel Kovel's volume *The Enemy of Nature* (2002), and particularly its second edition published in 2007, that 'carbon emissions,' 'greenhouse gases,' and 'global warming' became prominent topics in a book on the contradiction between capitalism and the biosphere. Like McKibben and Martinez-Alier, Kovel refers to the 1988 drought in the United States as the impetus to concerns about global warming. Climate change, he writes already in the preface to the first edition, is 'another kind of imperialism.'[30] In the second edition, he is even more convinced that climate change is happening, as illustrated by the heat wave in Europe in 2003 and the flooding of New Orleans by Hurricane Katrina in 2005. Kovel traces the destructive inertia of capitalism to the abstract idea of exchange-value, which in the form of money humans seek endlessly to accumulate.[31] Money, he writes, is the 'most strange and interesting concoction of the human mind.'[32] Since jeopardising monetary profits is 'unthinkable,' he asserts, 'nothing substantial will be done about global warming under the present regime.'[33] In extensively incorporating the topic of climate change into Marxism's indictment of capitalism, Kovel's conclusions must be regarded as significant. A lasting contribution is also his recognition of the very idea and artefact of money as generative of the logic usually referred to as capitalism.

In *Marx and Nature: A Red and Green Perspective* (1999), the economist Paul Burkett inaugurates what sociologist John Bellamy Foster in his foreword to the 2014 edition calls the 'second stage of ecosocialist analysis,' the aim of which is to refute 'first-stage' ecosocialist criticisms of Marx's approach to nature (by thinkers such as André Gorz, Ted Benton, James O'Connor, Alain Lipietz, and Joel Kovel).[34] Burkett attempts to dismiss these criticisms – of Marx's productivism, labour theory of value, and purported neglect of the natural conditions of production – by arguing that Marx's materialism was grounded in thermodynamics and thus indisputably ecological. He thus proposes, for instance, that Marx's concept of use-value refers to the 'natural-material' aspects of a commodity – Foster calls it 'ecological-value analysis'[35] – and that the appropriation of surplus-value from labour – 'the whole basis of capital accumulation' – is essentially a 'material, biological, and energetic extraction process.'[36] In support of this interpretation, Burkett cites Marx's occasional reduction of exploitation to energetics, as when Marx argues that all surplus-value production is contingent on labour productivity in agriculture,[37] and also adduces Elmar Altvater's energy input/output account of exploitation.[38] Against this background, it is remarkable to find Burkett – in a polemic with Martinez-Alier – endorsing Engels' assessment that Sergei Podolinsky, who suggested to Marx that surplus-value could be understood in terms of energetics, had 'confused the physical with the economic.'[39] Burkett's book thus inadvertently reveals the ambiguous position of eco-Marxist theory in between physics and economics. This ambiguity does not concern Foster, but he does reflect on the absence in Burkett's book of concerns about global warming, noting that 15 years after the original publication 'climate change is part of our everyday lives everywhere in the world.'[40]

Given the ascendancy of worries about global warming in the 1980s and 1990s, and Foster's urge to demonstrate the ecological relevance of Marx, the absence of concerns about climate change is equally conspicuous in his own book, *Marx's Ecology* (2000), published a year after that of Burkett. Its main mission is to unravel the deep intellectual roots of Marx's deliberations on the relation between humans and nature and to argue, as had Burkett, that Marx's materialism was solidly grounded in ecology. This meant rejecting the tradition of Lukács and the Frankfurt School, who had denied the relevance of Marxist theory for natural science. Foster discovered that Marx, in his critique of Malthus, had become keenly interested in agricultural chemistry, observing that there was a 'metabolic rift' between urban and rural areas, as nutrients flowed unilaterally to the towns from an increasingly impoverished countryside. Foster takes this interest in social metabolism as a refutation of critiques claiming that Marx's view of history tended to neglect nature. He claims that 'Marx made the concept of metabolism central to his entire system of analysis by rooting his understanding of the labor process upon it.'[41] As the concept of metabolism refers to exchanges of matter and energy, Foster is clearly pursuing the same line of argument as Burkett: that Marx's analysis of the capitalist's appropriation of surplus-value from labour pertains to a material and energetic extraction process. He writes that Marx's use of the concept of metabolism in the 1860s was consistent with the 'general shift toward energetics in science.'[42] Foster shows that Marx identified metabolic rifts also on a global level, but his quotations from Marx on this topic refer exclusively to the appropriation, through colonialism, of the nutrients required for soil fertility.[43] No evidence is presented to suggest that Marx thought of the metabolic rift as involving one-way flows not only of materials but also of energy. Given how familiar Marx was with the fact that plantations used slave labour to supply British mills with cotton fibre, and how Foster appears to agree with Burkett that the appropriation of surplus-value from labour is a process of energy extraction, it is puzzling that Foster does not fulfil his metabolic understanding of Marx's materialism by considering the shipments of raw cotton in terms of embodied labour.[44] Not even when Foster quotes Marx on the historical 'conversion of Africa into a preserve for the commercial hunting of blackskins'[45] does he frame the exploitation of colonial labour in terms of metabolism. He thus hesitates, in this context, to consider the appropriation of labour-power as an extraction of energy, although this approach, as we shall see, is explicit in his collaborations with Burkett. Foster's argument in *Marx's Ecology* finally raises the question why Marx's interest in soil fertility should render his labour theory of value more ecological. Although the book demonstrates that Marx had an interest in social metabolism, it does not address the value-theoretical foundations of Marxist social theory, which are essential to its understanding of exploitation, class struggle, and the historical trajectory of capitalism.

In Burkett's second book, *Marxism and Ecological Economics: Toward a Red and Green Political Economy* (2005), global warming is mentioned, if only in passing, as an addition to 'the growing list of metabolic rift mechanisms.'[46] Burkett here refers to the analysis of sociologists Brett Clark and Richard York (2005), which applies Foster's development of Marx's concept of metabolic rift to global carbon metabolism under capitalism. In approaching the emissions of carbon dioxide into the atmosphere in terms of metabolic rift theory, this article represents a pioneering effort to apply Marxist theory to climate change. It simultaneously, if briefly, illustrates the limitations of Marxist value theory. Clark and York reiterate the Marxian conviction that a commodity's value in capitalism is determined by the socially necessary labour time (SNLT) required to produce it. Contrary to what is often intimated, the Marxist position does not simply dismiss this notion of value as a capitalist mystification of material processes but contributes to its reification by treating value as an *objective* property of commodities. The discrepancy between economic valuation and material processes is presented as a contradiction between value as SNLT and 'value in the form of the accumulation of material processes.'[47] This phrasing, like Foster's reference to 'ecological-value analysis,' suggests that value is a material feature, rather than simply deriving from the measuring-rod of money. A consistently materialist approach, however, would recognise valuation as an entirely perceptual phenomenon, which obscures – while *organising* – the objective material metabolism of human societies. Although their account of how human activities – most prominently the use of fossil energy – are generating climate change is incontrovertible, as are their observations on how the material processes promoted by the world market are generating severe global inequalities, their analysis raises questions about how the specific logic of what Marxists refer to as capitalism differ, in these material respects, from *non*-capitalist societies based on industrial production and the use of all-purpose money. After the collapse of the Soviet Union and the ascent of China, we might ask if industrial societies using money could ever be anything *but* capitalist, and if the target of critique instead ought to be industry and money in themselves? To consider whether global warming and metabolic rifts can be connected specifically to a 'capitalist mode of production' as conceptualised by Marx in the 1860s, we shall return to Burkett's (2009) deliberations on value, energy, and entropy.

Marxist value theory as torn between economics and physics

Of particular relevance for this issue is Burkett's discussion of Marx's assessment of Physiocracy.[48] According to Marx, the Physiocrats confused nature's material substance with value, but Marx himself appears to have recurrent problems in keeping them apart, not least because he equated such material substance with 'nature's real wealth' or 'use-value.'[49] To apply the concept of 'wealth' to a material substance is clearly to engage in valuation. The concept of use-value is a misleading hybrid between physics and economics, deriving human valuation from material properties. Humans will obviously value a given commodity's material properties, but there is no way in which such valuation could be predicted or derived from those properties.[50] As Marx himself observed, beef is not food to a Hindu. Neither can the values circulating in a human economy be shown to derive from specific material inputs, whether of energy or labour. As in his earlier book, Burkett notes that Marx ultimately traces all surplus-value production to the physical productivity of labour in agriculture. In this sense, Burkett agrees, 'surplus-value has a natural basis.'[51] In a chapter originally co-authored with Foster and reiterating their rejection of Podolinsky, he refers to Marx's assertion that '[l]abour-power itself is energy' and adds that energy considerations are 'central to Marx's analysis of the value of labour-power.'[52] Indeed, these two meticulous students of *Capital* conclude that

> Marx considers the creation of surplus-value in terms of the difference between: (i) the *energy equivalent* of the value of labour-power, as determined by the labour required to produce the means of subsistence purchased with the wage, and (ii) the *energy expended* by labour-power, insofar as it corresponds to the *energy content* of the commodities in which value is objectified.[53]

They explicitly find that, 'by considering Marx's application of the energy income and expenditure approach to the production of surplus-value,' they are able to demonstrate the 'thermodynamic consistency of his theory.'[54] The result of the exchange between worker and capitalist, they assert, is 'an energy subsidy for the capitalist.'[55] Burkett and Foster refer to the 'value (*energy*) surplus' appropriated from the worker by the capitalist and to 'Marx's metabolic-energy analysis of surplus-value.'[56] All these formulations unequivocally indicate that Burkett and Foster conceive of the exploitation of labour under capitalism as an asymmetric transfer of energy. This position is difficult to reconcile not only with that of mainstream Marxian value theory – which simply does not need thermodynamics – but also with their vehement rejection of Podolinsky and his modern exponents.[57] In countering the challenge that Marx neglected nature, these proponents of ecological Marxism reinterpret his framework in a way that invites charges of energy reductionism. It is ironic that Burkett's critique of an energy theory of value is equally applicable to the labour theory of value that he himself would defend: he deplores how 'the energy theory's search for a primary input is driven by its reduction of the question of value to that of finding some common measure,'[58] regardless of historical context. Yet, this is precisely what energy and labour theories of value have in common.

These deliberations on the purportedly ecological foundations of Marxian theories of labour value and metabolic rifts may seem marginal to discussions on the relation between capitalism and climate change, but what they illuminate is Marx's and Engels' problematic efforts to integrate society and nature in a common analytical framework. Instead of wholly rejecting the concepts of 19th-century political economy as a veil that obscures the material and energetic metabolism of global society, the founders of Marxism felt compelled to retain the concept of 'value' and give it an objective and seemingly materialist definition, as SNLT. Instead of revealing the Industrial Revolution in Britain as a process of accumulation of embodied biophysical resources – including energy, materials, land, and labour – appropriated from Britain's colonial periphery, Marx and Engels marvelled at its new productive forces and focused on the local exploitation of the working class. In neglecting, like most Britons at the time, how contingent the productivity of British labour was on the asymmetries of *global* social metabolism, they did not problematise this global metabolism in material terms. It was thus far from evident to them that the expanding, fossil-fuelled industrial infrastructure that they celebrated was a source of atmospheric entropy that would ultimately contribute to global climate change.

The article by Clark and York (2005) is incorporated in a volume called *The Ecological Rift: Capitalism's War on the Earth* (2010) by Foster, Clark, and York, which completes the transmutation of Marxist theory into a platform for radical ecology. Ecologically, the book argues, the system of capital accumulation 'draws ever more destructively on the limited resources and absorptive capacity of nature, as the economy continually grows in scale in relation to the planetary system.'[59] The authors assert that Marx's analysis 'can be seen as a key to the whole problem of planetary boundaries.'[60] The paramount issue pervading the book – even its cover – is climate change. 'It is becoming increasingly evident,' the authors proclaim, 'that capitalism, given its insatiable drive for accumulation, is the main engine behind impending catastrophic climate change.'[61] The ecological elaboration of metabolic rift theory is indisputably valid, even if it can hardly be said to convey the main message of Marx's *Capital. The Ecological Rift* does accomplish the merging of 'red' and 'green' that ecological Marxists have long desired, but only a very selective reading of *Capital* can lead to the conclusion that it is the 'key' to the problem of global warming. Remarkably, although abundantly criticised throughout the book, there is no mention of the extent to which some misguided components of 19th-century European ideology – such as an *ontological* nature/society dualism and the faith in technology – were obstacles to Marx's own grasp of the human predicament. As in *Marx's Ecology*, the relevance of Foster's exercises in intellectual history to contemporary problems of global sustainability ultimately seems tenuous.

Although Marx may not have deserved to be called an ecologist, as Burkett and Foster maintain, Foster's development of metabolic rift theory certainly has profound ecological implications. Its focus is on asymmetric material transfers of various kinds: the appropriation of biophysical resources as well as the displacement of waste and other forms of entropy, including greenhouse gases. Such global transfers – empirically demonstrated by the burgeoning research on ecologically unequal exchange (EUE) – are socially organised but can only be conceptualised using physical metrics such as tons, Joules, hectares, and hours of labour time. They thus require a theoretical framework that transcends the conceptual boundary between social and natural phenomena, rather than reducing either to the other. The market – and all the levels of politics with which it is associated – determines 'values' measured in money that clearly do not systematically reflect inputs of certain quantities of resources such as energy or labour time, but instead (*because* of the discrepancies) generate asymmetric transfers of embodied materials, energy, land, and labour. To the extent that metabolic rift theory is synonymous with ecologically unequal exchange, it thus does not harmonise with a labour theory of value. Foster, Clark, and York equate the metabolic rift with 'unequal ecological exchange'[62] but evade its contradictory relation to Marxian value theory. They provide ample evidence of asymmetric global transfers of resources and disorders but finally do not present a theory of unequal exchange. Such a theory must be based on a consistent analytical distinction between the social sphere of valuation and the natural sphere of material substances. This is not dualism in the Cartesian sense, as it recognises the inextricable real-world interfusion of valuation and materiality, but refrains from theoretically attributing value to material phenomena such as energy or labour time. In not acknowledging the analytical mistake of making such an attribution, the frequently voiced ecosocialist argument that there are values in nature is misguided, but not more so than the labour theory of value that it means to complement. Marxist theorists tend to impute the labour theory of value to the operation of 19th-century capitalism rather than to Marx's analysis of it, but if so, his analysis confines itself to the conceptual universe defined by the capitalism of his time. It does so in positing 'value' as an objective phenomenon based on labour input, rather than a cultural phenomenon occupying an analytical level distinct from that of material substances and flows of labour energy. To fully grasp the global ecological predicament of humankind, we must acknowledge the unsustainable *interaction* of society's valuation and nature's materiality, approaching both with the same objective distance rather than trying to derive the former from the latter.

A crucial topic introduced but insufficiently elaborated in *The Ecological Rift* is 'the black box of technology as constituting the solution to all problems.'[63] The authors' scepticism about dematerialisation and other technological fantasies promoted by ecological modernisation theorists is as valid as their concerns about global asymmetries, but they do not explain how the two are connected. The concept of technology is fundamental to industrial capitalism, which they show is based on global metabolic rifts and ecological asymmetries. Technological progress in the core of the world-system, we should conclude, is the flip side of impoverishment in the periphery. Foster, Clark, and York note that '[t]he idea that technology can solve the global environmental problem, as a kind of *deus ex machina* without changes in social relations, belongs to the area of fantasy and science fiction,'[64] but they do not elucidate how the historical emergence of technological fetishism has been contingent precisely on the asymmetric resource flows – the ecologically unequal exchange – of world trade. To make this connection requires a full acknowledgement of the materiality of both technology and trade. Rather than presenting technology as productive forces magically emerging from ingenious ideas and free gifts of nature, or world trade being measurable in terms of disembodied values, such idealist conceptions of historical developments must be replaced with the genuinely materialist insight that the technological infrastructures of wealthier parts of the world-system are being accumulated at the expense of embodied labour and resources appropriated from their peripheries. There is a pervasive inclination among Marxists to attribute environmentally destructive technologies to the specific avariciousness of capitalism, as when Magdoff and Foster assert that 'capitalism systematically gives rise to technologies that produce waste in vast quantities,'[65] instead of acknowledging that it is in the physical nature of modern technology itself to produce waste. It is not sufficient to say that the 'underlying problem' of environmental degradation is 'an economic system that causes environmental and social damage in the very way it functions,'[66] which is to ignore the thermodynamic implications of *any* industrial economic process.

In *Marx and the Earth* (2016), Foster and Burkett resume their agenda of adamantly defending Marx against charges of neglecting nature and reinterpreting him as a pioneer ecologist. Some of the chapters draw on their articles, published between 2004 and 2008, on the intervention by Sergei Podolinsky. There are thus verbatim reiterations of sections of Burkett's 2005 book. As we have noted, their account of the 'Podolinsky business' is profoundly paradoxical. On the one hand, they strongly emphasise the extent to which Marx's conceptualisation of surplus-value extraction is steeped in thermodynamics; on the other hand, they argue that Podolinsky's proposal – providing 'a potential thermodynamic basis for value analysis' – 'adopts an energy-reductionist, crude materialist, and nondialectical approach to value that is completely alien to Marx's approach.'[67] The contradiction between these two positions is puzzling. If there indeed is a 'tremendous gulf between...energy reductionism and Marx's dialectical and material-social approach to capitalist value relations,'[68] it is difficult to see why Burkett and Foster should find so much evidence in *Capital* for 'Marx's metabolic-energy analysis of surplus-value.'[69]

A truly dialectical interpretation would understand Podolinsky's suggestion as a relevant reflection on Marx's own aspirations to merge value theory and energetics, but one revealing both to be misguided. It would acknowledge that energy indeed is relevant to the analysis of exploitation, not as a measure of value but rather the opposite: as a measure of what value *conceals*. Marxian value theory as encapsulated in the formula M–C–M^1 is an economic argument and has very little to do with thermodynamics. Yet, Foster and Burkett refer to 'the *enormous* extent to which Marx built thermodynamic concepts and other elements of contemporary physics into his critique of political economy.'[70] 'Thermodynamics,' they continue, 'is to be found in the very pores of an analysis that to the superficial reader addresses the capitalist laws of exchange value alone.' There is no doubt that Marx wanted to connect economics and thermodynamics, but to claim that he succeeded 'enormously' well in doing so is quite misleading. To refer to 'the energy equivalent of the value of labour power'[71] is to suggest that economic value can be translated into energy. But the surplus economic value extracted by capitalists from workers can hardly be thought of as an 'energy subsidy for the capitalist.'[72] In referring to 'Marx's metabolic-energy analysis of surplus-value,' Foster and Burkett suggest that he has unearthed a relation between thermodynamics and economics that simply does not exist. If anything, the Second Law of Thermodynamics tells us, it is the *disparity* between surplus-value and energy that characterises capitalism: the growth of monetary profits correlates with a *dissipation* of energy from the moment of resource extraction through the entire production process.[73] Foster and Burkett's efforts to demonstrate Marx's grounding in natural science backfire because they illustrate why an ecological Marxism must run into such contradictions.

The conundrum highlighted by Podolinsky has spurred Foster's and Burkett's prolonged engagement with the dilemma of Marx's relation to thermodynamics, which unfortunately could never benefit from the Second Law and the concept of entropy. It is of course a fact that '[t]he very concept of "labour power," so central to Marx's analysis, arose in part from the new thermodynamics, beginning with Helmholtz,'[74] but this in no way justifies an attempt to propose a linkage between economic value and energy. On the other hand, Podolinsky's observation that human labour in agriculture can augment the accumulation of solar energy on Earth – for instance, through irrigation[75] – is incontrovertible. Foster and Burkett attempt to undermine this valid observation by suggesting that, through the devastating process of global warming, 'humans have finally achieved the goal that Podolinsky sought (and confused with progress) of increasing the energy stored on the earth,'[76] but this is hardly a fair disavowal of his argument. Interestingly, Marx's lost letter of response to Podolinsky had given the latter 'deep joy.'[77] This suggests that the two theorists of exploitation, contrary to Foster's and Burkett's assertions, had something significant in common. Both had valid intuitions about asymmetric social transfers of energy, but both also failed to correctly account for the relation between energy and economic value. Rather than being positively correlated, there can only be an *inverse* relation between useful energy and value, as a production process will simultaneously increase economic value and entropy.[78] To understand production in terms of thermodynamics, we must acknowledge that all the energy inputs – from the meals that feed the worker to the fuels that propel the machinery – are subject to the Entropy Law. The relevance of this fact for the phenomenon of global warming is fundamental, as it means that the aggregate expansion of production in the world – euphemistically referred to as 'economic growth' – must inexorably increase greenhouse gas emissions and other forms of entropy. George Caffentzis observes that, in 'capital's struggle against entropy,' it is crucial that entropy be *localised and expelled*,[79] but the insuperable problem with global warming is precisely that greenhouse gases *cannot* be localised or expelled.

In *The Return of Nature* (2020), Foster meticulously traces the social and intellectual biographies of several 19th- and 20th-century British scholars and writers who combined socialist ideals with strong concerns about environmental degradation under capitalism. In terms of biographical detail and the sheer mass of documentation, the book is monumental and immensely impressive. It demonstrates how socialist and environmental concerns were connected in figures such as Ray Lankester, William Morris (three chapters), Friedrich Engels (three chapters), Arthur Tansley, Lancelot Hogben, Desmond Bernal, J.B.S. Haldane, Joseph Needham, and Christopher Caudwell. Foster's argument is that this line of thinkers can be understood as the early history of the modern environmental movement, genealogically linked to iconic environmentalists of the 1960s like Barry Commoner and Rachel Carson. The story that he tells is filled with polemics and political intrigue. It is invaluable in its own right, but it does not absolve *Capital* or *The Communist Manifesto* from productivism. Nor is it likely that its vindication and revival of Engels' metaphysical dialectics of nature are of much help for scientists. It is significant that the only sense in which a dialectical materialist account of evolution could be prepared to acknowledge teleology – the recognition of the Entropy Law[80] – was never rigorously contemplated by the original authors of *Capital* and Marxian value theory. For similarly understandable historical reasons, there is very little mention in *The Return of Nature* of anthropogenic climate change.[81] Given the thermodynamic foundation of global warming, the full theoretical argument against fossil energy cannot be retrieved from the conceptual framework of classical Marxism. The labour theory of value and the formula M–C–M^1 say nothing about entropy.

In their preface to the 2007 volume of the *Socialist Register*, the editors Leo Panitch and Colin Leys recognise that 'climate change is the most general environmental effect of capitalist growth,'[82] yet their work on a volume devoted to the topic *Coming to Terms with Nature* revealed a 'lack of coherence in eco-socialist theory.'[83] The volume includes a very diverse set of chapters, some of which are completely divorced from considerations of physical nature while others[84] focus on the implications of thermodynamics for fossil-fuelled capitalism. Altvater, for instance, observes that the expansion of capitalism has been contingent on the use of fossil energy but that the combustion of fossil fuels 'produces so much harmful emission that living conditions on earth are deteriorating.'[85] The differences between chapters indicate that some Marxist understandings of capitalism can do without thermodynamics while others cannot. Given how pivotal a role eco-Marxists such as Foster and Burkett attribute to thermodynamics in the Marxist analysis of capitalism, the question is whether analysts who fail to consider physical nature – which would include virtually all of mainstream 'Western Marxism' – even deserve to call themselves Marxists. *Contra* Foster and Burkett, it has obviously been feasible for countless theorists over the years to engage in a voluminous discourse on Marxian value theory without the slightest consideration of the Entropy Law.

The Capitalocene with or without a nature/society distinction

In his magisterial history of the turn to steam power in early industrial Britain, the human ecologist Andreas Malm (2016) shows how the shift of technology from waterpower to steam engines was driven primarily by the imperative to enhance the control of labour. This incentive itself derived from the imperative, inscribed in the logic of capital, to increase productivity and profits. Malm confirms and extensively elaborates Marx's observation that the steam engine 'permitted production to be concentrated in towns instead of – like the water-wheels – being scattered over the countryside.'[86] In thus tracing the roots of global warming to the incentives of early industrial capitalists, Malm reveals the historical connection between capitalism and climate change. '[C]onstantly increasing quantities of CO_2,' he affirms, 'are a no-less necessary aspect of the production of surplus-value than market transactions.'[87] Deploying a Marxist terminology, he argues that, rather than illustrating 'productive force determinism,' the turn to fossil energy illuminates how 'the relations of production ... enforced the selection of steam power and not vice versa.'[88] This is clearly a valid conclusion, to which should be added that those relations of production were not confined to factories or industrial centres but arguably encompassed the whole global economy. Although most of his account focuses on developments in Britain, Malm recognises the crucial role of steam engines in integrating the metabolism of the capitalist world-system, observing that steam-powered machines and vehicles 'could fabricate and distribute the widest imaginable range of commodities' and that they 'had the power to project the fossil economy out from the British Isles, through the pressures of economic competition and military invasion.'[89] He asserts that '[a] sequel to [*Fossil Capital*] entitled *Fossil Empire* will deal with mobile steam power on a global scale,'[90] but unfortunately has not pursued this relation between fossil energy and the emergence of an increasingly globalised economy. Such an inquiry should begin by examining for which markets the intensified British production of cotton cloth was destined in the first place, and not least how the cotton fibre was procured. Clearly, both questions would implicate colonialism and slavery.

Adducing a rich range of contemporary commentators, Malm shows that early and mid-19th-century Britons were prone to be awed by the seemingly magical animateness of steam engines.[91] Although in the 17th century machines had been 'purged of their magic,' the British bourgeoisie in the 19th century 'could allow itself to resurrect the spirits,' relapsing to romanticism and mysticism.[92] As a complement to Malm's eminent portrayal of the new machine fetishism that was pervasive at the time, we can add that the magical power of machinery ultimately derived not simply from the thermodynamic properties of coal and steam but from the global terms of trade that enabled British capitalists to invest in steam engines. The mechanical instruments for harnessing steam power were physical manifestations of globalised capital accumulation. The most obscure aspect of 19th-century machine fetishism was thus the illusion that Britain could adopt steam technology regardless of the structure of international trade. Given the volumes of embodied labour and other resources imported to Britain, not least in the uncounted bales of raw cotton, what Malm refers to as 'the slave trope of machine fetishism'[93] has an eerie appositeness. Just to give an additional example, the physical operation of the machinery was *literally* contingent on imported lubricants like palm oil, which Max Haiven aptly refers to as 'the grease of empire.'[94] The fact that the steam engine was perceived as 'the ultimate substitute for labour'[95] is related to the fact that it was a transmutation, through the medium of money capital, of real human labour on plantations beyond the British horizon. As Malm observes, 'power was *in* the engine, but only insofar as it was used by some against others.'[96] These 'others,' it must be added, included workers on distant plantations. His point that the roots of global warming should be sought in capitalist social relations is clearly on target, but particularly when such relations are recognised as extending very far beyond the British cotton mill. The machine became the private property of the mill-owner through the disenfranchisement not only of the industrial proletariat, but also of populations in the margins of the capitalist world-system. Since they are geared to international trade, capitalist property relations – the estrangement of producers from the means of production – are always mediated by the 'universal equivalent against which *anything* can be exchanged ...: what we know as money.'[97] The monetary profits accrued by capitalists derive from the difference between the costs of and the income from production, and the costs include not only the wages of industrial workers but also expenditures for labour and other resources embodied in inputs such as raw materials. As Malm finally concedes at the end of his book, 'we have not even glanced at the inhabitants of the distant shores where British steam power landed.'[98] Compared to the British workers 'trampled underfoot by the steam demon,' he continues, their losses 'were of another order of magnitude.'

Yet, the economic asymmetries inherent in industrial capitalism are generally not permitted to contaminate our understanding of machines – although machines are material *manifestations* of capital accumulation. This conceptual boundary between socially orchestrated resource flows and technological development is maintained by the mystifying language of money prices. It is by making more money that capitalists can increase their claims on labour and other resources. In other words, it is only by considering capital accumulation in the context of the world market that the mystified connection between global resource flows and the accumulation of machinery can be unveiled. Machinery does not coalesce in isolation. The processes within a given factory are a component in a much wider field of social metabolism. The money made by the British mill-owners represented expanding claims on labour and other inputs deriving from various parts of the 19th-century world-system. Through engineering and trade, that money was transmuted into the industrial technology that inaugurated global warming. Malm concludes that climate change is 'a *lifting of the veil* on two centuries of fossil capital – which is, of course, the literal meaning of the Greek word *apokalyptein*.'[99] Ultimately, we might add, this unveiling should illuminate the social essence of the machine itself.

Consistent with Malm's analysis is his proposal that the Anthropocene should really be designated the Capitalocene.[100] First proposed by Malm at a seminar in Lund, Sweden, in the spring of 2009,[101] the term has since been championed by – and become associated with – the environmental historian Jason W. Moore. In the process, the concept has been given posthumanist connotations that Malm had not intended, not least through Moore's edited collection *Anthropocene or Capitalocene?* (2016), which includes a chapter from Donna Haraway's (2016) book on what she calls the 'Chthulucene.' Moore's book *Capitalism in the Web of Life* (2015) aims at understanding capitalist social processes as undistinguishable from what he calls 'world-ecology.' It ambitiously fuses the global perspective of world-system analysis with a consideration of environmental degradation – much as the 2003 conference *World-System History and Global Environmental Change*[102] that brought him to Lund – but struggles vainly to maintain analytical coherence. In addition to world-system history and ecology, Moore's version of Marxist theory attempts to incorporate ecofeminist critiques of Cartesian dualism[103] and posthumanist perspectives such as Haraway's critique of human exceptionalism[104] and Bruno Latour's attribution of agency to inanimate objects.[105] This has yielded a highly amorphous line of reasoning, based on an unconditional jettisoning of the Nature/Society binary. Although Moore at one point concedes that 'Cartesian dualism as a mode of distinguishing confuses the difference between ontological dualism and analytical distinction within evolving wholes,'[106] he is consistently unable to retain – much less define – the analytical distinction between nature and society. Not least for political reasons, however, it remains crucial to be able to distinguish natural aspects of planetary metabolism that would be identifiable even in a biosphere unaffected by sociocultural processes (as it must have been up until the arrival of humans) from aspects introduced by such processes. Moore's inability to handle this distinction is illustrated by his injunction,

> Try drawing a line around the 'social' and the 'natural' in the cultivation and consumption of food. In a rice paddy or a wheat field, in a cattle feedlot or on our dinner table, where does the natural process end, and the social process begin?[107]

Clearly, the social and the natural are *aspects* of socioecological, metabolic wholes that cannot be geometrically delineated but nevertheless must be recognised. Oddly, while posthumanists like Latour emphasise the monist implications of anthropogenic climate change,[108] Moore claims that '[t]he Anthropocene argument shows Nature/Society dualism at its highest stage of development.'[109]

Moore recognises contradictions between environmentalist and feminist approaches to capital accumulation, on the one hand, and Marxist value theory, on the other hand,[110] but his recipe for solving the dilemma is inadequate. In assimilating human labour with the 'work/energy' of nature, he predicts that '[t]here are limits to how much new work capitalism can squeeze out of new working classes, forests, aquifers, oilfields, coal seems, and everything else,'[111] apparently equating working classes with forests, aquifers, and oilfields. The metabolic perspective of Foster and others, he argues, has 'driven a wedge between Marx's historical materialism and Marx's theory of value.'[112] Moore writes that the contributions of Foster and Burkett had promised 'the renewal of value-relational thinking – the law of value as co-produced by humans and the rest of nature,' and '[t]he incorporation of an ecologically informed theory of value into historical materialism.'[113] However, given the Second Law of Thermodynamics, Moore's anticipation of an 'ecological value analysis'[114] was fundamentally flawed from the start. Values are always attributed by humans and do not have an objective existence either in nature or in labour. In finally rejecting Foster's approach, Moore concedes that '[h]istorical natures *are* subject to broadly entropic processes – the degradation of nature – but these are ... reversible within certain limits.'[115] Further on, he repeats that 'entropy is reversible and cyclical.'[116] To suggest that entropic processes may be reversible is, of course, to reveal an obvious ignorance of thermodynamics. But the central weakness of Moore's analysis is his constant reference to capitalism's sources of 'unpaid' or 'cheap' work/energy, as if higher monetary compensation could alleviate its tendency to generate ecological crises. 'The great secret and the great accomplishment of capitalist civilization,' he says, 'has been to *not* pay its bills.'[117] The notion that some labour time is unpaid is fundamental to Marx's labour theory of value, but in Moore's account it is extended to natural resources and ultimately converges with the approach of mainstream environmental economics: for Moore, the emission of greenhouse gases exemplifies the 'externalization of costs' as the atmosphere is 'put to work as capital's unpaid garbage man.'[118] Given that, as Moore himself concedes, 'no metric can capture the differentiated activity of the web of life,'[119] it should be meaningless to speak of 'unpaid' work/energy or the 'true costs' of resource-use. Yet, the language of money – not thermodynamics – pervades Moore's conceptualisation of ecological degradation, including climate change.

The posthumanist proposals on the dissolution of nature/society distinctions and the attribution of agency to non-living matter are related to the critiques of Cartesian dualism and 'objectification' voiced by ecofeminists like Plumwood and ultimately by critical theorists like Lukács and Horkheimer and Adorno. While at first glance democratic and anti-capitalist, they muddle our capacity for rigorous analysis of the drivers of anthropogenic climate change. It is to be deplored that these proposals are being so widely adopted in the humanities and social sciences at a historical moment when it has never been more essential to distinguish (analytically) between the natural and the social.[120] In *The Progress of this Storm* (2018), Malm forcefully argues against such currents of thought in social constructionism, hybridism, and neomaterialism. He recognises that both constructionism and neomaterialism represent ways of dissolving the nature/society divide, the first by collapsing nature into society and the latter by doing the reverse.[121] He suggests that notions of a disappearing nature reflect how global warming has made us more aware of the power of social relations, but that, as the climate continues to deteriorate, 'nature comes roaring back into society.'[122] Malm finally concludes that the 'theoretical obliteration of nature'[123] has been made possible by the real-world economic processes through which it has become commodified and defiled. As the historians Christophe Bonneuil and Jean-Baptiste Fressoz observe, '[i]nternalization into the market is backed by the ontological dissolution of nature by constructivist philosophies that deny its alterity in relation to humans.'[124]

The consequences of such blurring of analytical boundaries between the social and the natural are illustrated by the prominent exponent of Western Marxism – yet professed anti-constructionist – Neil Smith, who holds that

> the attempt to distinguish social vis-à-vis natural contributions to climate change is not only a fool's debate but a fool's philosophy: it leaves sacrosanct the chasm between nature and society – nature in one corner, society in the other – which is precisely the shibboleth of modern western thought that [his] 'production of nature' thesis sought to corrode.[125]

Malm's (2018) objections to such efforts to block the identification of specifically *social* drivers of climate change are an eloquent reminder of the continued reality of both biophysical nature and the processes of commodification through which it is degraded. While clearly entangled in the modern world, the laws of thermodynamics and the logic of money are distinct and separately constituted phenomena. It is only by analytically recognising how these two aspects of reality are intertwined that we can grasp the predicament of global warming.

Unveiling the global machine

As climate change deepens, so do Marxist deliberations on the ecological trajectory of capitalism. While Moore's recognition that capitalism is an inherently global phenomenon is important, his inclination to bury this insight in posthumanist jargon has provoked serious objections from several ecological Marxists, including Foster (2016), Malm (2018), and Ian Angus (2016b), who in 2007 founded the journal *Climate & Capitalism*.[126] Angus has also published the highly readable and comprehensive *Facing the Anthropocene: Fossil Capitalism and the Crisis of the Earth System* (Angus 2016a), which provides a transdisciplinary overview of the climate crisis. Particularly useful is his discussion of how the globalisation of production since the 1980s has outsourced not only jobs but also greenhouse gas emissions and other forms of environmental degradation to the global South.[127] These developments underscore the fact that the accumulation of the fossil-fuelled infrastructure responsible for climate change is inextricably entwined with global social metabolism. It has been so from the very start.[128] The implication appears to be that the prime target of denunciation should be the very productive forces of capitalism that Marx celebrated, and that his classical analysis of 19th-century British industrialism – in being confined to that context – thus needs to be revised. The current confusion surrounding that analysis confirms such a conclusion. Interpretations of Marxism now range from extreme ecomodernist techno-fetishism[129] through calls for an increasingly unlikely ecosocialist revolution[130] to despondency,[131] ecosabotage,[132] and degrowth.[133] It is remarkable to observe how the road to a better society, symbolised by a profound and prolific 19th-century writer, can be imagined in so strikingly different ways. When Marx is variously portrayed as Promethean, as an ecologist, or even a 'degrowth communist,'[134] it raises the question whether the most important issue is 'what Marx really said' or the future of the world. Rather than directing our efforts at revisionist historiography, the most urgent task for radical scholars today must be to grasp in which ways climate change has revealed both mainstream and heterodox understandings of economic development and technological progress to be fundamentally flawed. To reiterate a conclusion drawn in chapter 3, the world-historical significance of the Industrial Revolution is that it represents *the point at which human ingenuity no longer suffices to account for the advance of technology*. From now on, technological progress would be contingent also on global displacements of environmental loads and workloads through the world market.

Over the second decade of the 21st century, the relentless course of climate change has generated an intensification of anxieties, indignation, and frustration among researchers, activists, and people in general. An initial optimism about the capacity of modern society to reduce greenhouse gas emissions and shift to renewable energy has lost ground to widespread feelings of despair. There is pervasive exasperation over the seemingly inexorable inertia of global warming, unyielding to countless political commitments and massive investments in putatively carbon-free technologies. This blend of panic, anger, and resignation is reflected in a series of startling book titles like *Requiem for a Species* (Hamilton 2010), *This Changes Everything* (Klein 2014), *Learning to Die in the Anthropocene* (Scranton 2015), *How Did We Get Into This Mess?* (Monbiot 2016), *The Uninhabitable Earth* (Wallace-Wells 2019), and *How to Blow Up a Pipeline* (Malm 2021). Whether despondent or agitated, the prevailing conclusion among left-leaning writers on climate change seems to be that whatever is propelling the world towards climate disaster is politically unstoppable. There seems to be something about the way people in modern societies conceive of the world – and the way they conduct their everyday lives – that implacably condemns them to catastrophe. The sentiment is well captured by George Monbiot's observation that, '[i]f the biosphere is wrecked, it will be done by nice, well-meaning, cosmopolitan people who accept the case for cutting emissions, but who won't change by one iota the way they live.'[135] In other words, the drivers of climate change are so inextricably entwined with modern existence that abandoning them is literally unthinkable. This is not simply a matter of reducing modern mobility and other forms of energy use – although even that is a political message that would be difficult to sell – but of intangible aspects of the modern worldview like the magical trust in money and technology. It would not be the first time in human history that a civilisation has been too entrenched in its commitment to its fetishised obsessions to be able to avoid collapse.

A pervasive modern illusion, shared by mainstream and heterodox thinkers alike, is the failure to grasp the fact that advanced technologies – including 'green' ones based on renewable energy – are products of capital accumulation. The fictive reciprocity of market prices – or money, for short – mystifies the asymmetric transfers of embodied material resources that are the substance of world trade and the prerequisite of technological expansion for those who can afford it. In not recognising the mutual entanglement of money and technology, and the global *distributive* dimension of that entanglement, critics of capitalism and the way it generates climate change continue to promote visions of the future that do not radically confront either money or technology. In none of the analyses and proposals reviewed here is there a fundamental critique of the money artefact or an acknowledgement of the *inherently* distributive logic of modern technology. These two quintessential artefacts and categories of modernity are thus never called into question, although their combination has arguably propelled climate change since the Industrial Revolution. Although there have been voluminous deliberations on what kinds of politics are required to mitigate climate change,[136] the main lesson that the Anthropocene might yet teach us is that politics should be largely a matter of how we design our artefacts.

The ecological crisis of the Anthropocene, most alarmingly manifest in climate change, has prompted Marxist theorists to fundamentally reinterpret the author of *Capital*. Attempts to reconcile Marxism and ecological concerns – such as by Burkett, Foster, and Moore – have often been contradictory and raised serious objections. Kohei Saito's (2022) claim that Marx in his final years became a precursor of the 'degrowth' movement is intriguingly paradoxical. The significance of Saito's hugely popular message – his book *Capital in the Anthropocene* sold over 500,000 copies in Japan – seems to lie not so much in being indisputable as in its appeal. A person who is radically critical of capitalism in the Anthropocene can hardly avoid being critical of growth. The success of Saito's claim no doubt largely derives from his explicit aim to 'finally resolve the tension between Red and Green.'[137] Whatever were the historical facts of Marx's leanings in his final years, Saito's message is politically impeccable. A turn towards global justice and sustainability can only spell degrowth in the global North. His study also succeeds admirably in countering the monism advocated by Moore. Finally, in consequence with his advocacy of degrowth, Saito convincingly rejects Marx's Eurocentrism and Promethean productivism, recognising that '[t]he traditional view fetishizes the productive forces developed under capitalism, regarding them as if they were neutral forces that can be taken over by the proletariat and utilised for establishing a socialist society.'[138] This critical approach to advanced technology opens new possibilities for combining the traditional Marxist focus on injustices with a critique of productivism and technological fetishism. It thus completes the liberation of Marxism from 19th-century political economy and its transmutation into a foundation for radical ecological activism.

Global warming is ripping apart the veil of economic value and money that has mystified social metabolism and technological progress for over 200 years. It forces us to acknowledge that the human economy is founded on a system of signs and abstractions devised in Victorian Britain but ultimately constrained by the Entropy Law and the material properties of asymmetrically traded biophysical resources. This demands a fundamental rethinking not only among mainstream economists but also among their critics, who navigate within the same conceptual universe but recognise how the world economy is inexorably pushing humankind towards increasing injustices and the biosphere towards disastrous climate change. For radical red-green theory, centrally concerned with global justice and sustainability, it means jettisoning technological fetishism as well as any attempts to derive value from material inputs in production. Value correlates with entropy and dissipation. There is no value beyond money. The machinery that congealed in 19th-century Britain continuously embodied and dissipated inputs of labour, land, energy, and materials appropriated from throughout its global empire. Ecologically unequal exchange today remains as rampant as ever. A vision of global justice and sustainability would need to grasp that local increases in productivity since the Industrial Revolution tend to occur at the expense of people and environments elsewhere, and that perpetual economic growth is incompatible with the Entropy Law. Ultimately, the challenge for the climate justice movement should be to visualise a way of redesigning the artefact – all-purpose money – that defines the destructive algorithms that generate both climate change and deepening global inequalities.

Notes

1 Hornborg *et al.* 2007.
2 Merchant 1980.
3 Plumwood 2002.
4 Naess [1976] 1989.
5 Evernden 1985.
6 Lukács [1923] 1971; Horkheimer and Adorno [1947] 1972.
7 Vogel 1996.
8 Vogel 1996: 9.
9 McKibben 1990: 154; emphasis in original.
10 Salleh [1997] 2017: 109.

11 Asafu-Adjaye *et al.* 2015.
12 McKibben 1990: 49.
13 McKibben 1990: 72, 76.
14 Lewis and Maslin 2015.
15 Soper 1995.
16 Soper 1995: 151–152.
17 Soper 1995: 249.
18 McKibben 1990: 118.
19 O'Connor 1994.
20 O'Connor 1994: 1.
21 Martinez-Alier 1994: 27.
22 Martinez-Alier 1994: 33.
23 Smil 2022: 180.
24 O'Connor 1988: 14.
25 O'Connor 1998: xii.
26 O'Connor 1998: 166.
27 O'Connor 1998: 44.
28 O'Connor 1998: 53.
29 O'Connor 1998: 135.
30 Kovel [2002] 2007: xii.
31 Kovel [2002] 2007: 4–5, 62, 74, 134–138.
32 Kovel [2002] 2007: 133.
33 Kovel [2002] 2007: 87.
34 Foster 2014: ix.
35 Foster 2014: xiii.
36 Burkett [1999] 2014: xvii–xviii.
37 Burkett [1999] 2014: 36–37.
38 Burkett [1999] 2014: 103.
39 Burkett [1999] 2014: 132.
40 Foster 2014: vii.
41 Foster 2000a: 157.
42 Foster 2000a: 160.
43 Foster 2000a: 164.
44 Walter Johnson (2004: 301, 304) observes that Marx evaded the role of slavery in British industrialization by discussing commodity fetishism through a detailed consideration of a bolt of *linen*, rather than cotton, thus staying clear of the fact that each bolt of cotton 'had been put in the ground, tended, picked, bagged, baled, and shipped by an American slave.'
45 Foster 2000a: 173.
46 Burkett [2005] 2009: 293.
47 Clark and York 2005: 408.
48 Burkett [2005] 2009: 30–36.
49 Burkett [2005] 2009: 54.
50 See Sahlins 1976.
51 Burkett [2005] 2009: 31, 36.
52 Burkett [2005] 2009: 185.
53 Burkett [2005] 2009: 190; emphases added.
54 Burkett [2005] 2009: 191.
55 Burkett [2005] 2009: 192.
56 Burkett [2005] 2009: 193; emphasis added.
57 Martinez-Alier and Naredo 1982.
58 Burkett [2005] 2009: 38.
59 Foster, Clark and York 2010: 29.

60 Foster, Clark and York 2010: 46.
61 Foster, Clark and York 2010: 107.
62 Foster, Clark and York 2010: 345–347.
63 Foster, Clark and York 2010: 42.
64 Foster, Clark and York 2010: 116.
65 Magdoff and Foster 2011: 33.
66 Magdoff and Foster 2011: 125.
67 Magdoff and Foster 2011: 92.
68 Magdoff and Foster 2011: 110.
69 Burkett [2005] 2009: 193.
70 Foster and Burkett 2016: 138; emphasis added.
71 Foster and Burkett 2016: 144.
72 Foster and Burkett 2016: 145.
73 Georgescu-Roegen 1971.
74 Foster and Burkett 2016: 199.
75 Foster and Burkett 2016: 102–103.
76 Foster and Burkett 2016: 238.
77 Foster and Burkett 2016: 118.
78 If, on the other hand, Marx and his followers would have spoken of *embodied* energy – that is, the amount of energy that has been *dissipated* in a production process – it would be reasonable to propose a positive correlation with exchange-value, but the concept of embodied energy (or 'energy memory'; Odum 1988) is the precise opposite of useful (free or available) energy. The closest approximation in Marx's terminology – although not correlated with value – is the concept of 'dead labour.' My initial problems with the concept of 'embodied energy' (Hornborg 1998) derived from the fact that dissipated energy cannot be *literally* embodied in a product, but in the general sense of denoting a product's history – representing its displaced resource requirements, such as the labour and land embodied in a bale of cotton imported to early industrial Britain – the concept is crucial to EUE theory.
79 Caffentzis 2013: 53.
80 Foster 2020: 378.
81 Foster 2020: 397, 462, 519, 612.
82 Panitch and Leys 2006: x.
83 Panitch and Leys 2006: ix.
84 Altvater 2006; Martinez-Alier 2006.
85 Altvater 2006: 45.
86 Marx quoted in Malm 2016: 275.
87 Malm 2016: 289.
88 Malm 2016: 36.
89 Malm 2016: 17.
90 Malm 2016: 17.
91 Malm 2016: 201–222.
92 Malm 2016: 210.
93 Malm 2016: 215.
94 Haiven 2022.
95 Malm 2016: 215.
96 Malm 2016: 221; emphasis in original.
97 Malm 2016: 281.
98 Malm 2016: 392–393.
99 Malm 2016: 393.
100 Malm 2016: 391.
101 See Moore 2016: xi, 5.
102 Hornborg *et al.* 2007.

103 Moore 2016: 84.
104 Moore 2015: 77.
105 Moore 2015: 196.
106 Moore 2015: 22.
107 Moore 2015: 47.
108 Latour 2017.
109 Moore 2016: 3.
110 Moore 2015: 53.
111 Moore 2015: 87.
112 Moore 2015: 81.
113 Moore 2015: 83–84.
114 Foster 2000b.
115 Moore 2015: 84.
116 Moore 2015: 97.
117 Moore 2015: 87; emphasis in original.
118 Moore 2015: 101.
119 Moore 2015: 145.
120 Hornborg 2011: 34. The cited chapter was previously published as Hornborg 2006.
121 Malm 2018: 149.
122 Malm 2018: 77.
123 Malm 2018: 217.
124 Bonneuil and Fressoz 2015: 220.
125 Smith 2010: 244.
126 Angus 2016b.
127 Angus 2016a: 163–167.
128 Hornborg *et al.* 2007; Bonneuil and Fressoz 2015: 222–252.
129 Phillips 2015; Bastani 2019.
130 Foster *et al.* 2010; Angus 2016a.
131 Scranton 2015.
132 Malm 2021.
133 Saito 2022.
134 Saito 2022.
135 Monbiot 2007: xvii.
136 For instance, Wainwright and Mann 2018; Dryzek and Pickering 2019.
137 Saito 2022: 172.
138 Saito 2022: 154.

Part III

Diversity, place, and resistance

7 The meltdown of diversity

As many have observed, economic globalisation is detrimental to both biological and cultural diversity.[1] The extinction of species and the extinction of languages are equally apparent and alarming. In promoting agricultural as well as mental monocultures, the logic of globalised capitalism appears to lead to both ecological and cultural homogenisation. In this chapter, I discuss the relation – similarities as well as differences – between the two processes. I outline how selective pressures generated by money and markets are conducive to both kinds of homogenisation, but then explore the differences between how biological and cultural diversity are created. My argument that there are significant differences between biological speciation and cultural diversification is supported by an overview of the histories of indigenous languages in Amazonia and the Andes. This overview also shows that extensive social integration does not necessarily mean homogenisation. Indigenous societies in pre-Columbian South America were able to retain their cultural specificity to an extent that has been impossible under the rule of colonialism, money, and the modern market.

The semiotics of homogenisation

One of the things that globalisation has taught people all over the world is to cognitively detach themselves from the specificity of their experience and to think about it – to objectify it – in terms of culture. To acknowledge this shift is intended not as a normative but as an analytical observation. The modern categories of 'culture' and 'tradition' exemplify what Anthony Giddens and other sociologists refer to as self-reflexivity. They are simultaneously examples of abstraction. To abstract is to decontextualise – to eliminate the particulars. To use abstract language is thus structurally related to the 'disembedding mechanisms' that Giddens identifies as diagnostic of the social condition of modernity.[2] A central disembedding mechanism, says Giddens, is money, which 'can be "passed around" without regard to the specific characteristics of individuals or groups that handle them.'[3] Money and expert systems are abstract sources of trust in modernity. The abandonment of context and particularity, observes James Scott, is also 'the necessary first premise of

DOI: 10.4324/9781032702186-11

any large-scale planning exercise.'[4] At the core of the modern condition, it seems, is an inclination to transcend specific contexts in favour of the general, whether in terms of how we think and talk, how we exchange things, or how we relate to people and places. As we saw in Chapter 2, historians such as Richard Seaford have traced this inclination towards abstraction and transcendence to the appearance of coined money during the Axial Age, and Marshall Sahlins characterised the early modern period and Enlightenment as a 'Second Axial Age.' Classical sociologists like Max Weber, Georg Simmel, and Ferdinand Tönnies emphasised how abstraction continued to transform Euro-American society through 19th-century modernity. From the perspective of the average person, it meant that a premodern attachment to *specific* things, people, and places was widely superseded by more abstract reference points in the form of *categories* of things, people, and places. By and large, specificity and uniqueness gave way to increasing standardisation and generalised interchangeability. This process continues to this day, as illustrated by George Ritzer's discussion of what he calls 'McDonaldization.'[5] The modern outlook was encoded in official ideology. A thesaurus from the apex of modernity, the early 20th century, would thus list 'uniformity' as the primary synonym of 'order' and 'diversity' as equivalent to 'disorder.'[6]

To many observers, the growing global convergences can be traced to the expansion of 'Western' dominance. In his bestseller *Sapiens: A Brief History of Humankind*, Yuval Noah Harari asserts that,

> [t]oday all humans are, to a much greater extent than they usually want to admit, European in dress, thought and taste. They may be fiercely anti-European in their rhetoric, but almost everyone on the planet views politics, medicine, war and economics through European eyes... Even today's burgeoning Chinese economy, which may soon regain its global primacy, is built on a European model of production and finance.[7]

Indeed, modern ways of thinking have historically been promoted by the expansion of Euro-American power since the 19th century, but its global logic is transcultural and transhistorical. It is propelled by the artefact of general-purpose money and what Karl Polanyi called the 'idea of the self-regulating market,'[8] which accompanied and buttressed that expansion. As James Scott observes:

> A market necessarily reduces quality to quantity via the price mechanism and promotes standardization; in markets, money talks, not people. Today, global capitalism is perhaps the most powerful force for homogenization...[9]

What we think of as modern capitalism is the aggregate logic generated by all-purpose money, which induces people to pursue the best deals they can on the world market. As we have seen in previous chapters, this means exchanging their labour time for products representing as low-wage labour and as lax environmental legislation as possible. If artefacts have powers suggesting 'agency,' money is the paradigmatic example. In making everything exchangeable, it tends to focus our attention on finding the lowest market price, which in turn inexorably increases global inequalities and environmental degradation.

What is the relation between such cultural processes and biological homogenisation – between the loss of cultural diversity and the loss of biological diversity? Given stable conditions, the diversity of species in an ecosystem tends to increase, as new, specialised niches are continuously generated through competition within populations and interaction between species. When conditions are severely disrupted, however, specialisation is a disadvantage, and generalists are more likely to survive. The radical environmental changes resulting from global capitalism over the past few centuries have led to the extinction of countless species, only a fraction of which have been recorded. Throughout the world, they have been supplanted by generalist species such as rats and dandelions, which seem to thrive almost anywhere. This process is indeed analogous to the disappearance of languages and other locally shared systems of meaning. We might use Richard Dawkins' concept of 'memes'[10] as the cultural counterpart of genes and suggest that generalist memes such as cheeseburgers and milkshakes tend to displace intricately designed ones, such as Japanese tea ceremonies or traditional manioc processing in the Amazon. In this general sense, the reduction of both biological and cultural diversity can be derived from the logic of capitalism.

We can probe deeper into the mechanisms through which the memes associated with modernity are being selected for in globalisation. Processes of selection are common to the survival of both genes and memes. In its most elementary form, the Darwinian theory of natural selection has been criticised for being tautological. If restricted to the observation that those individuals who are best equipped to survive are most likely to survive, the theory does not provide much of an explanation. But when complemented with information on genetic variation and selective pressures, the simple algorithm of natural selection can indeed help to explain why species evolve and in which direction. Gregory Bateson, who was both an anthropologist and a biologist, proposed that an explanation is a description mapped onto a tautology.[11] By way of illustration, the tautological assertion that those most likely to survive will survive assumes great relevance when applied to an ancient population of proto-giraffes with genetically varying neck-length on a drought-afflicted savanna. It helps to explain why genes for increasingly longer necks, enabling the animals to reach the leaf-bearing branches of trees, became more and more common among the ancestors of modern giraffes.

Perhaps, then, tautologies do not deserve their poor reputation. After all, they *are* always true. Indeed, those individuals who are best equipped to survive are most likely to survive. Are cultural memes similarly exposed to selective pressures? To begin answering the question, we need to consider the well-established anthropological insight that cultural phenomena – anything that conveys meanings – are always dependent on *context.* This is as evident from phonemes to myths. How does this relate to the inclination, in modernity, towards disembedding – that is, *de*contextualisation? In modern society, ideas, commodities, and people tend to be mobile, often moving great distances. In other words, they are expected to shift contexts. Modern money organises continuous exchanges of goods and services, regardless of context. Similarly, modern science and other expert knowledge is designed to be universally applicable, again regardless of context. Finally, even the modern person complies with the same pattern: she is designed to offer her services regardless of context, disembedded from kin and place, at home everywhere and nowhere, versed in the art of socialising with strangers.[12] The fundamental logic of modernity should thus be that *the ideas, artefacts, and personalities that gain the widest distribution are those that are least dependent on context.* While the explanation of evolution accepted by biologists includes a tautological reference to the survival of those most likely to survive, we can suggest that *cultural* selection in processes of modernisation can be represented in terms of the tautological insight that 'that which is most likely to spread is what spreads.' The ideas, objects, and persons that are most easily moved from one context to another can be expected to be favoured by the logic of cultural diffusion. We are more likely to encounter cheeseburgers – and the people who eat them – than Japanese tea ceremonies.

The biochemist and semiotician Jesper Hoffmeyer has suggested that the long evolutionary movement of life on Earth towards more biological complexity can be understood as an increase in 'semiotic freedom,' which he defines as 'the *depth of meaning* an individual or a species is capable of communicating.'[13] Hoffmeyer explains that this concept of 'freedom' refers to freedom from being determined by the constraints of natural laws. He exemplifies by comparing a microorganism's capacity to detect molecules of nutrients in its immediate environment, on the one hand, with a bird pretending to have a broken wing in order to distract a fox from its nest, on the other hand. Both are examples of communication, widely defined, but the difference in terms of 'depth of meaning' is enormous. The behaviour of the bird is a very specific and seemingly arbitrary mode of communication in the sense that it cannot be derived from biochemical or other natural laws. Hoffmeyer proposes that the biological evolution of complexity should be understood in semiotic, rather than morphological, terms. Citing the palaeontologist George Simpson, he points out that humans are not more morphologically complex than ancient species of fish living 400 million years ago, while human speech is immensely more complex – in terms of semiotic depth – than any other mode of communication that has emerged in the history of life on Earth. Persuaded by Hoffmeyer's approach, which urges us to rethink human language and culture in an evolutionary context, Thomas Hylland Eriksen proposes that the homogenising effects of globalisation suggest that this development towards greater complexity is now being reversed:

> Thousands of mutually unintelligible languages, unique religions and customs, kinship systems, cosmologies and economic practices produced a world of a fast growing number of differences. What seems to be happening today as a result of frantic human activity across the planet is nevertheless a reduction in semiotic freedom, a loss of flexibility and options. This seems to be the case both with respect to the nonhuman world and that of culture and society.[14]

The pervasive loss of indigenous languages, traditional ecological knowledges, and crafts – and their replacement with standardised outlooks and practices geared to modern technology – is nothing less than a systematic *deskilling* of most of humanity. We should recall that the much celebrated technical, scientific, and artistic expertise of modern society is reserved for a small minority of its population, while its overwhelming majority is compelled to perform tasks that are very rarely conducive to creativity. Semiotic freedom, in other words, is a matter of highly uneven global distribution. Moreover, whatever expertise is encouraged in modernity tends to be dependent on advanced technologies, which means that it is defined by those technologies rather than by the inherent skill of a human being. The outlook and worldview of modern people will thus tend to be permeated by the abstract rationality of technology, which might seem unobjectionable if it were not for the fact that access to modern technology is contingent on the abysmally uneven distribution of purchasing-power – or money, for short.

We can further explore this evolutionary perspective on globalising modernity by considering the relation between Hoffmeyer's concept of 'semiotic freedom' and what biologists call 'generalism.' Although at first sight equivalent, because both concepts suggest flexibility, semiotic freedom and biological generalism are different – and in a sense antithetical – parameters. If semiotic freedom is a measure of the complexity of meaning that is communicated, it may well be associated with specialisation, rather than generalism, if viewed from the perspective of an individual or population. Conversely, semiotically very simple microorganisms tend to be biological generalists. As mentioned, under stable ecological conditions, competition generates a tendency towards specialism, but when conditions rapidly change, generalists have an advantage.[15] Highly specialised, endemic species are attuned to unique sensory stimuli requiring sensitivity to very specific kinds of information regarding their ecological niche. The connection between semiotic and ecological specialisation was established by the Estonian zoologist Jakob von Uexküll through his concept of *Umwelt*.[16] The tendency towards specialisation is what has generated the intricate biodiversity of complex ecosystems, but it is also what makes specialised species so vulnerable to extinction, while generalists like rats and dandelions are able to survive major changes in ecosystems. Neither rats nor dandelions are dependent on specific and complex semiotic contexts. This makes them into not only survivors but also successful colonisers.

If we apply these perspectives to cultural processes, we discover that the relation between specialism and generalism is paradoxical and not as clearly geared to ecological viability as in biological processes. The unique semiotic freedom with which humans are equipped – through the capacity for language and culture – has made us into a generalist species, in the sense that we have been able to adapt to a great diversity of ecological settings from deserts and tropical rainforests to high mountains and the frozen Arctic. In this sense, semiotic freedom has indeed meant flexibility, from a species perspective. But from the perspective of individual human groups, it has encouraged specialisation, vulnerability, and a *loss* of flexibility. By and large, cultural diversity increased over hundreds of thousands of years, as humans colonised a wide range of habitats, up until the turn towards modern homogenisation that Charles Mann dates to the 16th century.[17] The rapid reduction of cultural diversity over the past few centuries has in part been a response to biological processes such as epidemics and environmental change in the form of deforestation, monocultures, and loss of biodiversity, but the primary impetus underlying all these processes has derived from a globalising social system pursuing the logic of general-purpose money.

As I showed in Chapter 1, money is a peculiar semiotic phenomenon. Unlike other kinds of signs – whether bird song, animal scent, or human words – money is a sign without a referent. It can mean whatever its owner wants it to signify. In this sense, it is certainly a source of freedom and flexibility, but it can hardly be seen as a means of communicating, to use Hoffmeyer's expression, a greater 'depth of meanings.' All other semiotic codes are composed of several characters, like the letters of the alphabet or the nucleotides of a DNA molecule, which generate meanings by being variously combined. Money is unique in having *one* single character. It thus cannot communicate meaning. It is paradoxical that the unique symbolic capacity of the human species, which has granted it unprecedented levels of semiotic freedom, has finally yielded a sign that is so devoid of meaning that it systematically undermines both the cultural and the biological diversity of the biosphere from which it emerged. It is as if money represents a threshold, where the evolutionary increase in semiotic freedom reaches a point at which it is reversed.

There is also a crucial difference between biological and cultural generalism in terms of how they relate to material metabolism. Biological generalism increases the chances of physical survival under conditions of sudden ecological disruption. It is a strategy for maximising the range of energy sources accessible to a species. But human malleability – our biological capacity for cultural diversity – has different implications depending on the level at which it is considered. At the level of the species, as we have observed, it has favoured a generalist colonisation of a wide range of ecosystems, but at the level of populations, which are culturally attuned to specific contexts and livelihoods, it has until historically recent times promoted specialisation.

To the extent that such cultural specialisation has implied vulnerability to rapid change, this is only in part a consequence of physical environmental disturbance. The loss of cultural diversity under the influence of globalised modernity has not so much been a matter of human populations failing to survive a competition for physical resources as of the socially organised dissolution of their systems of meaning. Integration into the abstract world of markets and money tends to corrode the cognitive and existential frameworks that have been geared to subsistence in particular places.

The transition to modernity can be viewed as a shift to cultural generalism in the sense that human outlooks are no longer as connected to specific contexts. In Hoffmeyer's terms, we have become semiotically shallower. In terms of material metabolism, for the global majority, modernity has narrowed the range of ecological resources. Modern people tend to derive most of their energy from a mere handful of industrially grown cereals, root crops, and species of livestock – a few domesticated strains of plants and animals that will thrive regardless of context. Of the 7,000 kinds of plants that have been grown or collected as food in human history, only '20 species provide 90 percent of the world's food and just three – wheat, maize, and rice – supply more than half.'[18] Paradoxically, then, our cultural generalism has favoured an increasing ecological specialism. This is a crucial difference between cultural and biological generalism – between modern customers at McDonald's and the flexibility of omnivores such as rats. Moreover, the dependence of most of humanity on the narrow ecological niche of fossil-fuelled, monocultural food production has not only increased our own vulnerability but also simultaneously radically reduced biological diversity.

Although affluent consumers in the global North will object that their culinary diversity is vastly greater than that of their premodern ancestors, we should again remind ourselves that this capacity to access edibles from all over the planet is contingent on their privileged purchasing-power, whereas most people in the world have no choice but to resort to a restricted selection of foodstuffs. More significant, from an evolutionary perspective, is that very few people have retained the skills and know-how required to derive their nourishment from the landscapes that they inhabit.

For two centuries, proponents of modern development have asserted that indigenous, nonmodern people represent cultural idiosyncrasies that must succumb to the progress of modernisation, in part because they are *inflexible* – much as highly specialised biological species may become vulnerable to extinction. However, if for some reason our global food system should fail, the tables would be turned and the inflexibility of modern civilisation would become disastrously evident. In having become completely dependent on the industrially produced groceries that we can purchase in supermarkets, most of us are entirely incompetent at deriving our subsistence from the natural environment.

Given that supermarkets have become our ecological niche, consumer behaviour can be understood as a form of foraging. Beyond the apparent abundance and diversity, it relies on an increasingly fragile global system of provisioning. It is noteworthy that the concept of 'consumption,' regardless of the type of commodity, is metaphorically based on eating. This is one reason why the paradigmatic example of globalisation is McDonald's fast-food restaurants. What Ritzer called 'McDonaldization' is literally about eating. Wherever we are in the world, we can have the same cheeseburger. Such globalised food habits require very little in terms of semiotic context, but they inexorably diminish both biological and cultural diversity. Most disturbingly, they have made us so dependent – so specialised in our reliance on industrial food production – that many people would be at a loss without it. The spectre of a global breakdown evokes the horrors of Cormac McCarthy's dystopic novel *The Road*, which depicts a post-apocalyptic world where humans resort to cannibalism. After all, it has been estimated that out of the total global biomass of terrestrial vertebrates, a stunning 36% now consists of human bodies.[19] Cannibalism perhaps represents the logical endpoint of a trajectory towards *zero* 'semiotic freedom.'

The case for biocultural analogies

In his popular book *1493: Uncovering the New World Columbus Created* (2011), Charles Mann vividly explains the homogenising consequences of the post-Columbian trade in tobacco, silver, rubber, and sugar, the expanding adoption of crops such as potatoes and sweet potatoes, and the entangled histories of diseases, slavery, and the fugitive communities of enslaved Africans. In these processes, reductions of biological and cultural diversity tend to be intertwined. After providing numerous examples of ecological degradation and cultural marginalisation that are hallmarks of what he calls the 'Homogenocene,' Mann finally reflects on the ambiguities of globalisation as deriving from human desires:

> [People] want to have what everyone else has, but still be aggressively themselves – a contradictory enterprise. ... As human desires bring the Homogenocene into existence, billions of people marching through increasingly identical landscapes, that special place becomes ever harder to find. Things feel changed and scary. Some people hunker down into their local dialects or customary clothing or an imagined version of their own history or religion. Others enfold themselves in their homes and gardens. A few pick up weapons.[20]

Mann's reflections on the contradictions between globalised capitalism and struggles for cultural identity are offered together with the observation that the biodiversity of purportedly 'traditional' vegetable gardens in the Philippines is 'a polyglot, cosmopolitan, thoroughly contemporary artefact.'[21] As elsewhere, some invasive species have ravaged ecosystems and extinguished several local species, while other novel imports have become symbols of tradition, arguably enriching garden plots and even their capacity to instil a sense of identity.

Twenty years ago, worries about simultaneously declining cultural and biological diversity were articulated in the UNESCO booklet *Sharing a World of Difference*.[22] The authors emphasise interlinkages between linguistic, cultural, and biological diversity and how globalisation tends to endanger them all through homogenisation.[23] Out of the world's almost 7,000 languages, they report, some scholars predict that as many as 90% may have disappeared by the end of this century. Their concept of 'biocultural diversity'[24] refers not only to the parallel trajectories of biological and cultural diversity but also to their common ecological significance: locally contextualised ecological knowledge, codified in endemic languages, is understood as having adaptive value similar to the biological adaptations of endemic species. In this view, traditional ecological knowledge codifies human adaptation to local conditions and simultaneously enhances the complexity of the local ecosystem.[25] As Tove Skutnabb-Kangas and David Harmon explain, 'much of the knowledge of how to maintain biodiversity is encoded in the small languages of Indigenous and local peoples, and it disappears when the languages disappear.'[26] Biocultural analogies at times evoke the anthropological school known as 'cultural ecology,' which in its more simplistic versions aspired to account for human culture as a functional adaptation to the environment.[27] In its more sophisticated versions, the approach might be referred to as 'contextualism,'[28] as it emphasises how local knowledge and worldviews tend to be calibrated with specific ecological contexts. Such observations are generally contrasted with the decontextualising forces of globalisation and modernity, as processes of modernisation hinge on the fact that ideas, objects, and persons that are most easily moved from one context to another are most likely to be diffused.

Luisa Maffi shows that biocultural perspectives can be traced back to Charles Darwin and recurs among anthropologists such as Boas, Sapir, Whorf, and Kroeber.[29] It was not until the mid-1990s, however, that there emerged 'a focus on the relationships between linguistic, cultural, and biological diversity, their global overlapping distributions, and the common threats they are facing.'[30] The significant co-occurrence of linguistic and biological diversity has strengthened proposals about their functional entanglement. Citing a 2005 study by Jonathan Loh and David Harmon, Maffi observes that 'core regions of exceptionally high biocultural diversity' include the Amazon Basin, Central Africa, and Indomalaysia/Melanesia.[31] Such correlations between linguistic and biological diversity have been verified in a global survey of 'biodiversity hotspots': 70% of the world's languages are found within the 25% of the Earth's land area that is classified as either biodiversity hotspots or 'high-biodiversity wilderness areas.'[32]

In their contribution to the *Routledge Handbook of Ecolinguistics*, Skutnabb-Kangas and Harmon provide a useful overview over the various parallels between biological and linguistic diversity. They begin by reviewing recent figures on ongoing processes of linguistic homogenisation and language endangerment. Just ten (0.001%) of almost 7,000 languages are spoken by around half of the world's population, while 88% of the world's languages are spoken by fewer than one million speakers and around 21% (1,537 languages) by fewer than a thousand speakers. Skutnabb-Kangas and Harmon observe that 'languages are today being killed at a much faster pace than ever before in human history.' It is well known that a parallel process is afflicting biological species: the rate at which vertebrate species have been lost over the last century is at least eight – perhaps as much as 100 – times higher than the so-called background (that is, natural) rate. Edward Wilson estimates the background extinction rate as 'about one species per one million species a year.'[33] Biologists reckon that somewhere between 5,000 and 150,000 species become extinct every year. The great variation in these assessments depends on differences between various estimates of the total number of species, most of which are undocumented, but pessimistic predictions suggest that around 20% of species may disappear by the end of this century.

The analogies between the trajectories of biological and linguistic diversity have inspired extensive methodological and even conceptual transfers from biology to linguistics. As Skutnabb-Kangas and Harmon note, both forms of diversity

> are fundamentally evolutionary, with all living species and languages the result of descent with modification from, respectively, a common genetic or linguistic ancestor. The histories of species and languages are traced by similar taxonomic methods and result in similar phylogenetic trees that reflect an evolutionary branching process. Both kinds of diversity can be classified hierarchically, with the genes/species/ecosystem ladder of biodiversity matched by structural/language/lineage levels of linguistic diversity.[34]

These parallels seem incontrovertible, as is the authors' conviction that 'linguicide' and 'ecocide' share 'the same root cause: neoliberal globalization.' Uniformity and homogenisation, they conclude, appear to be requisite to the economic growth that is encouraged by 'dominant economic and political forces.'

Given the many parallels, however, it appears that not enough attention has been paid to the differences between how biological and cultural/linguistic diversity is *generated*. As we shall see, there is a sense in which the two processes are diametrical opposites. Although conceding that there are important differences, Skutnabb-Kangas and Harmon finally assert that 'the main driver of both speciation and language genesis is *isolation* (reproductive for species, communicative for languages),' and that 'the same biogeographic factors that give rise to species diversification are probably at least partly behind language diversification.'[35] This is an assertion that calls for closer examination in the light of anthropological and linguistic theory. First, however, we shall briefly review the theoretical model of biological diversification synthesised by Edward O. Wilson in his classic study over 30 years ago, and the main reasons why biodiversity is currently being diminished.

Biodiversity in the Anthropocene

Supporting his explanations with myriad examples, Wilson presents a compelling account of the forces of evolution. 'Reproductive isolation between breeding populations,' he writes, 'is the point of no return in the creation of biological diversity.'[36] Speciation (that is, the appearance of new species) results from the emergence of some kind of genetic difference between parts of the original population that precludes interbreeding. Such differences generally originate as genetically determined traits that increase adaptive fitness in specific environments.[37] They thus reflect variations in environment, including varying opportunities to generate new ecological niches in co-evolution with other species. Through natural selection over countless generations, minute genetic differences are incrementally enhanced until they become unbreachable. 'The two populations have turned into distinct species because they are reproductively isolated where they meet under natural conditions.'[38] The genetic variation which is subject to selection is generated by random mutations. Where completely new environments are colonised, such as when a breeding population of organisms reaches an isolated island and adapts to several new environmental niches, the speed of adaptive radiation can be comparatively rapid.

In addition to accounting for biological diversification, Wilson also explains how human activity tends to reduce biodiversity through alteration or destruction of habitats, introduction of invasive species, and overharvesting. These processes of biological homogenisation have more recently been illuminated by Elizabeth Kolbert.[39] She explains the vulnerability of tropical rain forest ecosystems by referring to the extreme specialisation of their constituent species. Prompted by intense competition, specialisation means that more organisms can coexist within the same space. High diversity of species means low population density of each species, which increases distances between organisms, chances of isolation, and further speciation – and finally vulnerability, since isolated populations are more susceptible to extinction.[40] Kolbert succinctly captures the contradictory imperatives imposed on the biosphere by the Anthropocene. It compels species to move in response to rising temperatures, yet it creates 'barriers – roads, clear-cuts, cities – that prevent them from doing so.'[41] Its intercontinental reshuffling of species is unprecedented in the history of life. It has made a 'hash' of geographic distribution as 'highways, clear-cuts, and soybean plantations create islands where none before existed,' while 'global trade and global travel do the reverse: they deny even the remotest islands their remoteness.'[42] The reshuffling of species increases local diversity but reduces the number of endemics: 'For the same reasons that local diversity has, as a general rule, been increasing, global diversity – the total number of different species that can be found worldwide – has dropped.'[43]

For many anthropologists and linguists, this observation is equally applicable to cultural diversity, and for some, it is equally alarming.[44] Regardless of how we value or define cultural diversity, we need to understand how it is generated and why it is being reduced. In the next section, we shall consider how some prominent 20th-century anthropologists have theorised the social mechanisms of cultural diversification.

Theorising cultural diversity

Several of the giants of 20th-century anthropology, like Claude Lévi-Strauss and Gregory Bateson, were deeply inspired by natural science, particularly biology. In his biography of the former, Patrick Wilcken mentions the significance of Lévi-Strauss' encounter with D'Arcy Wentworth Thompson's 1917 classic *On Growth and Form*.[45] D'Arcy Thompson had applied mathematics to describe morphological differences between species, such as the shapes of skeletal parts, animal horns, and shells. He showed how biological diversity can be understood, or at least mapped, in terms of quantifiable distortions of geometric coordinates. Wilcken writes that D'Arcy Thompson's book 'fit like a key' into Lévi-Strauss' evolving thought, as he was writing his thesis, *Les Structures élémentaires de la parenté*: 'It was from D'Arcy Thompson that Lévi-Strauss elaborated on one of the keystones of structuralism – the idea of transformations.'[46] In other words, one of anthropology's most prominent inquiries into cultural diversity was significantly inspired by the phenomenon of biological diversity. Lévi-Strauss was convinced that diversification is not an altogether random process but comprehensible in terms of structural regularities amenable to formalisation. In addition to his comparative studies on kinship systems,[47] he devoted the four volumes of *Mythologiques* to tracing structural transformations through a long series of myths recorded among indigenous peoples from Brazil to Alaska. Common to both these projects is the premise that seemingly diverse series of cultural phenomena can be analytically derived from underlying structures of human thought and classification. Much as landscape surfaces in part derive from geology, the structuralist approach views empirical cultural diversity as generated by invisible substrates that can only be revealed through analysis.

Lévi-Strauss' structuralism was fundamentally inspired by the linguistic theories of Ferdinand de Saussure and Roman Jakobson. He recognised language as a system of differences in which the meanings of individual phonemes derive from their relations to other phonemes. Approaching other cultural phenomena as cognate to language, Lévi-Strauss consistently sought to discover the smallest constituent units, the combinations and recombinations of which generate meaning. In his analyses of kinship systems, he identified relationship terms, marriage rules, and prescribed interpersonal attitudes as constituting such 'atoms of kinship.'[48] In the structural study of myth, he similarly defined the basic 'mythemes' that recur in various transformations.[49] He was convinced that the empirical diversity of kinship systems and myths was generated by structures of human consciousness whose transmutations were ultimately as comprehensible in terms of mathematical formulation as the diversity of biological forms that had preoccupied D'Arcy Thompson.

Lévi-Strauss' intuitions about the affinities between the biological diversity mapped by D'Arcy Thompson and the linguistic diversity theorised by Saussure and Jakobson prompt us to ask what species and languages have in common? We have mentioned several biocultural analogies such as radiative branching, extinction rates, and similar methodological approaches (for instance, phylogenetic analysis, or cladistics). From an evolutionary perspective, it could be argued that the capacity for language emerged as a trait that accelerated and fine-tuned the adaptive advantage of early humans, as in the social collaboration required in hunting big game. Both species and languages are expressions of *codes* (genetic and phonetic, respectively) and can thus be approached as communicative phenomena. If genetic codes are transformed by the interaction of random mutations and varying selective pressures, we may ask through which mechanisms languages change? Are the kinds of phonetic shifts that can be traced by historical linguists the counterpart of genetic mutations? What are the pressures that select for the maintenance and reinforcement of certain phonetic or other cultural shifts? In other words, what produces diversity in linguistic and other cultural phenomena?

In his analyses of kinship systems, Lévi-Strauss approached congruities between alternative representations of social organisation not as implicating separate historical stages – as had the 'inventor' of kinship studies, Lewis H. Morgan, as well as other 19th-century evolutionists like Edward Tylor and James Frazer – but as coeval transformations. The intriguing redundancies that characterise indigenous social structures of central and eastern Brazil, which was the focus of much of his research, were a source of inspiration for his structuralist methodology:

> [The various types of groupings found in these societies are] a series of expressions, each partial and incomplete, of the same underlying structure, which they reproduce in several copies without ever completely exhausting its reality.[50]

Cultural diversity cannot be exhaustively derived from universal properties of the human mind, but results from diverging trajectories of interaction between mind and the varying social and ecological worlds with which it becomes entangled. A group's kinship terminology, for example, may reflect the group's position within an extensive regional system of exchange.[51] Neither kinship systems nor myths are completely confined to human consciousness – they are inextricably entwined with the social regularities and natural environments that they reflect. This becomes particularly evident as we follow Lévi-Strauss in deciphering the shifting zoological and other components of common mythological themes that he thought could be traced through countless campfire narrations over the millennia from Brazil to northwestern North America. The variations derive not only from successive mutations in the replication of myths over time but also from the introduction of new elements inspired by shifting social and ecological contexts. Yet, the structuralist approach is rarely explicit about the social agency underlying the cultural variation that it aspires to account for. We are finally left with the question of how cultural diversity is produced: what are the incentives for distinguishing a group's identity against another?

Although famous for his references to universal features of the human mind, Lévi-Strauss sensed a pervasive human preoccupation with *difference*. He has been vilified for maintaining that cultural identity is inextricably connected to ethnocentrism and an emphasis on contrasts vis-à-vis other groups, which Didier Eribon refers to as the idea that 'cultures want to be opposed to one another.'[52] Lévi-Strauss' position follows from the fundamental linguistic and structuralist observation that meaning, like information in general, derives from difference. It harmonises well with Gregory Bateson's theory of schismogenesis, that is, processes through which two individuals or groups reinforce the distance between them by increasingly entrenching and emphasising their distinctness.[53] Paradoxically, it also harmonises well with Fredrik Barth's interpretation of how ethnic or cultural differences are organised, which arguably offers a foundation for the theorisation of ethnogenesis.[54] This convergence between Lévi-Strauss and Barth is paradoxical, as the former has been accused of cultural essentialism while the latter considers his argument constructionist.[55]

Barth observes that 'the simplistic view that geographical and social isolation have been the critical factors in sustaining cultural diversity persists.'[56] As against this view, he affirms that 'ethnic distinctions do not depend on an absence of social interaction and acceptance, but are quite to the contrary often the very foundations on which embracing social systems are built.'[57] Barth shows that ethnic differences and boundaries may be emphasised precisely where the interdependence of groups is particularly strong, as when they occupy distinct ecological niches or positions in a traditional division of labour, regularly exchanging goods or services. While recognising the parallels between biological populations and ethnic groups, he emphasises the quite different role of boundaries in the two contexts. There is today a broad consensus among anthropologists that cultural or ethnic identity is not an objective, primordial essence but an actively communicated experience implicating and reinforcing contrasts with other such identities. The significance of such cultural contrasts is, for instance, a recurrent theme in David Graeber's and David Wengrow's narrative of the history of humankind, in which they explain and abundantly illustrate processes of schismogenesis.[58]

Given that language is a quintessential marker of ethnic identity – as reflected in the widespread concept of 'ethnolinguistic' groups – this anthropological understanding of ethnogenesis as founded on cultural contrasts should have significant implications for historical linguistics. It should be an important consideration in any attempt at explaining linguistic diversity.

As we have seen, however, a common assumption is that linguistic diversity, like biodiversity, reflects periods of relative isolation of the adjacent populations.[59] Increasing social interaction, in this view, will lead to homogenisation. In a similar vein, the biologically inspired Punctuated Equilibrium Model developed by R.M.W. Dixon posits that during long periods of equilibrium, 'as a result of linguistic diffusion, all the languages in the geographical area would become more similar in structural profile.'[60] Only when such periods of equilibrium are punctuated by some 'cataclysmic' natural or social event, the model suggests, there is a diversification of languages, until equilibrium is reestablished and the tendency towards homogenisation resumes. Such events might be a flood or drought, a new means of producing food, conquest by an expanding neighbour, or migration into uninhabited territory. The assumption is that, during most of history, the interaction of politically equivalent groups will, as a normal course of affairs, enhance linguistic convergence. This assumption seems difficult to reconcile with the abovementioned perspectives of Lévi-Strauss, Bateson, and Barth. In the latter view, cultural diversification is actively generated by humans seeking to distinguish their own identities from those of others – not as a result of cataclysmic events or isolation but as a regular aspect of social life. In this view, it is not diversification but homogenisation that needs to be explained in terms of historical political processes.

These two perspectives suggest contradictory or at least divergent accounts of the sources of ethnolinguistic diversity. To test their relevance, we now turn to general overviews of the post-Columbian linguistic histories of Amazonia and the Andes, respectively. The final section of this chapter will suggest some conclusions on the applicability of anthropological models of diversification in the linguistic histories of these two regions, and on the general conditions for cultural diversity.

Ethnolinguistic diversification and homogenisation in indigenous South America

At the time of European contact, there may have been around 700 languages spoken on the South American continent. Of these, only slightly over half have survived until today, 'a number, however, that is rapidly dwindling.'[61] Recent attempts at classification of currently spoken languages have reached varying estimates of the number of 'genealogical units' (language families and isolates), ranging between 107 and 118. Linguists recognise around 50 families and a slightly larger number of language isolates. Pieter Muysken and Mily Crevels observe that 'there is a broad consensus of linguistic diversity rivalled by only a few other places in the world.'[62] Because of the difficulties of distinguishing effects of language contact from those of common genealogy, they find that 'the linguistic diversity of South America...poses problems similar to that of a 500-piece jigsaw puzzle, of which neither the colour nor the shape of the pieces is fully specified and the model is absent.'[63] Much of the difficulty of reconstructing the historical linguistics of South America derives from the disastrous demographic collapse following European contact: it is frequently estimated that indigenous populations during the colonial period were reduced by around 90%, compared to what they had been in 1492.

Amazonia

A similar sense of bewilderment is conveyed by the editors of an authoritative volume focusing on the indigenous languages of Amazonia. 'The Amazon basin,' they observe, 'is the least known and least understood linguistic region in the world': maps of language families give an impression of anarchy, as their distribution is more discontinuous than in any other part of the world.[64] Yet, they note that 'each language family tends to have a characteristic profile in terms of the type of territory it is found in, methods of food procurement, and material culture,'[65] observing that groups speaking Arawak, Carib, and Tupí languages tend to be found in the rainforest, practice horticulture, and make canoes, hammocks, and pottery, while Gê-speakers generally inhabit grasslands, have little agriculture, and lack canoes, hammocks, and pottery. In between horticultural groups in the rainforest are predominantly foraging groups belonging to smaller language families, some of which engage in symbiotic exchange relations with the cultivators. Dixon and Aikhenvald propose that 'some of these may be the remainder of earlier populations that occupied larger tracts of land before the agricultural expansion.'[66]

There have been attempts to explain the expansions of at least two of the largest language families in the South American lowlands – Arawak and Tupí – in terms of migrations reflecting the competitive advantage gained by populations practicing agriculture.[67] However, the distribution of ethnolinguistic groups and the prevalence of multilingualism suggest a more complex history of interaction.[68] In 1492, the Arawak languages had a wider distribution than any other language family, ranging from Central America to Paraguay. In comparison with other groups, speakers of Arawak languages have been conspicuously focused on long-distance exchange, river navigation, intensive agriculture, ceremonial feasting, social hierarchy, and geographically extended, patrilineal identities.[69] This cosmopolitan, Arawakan 'ethos' may have been first established in the northwest Amazon, from which it was conveyed by Arawak-speakers along the Orinoco to the Caribbean and along the Río Negro to the central Amazon and beyond, downriver to the mouth of the Amazon and upriver to the Andes. The emphasis on long-distance alliance-making, suppression of endo-warfare, and prestigious ceremonialism generated a cohesive network of densely populated, Arawak-speaking chiefdoms that dominated the fertile floodplains and main rivers of Amazonia during the first millennium CE. The extensive cartographic knowledge of such riverine traders is reflected in a list of ceremonially chanted toponyms recorded among the Arawak-speaking Wakuénai in the northwest Amazon, which reaches across the continent from the mouth of the Orinoco over the Río Negro to the mouth of the Amazon.[70] The prestige and affluence of Arawak settlements may have attracted speakers of other languages along the rivers to adopt an Arawak language and identity, as Arawak men frequently married non-Arawak women, and their offspring generally identified with their fathers.[71] Multilingualism was widespread, while Arawak may have served as a lingua franca that mediated exchange and other interaction along the river systems from the Orinoco to the lower Amazon. Five hundred years before the arrival of Europeans, Arawakan languages may thus have had an integrating function similar to that of Nheengatú (or *Língua Geral*) during the colonial period.[72] Although tentative, this hypothesis would explain the widespread distribution of Arawakan languages in combination with pervasive bi- or multilingualism, which illustrates how homogenisation at one level can be compatible with diversity at another.

While Arawak-speakers have an ancient connection to rivers and water transport, the Tupí, Carib, and Gê language families all appear to have originated in upland areas: Rondônia, Guyana, and central Brazil, respectively. Perhaps consonant with Aryon Rodrigues' suggestion that Tupí, Carib, and Gê may share a common linguistic ancestry (the 'Tu-Ca-Gê hypothesis'), it could be speculated that the routes of expansion of Arawakan languages created ethnic wedges that led to the demarcation of these and other, less dispersed families. Indeed, the distribution of Arawak languages is broadly aligned with the barriers that have historically separated other linguistic families: the Orinoco, Río Negro, Amazon, Ucayali, Purús, and Madeira Rivers, the *llanos* of Venezuela and Bolivia, and the coastal areas of Guyana. Several of the other language families, such as Carib, Pano, and Gê, may at one time have been denied access to the Arawak-dominated floodplains and other resource-rich areas. Variously engaged in warfare and trade, populations on both sides of such socioecological boundaries would have entrenched their markers of ethnolinguistic distinctness over time. Both the expansive, Arawak-speaking groups and other ethnolinguistic categories (such as Tupí, Carib, Gê, Pano, Tucano) that may have emerged in opposition to them were in their own ways ethnogenetic products of the overarching regional system. While displacing some older languages, the expansion of language families through Amazonia would thus also have generated new ethnolinguistic groups, through fragmentation of previously homogenous populations, circumscription of newly isolated groups, and various forms of inter-group boundary maintenance.

Rather than assuming that ethnolinguistic diversity in general is the result of an *absence* of interaction, the approaches of Barth, Lévi-Strauss, and Bateson instead suggest that it may be a consequence of the intensity of exchange between groups occupying different socioecological niches. Although linguistic and social cohesion at one level unified wide expanses of the Arawak exchange network, integrating riverine populations through much of Amazonia, its expansion encompassed diverse, bi- or multilingual ethnic groups and generated pervasive ethnic differences at its boundaries. Whether assuming the form of trade or hostilities, such cultural differences were actively reinforced by the groups involved. From an anthropological perspective, the general expectation should be that linguistic diversification is enhanced by interaction among groups rather than by their isolation.[73]

The linguist Patience Epps has systematically tested this perspective by examining the evidence from six regions in Amazonia with particularly high linguistic diversity: the Upper Río Negro, the Upper Xingú, the Southern Guianas, the Caquetá-Putumayo, the Guaporé-Mamoré, and the Gran Chaco. 'Despite common assumptions,' she concludes, 'one explanation that does not appear to hold up to closer scrutiny is that Amazonian linguistic diversity is simply a factor of isolation.'[74] She shows how the various groups in these linguistically diverse areas tend to actively promote their various cultural differences, for example by specialising in the manufacture of different trade goods, even though the materials may be equally available for all. Epps understands the linguistic exogamy of the Upper Río Negro as an expression of a widespread Amazonian equation of language and identity.[75] Despite pervasive multilingualism, each person inherits an essential linguistic identity – patrilineally in the Upper Río Negro[76] – and is expected to keep that identity distinct, for example by avoiding to mix languages (code-switching) within a single sentence or to borrow words (or even sounds) from other languages. The recurrent pattern throughout the linguistic areas examined by Epps is that there is more resistance to lexical borrowing than to diffusion of grammatical structures, which no doubt reflects the fact that speakers tend to be more aware of the former than the latter. Epps also suggests that there may be 'active processes of [phonological] diversification' at play in these areas.[77] Such diversification of sounds and accents, generating local dialects and ultimately separate languages, differs fundamentally from biological speciation in being the result of active identity construction rather than ecological specialisation.

The maintenance of linguistic diversity in several areas of Amazonia, as Epps suggests, probably reflects the 'absence of profound differences in socio-economic dominance between communities, such that groups were not normally drawn into top-down social structures imposed by other groups.'[78] In this respect, the linguistic history of much of Amazonia has differed from that of the prehispanic Andes, where states and empires have repeatedly subjugated populations over wide areas. Nevertheless, the expansion of Arawak-speaking chiefdoms along the floodplains of Amazonia must at times have imposed highly hierarchical relations between adjacent groups. Such expansions could be expected to create conditions that were conducive to linguistic homogenisation, much as has the imposition of European colonial languages and trade languages such as Nheengatú. As Epps observes, the latter contexts have generated a quite different pattern of linguistic borrowing, with many examples of strong lexical diffusion, frequent code-switching within sentences, and complete language shifts.[79] As we shall see, however, precolonial indigenous language expansions appear not to have significantly reduced ethnolinguistic diversity.

Based on her detailed case study of recent language change among Arawak- and Tucano-speaking groups in the northwest Amazon, Alexandra Aikhenvald usefully distinguishes three kinds of language contact situations: a 'traditional' areal contact without a relationship of dominance; a 'more recent' contact between two languages where one is dominant (in this case Tucano); and 'current language contact with diglossia,' where Portuguese and indigenous languages have a complementary distribution (Portuguese being used primarily in schools, written communication, and media).[80] In the first case, there is a tendency towards convergence of grammatical structures but a general disapproval of code-switching and lexical borrowings. In the second case, the Tariana language is suffering from attrition and gradual replacement by Tucano. Finally, the diglossic relationship between indigenous languages and Portuguese can to some extent contribute to keeping them apart.[81] As a whole, however, the long-term prospects of indigenous Amazonian languages are assessed as somber:

> Every year the indigenous languages are used less and less, and Spanish and Portuguese more and more. Every year another few languages pass into oblivion. Of the estimated 300 languages now spoken in Amazonia, only a small fraction are likely to be still actively used in 100 years' time. ... In lowland Amazonia there is little hope for even medium-term survival of any language.[82]

A conclusion from the evidence surveyed here is that linguistic diversity and biological diversity are promoted by quite different kinds of factors. Rather than reflecting biogeographical isolation, linguistic diversification may be enhanced by regular interaction between groups. A significant consideration, however, is the nature of this interaction: where reciprocity and political equality is the norm, cultural diversity tends to be entrenched, whereas hierarchy and political dominance, unless tempered by diglossia, may be conducive to homogenisation. With this observation in mind, we turn now to the linguistic history of the Andes.

The Andes

When the first Europeans arrived in the 16th century, most of the Andean area from northern Ecuador to central Chile was under the control of the Inca Empire (*Tawantinsuyu*). For several millennia prior to the Inca, the area had experienced a series of expansive social systems that dominated parts of the coast and highlands. Judging from archaeological evidence, the periods 900–200 BCE and CE 600–1000 were times of extensive cultural, economic, and/or political unification, referred to as the Early and Middle Horizons, respectively (the Inca Empire being the Late Horizon, customarily dated CE 1438–1532[83]). Given the homogenising influences that we expect of these horizons, the formidable linguistic diversity of the Andes on European arrival suggests that ethnic groups were generally less vulnerable to language loss in prehispanic times than in the centuries thereafter.

In his classic account of Inca culture at the time of the Spanish conquest in 1532, John Rowe lists a total of 86 'tribes and provinces' mentioned in historical sources.[84] He frequently notes in passing that a group in the list 'had their own language' or even that 'a number of local languages were spoken,' but estimates that dozens of languages perished without leaving a trace in Spanish documents. Linguists observe that the 'wealth of mutually unrelated languages' in the Andean area is 'as opaque as ever,' and that 'scores of native languages, including entire families, have disappeared, often without leaving a trace.'[85] They estimate that 'maybe more languages became extinct here during the last five centuries than anywhere else on the continent. In most cases, such languages have remained undocumented.'[86]

Areas where several local languages disappeared during the colonial period include highland Ecuador and the north Peruvian coast.[87] In many cases, such local languages were not displaced by the two major native languages (Quechua and Aymara) until the end of the colonial period or even the 20th century. The spread of Spanish has further reduced linguistic diversity in the Andes, as exemplified by its replacement of Mochica (spoken on the northern coast around Chiclayo and Lambayeque) and other languages in northern Peru.[88] Other examples of languages that appear to have been lost in the colonial period or later include Quingnam (the language of the pre-Inca Chimú polity, spoken on the coast between Trujillo and Lima), Culli (in the highlands between Trujillo and the Marañon), Cholón (in the upper Huallaga valley), and Puquina (the language of Tiwanaku, spoken around Lake Titicaca and some areas in southwestern Peru and the Bolivian highlands).

Quechua has been referred to as the lingua franca of the Inca Empire.[89] The dialect of Quechua promoted by *Tawantinsuyu* was that of Chincha, a trade-oriented polity on the south coast that had once been part of the Wari sphere of influence. Although Quechua was used in official matters throughout the Inca Empire, much of the population was bi- or multilingual, conducting their everyday social life in non-Quechua languages.[90] This diglossic situation preserved smaller languages in a way that Spanish colonialism and recent globalisation has not. Given the pervasive equation of language and identity, linguistic diversity was undoubtedly promoted by the Inca enforcement of ethnic identity.[91] The Spanish chronicler Bernabé Cobo reported that

> the men and women of each nation and province had their insignias and emblems by which they could be identified, and they could not go around without this identification or exchange their insignias for those

> of another nation, or they would be severely punished. They had this insignia on their clothes with different stripes and colors, and the men wore their most distinguishing insignia on their heads; each nation was identified by the headdress.[92]

Archaeologically documented cultural and political expansions through Andean prehistory no doubt fundamentally influenced the distribution of language families in the region. Increasingly concerted efforts at cross-disciplinary collaboration have offered plausible accounts of such processes.[93] By and large, the archaeological, ethnohistorical, and linguistic evidence appears to support the proposal of David Beresford-Jones and Paul Heggarty that the first major spread of Quechua was propelled by the Middle Horizon expansion of the Wari Empire, centred in the Mantaro basin, and their suggestion that the spread of Aymara was associated with the Early Horizon influence of Chavín, emanating from the site of Chavín de Huántar in Ancash.[94] The many linguistic affinities between Quechua and Aymara may derive from their long coexistence in adjacent ecological zones, the former associated with terraced maize cultivation in the valleys and the latter with camelid pastoralism at higher altitudes.[95]

Wari influence (and the distribution of Quechua around CE 1000) did not extend much further south than Cuzco (destined to be the Inca capital); immediately to its south was the domain of Tiwanaku, which dominated the Titicaca basin during the Middle Horizon. The main language spoken in Tiwanaku was Puquina.[96] Following the collapse of Tiwanaku at the end of the Middle Horizon, the Puquina language declined and was largely replaced by the spread of Aymara from the northwest. Yet, as late as 1575 it was recognised by the Spaniards as one of the three 'general languages' (along with Quechua and Aymara) of Peru.[97] By the end of the 16th century, Puquina was spoken in an area north and east of Lake Titicaca and was still significant enough to count as one of the indigenous languages that parish priests in the area should be familiar with.[98] Its fragmented occurrence in other parts of the southern Andes at this time may have reflected other remnants from the Tiwanaku period, prehispanic (Inca or pre-Inca) settlements of Puquina-speakers beyond their *altiplano* heartland, and/or dislocations due to the Spanish labour tax.[99] Although, as mentioned, the Inca generally enforced the maintenance of ethnic differences, their extensive *mitma* resettlement schemes contributed to the decline of Puquina, as did their violent subjugation of the Puquina-speaking Colla north of Lake Titicaca, who eventually shifted to Quechua.[100] Nevertheless, it was not Inca policy that finally extinguished Puquina as an ethnolinguistic identity, but Spanish colonialism. The only traces of Puquina that survived the 19th century are widespread toponyms[101] and a ceremonial language preserved by Callawaya herbalists in the formerly Puquina-speaking Charazani area, east of Lake Titicaca.[102]

When the Inca Empire emerged in the 14th century, its four subdivisions (*Tawantinsuyu* = 'the four parts together') appear to have been conceived in terms of the dominant ethnolinguistic categories recognised in Cuzco at that time: the Puquina-speakers of Collasuyu to the southeast, the Aymara-speakers of Condesuyu to the southwest, the Quechua-speakers of Chinchasuyo to the northwest, and the speakers of Arawak and other languages of Antisuyo to the northeast.[103] These categories could thus perhaps be understood as sediments of past cultural and linguistic expansions: Tiwanaku (Puquina), Chavín (Aymara), Wari (Quechua), and Arawak, respectively. Of these four, only Wari can with some certainty be characterised as having been largely propelled by political and military means, as was the further promotion of Quechua by Wari's successor, the Inca Empire. The remaining three were primarily associated with the spread of trade relations, ideologies, and prestigious cosmopolitan identities through extensive areas of South America. Although they might be viewed as early precursors to globalisation, they clearly did not have the same devastating consequences for linguistic diversity. We shall now consider some possible reasons for this difference.

Conditions for diversity

We have seen that ethnolinguistic diversity in South America was formidable in 1492, regardless of whether populations had been integrated into hierarchical political systems. The equation of language and identity was fundamental not only among groups of horticulturalists and foragers in Amazonia but also among the millions of ethnically diverse peasants subordinated by the Inca Empire. In the five centuries since the European conquest, however, almost half of the around 700 languages spoken in 1492 have been lost, and most of those remaining are falling into disuse and in danger of complete abandonment. Linguists have been prone to think of this loss of ethnolinguistic diversity in terms of concepts and models strongly influenced by established approaches to biological diversity: phylogenesis, genetic relations, endangerment, extinction, and so on. However, to account for the loss of indigenous languages – beyond the tangible historical forces of epidemics, colonialism, and genocide – we must transcend biological analogies and acknowledge that the maintenance of ethnic identity is contingent on social-structural conditions that allow for a certain level of local cultural autonomy. As indigenous peoples are abundantly aware, the continued vitality of their identities and languages today pivots on their capacity to safeguard their cultural specificity vis-à-vis the homogenising forces of globalising modernity. Pervasively, such preservation of linguistic diversity can be understood in terms of *diglossia*: the local language is reserved for social contexts in which ethnic specificity can continue to be cultivated, alongside but delimited from one's engagement in globalised social relations. A corollary of this observation is that the cosmopolitan lingua franca is also restricted to delimited social contexts.

It can be argued that the difficulties of upholding such boundaries between local and global social contexts are diagnostic of colonial and modern conditions. Ever since the arrival of Europeans in South America, there have been fervent efforts to 'convert' indigenous peoples to globalised identities, whether in the guise of Christianity, modern 'civilisation,' European languages, or the capitalist world economy. The colonial exertion of power has thus been markedly different from that of the Inca, who instead enforced the maintenance of ethnic identities among its subjects. Various ethnolinguistic groups were incorporated into *Tawantinsuyu* without any expectation of cultural assimilation. Both the Inca expansion in the Andes and the extension of Arawakan trade networks in Amazonia illustrate how, in principle, far-flung geographical integration can coexist with ethnolinguistic diversity. In contrast to pre-Columbian patterns, the currently ongoing abandonment of indigenous languages reflects the loss of social contexts for cultivating ethnic specificity. Complete language shifts can take place over the course of two generations, as when indigenous elders are finding it difficult to communicate with their grandchildren. The homogenisation of public discourse – through media, schools, employment, commercials, and political administration – colonises the entire modern individual, leaving dwindling spaces for cultural resistance.[104] Abstract, national or global identities make local or cultural identities increasingly superfluous by extinguishing the social contexts in which they might be reproduced. This is ultimately a consequence of how the logic of abstract exchange-value – that is, *money* – currently organises the world economy, penetrating human lives even into the innermost recesses of their local contexts.

Given the experience of modern globalisation, it is understandable that increasing interaction is often assumed to lead to cultural and linguistic homogenisation, but this assumption is clearly not applicable to premodern situations, in which the phenomenon of diglossic bilingualism appears to have enhanced ethnolinguistic diversity. As well understood by Barth, Bateson, and Lévi-Strauss, identity pivots on the expression of specificity as defined through contrasts. Arguably, a population that reserves a space for the expression of local specificity is less likely to submit to abstract identity assertion such as potentially devastating nationalism. The frequent observation that linguistic diversity may promote biodiversity also appears to be quite robust, as locally contextualised, ethnobiological classification systems and 'traditional ecological knowledge' may indeed be vital assets for sustainable resource management. To advocate the use of social theory – rather than biological analogy – to explain ethnolinguistic diversity is not to deny that cultural diversity may enhance biodiversity. While there are several other good reasons to safeguard the relative autonomy of local social life, such autonomy thus appears to be essential to both cultural and biological diversity, and perhaps ultimately also to world peace. In the next chapter, we shall examine how local autonomy was maintained in the Inca Empire, the only major civilisation in history that did not use money.

Notes

1 The discussion in this chapter is largely inspired by Thomas Hylland Eriksen's (2021) essay on 'The Loss of Diversity in the Anthropocene: Biological and Cultural Dimensions.'
2 Giddens 1990.
3 Giddens 1990: 22.
4 Scott 1998: 346.
5 Ritzer 1993.
6 Mawson [1923] 1946.
7 Harari 2011: 313.
8 Polanyi [1944] 1957.
9 Scott 1998: 8.
10 Dawkins 1976.
11 Bateson 1972.
12 Modern money has been developed as a means of managing 'urban sociality – the degree to which interactions occur between strangers on an everyday basis'; Green *et al.* 2024: 105, 122.
13 Hoffmeyer 2005: 222; emphasis added.
14 Eriksen 2021.
15 Dennis *et al.* 2011.
16 Uexküll [1940] 1982.
17 Mann 2011.
18 Wilson 1992: 287-288. Commenting on the effects of the Green Revolution on rice cultivation in India, Edward Wilson (1992: 301) warns that 'homogeneity means vulnerability.'
19 Bar-On *et al.* 2018.
20 Mann 2011: 507.
21 Mann 2011: 292.
22 Skutnabb-Kangas, Maffi, and Harmon 2003.
23 The prominence of language in these considerations on cultural diversity deserves reflection. Culture clearly includes much more than language, but no other cultural phenomenon is as readily identified, delineated, and quantified as language. This explains why so many scholars have invoked linguistic diversity as a proxy for cultural diversity. It should be kept in mind, however, that other significant but less easily identified aspects of cultural diversity may be equally threatened by globalisation.
24 Maffi 2001.
25 See, for instance, Posey and Balée 1989; Balée 1994.
26 Skutnabb-Kangas and Harmon 2017.
27 The most extreme version of this perspective is no doubt Marvin Harris' (1980) theory of 'cultural materialism.'
28 Hornborg 1996.
29 Indeed, the linguist August Schleicher (1821–1868) recognised analogies between linguistic and biological cladistics even before the publication of Darwin's book *On the Origin of Species* in 1859.
30 Maffi 2005: 601.
31 Maffi 2005: 611.
32 Gorenflo *et al.* 2012.
33 Wilson 1992: 280.
34 Skutnabb-Kangas and Harmon 2017.
35 Skutnabb-Kangas and Harmon 2017; emphasis added. This understanding of diversity as connected to isolation appears to be a widespread misconception even among philosophers. For example, Luc Ferry ([1992] 1995: 113) is

unwilling to share the 'praise of difference' because it evokes 'the romantic vision of communities viscerally closed onto themselves, incapable of surpassing their atavistic individualities to enter into communication with others.'

36 Wilson 1992: 50.
37 The classic case of speciation is the divergent evolution of different species of finches in the Galapagos Islands, which stimulated Charles Darwin's thoughts on evolution.
38 Wilson 1992: 62.
39 Kolbert 2014.
40 Kolbert 2014: 183.
41 Kolbert 2014: 189.
42 Kolbert 2014: 198.
43 Kolbert 2014: 212.
44 While some would argue that cultural diversity has increased under globalisation, Ernst Gellner (1983, cited by Eriksen 2021) has proposed that the new kind of diversity produced by modernity evokes the concept of 'entropy' rather than organised patterns of differences. It is arguable that the individualised, modern 'diversity' invoked by many recent culture theorists is a phenomenon more appropriately studied by psychologists than by anthropologists.
45 Wilcken 2010; see also Lévi-Strauss 1994: 427.
46 Wilcken 2010: 141–142, 261.
47 Lévi-Strauss [1949] 1969.
48 Lévi-Strauss 1963a.
49 Lévi-Strauss 1963b.
50 Lévi-Strauss 1963c: 130.
51 Hornborg 2013.
52 Lévi-Strauss 1994: 422.
53 For the theory of schismogenesis, see Bateson 1972: 35–46, 1958: 171–197. Bateson (1972: 457) also repeatedly refers to 'difference that makes a difference' as fundamental to communication, ecology, and evolution. From this bio- or ecosemiotic perspective, the reduction of diversity through globalisation can be regarded as a reversal of the evolutionary trend toward increasing complexity; Emmeche 2001; Eriksen 2023.
54 Although discussions of ethnogenesis such as Moore 1994 and Hill 1996 have shown surprisingly little interest in Barth's contribution, they similarly focus on the social construction of cultural identity.
55 Barth [1969] 1998: 6.
56 Barth [1969] 1998: 9.
57 Barth [1969] 1998: 10.
58 Graeber and Wengrow 2021.
59 Skutnabb-Kangas and Harmon 2017.
60 Dixon and Aikhenvald 1999: 17.
61 Muysken and Crevels 2020: 254. Another overview gives the figure 574 South American languages in 1492, reduced to around 420 today; Lev 2021: 330.
62 Muysken and Crevels 2020: 257.
63 Muysken and Crevels 2020: 267.
64 Dixon and Aikhenvald 1999: 1.
65 Dixon and Aikhenvald 1999: 4.
66 Dixon and Aikhenvald 1999: 4
67 Lathrap 1970; Dixon and Aikhenvald 1999: 4, 17.
68 Hornborg 2005; Hornborg and Hill 2011; Eriksen 2011.
69 Hill and Santos-Granero 2002.
70 Hill 2002: 229, 235–236.
71 Schmidt 1917.

72 Nheengatú is a Tupí-based trade language that spread throughout the Amazon basin in the 17th and 18th centuries and is still spoken as a first language by some populations on the upper Río Negro; Jensen 1999: 127; Campbell 1997: 23.
73 Hornborg and Hill 2011: 11.
74 Epps 2020: 275.
75 The phenomenon of linguistic exogamy, in materialising cultural fictions of unilineal genealogy, illustrates how problematic it is to assume that languages and genes are aligned over time.
76 Aikhenvald 2002: 21, 27.
77 Epps 2020: 286.
78 Epps 2020: 287.
79 Epps 2020: 289.
80 Aikhenvald 2002: 274–276. In diglossic situations, two languages with different social prestige are used in separate contexts. The term diglossia was originally coined by Charles A. Ferguson (1959: 325) for situations 'where two varieties of a language exist side by side throughout the community, with each having a definite role to play.' More recently, it has been applied to the similar coexistence of two unrelated but functionally complementary languages, 'where – for example – one language, or dialect, may be used in the home and in religious observances, and another in all other circumstances'; Aikhenvald 2002: 10.
81 Aikhenvald 2002: 186, 241.
82 Dixon and Aikhenvald 1999: 7, 19.
83 The dating of the earliest Inca expansion is being revised. Based on radiocarbon dates, it is now estimated to have begun in the early to mid-14th century; Lane and Marsh 2024.
84 Rowe 1946: 185–192.
85 Adelaar and Muysken 2004: 2.
86 Adelaar and Muysken 2004: 22.
87 Adelaar and Muysken 2004: 12, 23.
88 Adelaar and Muysken 2004: 23.
89 Mannheim 1991; D'Altroy 2002: 44.
90 Mannheim 1991: 44–46.
91 Sillar 2012: 307.
92 Cobo cited in D'Altroy 2002: 295.
93 Heggarty and Beresford-Jones 2012.
94 Beresford-Jones and Heggarty 2012. Richard Burger (2012: 150–151) points out that the identification of the Chavín sphere of interaction with the expansion of Aymara precludes traditional explanations of linguistic expansion, as archaeology shows that the Chavín phenomenon was not associated with agricultural expansion, warfare, or demographic displacement, but with the spread of a cosmopolitan identity and long-distance exchange requiring a prestigious lingua franca. The same observation can be made, for instance, regarding the expansion of Arawak throughout Amazonia and the identification of Tiwanaku with the expansion of Puquina.
95 The connection between Chavín, Aymara, and llama pastoralism suggests that the intensification of long-distance exchange that characterised the Early Horizon was made possible by the expanded use of llama caravans.
96 Torero 2002; Cerrón-Palomino 2012. Several linguists maintain that Puquina was affiliated to the Arawak language family; Torero 2002: 488–489; Adelaar and Muysken 2004: 175, 353; Muysken and Crevels 2020: 259.
97 Torero 1987: 343.
98 Bouysse-Cassagne 2010; Domínguez-Faura 2014.
99 Domínguez Faura 2014: 196.

100 Sillar 2012: 307–308, 314. The Inca elite traced their mythological origins to Lake Titicaca and may have spoken Puquina among themselves as a 'secret language'; Cerrón-Palomino 2012. In other words, even the Inca nobility relied on diglossia to maintain its ethnolinguistic identity. Cobo reports that, 'besides the language of Cuzco, which is the general language introduced by the Incas in their empire and was spoken by all their subjects, they knew another, which they used solely when they were dealing with and conversing with those of their own lineage'; Cobo cited in Cerrón-Palomino 2012: 266.
101 Torero 2002; Adelaar and Muysken 2004: 175, 350–351.
102 Stark 1972; Adelaar and Muysken 2004: 351, 356. The survival of these fragments of Puquina can again be attributed to diglossia.
103 Hornborg 2014. For an identification of Antisuyu with Arawak languages, see the recent argument of Darryl Wilkinson (2022).
104 According to Couldry and Mejias (2019: 107), the phenomenon of 'data colonialism' currently exacerbates mass media's project of homogenisation.

8 Civilisation without money

When Europeans first encountered the indigenous societies of the Americas, both natives and newcomers acknowledged that the pervasive rift that divided them was money. Although many Native Americans recognised valuables, prestige goods, or even 'special-purpose currencies' such as wampum, the notion of an abstract, general exchange-value embodied in gold and silver coins was alien to them. The closest thing to European money were the currencies – such as copper 'axe-money'[1] and cacao beans – that were used by the Aztecs in their markets in Mexico, but throughout North and South America economic exchange was generally organised very differently than in Europe. Karl Polanyi observed that exchange in such premodern societies was 'embedded' in social relations such as kinship or rank, rather than constituting an autonomous sphere of pure commerce pivoting on the management of money. For Polanyi, the latter condition was encapsulated in the concept of *market*.[2]

Yet, market exchange must be distinguished from the management of money. In the Mediterranean, markets – in the sense of congregations of people exchanging goods with each other – predated money by millennia. The fact that there clearly were barter markets even in the Inca Empire indicates that the exceptional character of ancient Andean economy, compared to other premodern civilisations, was not a complete absence of markets.[3] The 'disembedding' or autonomisation of the economy that was Polanyi's ultimate target no doubt instead hinged on the fetishisation of *money* as a distinct and socially acceptable preoccupation. The Enlightenment critique of European society in the 17th and 18th centuries was in part inspired by the encounter with significantly more egalitarian societies in the Americas, and a recurrent topic in this critique – sometimes expressed by the Native Americans themselves[4] – was the destructive social repercussions of money. The critique of money continues to be fundamental to indigenous identities and movements today.

Andean exceptionalism?

To some extent, the Spanish invaders in Mexico were able to recognise the bustling Aztec markets as familiar to European eyes, but in Inca Peru they

DOI: 10.4324/9781032702186-12

found very few indications of commerce. The empire of Tawantinsuyu has thus posed a conundrum to Europeans ever since the Spanish invasion in 1532. Here was the greatest civilisation of the New World, extending from northern Ecuador to Argentina and halfway through Chile, with perhaps as much as 14 million inhabitants, yet unacquainted with money. The encounter between Spaniards and Inca is particularly emblematic, as it epitomises the subjugation of a moneyless society by another for which money is the paramount concern. Like Cortés before him, Francisco Pizarro was pursuing gold and silver, which were the very substance of money in the Old World.

A mystery for Europeans was how it was possible to coordinate an economy encompassing several million people without using money. This question inspired the ethnohistorian John Murra to reconstruct the economic organisation of Inca society, based on meticulous studies of Spanish chronicles and thorough archival research.[5] Murra shared Polanyi's readiness to understand premodern economies as fundamentally different from modern economies and was thus conceptually prepared to examine the unique operation of this society that seemed to have been the very antithesis of modern capitalism.[6] He famously developed the 'vertical archipelago' model of Andean exchange, showing how social groups at various scales strive to achieve self-sufficiency by securing access to resources in different ecological zones, not through trade with other groups but by setting up their own colonies in different environments. This understanding of Andean exchange systems has been abundantly confirmed by archaeologists, ethnohistorians, and ethnographers from the 1960s and on.[7] Although independent merchants engaged in long-distance trade have operated at the northern margins of the empire[8] as well as in the Southern Andes,[9] the Inca consistently repressed such entrepreneurial trade within their boundaries.

The Inca state, personified in the emperor, based its administration of imperial resource flows on traditional, pre-Inca conceptions of reciprocal labour exchange. The relation between each community or kinship group (*ayllu*) and the state was conceived as reciprocal: the *ayllu* delivered various kinds of labour service[10] to the emperor in return for grants of agricultural land, raw materials for crafts such as weaving, gifts of cloth and other items from the royal warehouses, and the ritual hospitality of *chicha*-drinking feasts.[11] Murra writes of such obligations to the state:

> We are told that the occasion was defined as a joyous one, the families going to work singing, in their best clothes... It is obvious that an attempt was made to extend to such *corvée* duties the feeling-tone of community reciprocal aid; while at work the peasants were...provided with food and beer by the state... All they owed was their labour; whatever they harvested was stored by the state.[12]

Murra showed that evidence of entrepreneurial trade in the prehispanic Andes pertained either to pre-Inca exchange that had been converted into state-controlled redistribution, or to marginal activities at the frontiers of the empire. He argued that pre-Inca arrangements whereby highland colonists cultivated maize and other crops at lower altitudes for exchange with their high-altitude relatives were incorporated into the administrative apparatus of the Inca state.[13] Murra acknowledges that the highly valued reddish shells of the Thorny Oyster (*Spondylus*), which were referred to as *mullu* and commonly served as sacrificial offerings at 'springs, wells, rivers and other watery shrines,' seem to have been 'the major object of coastwise trade.'[14] He believes that, in pre-Inca times, village communities lacking llamas and alpacas of their own probably got their wool through 'trade and barter.'[15] Murra proposes that the Inca 'state revenue set-up as an exchange system must have affected the ancient, pre-Incaic trade and barter patterns [of high- for low-altitude commodities] and in some cases reduced them to insignificance.'[16] He does not hesitate to conclude that many of the cultural continuities in the archaeological record indicate trade, and that excavations in Ecuador 'also indicate the importance of coast-wise migration and trade.'[17] Further on, he refers to 'the hard fact that archaeology indicates extensive trade in pre-Incaic times' and suggests, citing a chronicle from 1561, that long-distance barter trade dwindled in importance under Inca rule.[18] However, Murra concludes, 'there had always been barter at a local level and this did continue in Inca times.' For most people, he continues, 'this was the only kind of trade known.' A 1590 chronicle cited by Murra reported that every five days there was a barter market at Cuzco engaging 100,000 people. He also cites the chronicler Cobo's significant observation that the words used by indigenous Peruvians for 'selling, buying, paying' simply meant bartering. In all this local bartering, mostly of foodstuffs, there was no money used.[19]

Whereas local barter markets were significant in Tawantinsuyu, most of the long-distance trade that can be traced to pre-Incaic times had been converted into state-administered resource flows. Murra suggests that the llama pastoralists of the high *puna* would have been the main traders prior to the Inca expansion. Llama caravans carried camelid wool and other highland products to the coast in exchange for maize, coca, peppers, fruit, fish, and cotton. There was also an ancient trade in tropical forest products from Amazonia, such as colourful bird feathers. Prefiguring his later work, Murra in his 1955 thesis provides several examples of the 'vertical archipelago' strategy, whereby highland groups established colonies at lower altitudes to procure products such as maize, coca, and peppers, for which they bartered quinoa and freeze-dried potatoes and meat. This pattern was regulated through the Inca institution of *mitima* colonies, who produced maize for the state rather than for their kin, but Murra acknowledges the possibility that 'such an attempt to control barter by putting it in the hands of one's kin is pre-Incaic.'[20] Like the state-sponsored work parties, the *mitima* institution emulated long-familiar Andean practices. Murra repeatedly suggests that long-distance bartering was more widespread in earlier times, but that much of it was curtailed as the flow of goods came under Inca control. He nevertheless mentions several early Spanish references to barter markets and 'merchants' which 'indicate that some trade and barter survived well into the Inca era.'[21]

Why is the Inca economy significant?

We should be careful not to duplicate the many romanticised images of Inca society as a socialist welfare state,[22] but there are clearly some unique aspects of its economic organisation that deserve consideration in an age when globalised capitalism is generating growing inequalities, loss of biological and cultural diversity, and devastating climate change. Regardless of the incentives, the principles that organised Tawantinsuyu represent a social experiment from which humanity might derive some useful ideas today. Of central importance is that it illustrates that it is feasible to coordinate the lives of millions of people without the use of money. A corollary of the absence of money in the prehispanic Andes was the extent to which local and state levels of economy and social metabolism were kept distinct at the conceptual level. Commenting on the limited extent to which state projects such as military campaigns were prioritised at the expense of the concerns of the *ayllu*, Murra remarks on 'the inability or unwillingness of the Inca system to interfere with the self-sufficiency of the Andean village community.'[23] The picture that emerges from his classic analysis of ancient Andean economy is that of a two-tiered society, in which local and supra-local concerns are clearly delineated ideologically. Exchange at both levels is conducted through barter and reciprocation, whether the trade partners live in the vicinity or at great distance from each other. Long-distance trade has for millennia conveyed exotic foodstuffs, prestige-goods, and other desirable items from remote ecological zones along the Andean slopes. Such flows of goods were monopolised by the Inca redistributive apparatus and can be understood as the foundational 'niche' of Tawantinsuyu. In presenting prestigious gifts to subordinate elites, the emperor *indirectly* converted valuables into labour (*corvée*) and thus also staples,[24] but given the organisation of land tenure, through which he laid claim to a third of all agricultural land, the only *apparent* state demands on the *ayllu* were on labour, whether in agriculture, craft production, construction, or military service. In the absence of money, there were no other social means of disembedding local resources for appropriation by the state. The goods that circulated in local barter markets were generally not directly convertible into those that were transported along the arteries of imperial metabolism. These two economic levels were thus understood as distinct *spheres of exchange*, as conceptualised by economic anthropologists studying premodern societies in various parts of the world.[25]

This two-tiered structure is key to several salutary aspects of Inca society, including the economic and cultural resilience of the *ayllu* and the maintenance of diversity. The relative autonomy of the *ayllu* was conducive to local egalitarianism and democracy[26] and to the frequently lauded welfare concerns in Tawantinsuyu. Contrary to a widespread misconception, Murra asserts that Inca society was *not* a welfare state:

> The village community *did* assume considerable responsibility for welfare. The state did not, nor could it do the job.[27]

We can conclude that the absence of money, in securing the *ayllu* against excessive external exploitation, largely prevented local-level accumulation, hierarchy, and impoverishment. In maintaining a largely kin-based local group as the basic source of subsistence, congeniality, and identity, the Inca system fortuitously restricted the kinds of severe inequalities that were generated in the monetised societies of Eurasia. This is not to say that the Inca elite and administrators had such benevolent intentions, only that the consequences of suppressing entrepreneurial trade had some long-term advantages for the mass of the population.

It is revealing to compare the suppression of entrepreneurial trade in Inca society with the ambivalence or outright hostility shown by the Maya elite towards their merchants. The Aztecs, Maya, and Inca suggest a spectrum in this regard, with the Aztecs representing the commercial extreme and the Inca the opposite, administrative end.[28] Among the Maya, as elsewhere in premodern civilisations, the merchants were the source of the distantly procured prestige goods that were emblematic of elite power, but 'they could not be allowed to accumulate these power symbols for themselves, lest they threaten the ruling stratum's power.'[29] Barry Isaac observes that this pervasive tension between political and economic power 'occurred widely in preindustrial states with elite-oriented traders.'[30] It ultimately illuminates the semiotic inversion by which the signs of power risk being transformed into autonomous signifiers, illustrating the *power of signs*. It is crucial for premodern elites to maintain an essentialist view of power as inherent in certain human bodies rather than in their insignia. Their dress, ornaments, and other regalia – whether golden crowns or macaw feathers – are to be understood as *symbols* of legitimate status, as justified by genealogical or other means, but when power is contested, as when such insignia are usurped by an impostor, they risk being perceived as *indexes* of power. This is tantamount to what Jean Baudrillard has called 'the autonomization of the signifier.' As we have seen in Chapter 3, it is also a way of defining fetishism. It is finally what distinguishes money.

Premodern insignia are meant to communicate the inherent power of some people over others. In volatile situations, an impostor who wears a royal crown may be able to use it as a source of power, as it indexically communicates his or her ability to win it. Money artefacts complete such a semiotic transformation by granting their owners power, regardless of any other criteria of legitimacy. The transformation of prestigious insignia into impersonal money objects implies a displacement of their *capacity to empower* from the person whose power they were originally meant to signify to the objects themselves. Like all fetishes, they became indexical signs. This fetishisation of power in the form of money was simultaneously a reification of quantifiable exchange-value. The insignia of a premodern monarch legitimised virtually unlimited demands on his or her subjects, including the right to take their lives,[31] but to serve as a regulator of social interaction, the purchasing-power of money – the extent to which it grants its owner the right to make demands on others – must be delineated and predictable. The emergence of money can thus be understood from both perspectives: as a fetishisation of prestigious insignia and as a measure of abstract exchange-value.

In restricting mercantile trade, the Inca elite effectively abolished competition in the accumulation of power symbols. The suppression of trade ultimately precluded the adoption of money. As we have seen, what to the Inca elite was a strategy to secure its own power simultaneously – and inadvertently – had beneficial consequences at the *ayllu* level. Rather than imagining Inca society as a utopia, we can think of it as a unique social experiment in organising a civilisation without money – and draw conclusions on what the absence of money *in principle* might mean for the feasibility of promoting egalitarianism, democracy, diversity, and resilience. In situating money objects in a comparative context, as the endpoint of a series of semiotic transformations, we are also able to see money in a new light: as artefacts signifying power over other people, disembedded from other aspects of social relations. We turn now to historical and archaeological indications of trade and incipient money at the margins of the Inca Empire, to examine Murra's thesis that the Inca elite actively suppressed mercantile accumulation.

Accumulation at the margins

The most compelling evidence confirming that the Inca state did convert pre-existing trade into politically controlled resource flows derives from Frank Salomon's extensive archival studies on the political economy of chiefdoms at the northern margins of Tawantinsuyu.[32] He found that highland chiefs in Ecuador in the 16th century relied on distinct groups of trade specialists (*mindalá*) who procured exotic produce and prestigious valuables for them from the lowlands. Salomon proposes that such north Andean merchants had more in common with the relatively independent *pochtecas* of Aztec Mexico than the state-sponsored *kamayuq* (delegated specialists) appointed by the Inca.[33] Significantly, the less the chiefdom had been assimilated into the Inca Empire, the more autonomous and entrepreneurial were the *mindalá*. The differences between northern and southern chiefdoms in mid-16th century Ecuador were 'in part fossil evidence of a diachronic process occurring under Inka rule.'[34] This indeed suggests that the Inca economy should be viewed not as underdeveloped or embryonic, but as representing a development *beyond* the more autonomous trade that characterised other stratified polities from Mexico to Colombia. Given that historical evidence from the north Andean chiefdoms indicates the pre-Incaic occurrence of such trade, a crucial question must be whether there are also indications of money.

Salomon describes some of the items purveyed by the *mindalá* as 'wealth objects' with 'quasi-monetary exchange value,' such as *chakira* (or *chaquira*), that is, strings of small beads made from bone or *Spondylus* shell from the coast.[35] In an article comparing the *mindalá* with the Aztec *pochtecas*, Salomon writes:

> There is a strong likelihood that certain wealth objects played a role as special-purpose money among prehispanic Ecuadorians. To the already-mentioned bead wealth and cotton mantles, one might add gold buttons (*chaguales*) from Colombia, and possibly hatchets, which are known to have been used as nuptial prestations.[36]

Whereas the Inca generally tried to abolish tribute in kind, Salomon mentions that in the Pasto area, 'where Inca pressure was far less pronounced the payment of strings of *chaquira* to ethnic lords paralleled the Mexican levies of money-like goods.'[37] As evident from a testament from 1598, the insignia of a native noble consisted largely of bead wealth.[38] According to a price list from 1570, the exchange-value of strings of bead wealth could be expressed in terms of gold, cotton mantles, cotton thread, or pepper.[39] Salomon affirms that the beads were 'bartered for goods of all sorts.' [40] *Chakira* beads are similar to the *carato* bone bead currency used in the Amazonian foothills. Citing Udo Oberem, Salomon mentions that the value of a string of 24 *carato* beads in 1577 was equivalent to one day of work.[41]

Valuable beads were manufactured in great quantities from *Spondylus* shell on the Ecuadorian coast. The Thorny Oyster shells and items manufactured from them were in high demand along the Pacific coast from southern Peru to Mexico.[42] *Spondylus* shell (*mullu*) had for millennia been a highly valued substance throughout the Andes, used for sacrifice as well as prestigious ornaments. The different kinds of 'quasi-monetary' bead wealth circulating in the northern Andes to Salomon suggest 'different glosses of a common concept.' Also suggesting common concepts, different kinds of hatchets and stacks of miniature, hatchet-shaped copper sheets were used as bride wealth as well as grave wealth in Ecuador.[43] Salomon finds convincing the conviction of Olaf Holm that they were used as 'some sort of currency.'[44] Similarly stacked and shaped copper objects (*naipes*) have been discovered in graves at Lambayeque on the north coast of Peru.[45] Records of the contents of an Ecuadorian tomb looted by Spaniards in 1563 show that great quantities of *chaquira* beads, many hundreds of copper hatchets, and some plume-shaped metal ornaments (for high-status headgear) served as grave wealth for a non-Inca lord.[46] Like *Spondylus* shell beads, 'axe-monies' have been found in both western Mexico and the northern Andean area, suggesting that they are indicative of long-distance trade along the coast.[47] Based on a 16th-century document, it has been suggested that merchants from Chincha on the south coast of Peru traded copper for *Spondylus* from Ecuador.[48] Jorge Marcos has proposed that *Spondylus* outside of Tawantinsuyu served as 'primitive money.'[49] Within the realm of the Inca, however, there are no indications of money. As Richard Burger asserts, throughout the Central Andes, '[t]he absence of an accurate system of weights and measures would seem consistent with a tradition of exchange that emphasized barter and lacked specialized merchants.'[50]

Money or no money?

Not content with the identification of embryonic money at the northern margins of the realm, Terence D'Altroy and Timothy Earle have understood the role of prestigious valuables even within the Inca economy as 'semi-monetary goods.'[51] They argue that, in being convertible into *corvée* labour yielding agricultural staples, such 'wealth items' were a means for the Inca elite to 'finance' their empire. They repeatedly use expressions such as 'valuable/monetary goods,' 'monetary objects,' 'valuables, primitive money, or currency,' and 'goods with monetary characteristics.'[52] Consistent with this perspective is the view that the Inca economy represents an archaic stage in the development of money and the evolution towards a modern economy. This assumption is explicit in the authors' assertion that the central Andean pattern can be contrasted with those of coastal Peru and the Ecuadorian highlands, 'where economic specialization in production and exchange was more highly developed,' qualifying as 'incipient market exchange.'[53] This evolutionist framing of the contrast clearly contradicts Murra's and Salomon's conviction that mercantile trade *predated* Inca economic organisation.

Without aspiring to rekindle the old formalist-substantivist debate, I find it important to unpack the assumption that money and commercial markets represent a more 'highly developed' economy, as if necessarily more advanced along a unilinear trajectory. The artefact of all-purpose money pervasively tends to shape our conceptualisation of exchange, as evident in D'Altroy and Earle's phrases referring to 'the development of new forms of *finance*,' 'state *investment* in political and economic security,' 'transport *costs*,' '*disbursement* of staple support,' '*payment* for services,' '*funding* of personnel,' '*cost*-effective' means of integration, and so on.[54] All such abstract concepts invoke the management of money, as if modern researchers have access to a master terminology that captures what the natives' concerns *really* were. When applied to a civilisation that appears to have abolished money, they risk stripping it of the cultural nuances in which it had painstakingly immersed itself. Even to classify Inca *kumpi* cloth as 'a special-purpose money'[55] is to reduce an intricate universe of time-honoured meaning[56] into a mere instrument. A fundamental conviction in Inca cosmology was that all values are *not* commensurable. This is tantamount to rejecting the very idea of money. Although D'Altroy and Earle correctly show that there were complex social exchange relations through which prestige objects could *indirectly* be converted into staples, the absence of money – and the cultural recognition of incommensurable values – is unequivocal and significant, because it restricted external interference with the *ayllu* as well as individual accumulation and impoverishment. The cultural organisation of exchange and categories of value in Tawantinsuyu are not to be understood as indications of an underdeveloped economy, but as founded on genuine and legitimate convictions that deserve to be taken seriously. Particularly noteworthy are the several indications that money and commerce appear to have predated the economic organisation of Inca society.

Some of the commentators on D'Altroy and Earle's article express similar hesitations about their interpretation of the Inca economy. Murra, John Topic, and Darrel La Lone doubt that the Inca were overly concerned about 'prohibitive transport costs.' Salomon incisively asks why Amazonian and coastal peoples – and the 'tiny Pasto polities' in Colombia – should have possessed 'better-developed currencies than any Andean empire.' Thomas Myers emphasises the indisputable lack of direct convertibility between valuables and staples. In a volume documenting the results of the archaeological research project on which D'Altroy and Earle had reported, Bruce Owen defends their proposition of 'market-like convertibility' in the Inca economy, arguing that 'convertibility and status legitimation are really two sides of the same coin.'[57] He observes that 'the utility of wealth goods for establishing high status' is that high status provides access to other resources such as labour. 'To function in this way,' he continues, 'wealth goods need [not] be literally and directly convertible in the sense of currency in a marketplace.'[58] In other words, he seems to say, beyond the appearance of being fundamentally different, reciprocal gift-giving, redistribution, and market exchange can analytically be conflated, as their common rationale – although in non-commercial societies it is convoluted – is convertibility. While it has been abundantly established that insignia of high status in premodern societies are associated with the capacity to appropriate goods and services provided by others, Owen's conclusion does not grant proper significance to the difference between such insignia and money objects. The former are *symbols* of a person's position in a status hierarchy, the latter are *indexes* of fetishised exchange-value conceived as intrinsic to the objects and detached from other criteria of power.

Many years later, in a conference volume to which both he and I contributed, Earle admits that the main idea on which his research project had been founded was 'the accepted economic principle that humans were fundamentally traders, simply waiting for opportunities to exploit regional comparative advantages.'[59] However, in showing that the Inca conquest did *not* encourage long-distance trade, the archaeological evidence proved the idea to be wrong. Nevertheless, it seems that he and his colleagues continued to embrace the 'formal logic' of some fundamental 'economic principles,' such as the universal rationality of convertibility. Paradoxically, while originating in a universalist approach, his chapter ends up arguing for Andean exceptionalism, while my chapter, which contests such exceptionalism by framing Andean political economy in terms of world-system analysis, now strikes me as overly universalist.[60] What I currently find missing in both chapters is a serious consideration of the absence of money in Tawantinsuyu. Given this absence, there were few incentives for long-distance trade and few opportunities to accumulate individual wealth in the Inca realm. From this perspective, the results of the archaeological excavations reported by D'Altroy, Earle, Owen, and their colleagues are quite predictable. For my part, I have come to realise that world-system dynamics will operate very differently where there is no money.

Some theorists of money downplay the social significance of physical money tokens such as coinage, emphasising that 'credit systems and debt obligations were operating in Bronze Age Mesopotamia and Egypt long before physical currencies ever circulated.'[61] Robert Rosenswig proposes that '[w]hat is called money in common parlance – metal coins and paper bills – is more accurately currency.'[62] Money, he continues, is an accounting system that should be kept analytically distinct from the 'counting units' or currencies that are used to measure it, like weight is distinguished from kilograms.[63] Among such currencies, Rosenswig counts medieval tally sticks, coins, paper bills, and electronic bank balances. In his exploration of how Mesoamerican currencies and monetary systems might contribute to a comparative economic history of the world, he rejects 'Polanyi's unfounded insistence that capitalist and noncapitalist states were organized qualitatively differently, and the related unhelpful dichotomy between special purpose and general purpose money.'[64] More than a millennium before the appearance of coinage, he asserts, a 'monetized state economy without any monetary tokens was...a stable and long-lasting basis for economic organization in the ancient Near East.'[65]

Such accounts underestimate the momentous difference implied by the introduction of coinage, which we have traced in previous chapters. In declaring that '[m]arket exchange presupposes the existence of money, so the latter necessarily existed first,'[66] Rosenswig's argument raises questions about the occurrence of markets and money of account in the prehispanic Andes. He suggests that the accounting and scheduling of *corvée* labour 'can be envisioned as *protomoney* in the sense of laying the organizational and accounting groundwork from which money could emerge.'[67] Indeed, he is doubtful that it would be possible for a state to function without a monetary accounting system, and suggests that 'the possibility of double-entry accounting by the enigmatic khipu makes it possible that this Andean empire had a monetary system similar to that of Bronze Age Egypt and Mesopotamia with accounting and no currency tokens.'[68] The implication is that *khipus* were a form of money. Rosenswig's argument that we should distinguish between money as an idea and as physical form is perfectly reasonable, but the proposal that physical forms like coins and banknotes should no longer be called money, but currencies, finally suggests only a semantic shift.

In many societies through history, accounting systems and tokens of exchange are obviously two co-existing aspects of money, but it is not helpful to confine the meaning of money to the former and identify its existence even in the absence of the latter. As Christine Desan observes in her comment,

> While the unit of account can be conceptualized abstractly, making a money is a material political project. The worldly container for monetary value can indeed take different forms, but *those forms critically inform the dynamics of the unit.*[69]

Tally sticks and gold coins clearly generate different kinds of social processes. We have seen how the repercussions of the 'military-coinage-slavery complex' transformed Eurasian societies during two millennia before reaching the Americas in 1492. *Khipus* may have been used for double-entry accounting, but they were not money.

Can we imagine the end of money?

Research on prehispanic exchange in the Andean area tends to underscore Murra's thesis that the Inca elite actively restricted mercantile activity. Some scholars believe that indications of long-distance transports, barter markets, or rudimentary currencies (such as coca leaf) contradict Murra's 'verticality' model of the Andean economy,[70] but they thus underestimate how his 1955 thesis acknowledged the extent of pre-Inca commerce and the determination of the Inca elite to suppress it. The appearance of a contradiction was no doubt amplified by Murra's tendency over the years to harden 'his antimarket position, staking a lot on his verticality idea.'[71] The contradiction has also been entrenched by a misleading equation of markets and money. As Charles Stanish and Lawrence Coben demonstrate, this equation must be abandoned if we are to 'understand how one of the great empires of world history – the Inca – functioned without price-making market mechanisms while simultaneously existing in an economic landscape structured by regional fairs, intense specialized production, and vigorous interregional trade.'[72] They conclude that 'our debate is effectively over:'

> [T]here were markets in the prehistoric Andes. Andean markets were based on barter exchange without the use of currencies, price swings, and an independent class of traders.[73]

Price-making markets, Stanish and Coben observe, require some kind of currency. Variations in supply and demand affect the rates at which goods are exchanged even where there is no money involved, but in barter markets fluctuations are slower and equivalences more stable. While acknowledging the significant difference between price-making and barter markets (primarily that the latter do not provide opportunities – that is, generate incentives – to profit from price differentials), Stanish and Coben adopt a 'neo-formalist' approach. They argue that in barter, too, people tend to maximise advantages or utilities, but what they maximise is not profits but the number of trading partners. In focusing on the economic behaviour of humans, however, they fail to consider the social repercussions of the *objects* of their maximising strategies. To maximise the number of exchange relations a person has can hardly create disadvantages for others, but incentives and opportunities to maximise monetary profits can, as we have seen in earlier chapters, generate a global system of accumulation and exploitation. To accumulate money is to accumulate claims on other people. In considering the difference between societies with or without money, the crucial point is not the behaviour of humans but the inherent social logic of the money artefact itself. It is this 'agency' of money that tends to escape not only economists but also economic anthropologists. This is finally the reason why I would contest the often-declared victory of formalism over substantivism in economic anthropology. Economics has myopically concentrated on human rationality and maximisation, while ignoring the social logic that is inscribed in *that which is being maximised*. Barry Isaac is justifiably relieved that anthropologists are 'resisting the urge to make capitalists or socialists out of the ancient Americans,'[74] yet the question of whether a major civilisation can be organised without money must continue to be of the utmost relevance.

Formalism is to substantivism not simply as abstract is to concrete. Formalist accounts of premodern economies focus on the human transactors and how their behaviour could be understood as maximisation, but they do not consider the features of *the objects exchanged*. The gold and silver that Pizarro's pilot Bartolomé Ruiz was seeking had different social ramifications than the *Spondylus* shells that were being collected by the merchants on the balsa raft that he encountered off Ecuador in 1526. Macedonian and Roman soldiers were compensated in silver coins, Inca soldiers in cloth. The former were paid wages in money, the latter reciprocated for their services to the Inca emperor. As we have seen, these two kinds of compensation for labour had very different repercussions for the societies in which they occurred.

The purported victory of formalism, and the pervasive debunking of 'myths' about money, are generally based on ethnographies of societies that have already become entangled in money; such statements do not refute the *possibility* of alternative forms of social organisation that some accounts of premodern societies inspire. Polanyi's and Murra's studies of premodern societies have not been proven wrong, just ideologically unfashionable in the era of neoliberalism. It is not evident that the inclination of anthropological discourse today is more relevant for the future of humankind than it was four decades ago. If the economic anthropology of the Inca or indigenous experiences of the environment seem obsolete discourses in 2025, it is not because these topics have lost their critical relevance, but because they are so blatantly at odds with globalised capitalism.

Can Tawantinsuyu tell us something about how social life can be experienced in the absence of money? Or does the very idea imply naïve romanticism? Graeber and Wengrow's *The Dawn of Everything* has rekindled my hope that the efforts of anthropologists and archaeologists to document the myriad human experiments with social organisation might fulfil some purpose, as we imagine how a just and sustainable society might be designed. More than just quaint stories about cultural idiosyncrasies, the vast record of human history and prehistory does have much to teach us. But are we collectively capable of learning from the past? Or are we prone to doubt that people have ever been otherwise? Maurice Bloch and Jonathan Parry have questioned critical approaches to money since Aristotle – through Aquinas, Marx, and Simmel to Polanyi, Bohannan, and Kopytoff – by invoking ethnographies of people who are already monetised.[75] They seem to deny the scope of historical transformations caused by general-purpose money based on modern observations that 'the vast majority of cultures make some space for exchanges which display many of the features which are sometimes, as in our own society, associated with monetary exchange (a degree of impersonality, considerable scope for individual gratification and a concern for pure instrumentality, for example).'[76] But how are these 'cultures' to be distinguished from 'our own society'? Such an essentialist approach to 'cultures' now seems outdated, as we recognise that virtually everyone in the world is currently incorporated in the monetised world economy. It also suggests an illustration of neoliberal ideology, as if all people *always* have had an aspect making them inclined towards 'impersonality,' 'individual gratification,' and 'pure instrumentality.' Bloch and Parry's argument exemplifies a widespread modern scepticism, once associated with the formalist pole in the debate that divided economic anthropologists in the 1960s, about claims that non-monetised people are or were radically different from those who use money.[77] Such scepticism tends to be distrustful of historical accounts suggesting significant differences and is instead prone to remould the historical Other in the image of the modern. Like Bloch and Parry's intervention, this kind of reasoning largely relies on references to contemporary ethnographies of recently monetised populations.[78] In the Andean context, it tends to understand a purported absence of commerce in essentialist terms, implying that the introduction of money in these societies would be difficult, and that it would contradict Murra's interpretation to adduce 'contemporary studies in the Andes [that provide] excellent descriptions of success stories in market-oriented ventures.'[79] *Contra* such assertions, we may recall Lévi-Strauss' advice to anthropologists in 1966:

> [W]e should probably be more cautious when tempted to dismiss the work of our great predecessors in the light of new outlooks or recent observations. What they have seen and recorded is gone and we cannot be sure that we are actually observing the same kind of evidence.[80]

The fetish that superseded animism

The significance of precious metals obviously differed between Spain and the Inca realm which it subjugated. Mike Sallnow observes that 'the gift-symbols of political power in native Andean society were transmuted after the Spanish conquest into the global commodity-currencies of mercantile capitalism.'[81] Under the Inca, gold and silver – representing, respectively, the sweat of the Sun and the tears of the Moon – had been largely monopolised by the elite as symbols of state power. Drawing on Mary Helms' contrast between the Northern and Central Andes, Sallnow shows how precious metals were transformed by the Inca from prestigious ornaments into emblems of political power and by the Spaniards from emblems of power to money. Rather than items of personal adornment, which in the Northern Andes were worn to express kin-based rank, precious metals in Tawantinsuyu became a state monopoly, used to legitimise the superiority of the Inca elite.

> As regional polities were drawn into the ambit of the state, precious metals ceased to be merely the markers of personal rank and standing within independent chiefdoms and became the universal symbols of state power and vassalage.[82]

'Today,' Sallnow continues, 'gold is pure profit, disposed of for cash.'[83] This sequence of transformations illustrates the pervasive semiotic shift through which signs of power are transmuted into powerful signs. Having symbolised the rank-based claims of certain people on others, precious metals became autonomous and impersonal signifiers, granting whoever controls them the power to claim other people's services or resources. To become money, gold and silver were attributed *intrinsic* power in the form of abstract exchange-value. In semiotic terms, the precious metals shifted from a symbolic to an indexical mode of reference. Such shifts, we have argued, are diagnostic of fetishism.

Given Richard Seaford's suggestion that the appearance of money in Old World civilisations has been associated with Axiality,[84] it is finally intriguing to consider Andean societies in this light. We have seen that the notion of an abstract exchange-value making everything convertible was fundamentally alien to the worldview cultivated in Inca society. In this respect, prehispanic Andean cosmology serves as a definitive illustration of pre- or non-Axiality as conceived by Seaford. Could it be a coincidence that it also perfectly exemplifies what Sahlins has referred to as an 'immanentist' worldview?[85] Ever since they invaded Tawantinsuyu, Europeans have been astonished by the extent to which indigenous Andeans attribute unique and immanent identities to seemingly lifeless things such as mountains, rocks, lakes, fields, springs, buildings, and dead ancestors. In the 16th and 17th centuries, the Spaniards who colonised the Andes were frustrated by and intensely engaged in extirpating what they considered to be the natives' idolatrous worship of inanimate objects, including the mummies of their ancestors.[86] Following Tylor, historians of religion have condescendingly referred to such practices as animism.[87] In the late 20th and early 21st centuries, anthropologists, archaeologists, and ethnohistorians are instead intrigued by how traditional Andean cosmology fits the ongoing reassessment of animism in terms of 'relational ontology' and the 'social agency of things.'[88] The ethnographic and historical documentation of Andean animism pervasively describes a propensity to experience non-living things as sentient and responsive 'persons' that are included in a cosmic sphere of *sociality* and reciprocity. As Bill Sillar succinctly puts it, '[a]nimism is an ontology which has at its core the simple philosophy that people have an inter-dependent social relationship with the material world.'[89] It is clearly important to ask under which conditions such relationships are cultivated and codified in ritual, and under which conditions they deteriorate.

A core element of pre-Axiality is an expectation of balanced reciprocity vis-à-vis significant aspects of the environment. To embed unpredictable and uncontrollable forces such as weather in a framework of personal social relations makes uncertainty manageable. An undertaking that yields beneficial outcomes is understood as an indication of harmonious relations, whereas setbacks are interpreted as consequences of insufficient propitiation or other transgressions. In either case, the inevitable vicissitudes of life are made comprehensible and meaningful. In a very general sense, this human pursuit of meaning, explanation, and manageability no doubt accounts for the universality of animism – or what Sahlins has called 'immanentism' – prior to the Axial Age. If Seaford is right in that Axiality is associated with the appearance of money in Greece, India, and China around 600 BCE, we must ask how money changed the fundamental social conditions that had previously been extended to relations with the natural world. A plausible answer is that the inherent logic of the money artefact tends to lead to expectations, not of balanced reciprocity, but of what Sahlins called 'negative reciprocity.'[90] Money encourages accumulation. In a society where all people are constantly pursuing the best deals, they are also always at risk of being shortchanged, exploited, or swindled. The pre-monetary social logic is inverted. If animism is the extension of social relations to nature, it can be argued that so is modern 'naturalism.' A society in which most other human beings are experienced as unpredictable strangers will produce natural aliens, existentially disconnected from their environment. The increase in technological efficacy and control propelled by money since the first Axial Age has occurred at the expense of congeniality and meaning.

This rather tragic understanding of human history has not diminished modern people's curiosity about the pre-Axial condition, leading to questions like, what cognitively distinguishes Axial from non-Axial cultures? Sillar refers to James Frazer's classic concepts of 'homeopathic' and 'contagious' magic to explain the underlying principle of Andean ritual offerings to the rain-giving mountain peak divinities (*apus*).[91] To use a semiotic terminology, these two variants of Frazer's 'sympathetic magic' are based, respectively, on iconic and indexical modes of reference. Frazer, like Tylor, expressed the perennial urge among representatives of Axial civilisation to account for the beliefs and practices of non-Axial cultures as based on primitive and erroneous conceptions of the world. Modern theorists of religion are no less curious to understand the differences between Axial and non-Axial worldviews, but not as prone to assume that the former represents a more advanced evolutionary stage than the latter. Frank Salomon has reviewed some theories of religion drawing on cognitive and evolutionary theory, which propose that the human inclination to interpret impersonal natural events as *intentional* is universal.[92] He cites Pascal Boyer's suggestion that such religious perceptions derive from a blurring of boundaries between different domains of experience, that is, 'when multiple mental "modules" simultaneously process a phenomenon but in different ways.'[93] The attributions of agency and personhood to inanimate entities are '*partly* abnormal' and '*minimally* counterintuitive' perceptions that catch attention and are shared in groups as markers of common identity. What begin as cognitive 'glitches' can thus become the cores of socially significant perceptions that foster solidarity and cooperation. Cognitive and social theory here find common ground. As culturally shared meanings, perceptions that attribute intentionality to natural phenomena can be socially integrative.

To conclude that animism can be socially integrative is to situate it in an evolutionary context. For hundreds of thousands of years, it contributed to the success of our species. Against this background, the dilemma of modernity appears uncomfortably clear. The exclusion of nature from society has been fundamental to scientific and technological progress, but this 'progress' has simultaneously alienated modern people from the world – and is currently in the process of destroying it. If animism is ultimately the result of a cognitive or semiotic 'glitch,' then so is money. It is arguably not more magical or metaphysical to attribute agency to a mountain than to attribute intrinsic value and purchasing power to a piece of paper. The question is which of these attributions is more sustainable in the long run. A corollary to the interpretation sketched here is that a reestablishment of moral relations to the natural world would have to begin with a reorganisation of social relations, and that such a social transformation must hinge on a transformation of money.

Notes

1 Hosler *et al.* 1990: 39–40.

2 This distinction between non-market and market economies was the fundamental contention that provoked the debate between Polanyian 'substantivists' and mainstream 'formalists' in economic anthropology in the 1960s. As many commentators have observed, the debate – notably as regards Andean society – was largely an ideological confrontation between left and right; Mayer 2013; Isaac 2013: 444.

3 Stanish and Coben 2013. Note, however, that some scholars reserve the term 'market' for 'a more capitalistic structure, which is generally inappropriate for the ancient Americas,' suggesting instead that we distinguish between 'commercial' and 'non-commercial' societies; Hirth and Pillsbury 2013: 17, n1. Even more problematic is the concept of barter. I fully agree with Graeber (2011) and others who debunk the economists' 'myth of barter' – as a cumbersome means of procuring goods before the convenience of money – but I retain the term as in a wider sense denoting various forms of reciprocal exchange unmediated by money. This is consistent with its application to prehispanic Andean exchange by many specialists including Murra, Salomon, Burger, Stanish, and Coben. As used here, barter does not signify an impersonal and instrumental act of acquisition focusing on the goods exchanged and stripped of social context but *a whole range of gift-giving, granting of credit, compensation, and debt cancellation primarily concerned with managing valued social relations*. To understand economies as universally focused simply on the transfer of goods, rather than on the maintenance of social relations, is arguably the quintessence of fetishism.

4 Graeber and Wengrow 2021: 54–55.

5 Murra 1955.

6 Mayer 2013.

7 See, for instance, Masuda *et al.* 1985; Goldstein 2013.

8 Salomon 1986a.

9 Nielsen 2013.

10 Such labour service is often referred to as a tax or tribute comparable to Roman and feudal European *corvée*.

11 In emulation of traditional peasant practices, *chicha* (maize beer) was brewed and consumed in large scale at work parties in connection with agricultural labour on land belonging to the emperor.

12 Murra 1955: 170.

13 Murra 1955: 24.

14 Murra 1955: 36. *Spondylus* occurs naturally no further south than the very northern coast of Peru. It is significant that Pizarro's pilot Bartolomé Ruiz in 1526 off the coast of Ecuador encountered a traders' raft bartering ornaments, fine cloth, and other valuables for *Spondylus* shells.

15 Murra 1955: 124, 131, n2.

16 Murra 1955: 229.

17 Murra 1955: 230.

18 Murra 1955: 235.

19 Murra 1955: 236.

20 Murra 1955: 239.

21 Murra 1955: 247.

22 Murra (1958) observes that 'the sociopolitical structure erected in the fifteenth century in the central Andes has consistently been viewed as unusual, and by some as utopian: here were *gente de razón*, civilized folk, with cities and temples, irrigation and elites; with warehouses to store the surplus. Nobody was "poor" or starving.'

23 Murra 1955: 220, 224.

24 D'Altroy and Earle 1985.

25 Even among the goods that were transported over long distances, there were different kinds of non-commensurable values recognised. Thus, cloth was 'placed in a different economic sphere from the luxuries of maize and coca leaves and so on'; Murra [1969] 2017: 54. This is not to say that conversions did not occur – for instance, through exchanges of gifts and obligations between elites at different levels – but that there was no all-purpose money with which to make such exchanges general and overt.

26 Throughout the Central Andes, indigenous communities have practiced local self-government through rotating offices known as *varayoq* ('staff-owner').
27 Murra 1955: 223; emphasis in original. See also Murra 1958.
28 Hirth and Pillsbury 2013: 1; Isaac 2013.
29 Isaac 2013: 439.
30 Isaac 2013: 440.
31 David Graeber (2007: 73) has argued that the sovereignty of the premodern monarch over his or her subjects has been transmuted into the power of the modern consumer over his or her objects.
32 Salomon 1986a, 1986b.
33 Salomon 1977/1978: 242.
34 Salomon 1986b: 94.
35 Salomon 1986a: 207, 1986b: 98, 111.
36 Salomon 1977/1978: 240.
37 Salomon 1977/1978: 241.
38 Salomon 1986a: 124.
39 Salomon 1986a: 207.
40 Salomon 1986a: 91.
41 Salomon 1986a: 91
42 Salomon 1986a: 92; for a comprehensive review of the literature on this trade, see Marcos 1977/1978.
43 Hosler *et al.* 1990. The stacks of copper pieces are regularly bundled in multiples of five.
44 Salomon 1986a: 92–93. For a different opinion, see Topic 2013: 350–351.
45 Shimada and Merkel 2021.
46 Salomon 1987: 220–221.
47 Based on metallurgical evidence, Dorothy Hosler, Heather Lechtman, and Olaf Holm (1990: 70) conclude that the phenomenon of axe-money 'seems to have had its technological beginnings in Lambayeque, was rapidly assimilated and transformed into something close to its final aspect by the growing chiefdoms of the central and southern Ecuadorian coast, and ultimately followed a maritime route to the Pacific coast of Mexico where it achieved its fullest expression.' Copper 'money-axes' have been unearthed in late prehispanic sites on the southern coast of Ecuador; McEwan and Delgado-Espinoza 2008: 509.
48 Rostworowski de Diez Canseco 1977. Less than a year after Rostworowski's discovery of this document in Madrid in 1968, Murra concurs and comments: '[W]e have predicted this all along, and now we have the information. There is long distance *administered* trade'; Murra [1969] 2017: 49, emphasis added. The extent to which such coastal trade between Peru and Ecuador would have been 'free' or 'administered' remains undetermined; D'Altroy and Earle 1985: 195; Dalton 2024: 8–9. It has been proposed that the Inca, after conquering the north coast Chimu polity around 1470, dismantled Chimu control over the *Spondylus* trade and granted it to Chincha; Sandweiss and Reid 2016. Many scholars today doubt the accuracy of the document; Burger 2013: 320; Topic 2013: 349.
49 Marcos 1977/1978: 118–11).
50 Burger 2013: 321. However, several balances have in fact been found in tombs in the Chincha Valley; Sandweiss and Reid 2016: 318; Dalton 2024. As Jordan Dalton (2024: 15) observes, balances may have been used for other purposes than trade, such as in craft production (for instance, to regulate yarn or create metal alloys) and measuring tribute or community obligations.
51 D'Altroy and Earle 1985: 189.
52 D'Altroy and Earle 1985: 189, 190, 193.
53 D'Altroy and Earle 1985: 189.
54 D'Aaltroy and Earle 1985; all emphases added.

55 D'Altroy and Earle 1985: 196. Referring to Murra, D'Altroy and Earle (1985: 203) argue that 'cloth, because of its skilled-labor investment, its visibility as a status marker in display, and its storability, was an excellent early wealth object.' As Toby Wilkinson (2018: 35) has pointed out, however, cloth is not suitable as a liquid medium of exchange.
56 Murra 1962.
57 Owen 2001: 282, 284.
58 Owen 2001: 284.
59 Earle 2018: 454.
60 Hornborg 2018.
61 Rosenswig 2024: 235.
62 Rosenswig 2024: 236.
63 As we noted in Chapter 3, the comparison between weight and monetary value is problematic, as the former is physically objective while the latter is not.
64 Rosenswig 2024: 237–238. Given this rejection of Polanyi, it is surprising to find Rosenswig arguing that '[s]ubstantivists could have waged a more effective battle' against the formalist position if they had provided a chartalist analysis of both capitalist and noncapitalist economies.
65 Rosenswig 2024: 238.
66 Rosenswig 2024: 237.
67 Rosenswig 2024: 242; emphasis added.
68 Rosenswig 2024: 249–250. *Khipus* were used to administrate large, centralised polities like Tawantinsuyu and Wari, not to manage trade; Green *et al.* 2024: 142.
69 Desan's comment in Rosenswig 2024: 251; emphasis added.
70 Hirth and Pillsbury 2013; Dillehay 2013.
71 Mayer 2013: 311.
72 Stanish and Coben 2013: 419.
73 Stanish and Coben 2013: 423.
74 Isaac 2013: 444.
75 Bloch and Parry 1989.
76 Bloch and Parry 1989: 29.
77 For another example, see Maurer 2006.
78 Mayer 2013: 312.
79 Mayer 2013: 312. Stanish and Coben (2013: 430) observe that 'native Andeans quickly adapted to the introduction of currency.'
80 Lévi-Strauss 1968: 351–352.
81 Sallnow 1989: 209.
82 Sallnow 1989: 223.
83 Sallnow 1989: 227.
84 Seaford 2004, 2020; see Chapter 2.
85 Sahlins 2022. Sahlins explicitly contrasts 'immanentist' and 'transcendentalist' societies as divided by the experience of the Axial Age.
86 Bauer 2004: 159–184. Sahlins (2022: 102–104) uses the Inca cult of royal mummies as an illustration of immanentism. Salomon (2017: 95) cites Peter Gose's suggestion that the Andean cult of ancestral mummies, as a consequence of the colonial efforts to extirpate idolatry, was transposed into the cult of mountains.
87 In Descola's (2013) quadripartite typology, Andean societies would exemplify what he calls 'analogism' rather than animism, but the opposition between animism and modern 'naturalism' represents the most fundamental contrast (Descola's 2013: 172–173, 201). Animism holds that all beings have similar interiorities but dissimilar physicalities, whereas naturalism assumes the diametrically opposite position (Descola's 2013: 122). Analogism, in this system of transformations, recognises discontinuities in both interiorities and physicalities. Descola's structural analysis reveals important differences between Andean analogism

and Amazonian animism, such as the Andean inclination to worship ancestors and perform sacrifices (Descola's 2013: 227–228), but it does not attach proper significance to the fact that both cosmologies may attribute personhood to abiotic things, which is unthinkable in naturalism. In this respect, both analogism and animism are variants of immanentism, as opposed to transcendentalism. As Sahlins (2014) has argued, it is reasonable to consider analogism a subcategory of what is conventionally referred to as animism. Descola's category 'dissimilar interiorities,' denoting a feature common to naturalism and analogism, does not do justice to the chasm that separates them. On the other hand, in classifying pre-Enlightenment Spanish Catholicism as a species of analogism, but with an absolute apex (God), his model explains the shifting 'transatlantic religious wrangle of which Peruvian extirpation of idolatry was a part'; Salomon 2018: 79. The movement toward monotheism corresponds to a drift toward abstraction and transcendence that must be at odds with all varieties of immanentism; Sahlins 2022: 130–131. In emptying the tangible world of immanent subjectivity, monotheism prepared the way for naturalism.

88 Sillar 2009; Bray 2015; de la Cadena 2015; Salomon 2018.
89 Sillar 2009: 374.
90 Sahlins 1972: 191–195.
91 Sillar 2009: 372–373.
92 Salomon 2018: 38–41.
93 Salomon 2018: 40.

9 Visions of indigenousness

The Eurasian civilisation that overran the indigenous societies of the Americas after 1492 was thoroughly monetised. It had calculated exchange-value in terms of the weight of silver for 4,500 years and used precious metal coins for over 2,000 years. Concepts of money and the value of gold and silver were as self-evident to the European colonisers of the Americas as water to fish. The hunger for precious metals that drove the Spanish conquests in Mexico and Peru in part reflected the demand for silver for use as money in distant China. For Native Americans, however, the European hunger for gold and silver was incomprehensible. Throughout the Americas, from Algonkian foragers in Canada to the agrarian empire of the Inca in Peru, the most irreconcilable cultural difference between Native people and the European colonisers was the latter's use of money. In this chapter, I hope to show how this difference has organised a pervasive conceptual divide between Native and non-Native Americans. From the earliest 16th- and 17th-century encounters until today, the nature and even the veracity of this divide has been debated on both sides, but the full extent to which it implicates the artefact of money is rarely acknowledged. Although there are innumerable accounts of the Spanish greed for gold in the 16th-century Caribbean, Mexico, and Peru, such accounts generally do not reflect on how the abstract notion of exchange-value had formed the persons and worldviews of the conquistadors, producing kinds of human incentives that to the natives were alien and inconceivable.

Any deliberation on the conceptual aspects of the post-Columbian holocaust and its aftermath must of course be trivial in relation to its unfathomable atrocities and centuries of repression. However, in examining how this historical process continues to shape the concept of 'indigenousness' throughout the world, we can trace the pervasive divide between Native and settler colonialist societies in the Americas to fundamental differences in how the two populations conceived of social as well as human–environmental relations. The confrontation between European and Native American societies was unilaterally genocidal, reducing indigenous populations in most areas by at least 90%, but its cultural ramifications worked both ways. The historical ambivalence of the settler colonists vis-à-vis the natives – a characteristic blend of fear, condescension, guilt, and admiration – has remained an

DOI: 10.4324/9781032702186-13

enduring component not only of American culture but also of the European worldview. In the late 17th and early 18th century, Native American critiques of European society strongly influenced French intellectuals whose ideas were foundational to the Enlightenment.[1] Critiques of European civilisation by Rousseau and others pervasively referred to indigenous Americans as a foil for the avarice and injustices of Europe. Such rhetorical polarisation of Amerindian and European cultures – rooted in real differences but elusively transmuted through the centuries – has been particularly prominent in the past few decades of deliberations on human–environmental relations. The different perspectives mentioned here are to be understood as strains of a discursive thread that runs from the Enlightenment to this day. Confrontations between capitalist civilisation and indigenous peoples have occurred on all continents, but the extent to which Native North Americans have come to serve as the antithesis of Europeans has granted this specific opposition a symbolic centrality that is emulated in indigenous struggles worldwide, from Polynesia to Scandinavia. In attempting to unearth the core of the opposition, we are arguably pursuing a transcultural and transhistorical definition of the very concept of 'indigenousness.' The discussion in this chapter is limited to how indigenousness has been represented among historians, anthropologists, and activists in North America during the 1980s, 1990s, and 2000s.[2]

In its most general form, the conventional stereotype states that Native Americans are ecologically wiser than non-Natives. This is the simplest and most essentialist approach to the issue, seemingly based on historical evidence, and widely popularised in Euro-American societies for centuries. It is essentialist in the sense that it attributes ecological wisdom to an ethnic category of people, without regard to cultural, historical, or individual variations. It also raises questions about how to define 'ecological wisdom.' Although a persistent trope, it is increasingly rare to find it professed in this simple, categorical form, except as part of political rhetoric. Such rhetoric has found support in several overly unqualified narratives written in the 1980s and 1990s by environmentalists, historians of religion, anthropologists, and environmental historians.[3]

The essentialist premisses of this approach prompted one environmental historian to propose that the Mi'kmaq participation in the 17th-century overhunting of beavers and other fur-bearers in eastern Canada is comprehensible only if understood as a 'revenge' on animals believed to be responsible for the devastating human epidemics derived from Europeans.[4] In other words, according to this interpretation, the ecologically unsustainable practices of indigenous people drawn into the fur trade were *generated by* their own ecological worldview, when their trust in human–animal reciprocity was distorted by epidemics. As argued by critics, this understanding of Native American overhunting essentialises and exoticises indigenous cosmology, rather than acknowledging the extent to which it was dissolved under the impact of the new commercial incentives of the fur trade.[5] Wherever they have penetrated, money and markets have disassembled premodern worldviews.[6] Yet, the pitfalls of essentialism are evident in our propensity to think of the 'people without history' as inherently governed by their premodern conceptions.

Introducing their collection of 'sacred Native stories of nature' from all over the world, environmentalists David Suzuki and Peter Knudtson assert that 'there is a fundamental division between Native and Western ecological perspectives.'[7] Within Native worldviews, they continue, 'the parts and processes of the universe are, to varying degrees, holy; to science, they can only be secular.' This distinct dichotomy between Native and non-Native understandings of the environment is a recurrent theme among environmental historians describing the ecological transformations of North America after European colonisation.[8] It is also frequently reiterated by historians of Native American religions.[9] Many historians have suggested that modern society, given its professed goal to become more sustainable, has much to learn from the ecological wisdom of indigenous people. Donald Hughes, for instance, asserts that 'we can gain much by studying our American Indian heritage and seeking modern applications of the wisdom we find there.'[10] Carolyn Merchant similarly writes that '[a] generation of ecologically conscious people have found inspiration in native American beliefs that nature is alive and the earth is a mother.'[11] By the early 1990s, such references to indigenous ecological wisdom were axiomatic in deliberations on environmental issues.

Indigenous identity, constructionism, and the modern longing for Place

During the 1990s, there emerged a general wariness about attributing essentialised features such as 'wisdom' to an ethnic category like Native Americans. In part, this reflected a growing awareness of the extent to which ethnic identities and attributes are to be understood not as primordial and objective essences but as continuously negotiated means of boundary maintenance vis-à-vis other ethnic categories.[12] Doubts about the authenticity of purportedly indigenous identities and sentiments were boosted by the academic turn towards social constructionism. At a more popular level, such scepticism may have harked back to how non-Native people and ideas had long infiltrated iconic 'Amerindian' figures and messages such as the fraudulent Grey Owl in the 1930s and the adulterated speech of Chief Seattle, which was ubiquitously cited and apotheosised by environmentalists in the 1970s.[13] Native and non-Native people alike had become increasingly aware of how the identities and ideal features of 'the American Indian' were being *produced* in the interaction between Native Americans and mainstream society.[14] Observations on the 'White Man's Indian' refer not only to stereotyped images of Natives that are prevalent among non-Natives but also to the influence of such projections on the actual formation of ethnic identity and personhood among Native people.[15] The dilemma of the 'positive stereotype' has generated much frustration among Native Americans, particularly as they have been idealised by the environmental movement.[16] The Lakota scholar Vine Deloria, Jr., whose compelling critiques of non-Native engagement with Native American societies have been pivotal ever since the publication of his first book *Custer Died for Your Sins* in 1969, saw nothing hopeful in the trope of 'the ecological Indian':

> American Indian delegations have been active in world environmental movements but have brought only a romantic sentimentalism as their contribution. It is totally disheartening to see Indians interviewed in the seemingly endless documentaries about the environment and find them telling us that the earth is our mother. The interviewer nods wisely, the Indian looks solemn, and the destruction continues.[17]

The turn towards 'deconstruction' of conventional, positive stereotypes of Native Americans has yielded at least two different kinds of investigations: historical reconstructions of how the stereotypes are created and entrenched, and critical examinations of the extent to which they are compatible with empirical reality. While sharing a common scepticism about such idealised stereotypes, the two projects – here represented by the work of Thomas C. Parkhill and Shepard Krech III, respectively – have different political implications.[18] As we shall see, the former study indisputably reveals how stereotypes have shaped the work of non-Natives writing about Native people, whereas the latter – in being read as a 'debunking' of praising generalisations about Amerindians – proved to be politically highly controversial.

Parkhill traces how the journalist and folklorist Charles Godfrey Leland (1824–1903) had allowed his own stereotype images and personal conditions to colour his documentation of Algonkian (Abenaki and Mi'kmaq) legends, published in 1884. Parkhill's study intertwines several disparate strands of thought relating to his struggles to grasp the cultural dynamics of representing 'the Indian.' He begins by referring to a heated 1993 email conversation involving, among others, Ronald Grimes, Sam Gill, Vine Deloria, Jr., and himself on the problems of representation raised by European-Americans' teaching courses on Native American religions. He then recalls the prominent role of fictive 'Indian' dramaturgy at a Boy Scout camp in Vermont that he attended as a teenager, before mentioning some of the many Euro-American movements and individuals who have dedicated themselves to imitating 'Indian' culture.[19] In Parkhill's words, these are examples of non-Natives trying to 'incarnate their own images of the "Indian" stereotype.'[20] He is perturbed not so much by such imitations being offensive as that they are inaccurate. This perspective informs his reconstruction of how Leland represented the Algonkian peoples whose legends he collected. Parkhill asserts that Leland's claims about the 'Indian's' close connection to nature in the 1880s, 'just as now, ...simply was not true for many Micmacs, Maliseets, Passamaquoddies, and Penobscots.'[21] But even if it is inaccurate, he asks, can an approving stereotype do any harm? Yes, he responds, citing several Native

Americans, including Vine Deloria, Jr., who confirm that the insuperable chasm between the imagined 'Indian' and the lives of real Native Americans is an obstacle in their struggle for better conditions.

Parkhill shows that Leland's goal was to instil among the settler colonialists a 'sense of belonging to the land,' a *sense of place*.[22] Citing Leland's biographer Elizabeth Robins Pennell, Parkhill agrees that Leland, in collecting the Algonkian myths, hoped to 'repeople his native land with the fairies of yore,'[23] reanimating a rural New England landscape that was rapidly being abandoned through the lure of urbanisation. In this work, he was inspired by German Romantics like Friedrich Schelling, who emphasised the long-term existential connections between humans and the land they experience as their place. Although most Native American activists would no doubt identify with this fundamentally anti-modernist stance, the infamous efforts by German Nazis to convert it into modernist politics of *Heimat* has made any postwar mention of the attachment of a people (*Volk*) to place politically suspect.[24] Leland's project also failed, says Parkhill, because it was 25 years too late. At the end of the 19th century, the romantic image of the 'Indian' had widely been eclipsed by a disparaging stereotype representing Native Americans as savages to be conquered by civilisation. As Parkhill concludes,

> No amount of editing and recasting, adding and improvising could make [Leland's] story attractive to the people of the United States in the late 1800s between Custer's defeat at the Little Big Horn and the massacre at Wounded Knee.[25]

Having identified the 'need for place' as characteristic of contemporary 'hegemonic culture,' Parkhill suggests that the United Nations' designation of 1993 as the International Year of Indigenous People reflects the fact that the need for place had become 'a global rather than national or continental matter.'[26] He proposes that the misleading, increasingly globalised stereotype of the ecological Native, reiterated by prominent environmentalists like Jerry Mander and David Suzuki, is ultimately a projection of modern 'Westerners,' generated by their pervasive sense of placelessness. Although Parkhill shares Mander's sense of loss and agrees that we have much to learn from different indigenous peoples, he maintains that the urge to conflate those peoples into a monolithic category of non-modern Natives, equipped with an essential closeness to nature, is a construction evoked by modern people's need for place. In representing a possible alternative to the alienation of modern life, the image of the 'Indian' fulfils an existential function in the modern worldview. Yet, as Parkhill observes, the gulf between mainstream modern people and the generic Native tends to be portrayed as unbridgeable. As a consequence of the idealisation of the ecological Native, relations between Natives and non-Natives 'will be fraught with unmet and unmeetable expectations at best, and charges of deceit and fraud at worst.'[27]

The politics of the ecologically noble Native

The intimation of fraud is implicit in much of the debate about 'the ecological Indian.' Rather than consider this stereotype a problem inherent in modernity, evoking the placelessness and unsustainability of mainstream society, the anthropologist Shepard Krech III set out to examine its empirical validity.[28] In other words, rather than approaching the stereotype as a misguided reflection of its flawed authors, he chose to highlight how its targets have failed to live up to its ideals. Krech thus finally gives the impression of disparaging the generic Native American for falling short of the non-Native fantasy. Adducing a range of circumstances from Pleistocene extinctions, buffalo jumps, and Hohokam salinisation to the 16th- to 19th-century trade in deerskins and beaver pelts, he is intent to rid the environmentalists of their illusions. Although the bulk of his book, *The Ecological Indian: Myth and History* (1999), seems a dispassionate review of historical and contemporary evidence suggesting that Native Americans have not conformed with the stereotype, parts of it are clearly polemical:

> [T]hroughout the five-hundred-year history of imagery of indigenous nobility is a rich tradition whereby the Noble Indian – including today's Ecological Indian – is a foil for critiques of European or American society. As Vine Deloria, Jr., the Lakota activist, remarked, white people '*destroyed planet earth*.' Writing as heatedly, many since 1970 have excoriated American society for all the environmental damage in Indian Country, and pointedly charged white people of environmental racism and 'radioactive colonialism.'[29]

Judging from such phrasing, Krech fuses two issues that both have significant political implications. The first is the assessment of the ecological trajectory of industrial civilisation, whether predominantly destructive or not; the second is the role of Native versus non-Native Americans in ecological degradation. Whereas the first boils down to whether there are reasons to be concerned about the future sustainability of industrial society, the second transmutes the contradiction between two divergent cultural traditions into a contradiction between two races. Leaving the first issue aside for the moment, we note that Krech's approach to the second issue commits the common error of mixing constructionist and essentialist perspectives: although recognising that the stereotype of 'the ecological Indian' is a 'projection of Europeans and European-Americans' that has become a 'self-image' embedded in the 'self-fashioning' of modern Native Americans,[30] his aim is to expose the poor fit between this image and the environmental record of a real population of humans extending throughout the continent from the Pleistocene until today. This approach has understandably provoked much indignation.

Prompted by Krech's book, a conference at the University of Wyoming in 2002 critically discussed its thesis and problematic political implications.

Michael Harkin and David Lewis write that 'he and his book have been called racist and politically incorrect, easily co-opted by those seeking to dismantle Native American lands, rights, and sovereignty.'[31] They note that Vine Deloria, Jr. had issued a call via internet discussion groups to 'attend the conference in protest.'[32] In a survey over the animated debate provoked by the book, Krech mentions that Deloria had called him 'the worst kind of racist.'[33] Krech writes that more than 90 reviews of the book had appeared in the first two and a half years after publication, many of which were positive, but some of which were harshly vitriolic. He recognises that his book 'was caught up in identity politics and charges of political incorrectness.'[34] The politically sensitive character of the topic is underscored by the fact that what is said may be less important than who says it. For example, Murray Wax had previously cited Deloria as saying:

> Our activists chastise the white man for his destruction of nature, and admonish people to respect the Sacred Mother Earth, while they themselves are throwing empty beer cans along the road. Many of our communities look like junkyards... While we are poor there is no excuse for being either destructive or dirty about the way we live.[35]

As Krech's book *The Ecological Indian* and the ensuing debate underscored, assessments of indigenous ecological wisdom or nobility had created a hall of mirrors, filled with contestation, credulousness, cynicism, and insults. The image of the ecological Indian has given indigenous people considerable political influence, helping them mobilise wide support for local struggles, for instance over land rights.[36] While there are many instances around the world in which environmentalists and indigenous people have created successful alliances, in other cases – such as the hunting of iconic wildlife like wolves, seals, or whales – they have been opposed. In such disputes, environmentalists have often expressed disappointment and anger, accusing indigenous people of betraying their authentic cultural values. Paul Nadasdy has shown that much of such controversy derives from the recurrent mistake among non-Native environmentalists to judge Native American positions on resource management in terms of a right–left spectrum ranging from anthropocentric 'Nonenvironmentalism' to ecocentric 'Radical Environmentalism.'[37] Nadasdy argues that this spectrum reflects Euro-American cultural categories that to many Native Americans are meaningless. He mentions both Calvin Martin and Shepard Krech among scholars who have argued 'not only that indigenous people's beliefs and practices can be incompatible with an environmentalist agenda, but that they can at times be distinctly *anti*conservationist.'[38] When environmentalists are angered or perplexed by such differences, their frustration and disillusionment reveal a gap between indigenous incentives and Euro-American assumptions. Michael Dove has reviewed the several kinds of problems that recur at the interface of indigenous movements and environmental politics, including charges of opportunism, inauthenticity, exclusivity, and racism.[39]

Adam Kuper has acerbically rejected the very concept of indigenousness, suggesting that Native Americans are as immigrant as Euro-Americans, that land claims based on descent imply a 'drift to racism,' and that spokespeople for indigenous identities paradoxically demand recognition 'in the idiom of Western culture theory.'[40] He goes beyond the argument that the image of the 'primitive' is constructed 'to suit the Greens and the anti-globalization movement,' finishing his reply to critical comments with a sarcastic crescendo that positions him as a frontline chauvinist of capitalist civilisation:

> Like the old enemies of civilization, those who inveigh against globalization seem to expect the Noble Savage to stand in its way, like Obelix the Gaul hurling menhirs at the Romans.[41]

Towards the end of the 2000s, the discourse on 'the ecological Indian' appears to have reached an impasse, in which the various arguments and incentives had become plain to see for most participants. This is not to say that the rhetorical use of the image would not continue to pervade popular and academic deliberations on environmental issues,[42] but that its proponents and critics alike had become familiar with the political strategies and contexts in which it is promoted and contested. It had become increasingly clear that the romantic stereotype of indigenous ecological wisdom is a Euro-American projection, but also that it continues to provide Native Americans and other indigenous people with a politically compelling platform, which at times leads them to confrontations with non-Native groups, including environmentalists. Given that the concept of 'indigenousness' is a product of modernity, the political tensions that it generates must be understood as internal to the self-critical modern civilisation from which it sprang.

Two readers in environmental anthropology from the late 2000s offer overviews of contemporary debates on the relation between environmental issues and indigenous cultures, knowledge systems, and movements.[43] While the positions range widely – from David Maybury-Lewis' essentialist nostalgia for the 'tribal wisdom' of the Xavante, through Peter Brosius' deconstruction of how environmentalists' distortions of ecological knowledge among the Penan are adopted by the Penan themselves, to Will Anderson's comment on the controversial resumption of whaling among the Makah – the fundamental tropes, relations, and political tensions reiterate a familiar pattern.[44] Through endless variations, the theme remains the same. Whether genuine or spurious, the invocation of the ecological Native continues to organise the modern worldview. Although put to different uses, the image of modernity's Other haunts us as a fantasy, a conscience, a desire for authentic wisdom. Beyond the myriad tangible ways in which it shapes the lives of people across the globe, it tells us something about our ambivalence regarding modern civilisation. Even if, over the course of three decades around the turn of the millennium – from the late 1970s to the late 2000s – we learned to be sceptical of essentialising attributions of nobility to specific ethnic groups, we are no less convinced that there must be an alternative to our own social and ecological deficiencies. Although less likely to be projected onto real people, the image of the 'noble savage' remains an integral part of civilisation itself.

Wisdom sits in places

Although they hardly mention the ecological predicament of humankind,[45] Graeber and Wengrow's intriguing world history *The Dawn of Everything* treats the image of the 'noble savage' as a powerful reminder that human life could be something much more agreeable than it is for most people. In the spirit of their conviction that hierarchy and inequality are not inevitable features of human societies but unfortunate conditions that can be rejected,[46] we must do two things. First, we must take very seriously the fact that we continue to imagine the possibility of an ecologically noble human existence. We must ask what it tells us about our dissatisfaction with modernity, the extent to which our collective limitations are self-imposed, and the potential of human imagination. Second, we must identify the source of our self-imposed limitations, persistently pursuing Graeber and Wengrow's most fundamental question about the shortcomings of modern civilisation: 'How did we get stuck?'

Beyond the struggle between essentialism and constructionism, anthropologists and philosophers trying to capture what the tenacious image of indigenous ecological wisdom might refer to have focused on either of two aspects, which seem divergent but are closely related. On the practical side, many have emphasised the fact that indigenous people tend to possess very detailed knowledge of their local ecosystems. This 'traditional ecological knowledge,' as it is commonly called, is often invoked in arguments for local self-governance. It is also understood as a potential asset for externally trained experts in sustainable resource management. On the experiential side, there have been numerous observations on the phenomenological dimension of indigenous people's relations to the landscapes and places to which they may feel intimately – even inextricably – connected. These two aspects generally engage two quite different kinds of scholars (resource managers versus philosophers), although both aspects derive from the same circumstances: people's long-term attachment to place. This illustrates how our understanding of what is clearly a single phenomenon is fragmented by the way knowledge production is organised in Euro-American society. Representations of the objective biophysical environment are conceived as fundamentally separate from subjective experiences of the same place, although both may have been formed through long and intimate involvement with that place. Even if studies of indigenous knowledge often evoke the sociocultural dimensions of local experience, they tend to gravitate towards a managerialist approach.[47] While regularly merged in environmental rhetoric,[48] ethnobiology and phenomenology belong to very different research traditions requiring radically divergent points of departure.[49] The notion that outsiders trained in resource management may incorporate local knowledge to enhance sustainability is to underestimate the essential difference between two systems of knowledge – specific versus abstract, experiential versus cerebral, local versus global, contextual versus decontextualised. Paul Sillitoe concedes that 'there are dimensions to understanding and living in the world other than the intellectual, for human experience and knowledge encompass far more than words can convey.'[50] Local knowledge is a *relation* between knower and known, not a resource accessible for extraction from its context. Although the ambition of resource managers, development agencies, and educators to incorporate the local in the global is no doubt well-meaning, the structural obstacles are formidable. It brings to mind the asymmetric relation between what Jürgen Habermas called 'system' and 'lifeworld' – and the aspiration of modernist schemes of social engineering to encompass and control their subjects, which, as James Scott showed in *Seeing Like a State*, must always fail.[51] The celebration by modern resource managers of 'traditional ecological knowledge,' 'indigenous knowledge,' or 'local knowledge' is finally as contradictory as the image of the ecological Native from which it derives. There is something profoundly incongruous about a civilisation eulogising the peoples, cultures, and knowledge systems that it is systematically destroying. The pervasive concessions about the vital contributions of indigenous knowledges to sustainability appear to have encouraged myriad marginalised people to believe that world capitalism is about to transform its essential logic.[52] Yet, their unlikely vision would require nothing less than our encompassment of the modern practice of encompassment – a veritable U-turn of modernity.[53]

If a fundamental condition of indigenous claims to ecological wisdom is their long-term attachment to place, it is clearly antithetical to a civilisation founded on decontextualisation and placelessness. Yet, as colonial and capitalist expansionism has been transmuted into the subtle logic of the global market, public discourse has admitted official concessions to indigenous peoples that were unthinkable a few generations ago. This has confirmed and augmented internal doubts about the sustainability of capitalist civilisation while providing opportunities for marginalised groups to assert their ethnic identities and land claims in new ways. This reorganisation of the discursive landscape has put many anthropologists in an ambivalent position. Having internalised the tenets of constructionism, it has been difficult for them to accept the new ethnic claims at face value. The dilemma is summed up by Michael Dove and co-authors:

> What do we make of the extraordinary coincidence that anthropology (and the other social sciences) began to critique the concept of indigeneity at the very time that it was being legitimised by mainstream global organisations like the United Nations and the International Labor Organization? How is academia's assault on locality related to the larger assault on locality of modernity?[54]

To the first question, the answer would be that global legitimisation has encouraged instrumental assertions of indigenousness that anthropologists are positioned to critically examine. The second question is more troubling. Having recently believed themselves to have jettisoned their ties to colonialism, anthropologists must now consider if they risk becoming accomplices of neoliberal modernity.

Attachment to place is a pervasive form of resistance to the decontextualising logic of modern society. Visions of sustainable connections to place have encouraged utopian social experiments among indigenous and non-indigenous people alike.[55] As previously noted, long-term familiarity and identification with a particular geographical space is conducive to two different aspects of what environmentalists have referred to as ecological wisdom: on the one hand, detailed knowledge of local ecosystems and, on the other hand, an existential and emotional connection to unique places. The former is often 'extremely sophisticated and of considerable practical value.'[56] It is this 'practical value' that has inspired externally trained experts, including commercial interests, to approach 'traditional ecological knowledge' as a resource to be tapped. The comprehensiveness of indigenous ecological knowledge is typically conveyed by means of quantification: the Hanunoo can distinguish 1,600 plant species; the Kayapó 'rely upon more than 250 different species of plants for their fruits alone, and hundreds more for their roots, nuts, and other edible parts'; traditional healers in Southeast Asia may use up to 6,500 kinds of medicinal herbs; and so on.[57] The modern documentation of such 'repositories of vast accumulations of traditional knowledge and experience'[58] is a distinctly different enterprise than anthropological attempts to fathom the experiential dimension of a profound engagement of humans with their local environment. The latter dimension is inherently difficult to study and communicate because it consists of perceptions and sensations that occur beyond the reach of everyday language.

Often drawing on the tradition of phenomenology as developed by philosophers like Martin Heidegger and Maurice Merleau-Ponty, some anthropologists have felt the urge to convey the tacit connection to place that they have sensed among the generally rural people who have hosted their fieldwork. Although largely unspoken, such connection is pervasive and discernible enough to have made strong impression on many anthropologists accustomed to more placeless lives. In the mid-90s, some of them addressed the phenomenology of 'place' as a focus of observation and analysis. Pioneering contributions to this discourse include a rich collection edited by Eric Hirsch and Michael O'Hanlon.[59] In his introduction, Hirsch notes that, in geography and anthropology, there is 'a tension evident in the relationship between the subject-position of place and the non-subject-position of space in the way landscape has been taken up as an analytical concept.'[60] Efforts by anthropologists to convey the attachment to place that they have noticed among their hosts have acknowledged the constraints of regular language – and the contradictory aspirations of anthropology – by consciously resorting to metaphor and poetry.[61] Significantly, their most thought-provoking ethnographies rely on a radical commitment to empiricism. Employing the concept of 'home' rather than place, Michael Jackson explains how fieldwork among the Walpiri in Australia led him to 'eschew thinking of home as an entity or essence that could be *defined*, and to focus instead on *describing* the lived relationship suggested by the phrase "being-at-home-in-the-world."'[62] In exploring the multi-layered relations to place among the Western Apache, Keith Basso similarly emphasises that, whereas 'sense of place is a universal genre of experience,' it everywhere 'hinges on the particulars.'[63] Jackson's and Basso's ethnographies are profound reminders that such attachment to place is not easily accessible to abstract theorisation. While pervasively evoked in images of the ecological Native, it remains tantalisingly out of reach for most modern people, for whom it would be inconceivable that 'selfhood and placehood are completely intertwined.'[64] Yet, the constitution of the thoroughly local person often does seem inextricable from context or place, which Richard Shweder and Edmund Bourne refer to as a distinctive mode of social thought among some 'non-Western peoples' that 'goes under a variety of cognate descriptions – concrete, non-abstractive, non-generalizing, occasion-bound, context-specific, undifferentiated, situational.'[65] To be profoundly *emplaced* means identifying oneself with points of reference that are concrete and particular rather than abstract and interchangeable.

This 'distinctive mode of social thought' appears to refer to what Claude Lévi-Strauss in *La pensée sauvage* famously called 'the science of the concrete':

> To be sure, the properties accessible to wild thought are not the same as those that hold the attention of scientists. In the two cases, the physical world is approached from opposite ends: one supremely concrete, the other supremely abstract; and either from the angle of sensible qualities, or from that of formal properties.[66]

If we understand 'sensible qualities' as immanent, indexical signs and 'formal properties' as transcendent symbols, we recognise not only that Lévi-Strauss' anthropological edifice addresses precisely the dichotomy that we have elsewhere referred to as non-Axial versus Axial but also that it illuminates the frustration of de Brosses and other transcendentalist Europeans with what they dismissed as African fetishism. In translating the concrete specifics of 'wild thought' into what he claims are their underlying, abstract meanings, Lévi-Strauss imposes on immanentist narratives a transcendentalist code. While skilful and persuasive, such acts of decipherment say more about the modern demand for abstract master narratives than about the cognitive and experiential conditions of emplaced, non-Axial humans.

To be embedded in relatedness

To invoke the extra-linguistic sensibilities that are implicit in any human bonding with a particular environment, some anthropologists have focused on the concept of 'emotion.'[67] Emotions are clearly important in a phenomenological approach to human–environmental relations, as they express the subjective states that such relations may engender, but of more fundamental analytical interest are the relations themselves. Like other phenomena at the level of individuals, emotions are derivative expressions of the relations in which they are immersed. In a much-cited article based on her fieldwork among Nayaka hunter-gatherers in India, Nurit Bird-David has proposed a rethinking of the foundational anthropological concept of 'animism' in terms of what she calls a 'relational epistemology.'[68] She argues that what Edward Tylor in 1871 had defined as a 'primitive' and erroneous understanding of the world, attributing animacy and spirit to inanimate things in the environment, is really a matter of *relating* to it, rather than clinically separating knower and known through a modern, objectivist stance committed to detached representation. 'Relational' ways of knowing stand for 'attentiveness to variances and invariances in behavior and response of things in states of relatedness and for getting to know such things as they change through the vicissitudes over time of the engagement with them.'[69] For animists, to know is to relate. It is to extend to all aspects of the environment the expectation that propitiation will be reciprocated with benevolence, that is, the cognitive skills essential to sociability. In this light, the modern objectivism epitomised by Descartes is quite simply correlated with alienation.

This is not to deny the many tangible successes of modern science since the Enlightenment, but to seriously ask if they have been achieved at the expense of the long-term viability of human society. There is no contradiction in observing that human civilisation has simultaneously accomplished what we think of as progress *and* invited disaster. Regardless of the feasibility of steering clear of disaster, it is essential to comprehend what 'civilisation' ultimately signifies, for the biosphere, for the scale of human inequality, and for each person's sense of being-in-the-world. This brings us back to where we started: what is it that makes our species unique in the evolution of life on Earth, and what was it that happened to human cognition in the Axial Age?

Having explored the pervasive image of indigenous ecological wisdom, rooted in the historical encounter between European and Native American societies and today reflecting widespread doubts about the sustainability of capitalist civilisation, we have tried to determine the core of the vacuity or inadequacy that haunts all those modern people who are prone to ennoble the generic Native. In identifying the modern sense of loss and placelessness that underlies such projections, we have rejected naïve essentialism as well as ironic versions of constructionism, both of which generate political and existential problems for indigenous people. We have unravelled a complex cluster of features that seem diametrically opposed to the premisses of modern civilisation: contextual versus general, concrete versus abstract, local versus global, experiential versus intellectual, relational versus objectivist, and so on. On closer examination, these oppositions can be understood as closely related to each other and as jointly traceable to the development of Eurasian civilisation after the onset of the Axial Age around 600 BCE. As we saw in Chapter 2, this was the point in history at which appeared the first coined money.

The literature on the Axial Age is voluminous, having engaged scholars in philosophy, sociology, psychology, history, anthropology, and several other fields.[70] Marshall Sahlins refers to 'the large cottage industry of scholarly commentary' that followed Karl Jasper's observations on the transition to 'transcendentalism' in several parts of Eurasia in the Axial Age.[71] To reiterate, cultures unaffected by the Axial shift to transcendence are pervasively characterised by what Sahlins calls 'immanentism': the world – including those parts of it that modern people would consider inanimate – is understood as fundamentally sentient. In Axial cultures, on the other hand, the turn to transcendent spirits left humans with 'an earth that had become a subjectless "nature."'[72] Sahlins rejects anthropology's traditional approach to the immanentist cultures encountered by Europeans, which has condescendingly treated their understandings of the world as erroneous 'beliefs' about a reality to which our own has privileged access. Exemplifying this stance with Raymond Firth's classic ethnography of Tikopia, Sahlins writes:

> All these identity-subtracting expressions – they are 'believed' to be the goddesses; he is the 'symbol' of the god, the 'representation' of the god, 'under the protection' of the god, and the like: all these are so many transcendental equivocations of simply, the god...[73]

Curiously, this is precisely the point that de Brosses made in 1760 about fetishism: in semiotic terms, divine status is not symbolic but indexical. Yet, de Brosses' excessive condescension regarding such convictions is the very opposite of Sahlins' commitment to taking seriously the natives' point of view. Inspired by Giambattista Vico, Sahlins advocates an anthropology that respects 'its informants' words as a distinctive ontology constituting worlds other than ours.'[74] Like Bird-David, he understands a pre- or non-Cartesian ontology as a pervasively attentive stance rather than a failed epistemology:

> Rather than a relation of persons to things, the human relation to the world was largely one of person-to-person. Otherwise put, rather than a sense of objectivity, it was a condition of intersubjectivity.[75]

As Philippe Descola, Eduardo Viveiros de Castro, Kaj Århem, and other ethnographers of animist societies have confirmed, what is characteristic of these societies is 'the attribution by humans to nonhumans of an interiority identical to their own.'[76] Their worlds are populated by nonhuman persons to be approached as subjects, rather than objects. Reviewing a vast range of ethnographic information on immanentist societies around the world, Sahlins demonstrates the ubiquity of such intersubjective relationism. This was the 'primitive' condition rejected by the Enlightenment and disparaged by de Brosses, but significantly also what some modern environmentalists glorify as 'sacred ecological wisdom.' Many modern people remain torn between what a modern approach *says* about the world and what it *does* to it. Knowledge based on dispassionate detachment may be useful but tends to be devoid of responsibility.

The Axial Age transition to transcendentalism, approached as a shorthand for the distinction between 'indigenous' and 'civilised,' clearly appears to have been correlated with changing social conditions. Charles Taylor proposes that pre-Axial humans were profoundly *embedded* in small-scale social contexts.[77] Björn Wittrock similarly views Axiality as 'a reaction to a new type of human condition where neither the structures of kinship and physical proximity nor those of a self-legitimizing empire suffice any longer to *embed* the individual in a context of meaning and familiarity.'[78] These observations harmonise with Bird-David's point that animism, understood as a relational approach to the nonhuman environment, is an extension of sociability beyond society. The same point has been made by Philippe Descola, who found that Achuar relations to garden plants and wild game had much in common with their relations to children and affines, respectively.[79] In these cases, human–environmental relations seem to be modelled on social relations, but given that plants and animals are perceived as nonhuman persons, it is arguably misleading to impute a projection of society onto nature to such relational ontologies, where no society/nature divide is recognised.[80]

To be profoundly embedded in local social and ecological contexts thus appears to be conducive to the kind of relational or immanentist outlooks that Tylor called animism. As Århem suggests, a 'participatory ontological stance' derives from 'deep practical and experiential involvement in the local environment,' a 'radical intimacy between humans and their environment, characteristic of an intensely localised mode of life.'[81] This agrees with the observation that the turn to transcendentalism and abstraction that defined the Axial Age was correlated with *dis*embedding, that is, decontextualisation. As David McNally notes, 'one of the oldest Latin meanings of the verb *abstract* is "to separate or pull away."'[82] Abstraction, in turn, is closely associated with money. With the capitalist market economy, McNally writes, comes

> the colonization of life by the abstract, quantitative metrics of commodities and prices. ... What guarantees connection to the land is not communal memory, but the (alienated) social synthesis of money. At the most fundamental of levels, monetization is thus a victory of the abstract over the concrete.[83]

If the Axial transition is correlated with changing social conditions, as argued in Chapter 2, monetisation is the prime suspect. The symbolic polarisation of capitalist civilisation and its indigenous antithesis is not to be understood as an opposition between different kinds of people equipped with different measures of wisdom or nobility. It is an opposition between two divergent human mentalities, reflecting the extent to which minds and social relations have submitted to monetisation. Graeber and Wengrow cite the French baron de la Hontan's rendering of the Native American (Wendat) thinker Kandiaronk's disparaging remarks in the 1690s on money as 'the devil of devils.'[84] The important thing is not whose exact words they were – the

French baron's or the Native's – but the fact that Native American societies provided the French Enlightenment with ideological levers with which to critique the obscene injustices of European society. The critique of the logic of money continues to this day, now more justified than ever.

As many have observed, money tends to truncate the social relations in which an exchange is conducted. Whereas a gift is an expression and confirmation of a continuing social relation between the giver and the recipient, most money transactions are understood to be concluded the moment payment is made, beyond which no relation exists between the parties in the deal. Money thus serves as a negation – a dissolution – of social relations. By extension, it dissolves our relation to the natural environment. The radical environmentalist worldview, which for decades has extolled the ecological wisdom of indigenous people, tends to be fundamentally sceptical of money, markets, and capitalism. Its praise of the ecological Native implicitly assumes that indigenous people are free from the insidious injunctions of money. Concluding a book that persuasively endorses the public influence of emotional attachments to nature, Kay Milton writes:

> The market systematically destroys whatever it cannot encompass. This includes, not only nature and natural things, but also health, family, friendship, spirituality, knowledge and truth.[85]

Given that Milton equates the modern market and money, this conviction summarises much of what has been said throughout the chapters of this book. In the next, final chapter, we shall address the problem of money head-on.

Notes

1 Graeber and Wengrow 2021.
2 This limitation stems from the author's fieldwork among Mi'kmaq environmental activists in Nova Scotia in the 1990s. It should not be interpreted as ignorance or diminishment of indigenous movements in other parts of the world. In Latin America, particularly in the Andean countries, indigeneity is a considerably more salient political issue than in North America, inspiring strong indigenous movements in their struggle for a *decolonial* future beyond extractive capitalism. In Peru, Bolivia, and Ecuador, *indigenismo* often invokes historical memories of Tawantinsuyu, which was the topic of Chapter 8.
3 For instance, Hughes 1983; Suzuki and Knudtson 1992; Merchant 1992: 110–131; Anderson 1996; Harrod 2000.
4 Martin 1978.
5 Calvin Martin's hypothesis was critiqued and rejected in a conference volume edited by Shepard Krech III (1987).
6 Wolf 1982.
7 Suzuki and Knudtson 1992: 18.
8 Cronon 1983; Hughes 1983; Merchant 1989.
9 Vecsey 1980; Hultkrantz 1979; Harrod 2000.
10 Hughes [1983] 1996: 139.
11 Merchant 1992: 121.

12 Sokolovskii and Tishkov 1996.
13 After his death in 1938, the internationally celebrated 'Apache' Grey Owl was revealed to be a pure Englishman by the name of Archie Belaney. The speech attributed to Suquamish/Duwamish chief Seattle (Si'ahl) in 1854 has been radically distorted through multiple non-Native translations and embellishments, finally granting it cult status among environmentalists throughout the world in the 1970s. Scepticism has even been voiced about the Lakota sage Black Elk, who had been a Roman Catholic for over 40 years and spent three years in Europe; see Parkhill 1997: 118. Significantly, non-Native projections of 'Nativeness' have pervasively denounced money.
14 Francis 1992; Hornborg 1994a; Bordewich 1996; Biolsi and Zimmerman 1997; Parkhill 1997; Krech 1999; Harkin and Lewis 2007; Hornborg 2008.
15 Parkhill 1997: 139–144.
16 For a nuanced discussion of the complex relations between radical environmentalists and Native Americans in the 1990s, see Taylor 1997.
17 Deloria, Jr. 1997: 213.
18 Parkhill 1997; Krech 1999.
19 Parkhill 1997: 9–16. Parkhill here refers to Daniel Francis' (1992: 157) observations on how Ernest Thompson Seton's Boy Scout movement 'gave expression to a persistent theme in North American culture, a desire on the part of Whites to go Native, a desire which is not, it seems, always confined to childish play.' Parkhill (1997: 147) is 'embarrassed by these Wannabees because they broadcast too garishly, too graphically, too clearly the Place-needs I feel too.'
20 Parkhill 1997: 15.
21 Parkhill 1997: 82.
22 Parkhill 1997: 91. Parkhill spells Place with a capital P. For an early and extensive discussion of place and placelessness, see Relph 1976.
23 Pennell's 1906 biography of Leland cited by Parkhill (1997: 103).
24 Parkhill (1997: 192, n28) finds In Vine Deloria, Jr., '[o]ne unexpected voice that resonates with German Romanticism.' For discussions of ecological sentiments in Nazi Germany, see Bramwell 1989 and Ferry [1992] 1995.
25 Ferry [1992] 1995: 107.
26 Ferry [1992] 1995: 110.
27 Ferry [1992] 1995: 129.
28 Krech 1999.
29 Krech 1999: 214; emphasis in original.
30 Krech 1999: 27.
31 Harkin and Lewis 2007: xxiv.
32 Harkin and Lewis 2007: xxii.
33 Krech 2007a: 6, 25, n5.
34 Krech 2007b: 348.
35 Wax 1997: 59, n3.
36 See, for instance, Conklin and Graham 1995.
37 Nadasdy 2005.
38 Nadasdy 2005: 308; emphasis in original.
39 Dove 2006.
40 Kuper 2003: 392, 395. Kuper (2003: 390, 395) claims that the propositions underlying indigenous land claims are 'popular with extreme right-wing parties in Europe' and are used to 'justify anti-immigrant policies.'
41 Kuper 2003: 395, 401. Alcida Rita Ramos (2003: 397) finds it puzzling that an anthropologist like Kuper should share the rhetoric of authoritarian governments who disclaim the political agency of indigenous peoples by 'attribut[ing] their actions to the manipulative powers of non-Indian agitators.' She also observes (Ramos 2003: 397) that, 'to put Western powers of conquest [e.g., Nazi racism

and South African apartheid] on an equal footing with ethnic demands for recognition is either to ignore or to minimize the violence of Western expansion.' As others have pointed out, given the uneven distribution of power in the world, anthropologists' representations cannot be neutral.

42 As recently as in his final, posthumously published book, Bruno Latour (2024: 30–31) writes: 'Whereas, just a few decades ago, indigenous peoples were considered to belong to the past of peoples who were unanimously marching toward progress, now those same indigenous peoples are *ahead of us* in the search for a way of caring for the world that we now share with them' (emphasis in original).
43 Haenn and Wilk 2006; Dove and Carpenter 2008.
44 Maybury-Lewis 2006; Brosius 2006; Anderson 2006.
45 I discuss this puzzling omission in a previous publication; Hornborg 2023: 208.
46 Graeber and Wengrow 2021.
47 Berkes 1999; Menzies 2006; Jessen *et al.* 2022; Gómez-Baggethun 2022.
48 For instance, Suzuki and Knudtson 1992.
49 Nazarea 1999; Sillitoe 2007. For phenomenological approaches to human-environmental relations, see Evernden 1985; Ingold 2000.
50 Sillitoe 2007: 12.
51 Scott 1998.
52 Tom *et al.* 2019.
53 Hornborg 1994b.
54 Dove *et al.* 2007: 148.
55 Maida 2007; Lockyer and Veteto 2013.
56 Suzuki and Knudtson 1992: 15.
57 Suzuki and Knudtson 1992: 15.
58 World Commission on Environment and Development 1987: 114.
59 Hirsch and O'Hanlon 1995.
60 Hirsch 1995: 9.
61 Jackson 1995; Basso 1996.
62 Jackson 1995: 123; emphases in original.
63 Basso 1996: 145, 148.
64 Basso 1996: 146.
65 Shweder and Bourne 1984: 166; emphasis in original.
66 Lévi-Strauss [1962] 2021: 306.
67 Anderson 1996; Milton 2002.
68 Bird-David 1999.
69 Bird-David 1999: S77.
70 Bellah and Joas 2012.
71 Sahlins 2022: 4.
72 Sahlins 2022: 4.
73 Sahlins 2022: 13.
74 Sahlins 2022: 21.
75 Sahlins 2022: 10.
76 Descola 2013: 129; Århem 1996, 1998, 2016; Viveiros de Castro 1998.
77 Taylor 2012: 31–32.
78 Wittrock 2012: 111; emphasis added.
79 Descola 1994.
80 Descola 2013: 107, 123–124, 250.
81 Århem 1998: 98–99.
82 McNally 2020: 39.
83 McNally 2020: 110–111.
84 Graeber and Wengrow 2021: 54.
85 Milton 2002: 150.

10 Meaningful money?

For more than 2,600 years of history, the pursuit of money has dominated the course of civilisation. It has shaped the incentives of countless generations of people in all walks of life. From the beginning, there have also been serious doubts about its effects on social life, morality, and the feasibility of human happiness. Money puzzled Aristotle and was denounced by Church leaders from St. Paul to Thomas Aquinas and beyond. While it was instrumental in integrating the capitalist world-system in the 17th and 18th centuries, money was disparaged by Native Americans whose societies and ecosystems it was dismantling and by Enlightenment Europeans who understood their anguish. In the mid-19th century, Marx and Engels condemned money's commodification of human time, hoping for an international workers' movement that would take control over the logic of capital. Today, the environmental movement, climate activists, and proponents of degrowth continue to criticise the seemingly inexorable logic of money. In this chapter, after reviewing some strands of this widespread critique over the past five decades, we shall consider how – *in principle* – it might be possible to reorganise that logic.[1] While it clearly seems unfeasible to revive pre-Axial social conditions of balanced reciprocity within restricted local groups – and the animistic projection of such reciprocity onto nature – the dire circumstances of the Anthropocene should prompt us to take stock of human history and seriously rethink our obsession with the magic of money.

Several distressing and seemingly irreconcilable contradictions of modern civilisation are evident in the 2020s: its urge to universalise modernity versus its awareness that this means destroying the biosphere; its pledge to abandon fossil energy versus its inability to do so; its celebration of its own progress versus its dread of extinction; its official aversion to consumerism versus its pervasive injunction to consume; its advocacy for the local and cultural identity versus its unyielding globalisation; its romantic affection for wildlife, wilderness, and indigenous peoples versus its relentless devastation of them all.

The contradictions between the professed values and the unremitting trajectories of our contemporary world invite reflection. They suggest that mainstream discourse does not recognise the driving forces of the destructive tendencies that we deplore. It seems unlikely that the official concessions

DOI: 10.4324/9781032702186-14

on inequalities, climate change, loss of diversity, and so on are a deliberate cover-up for continued devastation. The reason why public values – in support of justice, biodiversity, renewable energy, and other elusive ideals – are not winning over business as usual is that the mainstream modern worldview fails to fathom what ultimately propels what we call capitalism, or why it should be incompatible with justice and sustainability. Looking back at events and discourse over the past 50 years will help to illuminate the current impasse.

Five decades of critique

The early 1970s marked the end of three decades of growth and general optimism throughout much of the world. President Nixon's abandonment of the gold standard in 1971 unleashed the era of financialisation. The 1970s were years of recession, oil crises, and environmental alarms. Concerns over global inequalities and the environmental impacts of economic growth were formally recognised through events such as the UN Conference on the Environment in Stockholm in 1972. Several influential books were published that criticised mainstream economics for not acknowledging the social and ecological limits to growth.[2] The determination of mid-century movements celebrating ways to improve the future of humankind gave way to widespread post-modern hesitations about our dubious constructions of reality. Out of this collective loss of confidence in modernity emerged the neoliberal market fundamentalism that was established in the 1980s. Although misgivings about the future continued to be warranted, the official consensus was that economic growth had to be revitalised.

As critiques of neoliberal capitalism and growth have grown more pervasive, equally prevalent today is the feeling that the inertia of the capitalist economy appears to be unstoppable. While official alarm about climate change, biodiversity loss, inequalities, and other disturbing consequences of the world economy dominate contemporary media, the modern consciousness is plagued by a growing sense of hopelessness. If the years around 1970 alerted us to many of the failings of capitalism, the dominant assumption was that these shortcomings could be rectified through political campaigns and decisions. Such hopes have now largely withered. The ubiquitous rhetoric on sustainability and green transition inspires little enthusiasm as the annual COP meetings continue to deplore inexorably rising temperatures, escalating greenhouse gas emissions, and the indomitable combustion of fossil fuels.

In this book, we have traced the operation of the capitalist 'system' to the aggregate injunctions of the artefact of all-purpose money. To change the logic generated by the idea of money, our only option may finally be to redesign that artefact itself. The logic of money is unjust and unsustainable because it inexorably generates economic polarisation and accelerates the dissipation of resources. I will here consider a spectrum of approaches to the critique of modern civilisation and review some visions of how its ecological contradictions could be overcome. I shall argue that most of the currently suggested remedies fail to identify money itself as the problem and thus cannot provide much hope. Beyond mainstream 'solutions,' we must consider how far we are prepared to go in relinquishing what we have come to know as progress, to reinsert ourselves, as one species among others, in the organic cycles of local ecosystems. This is not to dispute the (unevenly distributed) advances in human health, food security, communication, mobility, science, or harnessing of nonhuman energy – as if such advances could be entered in a balance sheet and weighed against the threat of extinction – but to assess the viability of the human species under conditions of modernity. What is required of us if we are to remain long-term components of the biosphere?

Most people who have seriously considered the predicament of the human species in the Anthropocene conclude that the current trajectory of world society is unsustainable. If it is not fundamentally transformed, many acknowledge, it will lead to the collapse of civilisation. A substantial share of media space and national budgets are devoted to deliberations on various schemes for how to avoid such a disaster. Environmental economists have long proposed that problems can be alleviated if the 'costs' of environmental damages are 'internalised' in market prices, as if physical changes in ecosystems had a price that money could cover. As we saw in Chapter 6, this is a profoundly misleading notion that disregards the contradictory relation between the Entropy Law and economic processes. Heterodox economists have proposed various radical reforms of economics, but mainstream economists have responded with silence. Marxism has largely failed to dissociate itself from the productivism and technological optimism out of which it was born. Many people have hoped that the wished-for changes would result from a widespread shift towards more frugal, sustainable, and 'post-consumerist' values reflected in social movements and democratic decision making, but the tendency over the past 50 years has been diametrically opposite: the material intensity of the economy has increased.[3] For decades we have been aware of the average person's 'overshoot' and oversized 'ecological footprint' in the global North, but such measures have only grown more alarming.[4] Meanwhile, world population continues to increase, expanding the number of people aspiring to modern levels of consumption. Some visionaries have hoped for a world government that would deal with injustices and unsustainability, but a global government now seems further away than ever.

Ever since Schumacher and Illich, utopian thinkers have imagined localised, small-scale economies based on simpler technologies and organic agriculture.[5] Some of these attractive visions celebrate the premodern conditions that modern economies have displaced and continue to destroy, but they do not persuasively show how the inertia of modernisation and economic growth could be resisted or reversed. Given the threat of 'peak oil' and especially climate change, the imperative of abandoning fossil energy is very widely embraced, but the feasibility of decarbonising the entire world economy is a highly contested issue.[6] Considering that around 85% of global energy use is currently fossil, and that total energy use continues to rise with modernisation and population growth, it is not realistic to imagine a globalised modernity basing most of its energy demands – of which electricity is but a fraction – on non-fossil sources.[7] Technologies for harnessing renewable energy at that scale would require not only vast amounts of space but also absurdly huge volumes of rare earth minerals. The task of decarbonisation would necessarily mean abandoning hopes of universalising the modern, high-energy lifestyles that are conventionally seen as indexical of development.

Whether leaning towards the left or the right, ecomodernists express faith not only in new energy technologies but also in imaginative technological solutions such as geoengineering, asteroid mining, and the colonisation of other planets.[8] One of their recurrent mistakes is to neglect the astronomic amounts of energy that would be required to mechanically draw significant amounts of carbon dioxide from the air, transport minerals from asteroids, or travel in space. A fundamental flaw in ecomodernist visions is their disregard for the huge resource requirements of the miraculous new technologies, which would often derive from the very areas that they imagine could be 'rewilded' as humans retreat into their urban homes. They also ignore justice issues related to the fact that the appropriation of resources will generally implicate asymmetric material transfers between different social groups, to the disadvantage of extractive areas.

Conventional recipes for sustainability thus offer us little hope. Neither economists, engineers, climate activists, or degrowth advocates persuade us that modern civilisation can abandon its currently unsustainable trajectory, short of social collapse. While most people tend to repress such insights, it is not surprising that more drastic approaches emerge. Some analysts consider collapse to be an unavoidable scenario, but anticipate social renewal beyond the envisaged disaster.[9] Others have decided to accept or even embrace collapse.[10] Yet others have chosen to militantly confront the technological infrastructures through which capitalism usurps the planetary landscape, even advocating violence or sabotage.[11] These are the lengths to which people will go to alleviate their distress over the blind inertia of modern civilisation, mechanically pursuing its implacable course towards disaster.

What options finally remain but to open ourselves to a complete shift of perspective on human history? Is what we thought was the universal progress of humankind merely a series of strategies for the aggrandizement of privileged elites? Such a fundamental distrust of what we are accustomed to thinking of as 'civilisation' can find support in the efforts of anthropologists like James C. Scott, David Graeber, and David Wengrow to rethink the history of human progress.[12] When the inevitable crisis facing modern society can no longer be denied, we must be prepared to think of civilisation in new ways. To be able to fathom the future, we must renegotiate the past. Such a rethinking of history is intimated in the reflections of sociologist Zygmunt Bauman:

> It is high time to start wondering: are those forms of life-in-common, known to most of us solely from ethnographic reports sent back from the few remaining niches of bygone 'outdated and backward' times, irrevocably things of the past? Or is, perhaps, the truth of an alternative view of history (and so also of an alternative understanding of 'progress') about to out: that far from being an irreversible dash forward, with no retreat conceivable, the episode of chasing happiness through shops was, is and will prove to be for all practical intents and purposes a one-off detour, intrinsically and inevitably temporary?[13]

To contemplate such a rethinking inevitably means rejecting the worldview of mainstream economics. The excessive output of critique, not just over the past few decades but over the course of history ever since Aristotle's deliberations on money in the fourth century BCE, raises important questions. What does it ultimately signify, and why does the operation of human economies seem so impervious to it?

To be sure, the literature *defending* the virtues of business as usual is no less vast.[14] From Adam Smith to recent Nobel laureates in economics, deliberations on the advantages and possibilities of money and market exchange have been quite as voluminous, influential, and existentially compelling as the medieval theology that it displaced – and, I should add, quite as esoteric. The specialised modern discourse on why the economy must operate as it does tends to be as inaccessible to the layman as the scholastic meditations of the Middle Ages. To most people, it is probably as difficult to comprehend why the world economy must generate abysmal income gaps and financial crises as it is to fathom the mysteries of Genesis.[15]

What does all the critique of mainstream economics finally mean? Why have all the compelling, early objections of John Ruskin, Patrick Geddes, and Frederick Soddy been so completely disregarded?[16] Not to mention the radical critiques of economics launched by Karl Marx, Friedrich Engels, and their innumerable followers? In the mid-20th century, after 30 years of world war and an intervening depression, some of the most incisive objections against the failures of globalised market exchange were articulated by Karl Polanyi. The 1970s saw the elaboration of 'ecological economics' through the contributions of Nicholas Georgescu-Roegen, Howard Odum, Herman Daly, Robert Ayres, Barry Commoner, and many others. Their critique, mostly based in natural science, was recently reiterated by Vaclav Smil, who finds it 'hard to understand why modern economics, that body of explanations and precepts whose practitioners exercise more influence on public policy than any other experts, has largely ignored *energy*.'[17] Rejections of neoclassical economics voiced by natural scientists have converged with those of scholars based in the humanities and social sciences. In the 1970s, influential critiques of mainstream economic rationality were presented by Friedrich Schumacher, Ivan Illich, and Manfred Max-Neef, while André Gorz and Serge Latouche launched the idea of 'degrowth.' Since then, a long line of thinkers have continued to identify destructive features of the economy and proposed various ways in which it could be made more sustainable. A list of globally prominent voices over the past few decades would include Margrit Kennedy, Lester Brown, Wolfgang Sachs, Bill McKibben, Peter Victor, Tim Jackson, Steve Keen, Anitra Nelson, Naomi Klein, Mary Mellor, Kate Raworth, George Monbiot, and Giorgos Kallis.[18] All of them have published influential books criticising mainstream economics. Yet, they are only the most audible voices of an extensive global movement concerned that modern society's preoccupation with the management of money is socially and ecologically ruinous.

Given how massive the criticism of mainstream economics has been, it is reasonable to ask why the operation of the world economy appears to be so unperturbed by all these objections? Is it because the powerful interests underlying the hegemony of economics are so invincible, or could it be because the objections and proposals do not address the problems at a pertinent level? Given the alarming economic polarisation and ecological degradation generated by the world economy, a radical critique of economics needs to address the semiotic and cultural dimensions of the money artefact itself.[19] Social power is ultimately contingent on a system of cultural beliefs.

The artefact that shapes our thinking

In his book *Economics as Culture* (1986), Stephen Gudeman showed that the categories and premises of mainstream economics, which most of us have been taught to think of as robust tools for understanding the world, are arbitrary cultural constructions, parallel to the myths and traditions of any society ever studied by anthropologists.[20] In relativising the language of Wall Street, we can use anthropology to question the assumptions that are propelling humankind towards ever deeper inequalities and ecological disaster. Gudeman has suggested that the concept of *fuerza* (Spanish for 'strength' or 'force') that he encountered among small-scale farmers in Colombia had affinities with notions of land fertility among the 18th-century Physiocrats.[21] It seemed that both these worldviews, although 200 years apart, offered a very different understanding of economic processes than that of mainstream neoclassical economics. Moreover, their way of conceptualising the vital forces that animate human communities and the world as a whole has a lot in common with the ecological critique of economics. In this view, neither labour nor consumption are sources of economic value; ultimately, productivity derives from the crops, the soil, and the sun – or, to use a modern concept, from *energy*. The absence of this insight in the mainstream economic worldview shows how diametrically opposed economics is to fundamental material conditions established by the Second Law of Thermodynamics (the Entropy Law). Where economists see production processes as *generative*, a thermodynamic perspective must see them as *dissipative*. A corollary is that economists advocating growth are saying that they want to accelerate what in physical terms is dissipation.

What can anthropologists say about this? There is obviously not much they can do about the Second Law of Thermodynamics, but they can take a serious and critical look at the idea of money: what it means, and what it *does* to the biosphere from which it emerged. As Roy Rappaport has argued, what money means and what it does are not separate issues. 'Money,' he said, 'degrades meaning, but not only meaning. It also, and by the same token, degrades the objective world.'[22]

The ecological problem with money is not so much the occurrence of tokens of value as the belief in one single currency that measures *all* values along the same, abstract metric. Polanyi called such money 'all- or general-purpose money,' which he contrasted against 'special-purpose money.' The contrast is succinctly explained by Barry Isaac:

> Because special-purpose money (and the goods or services it purchased) circulated in only part of the economy, precapitalist economies were *multicentric*, having two or more 'spheres of exchange'; in contrast, capitalist (market) economies are by definition *unicentric*, because everything, even the factors of production, circulates in an economy unified by the market principle and the universal solvent, general-purpose money.[23]

For most of human history and in most societies known to anthropology, there have been cultural limits to what can be exchanged. An example of this is the economic system of the Tiv, a people of Nigeria studied in the 1950s by the anthropologist Paul Bohannan.[24] He argued that the Tiv had strong norms regarding what should be exchanged for what, and what kinds of exchanges were inappropriate. For example, foodstuffs should ideally be exchanged for other foodstuffs and prestige goods for other prestige goods, but not foodstuffs for prestige goods. Special-purpose currencies may be used within such spheres of exchange. In contrast to such special-purpose forms of money, general-purpose money is used for basically all kinds of exchanges. It makes all kinds of goods and services commensurable. Given this simple rule, general-purpose money has unleashed the modern, global market economy. Economists since the Marginalist Revolution in the 1870s have focused on studying the logic of the market: the mechanisms by which prices are determined, the ways in which market actors behave, the consequences of political interventions in markets, and many other aspects. In other words, the subject matter of economics is the way markets operate, *given general-purpose money*. The mandate of the economic profession is to understand the logic of such money.

In recent decades, there has been increasing interest among sociologists and other social scientists in recognising the causal role (or even 'agency') of non-living artefacts in organising social relations. This approach is particularly pronounced in the school known as Actor-Network Theory (ANT),[25] but it has so far been surprisingly disinterested in the 'agency' of money. A simple illustration of ANT thinking might begin by considering a game of chess. The outcome of the game will in part be determined by the features of the pieces as established by the rules of chess. The characteristics attributed to each piece generates the logic of the game and influences the relation between players. This perspective can be generalised to apply to the use of all the various artefacts and technologies that mediate relations between humans in modern society. Given this insight, it will be evident that a crucial consideration, if we are interested in influencing human behaviour, must be how artefacts are designed. As Arturo Escobar has emphasised, 'we design artifacts, and the artifacts design us back.'[26] Politics, in other words, should be recognised as very much a matter of how artefacts are designed.

The mandate of economists has not been to think about how money could be redesigned. Their task has been to understand how general-purpose money works. This means that the voluminous criticism of economics is not quite fair. The economists have meticulously and with great methodological sophistication traced how markets operate, given general-purpose money. Their concepts of 'efficiency' and 'rationality' have been conditioned by these circumstances. However, they have been at a loss to figure out how to deal with challenges such as increasing global unsustainability and inequality, because these trajectories are inscribed in the logic of the artefact that defines their field of vision and the operation of the world market. When maximum efficiency is defined in terms of making the best deals, and this in turn means buying goods produced with the lowest-paid labour and the least rigorous environmental legislation, market rationality will inexorably promote wider global wage gaps and increasing environmental degradation. These are ultimately consequences not of how economists think but of the design of the artefacts that *shape* how they think.

The countless critics of mainstream economics have rarely acknowledged that the problem is the design of the artefact that economics studies. Critiques have generally focused on other things such as who own the means of production, how money is produced, the conditions under which it can be borrowed, whether it yields interest,[27] whether its value is pegged to gold, the design of taxes and subsidies, and so on. All these aspects have their relevance, of course, but none of them changes the fundamental logic of general-purpose money. Modern money encourages people to make good deals at the expense of the biosphere and the global poor. To change this logic, the only option may be to constrain the global commensurability that is inscribed in general-purpose money.[28] To change the way the world market works, we must redesign money. To put it philosophically, humans must find a way of mastering the artefact that has become *their* master.

Cultural incentives and natural ramifications

To the extent that current tendencies towards greater global inequality and unsustainability are being generated by the design of regular, all-purpose money, it is important to show how this occurs. We can begin by considering Gudeman's explanation, in his book *The Anthropology of Economy* (2001), why he is not willing to accept mainstream models of market efficiency and rationality.[29] He writes that his hesitation at accepting the typical market model derives from 'its inability to account for accumulation.'[30] Indeed, the phenomenon of accumulation, profit, or surplus seems to be difficult to theorise from the perspective of neoclassical economics. Gudeman proposes that profit-making is based on value creation, which shifts the question to matters of evaluation and the origins of value. Contrary to neoclassical models, he writes, premodern mercantilists, Physiocrats, and contemporary rural communities in Latin America all view value or wealth as deriving from *outside* the economy. For the mercantilists, international trade was a zero-sum game around the management of gold and silver, which ultimately derive from nature. For the Physiocrats in 18th-century France and Latin American peasants today, wealth is also understood as a product of nature.[31] David Ricardo originally shared this view, but his labour theory of value, says Gudeman, 'shifted the agent of profit from nature to humans.'[32] Karl Marx further developed the labour theory of value by explaining that surplus value and monetary profits derive from the difference between the output and the cost of labour-power, given that the exchange-value of the products of labour is higher than the exchange-value of the goods needed to maintain that labour (the cost of food, housing, and so on). Marx considered this capacity of humans to produce more value than they require for maintenance as a 'gift of nature.' In this sense, Marx followed in the footsteps of the mercantilists, the Physiocrats, and the early Ricardo. It is telling that Marx could even write that 'labour-power itself is energy.'[33] Like Hermann von Helmholtz, who coined the concept of labour-power (*Arbeitskraft*), Marx understood the human capacity for value-generating work as a natural force.

But the problem with looking for an objective source of value – whether based on land, energy, or labour – is that such an approach neglects the difference between material force and cultural exchange-value. For a farmer, it is reasonable to think of soil fertility and good harvests as being transformed into money, but beyond farming economies, material forces and economic valuation part ways. Physiocrats and Marxists both commit the error of confusing flows of biophysical resources with monetary values. Unlike neoclassical economists, they acknowledge that the economy does have a material dimension – and this, of course, is as commendable as the efforts of the ecological economists – but they make the mistake of tracing economic value to material factors, and ultimately to nature. This is misleading. We need to find a middle road, where we clearly distinguish economics from physics, while acknowledging that economic processes that enhance exchange-values do have detrimental physical consequences. This is abundantly evident. Suffice it to reiterate the point made in Chapter 6, that the greenhouse gas emissions now threatening the biosphere are an example of *entropy* produced by the capitalist world economy.

Neoclassical economists have tried to theorise the creation of value without reference to external nature. In the modern conceptual binary of nature-versus-society, economics is as detached from nature as technology is detached from world society. The challenge is to reconnect economics to ecology without basing theories of value on nature. Gudeman has acknowledged that his ethnographic information on the concept of 'strength' (*fuerza*) among Latin American smallholders indeed suggests the insights of thermodynamics.[34] In this sense, their agrarian worldview is more aware of the biophysical conditions of accumulation than the school of neoclassical economics that has dominated the discipline since the apex of British colonialism. However, this critique of mainstream economics for not acknowledging the physical implications of the economy should not be confused with an energy theory of value. The production of value tends to have physical consequences, but value cannot be derived from physics.

Technological advances obviously require human ingenuity, but this is not a sufficient explanation of technological progress. As technologies are material structures, they can only be kept operating through a continuous input of physical resources such as fuels and spare parts. Given the Second Law of Thermodynamics, as we have seen, technological infrastructures must rely on a *physically* asymmetric exchange with their environments. In other words, the input of resources to a unit of 'technomass' must represent more highly ordered matter and energy than the sum of products and waste that it generates. The Second Law of Thermodynamics thus has two important implications for human economies that neoclassical economists are inclined to neglect. One is that the maintenance of a growing socio-metabolic infrastructure of some sort ('technomass' or 'technosphere'[35]) inevitably generates increasing entropy, as illustrated by the rising global emissions of greenhouse gases. The other is that populations controlling such infrastructure must maintain, through trade, a continuous net import of the biophysical resources required to reproduce it. This is what we have referred to as ecologically unequal exchange. In other words, the centres of 'growth' and 'progress' celebrated by mainstream economists not only accelerate the dissipation of resources but also rely on asymmetric resource transfers from their increasingly impoverished peripheries.

To approach economy and technology from the perspective of physical resource theory is to revive the non-modern insight that accumulation must ultimately draw on nature. Neither economic nor technological growth can be accounted for exclusively in terms of human creativity. This shift of perspective helps us understand the world economy as a social *metabolism* that is necessarily entwined with the planetary biosphere of which it is a part. It explains why the phenomenon conceived of as economic growth must have implications for ecological sustainability. In explaining the reliance of advanced technologies on ecologically unequal exchange, it also illuminates the widening economic gaps between what Stephen Bunker called the 'extractive' and the 'productive' sectors of the world economy.[36]

These physical constraints on human economies cannot be circumambulated through impractical policies such as 'dematerialisation' or 'circular economy.' The dematerialisation of the economy envisaged a few decades ago has been thoroughly debunked.[37] The notion of a systematic recycling of materials is similarly misguided, as it neglects the great quantities of energy required for such recycling to take place, as well as the economic logic that makes it more profitable to use low-wage labour in the peripheries to extract new resources than to use high-wage labour in core areas to recycle them. The logic of regular money and economic growth is ultimately at odds with the Law of Entropy, but mainstream economists have been able to ignore this fact by cultivating their models in isolation from the implications of thermodynamics.

In focusing exclusively on the operation of general-purpose money, neoclassical economics since the 1870s has detached itself from the biophysical context that would need to be included in any account of deepening global inequalities and unsustainability. It is the generalised commensurability posited by general-purpose money that encourages people to buy distantly derived commodities produced with minimal wages and environmental controls. Practical efforts to reject such a rationality – and the mainstream economic definition of efficiency – must entail changing the design of the tokens through which we conduct our exchange. It must mean limiting the geographical reach of much of the money with which we provision ourselves. From the perspective of northern Europe, for instance, a special-purpose currency that genuinely promotes economic localisation should not be convertible into coffee from Colombia or human labour in sweatshops in Malaysia. In restricting the bulk of consumption to what can be locally sourced, the widespread use of such a currency would inhibit both global transports and unequal exchange, while enhancing local food security, diversity, and resilience.

Since its inception in 18th-century Europe, the mandate of economics has been to study the frameworks shaping economic behaviour – for instance, markets, banks, all-purpose money – as scientific objects comparable to gravity and thermodynamics, rather than to reflect on the extent of their arbitrariness and malleability. Now that we must acknowledge the destructive impacts of our economic behaviour on global ecology and climate, it is no longer feasible to approach the premises of economic organisation with the detached objectivity fostered in natural science. We need to think about how economic institutions, principles, and artefacts could be redesigned to avoid disaster. Such a readiness to reconsider what we thought was written in stone is precisely what we can learn from economic anthropology. To understand the categories of economics as cultural is to recognise that they represent a particular perspective that to some extent is arbitrary and should be open to discussion. It means being able to challenge the reification or objectification of the products of cultural processes that is at the conceptual foundation of mainstream economics. As discussed at length in Chapter 3, such reification is encapsulated in the concept of *fetishism*. Graeber has provided a succinct and accessible perspective on fetishism:

> The social (even, to a large extent, the natural) world we live in is something we have made and are continually remaking. Our problem is that we never seem to see it fully that way and therefore can never take control over the process; everywhere, instead, people see their own creations as controlling them.[38]

Marx's arguably most seminal insight was that European economists, too, are fetishists, in the sense that they attribute autonomous agency to money and commodities, obscuring the asymmetric social relations through which these artefacts are generated. The most tangible forms of fetishism are when material objects ('things') are endowed with imaginary powers of their own.[39] In Marx's words, relations between people are represented as relations between things. For economic anthropologists, it has long been intriguing to view modern banknotes as somehow related to the exotic shell valuables that were traded between islands in premodern Melanesia.[40] In both cases, attention is deflected from social relations to focus excessively on the manipulation of *things*. Such fetishism evokes games like chess, in which the rules seem unnegotiable, and players become completely preoccupied with handling their tokens. From this perspective, it is frustrating to find the operation of the modern economy to be both constructed and unyielding at the same time. It is propelled by arbitrary human categories, yet it seems to be capable of destroying the biosphere.

A theory that proposes to provide a universal account of economic value, whether based on labour, land, energy, or some other metric, implicitly endorses the fetishism of money. It tacitly accepts that there is a single measure of value applicable to all commodities. In accepting the continued use of all-purpose money, Marx in a sense accepted *capital*, which, as Keith Hart has noted, is arguably 'another word for money.'[41] Graeber pertinently asks how radical a break with capitalism Marx's vision of socialism really was?[42] If, however, we invert the way we understand the relation between money and value, we can imagine new possibilities for challenging capitalism. In semiotic terms, this is to invert the relation between signifier and signified. Rather than saying that money is a measure of value, we might acknowledge that the concept of value, in denoting the amount of money that a commodity can fetch, derives from the artefact of money.[43]

This would make it possible for us to establish different *kinds* of value and to problematise the assumption that everything can be valued in terms of a single monetary metric. To assert that 'ecosystem services,' women's labour, or other so-called 'externalities' are 'unpaid' or 'underpaid' is to implicitly suggest that they do have a correct price. Referring to Chris Gregory's work on the Mae-Enga, Graeber notes that we can only talk about value where there is a common metric for measuring all the items exchanged.[44] Where different kinds of value are recognised, they can be compared in terms of hierarchical rank, but not in terms of abstract quantity. Money fetishism projects the peculiar notion that everything in the universe can be measured along a single, quantitative metric.[45] As James Scott puts it:

> The discipline of economics achieves its formidable resolving power by transforming what might otherwise be considered qualitative matters into quantitative issues with a single metric and, as it were, a bottom line: profit or loss.[46]

The seemingly unproblematic assumption that an hour of human labour in the global North should be convertible into several hours of labour in the South (whether expended in manufacture, food production, or resource extraction) is ultimately a notion as remarkable and insidious as the magical aspirations of alchemy. The difference is that it has very real, material implications throughout the world. To seriously address the mounting challenges of climate change, ecological degradation, and global inequalities, the mandate of economics must be not just to study the logic of general-purpose money, but to envisage ways of transcending it. Let us embark on a thought experiment on how that might be done.

Some design features of a special-purpose money conducive to sustainability

Aristotle acknowledged that money was merely a social convention. Since 'it had "come about by agreement, therefore it is within our power to change it or render it useless" if we all decide that that's what we want to do.'[47] Almost two and a half millennia later, this acknowledgement continues to inspire utopian ideas about how we might change the money system in which we are all entangled. Bjerg declares that,

> [i]f democracy is to mean anything in capitalism, it must include the right of citizens to have an influence not only on *how* the government spends the money of the community but also on *which kind* of money should be circulating in the community.[48]

Jack Weatherford's vision of a future with electronic, special-purpose currencies assumes a spiritual dimension:

> Throughout its history, money has become steadily more abstract. By moving at the speed of light, electronic money has become the most

> powerful financial, political, and social force in the world. Money has become even more like God: totally abstract and without corporeal body.[49]

When tokens symbolising specific social obligations are reified into impersonal, desirable objects that are counted, hoarded, and plundered, the result is what Marx called 'money fetishism.' Given the digital technologies for managing electronic money that have been developed since the abandonment of the gold standard in 1971, we may indeed glimpse the possibility of an economy where money serves humans, instead of the other way around. The system of complementary currencies that I shall outline here could potentially be managed without any physical tokens to fetishise.

In imagining a utopian currency reform, the first thing that comes to mind is 'local money.' The idea is simple and persuasive. In creating a special kind of money – a complementary or community currency – that only circulates within a given geographical area, it is assumed that people will be able to control the flows of labour and other resources that leave or enter their community. In reaction to the inherently destructive and exploitative consequences of general-purpose money, experiments with such money have been conducted since the early 19th century.[50] Over the past four decades, a great number of experiments with local community currencies have appeared throughout the world. Pioneering and famous are the so-called LETS systems originating in Canada in 1983.[51] A survey of community currencies in 23 countries, published in 2013, found a total of 3,418 local projects.[52] It is arguable that what they all have in common is the desire to safeguard what Gudeman calls a 'base' or 'community'[53] – a sphere of social and place-based relations that is experienced as threatened by the dissolvent logic of the market. They show how next to universal is the urge to resist the idea that everything can be exchanged for money. Their foundational message is that there is a *limit* to commensurability.

These efforts to localise economies are highly justified, but they generally have not accomplished what they were intended to do.[54] They have failed to decisively challenge the logic of globalisation. There are several reasons for this. One is that the category of people engaged in these projects tend to belong to arbitrary networks of dedicated acquaintances with limited goods and services to offer for exchange, which means that most of their provisioning will continue to be through ordinary money and the regular market – and that their engagement will only last as long as their enthusiasm. The possibilities of earning and spending the local currency will be very uneven, and the long-term viability of such projects quite dubious.[55]

Another problem is that there is no way of distinguishing local *purchases* from local *produce*. Even if a person restricts his or her purchases to a given locale, the products sold there may derive from the other side of the planet. 'Local money' thus does not effectively localise the economy in the way many expect.[56] While it may encourage people to turn to local retailers, there is nothing to stop those shops from using regular money to access their wares, which means displacing work and environmental loads in accordance with the general logic of globalised capitalism.

These two obstacles to using community currencies to create more sustainable and just economies – the marginal involvement of users and the inability to seriously challenge globalisation – can only be overcome by finding ways (a) to encourage most people to use them and (b) to link them to goods and services that are largely locally produced. To do both these things would be possible by combining two distinct ideas on how to challenge regular market exchange: that of (a) a universal basic income (UBI) and that of (b) a complementary currency. The *combination* of basic income and complementary currency has huge potential because each of the two proposals compensates for the shortcomings of the other: a society using a complementary currency can specify *how* it is to be used but may find that only a minority of people gain access to it (by offering their goods or services), while a society with a universal basic income will provide general access but is unable to specify its use (which means simply reinforcing globalised capitalism). In combination, however, the two ideas could make it feasible for a society to simultaneously promote general economic security and sustainability.

After decades of deploring the failure of individual nations aiming for social and ecological reforms to challenge the logic of globalisation, we can thus begin to see a possible way forward. By establishing a special-purpose complementary currency, national or municipal authorities would be able to promote consumption patterns that comply with democratically embraced ideals such as increasing sustainability, local diversity, or global justice. By distributing it as a basic income for all members of society, they can encourage universal use of the special-purpose currency and simultaneously provide a basic social security as protection against the vicissitudes of the world market.

One of the closest examples I have encountered of an initiative in this direction is a recent experiment with 'universal basic vouchers' (UBV) in Korea.[57] Distributed among unemployed youth in the form of paper or electronic vouchers, such tokens can be used to encourage specific kinds of consumption. The economist Joseph Stiglitz has praised the Korean initiative for devising a system that can benefit the local economy.[58] To counter the logic of globalisation, basic income must be paid in a currency with limited commensurability. The category of 'vouchers' is currently the closest concept at hand, but it would be theoretically possible to design a complementary currency that is similarly limited. Such a system would require that goods and services are *transport certified*, that is, marked not just in terms of the time elapsed since production, but also in terms of the distance between the place of production and the point of purchase – acknowledging space as well as time. The idea is a bit more complex than Expiry Dates and certification schemes such as Fair Trade or Organic, but it is not at all unfeasible. The maximum transport distance should vary depending on where in a country a person resides, with the category 'locally produced' being more generously defined in areas with less agricultural land and other resources. In contrast to the Korean vouchers, which are used only for one-way transactions, the tokens of exchange should be possible to recycle through an indefinite number of transactions, while retaining the limitation to specific kinds of goods and services. The crucial design feature of a currency established to localise the economy would be that it can only be exchanged for goods and services that are produced within a given geographical radius from the point of purchase.

A second consideration is the proportion of a commodity that derives from local production processes, rather than from distant sources. Such estimations are more problematic for manufactured products than for services and for agricultural and other primary products, which suggests that the system might initially focus on the latter. It is reasonable to expect the circulation of large quantities of a complementary currency seeking locally sourced purchases to encourage the development of diverse new local products and services. The establishment of such a complementary currency should thus stimulate a long-term transition towards an economy that generates less transports (and thus greenhouse gas emissions) and enhances local diversity and resilience.

A necessary condition for this kind of system is that it is administered by authorities, whether at the federal or local level, as this would be a feasible way of organising a system of universal benefits such as UBI or UBV. This in turn has several important implications. It means that it will need to have the support of a political majority and cannot simply operate as a bottom-up movement with ideological overtones challenging established economic institutions. The advantages of having such a foundation are numerous in terms of impact, efficiency, and fairness, but an obvious *dis*advantage is that such 'localising' money cannot be conjured as a grassroots initiative, without the support of political authorities.

There are, in other words, big differences between the system considered here and the idea of 'local money.' I am not suggesting local money in the sense of geographically delimited currencies, but *one single* national currency that can only be used for local transactions. There is no question of reverting to a cumbersome patchwork of local currencies as in premodern times, but of creating a currency whose reach is defined with reference to the geographical location of each individual. The main thing is not where goods are purchased but how far they have been transported before being purchased, which could be certified much as we are today accustomed to finding dairy products marked with packaging dates. As consumers we are arguably entitled to information not just about the time that has elapsed since production, but also about the distance that the product has been transported.

Given the utopian character of proposals for redesigning money,[59] it follows that such schemes must be based on imagined futures rather than limiting themselves to the study of past or existing experiments.[60] Although we certainly have reasons to scrutinise earlier experiments, the aim should be to learn from their shortcomings in order to develop new ways of avoiding them. Among recurrent failures reported from attempts to establish complementary or community currencies are: low levels of participation among citizens as well as enterprises; inefficient administration; instability over time, due to unpredictable commitment of key proponents; limitation of transactions to a narrow range of goods and services; negligible impact on consumption and resource flows; uneven distribution of credit, providing some individuals with unfair advantages; and confrontational rather than cooperative relations with authorities.[61] The system outlined here suggests how these deficiencies could be alleviated.

The challenge of designing an economic system that encourages sustainable practices is to envisage organisational features that provide incentives and rewards for various actors to engage in such practices. We thus need to ask what could motivate individual consumers to use the complementary currency (CC),[62] why an enterprise would accept payment in it, and why the authorities might want to promote it. Let us consider these stakeholders one by one. To begin with, we can assume that the individual consumer will view the monthly receipt of an allotted quantity of CC as a welcome addition to his or her income, even if its potential for purchasing goods is geographically circumscribed. At the outset of the reform, the range of purchases accessible with this currency may be restricted to services and locally produced food, but over time it would be likely to expand significantly. An immediate effect of the CC will be to liberate a portion of the person's regular income that had previously been spent on products and services that could in principle be provided locally – for instance, vegetables, carpentry, and baby-sitting. We can thus expect incentives to utilise the CC income to the greatest possible extent. One objective is to stimulate a diversification of local enterprise to the point where the monthly income in CC will be able to provide for an individual's most basic needs.[63]

As enterprises will be offered the opportunity to pay taxes in CC, and perhaps also to exchange, through the authorities, a proportion of their CC income into regular money, they can be expected to welcome additional transactions conducted in CC. Moreover, there will be incentives for the establishment of a wide range of new enterprises catering to the substantial new niche represented by the great demand for local products and services created by the CC. To encourage this process, the authorities may provide economic help to entrepreneurs starting up new local businesses, particularly in high-demand repairs (such as tailors, shoe repairs, bicycle maintenance) and recycling.[64] The creation of the CC economy as a distinct sector or 'sphere of exchange' would generate symbiotic, positive feedback processes linking individual needs and entrepreneurial initiatives at the local level. The CC distributed by the authorities would circulate between households and enterprises, organising local flows of goods and services while continuously being returned to the authorities as businesses pay taxes and convert some of their CC income into regular money. The rate at which CC is returned to the authorities can be increased or decreased by adjusting the exchange rate between CC and regular money, thus encouraging or discouraging conversion.[65]

The conversion of CC into regular money is pivotal, as it is the point at which the actual cost of the system is revealed. By depressing the exchange rate, the authorities can encourage enterprises to use their CC to source, as far as possible, their labour and other production inputs from the local market. In diminishing the input of regular money into local social metabolism, they correspondingly reduce the demands of the community on global resource flows. By modifying the conversion rate, the authorities can thus successively augment the economic diversity, autonomy, and resilience of communities. This should not only improve sustainability, global justice, food security, and community cohesion but also reduce the public costs of transport infrastructure, emissions reductions, waste management, social security, and undoubtedly also health care. In the long run, the implementation of a CC sector may prove to be less of a strain on public finance than the currently escalating costs of business as usual. A more immediate way of financing the reform would be to successively make a proportion of social security payments – such as pensions, sickness benefits, unemployment insurance, and family allowance – in the form of CC.[66] Faced with ever higher costs for mitigating climate change, reducing traffic accidents, counteracting eutrophication, maintaining biodiversity, and keeping people economically secure and healthy, there may come a time when national authorities would welcome a reform such as this, even for purely financial reasons.

Technically, the reform is not more complex than establishing the Euro; although aiming in opposite directions, both initiatives illustrate that money systems are not unnegotiable facts of life but can be dramatically transformed. A crucial point is that the CC is not offered as a challenge to globalised currencies, but as a complement to them. Sustainability should be sought in their relation. Rather than local versus globalised production processes competing on the same market, to the systematic advantage of those profiting from the lowest-paid labour and the least rigorous environmental legislation, they would complement each other in accordance with the conditions at hand. The use of the CC, to the extent circumstances permit, would make local economies more secure, resilient, and sustainable.

The key to redesigning the economy in this way is the recognition of a distinction between two separate kinds of values that are not easily commensurable. While general-purpose money and modern business as usual recognises no such distinction, the existence of a special-purpose money (CC) would signify that a distinction is made and codified in social institutions.[67] How the distinction should be characterised is a debateable point, but categories such as 'local' versus 'global' and 'long-term' versus 'short-term'[68] seem relevant. From the perspective of a philosophy of money, the distinction between two complementary kinds of money is requisite to curbing the runaway logic of general-purpose money, which inexorably pursues endless accumulation and growth, the flip side of which is ecological degradation and deepening inequalities. We need to understand that the notion of universal interchangeability of values is detrimental to the biosphere, human society, and culture. As we have seen, the magic of general-purpose money derives from a sign that can stand for anything at all that its owner wants it to represent – a sign, that is, without a referent. This is what drives ecological, economic, and existential impoverishment. In positing a significant difference between the local and the global and between the long-term and the short-term, a complementary currency designed along the lines sketched here would encode *meaning* into the fabric of our economy.

Notes

1 This utopian proposal for 'social engineering' has largely been developed within a research project on 'Special-purpose money for sustainability,' funded by Formas, the Swedish Research Council for Sustainable Development, grant number 2020-00402.
2 Georgescu-Roegen 1971; Odum 1971; Commoner 1971; Meadows *et al.* 1972; Schumacher 1973; Illich 1973.
3 Schandl *et al.* 2016.
4 Catton 1980; Wackernagel and Rees 1996; WorldWide Fund for Nature 2022.
5 Schumacher 1973; Illich 1973; Mander and Goldsmith 1996; Heinberg 2007; McKibben 2007; Greer 2008, 2011; Trainer 2020; Smaje 2020.
6 Heinberg 2004, 2005; Kunstler 2005; Smil 2015; Murphy *et al.* 2021.
7 Smil 2022.
8 Asafu-Adjaye *et al.* 2015; Phillips 2015; Bastani 2019.
9 Tainter 1988; Homer-Dixon 2006.
10 Hine and Kingsnorth 2009; Scranton 2015.
11 Kaczynski 2016; Zerzan 2002; Malm 2021.
12 Scott 2017; Graeber and Wengrow 2021.
13 Bauman 2012: xix.
14 Just to give one example, Yuval Noah Harari (2011: 207) calls money 'the apogee of human tolerance.'
15 The byzantine complexity of our entanglement in our own sign systems is well illustrated by contemporary deliberations on the implications of financialisation and financial crises, as well as by attempts to decipher the intricate convolutions of Marx's ruminations on money; de Brunhoff [1973] 2015; Moseley 2016.
16 For an overview of these objections, see Martinez-Alier 1987.
17 Smil 2022: 21; emphasis added.
18 Among these influential critics of mainstream economics, only Anitra Nelson (2022: 45) has resolutely concluded that the idea of money itself is the problem: 'The conclusion is clear: we need to do away with money, not simply capital.'
19 Eisenstein (2011: 214) observes that '[m]oney is so fundamental, so defining of our civilization, that it would be naïve to hope for any authentic civilizational shift that did not involve a fundamental shift in money as well.'
20 Gudeman 1986.
21 Gudeman and Rivera 1990.
22 Rappaport 1979: 131.
23 Isaac 2005: 16; emphasis in original.
24 Bohannan 1955.
25 Latour 2005.

26 Escobar 2018.
27 The charging of interest on loans is the target of one of the oldest critiques of money. Condemned as 'usury' in the Middle Ages, it is also often denounced as a driver of compulsive economic growth leading to ecological degradation. Paradoxically, proposals on its antithesis – 'decaying' or negative-interest currency – have been conceived as a means of increasing the velocity of economic transactions (that is, *stimulating* economic growth). Rather than aligning the economy with the Entropy Law, decaying money could thus be expected to accelerate the dissipation of resources. Adjustments of interest rates – whether positive, zero, or negative – can affect the speed of economic processes but not their fundamentally dissolvent ramifications.
28 Jean-Michel Servet (2009) observes that recent efforts to organise alternative currencies can be seen as an affirmation, in the age of neoliberal globalisation, of Polanyi's denunciation of the generalised fungibility of general-purpose money and the world market. Hart (2009: 97) and Graeber (2009: 106) note that the relevance of Polanyi's work has never been greater than now.
29 Gudeman 2001: 97–107.
30 Gudeman 2001: 97.
31 It is significant that Gudeman discovers this affinity between 18th-century Physiocracy and contemporary peasants living off the land; Gudeman and Rivera 1990. Whereas the economies of nonmodern societies have always struggled with local, natural constraints, it can be argued that the technologies of the Industrial Revolution represent the emergence of strategies to displace such constraints to other parts of world society.
32 Gudeman 2001: 100.
33 Marx cited in Burkett and Foster 2006: 120.
34 Gudeman 2012.
35 Zalasiewicz *et al.* 2017.
36 Bunker 1985.
37 Schandl *et al.* 2016; Parrique *et al.* 2019.
38 Graeber 2001: 239.
39 Graeber 2001: 65. Graeber (2005: 451) writes that '[f]etishism occurs when we assume that the value comes from the token, rather than ourselves.'
40 Graeber (2001: 81) observes that, '[j]ust as value seems to come from money, so fame and glory seems to emerge from the armshells and necklaces exchanged between kula partners.'
41 Hart 2009: 95.
42 Graeber 2001: 248.
43 Eisenstein (2011: 164) similarly suggests that, rather than dollars (pegged to gold) being valuable because they could be exchanged for gold, 'gold was valuable because it could be converted into dollars.'
44 Graeber 2001: 41.
45 Graeber 2001: xi. In practice, however, even modern people tend to maintain 'cultural values denying that all goods are commensurate'; Hart 2005: 165.
46 Scott 1998: 346.
47 Aristotle cited by Graeber 2011: 298.
48 Bjerg 2014: 259; emphasis in original.
49 Weatherford 1997: 248–249. Some modern deliberations on money illustrate the enduring connection between money and metaphysics, as suggested by Seaford (2004). The messianic visionary Charles Eisenstein (2011) juxtaposes reasoned proposals for monetary reform with a spiritual idiom that jars with his generally rigorous denunciation of contemporary money. His book *Sacred Economics* thus intersperses valid critiques of standardisation, limitlessness, degradation,

impersonality, and avarice – all traceable to money – with implausible fantasies and millenarian prophecies bordering on New Age. His level-headed advocacy of negative-interest currency, localisation, and degrowth is presented alongside astonishing speculations on connections between solar activity and financial crisis (Eisenstein 2011: 183, n7), secretly repressed energy technologies that violate the Second Law of Thermodynamics (Eisenstein 2011: 443), and – 'by the end of our lifetimes' – the restoration of the Sahara Desert to rich grassland (Eisenstein 2011: 445).

50 North 2007.

51 Bowring 1998; Dobson 1993.

52 Seyfang and Longhurst 2013.

53 Gudeman 2001.

54 Blanc 2012; Dittmer 2013, 2015.

55 Eisenstein (2011: 298) observes that 'local currencies only work if there is a local system of locally circulating production' that is not forced to compete with inexpensive imports.

56 Marshall and O'Neill 2018.

57 Seung-Yoon Lee *et al.* 2020. I thank Ester Barinaga for bringing this initiative to my attention.

58 Stiglitz 2021.

59 Dodd 2015.

60 In a more general sense, because the phenomenon of money transcends the local case study, it largely remains inaccessible to ethnography; Hart and Ortiz 2014.

61 Blanc 2012; Dittmer 2013, 2015.

62 Although I am averse to acronyms, I shall henceforth write CC instead of the rather cumbersome 'complementary currency.'

63 To the extent that this objective is accomplished, it should in principle be possible for individuals wishing to do so to subsist largely or even entirely on CC. This would mean not having to rely on formal employment or social security, but liberating individuals to pursue whatever social and creative activities they prefer. In effect, this would dissolve the proletarian condition – the imperative to sell one's labour in order to survive – that Marx identified as the foundation of capitalism.

64 Visions of a 'circular economy' may thus be more likely to materialise through such structural changes of the economy than through attempts to technologically reorganise production.

65 This would be the main tool through which the authorities could regulate inflation in the CC economy.

66 Note that this would only apply to a *proportion* of such payments, as it is crucial that everyone has adequate access to both currencies.

67 An early precursor unearthed by archaeologists might be Bronze Age Mesopotamia, where '[w]e should, perhaps, see grain as a parallel currency to silver, used purely in domestic, as opposed to international, exchanges'; Green *et al.* 2024: 138.

68 See Bloch and Parry 1989.

Afterword

Throughout its ten chapters, the underlying theme of this book has been the repercussions of money. We have seen how the money sign emerged out of the human capacity for symbolic thought. Viewed from an evolutionary perspective, it was a completely new semiotic phenomenon with convulsive social and ecological ramifications. Money integrated vast empires and predatory systems of trade, enabling kings and emperors to muster great armies to conquer new territories and enslave their populations. Beyond the age of overt political imperialism, exploitation was delegated to the seemingly neutral operation of the world market. In making all things commensurable, money has made human labour and other resources throughout the world accessible for extraction by successful accumulators.

We have argued that money fundamentally transformed the relations that humans have to each other and to the natural environment, shaping the social condition of modernity as well as the detached and objectifying worldview of modern science. While conducive to abstract philosophies and religions that supplanted animism, money simultaneously entangled us in its fetishism. Specialists entrusted with understanding the ways of money have become so preoccupied with its logic that they remain peculiarly oblivious about the materiality of the social and ecological world that it is transforming. Money obscures the uneven global transfers of embodied labour and other resources from areas where they are cheap to areas where they are accumulated in increasingly advanced technologies. The materiality of technologies sustains the illusion that they are not based on such unequal social relations of exchange. As we discover that our technologies are devastating the biosphere and the atmosphere, the standard response is to aggravate our fetishism by proposing that we invest in yet more technologies. Even the most radical critics of modern society tend to think in terms shaped by the concept of money and trust in the corrective powers of technology. The fetishism of money and machines, obscuring their dependence on asymmetric global exchange, thus continues to delude mainstream recipes for sustainability.

Meanwhile, money-propelled processes of trade and globalisation undermine biological and cultural diversity. The extent to which such

DOI: 10.4324/9781032702186-15

homogenisation is a result of the logic of money is evident when we contrast current conditions with those of premodern societies that lacked money. They give us insights on how social and human–environmental relations can be organised when they are not dominated by general-purpose money. Such insights continue to haunt many modern people, who sense that the global expansion of commercial civilisation in many ways has been detrimental to the long-term good of humankind. While it would be naïve to consider revitalising premodern conditions, we have much to learn from anthropology's comparative study of human societies through time and space. The documentation of different forms of non-modern social organisation indicates how creatively humans have explored a wide range of options and how some of those options could inspire contemporary efforts to envisage just and sustainable societies. A compelling conclusion regarding the history of money is that its inherent tendency to degrade both social and ecological relations has been underestimated and widely misunderstood.

In some respects, the perspectives that I have evoked in this book share concerns that are frequently voiced by proponents of the so-called ontological turn in anthropology and other social sciences. This is not to say, however, that I share its excessive relativism. Some of its foremost exponents – for instance, Bruno Latour, Eduardo Viveiros de Castro, and Philippe Descola – reject the Enlightenment understanding of cultural diversity as representing different interpretations of a single objective reality, proposing instead that the premisses of non-modern cultural worlds should be understood as no less valid than those of modern science. While perhaps commendably open-minded and unprejudiced, this is a position that I cannot subscribe to. It is significant, however, that the radical rejection of the modern worldview by proponents of the ontological turn may have been provoked – as is the current book – by the global ecological crisis of the Anthropocene.[1]

One aspect of the ontological turn that I sympathise with is the persuasion that anthropology must find ways to illuminate the trajectory of modern society within the context of the global biosphere *beyond the realm of the human*.[2] Driven by this conviction, I have approached money as an eco- or biosemiotic phenomenon with dramatic ramifications. As I argue in Chapter 1, to treat humankind as one species among many is not tantamount to abandoning analytical distinctions between the semiotic agencies of different species.

Another theme that I share with some proponents of the ontological turn is the aspiration towards a *renewed materialism*. Concerns with the interpenetration of human societies and their biophysical environments are imperative. Rather than confine itself to philosophy, the new materialism must be prepared to address the asymmetric global transfers of material resources that are veiled by what mainstream economists approach as balanced flows of money. Again, acknowledging the ubiquitous interpenetration of society and physical nature does not mean abandoning the *analytical* distinction between them.

The concurrence with ontological anthropology on these two seemingly antithetical points is not a coincidence, because both are aspects – the eco-semiotic and the material – of the world economy that have been omitted from the modern worldview. Modern humans have been too preoccupied with their monetary signs to see how starkly they differ from the other sign systems of the biosphere, or to trace their devastating material repercussions. Juxtaposed with the Second Law of Thermodynamics, the inexorable logic of general-purpose money is to reward activities that accelerate the dissipation of resources and the production of entropy. Yet, of the vast numbers of philosophers, historians, sociologists, and anthropologists who have addressed the modern environmental predicament, very few even mention money as a problem.

A third concern that this book shares with the ontological turn is the conundrum of animism. It can be argued that shifts from animistic to transcendentalist worldviews are related to transformations of social relations – from balanced to negative reciprocity – generated by the logic of money. The fetishisation of money is itself an illustration of the immanentism that is fundamental to animism, yet money appears to have historically contributed to the displacement of such relational ontologies. However, ontologically oriented anthropologists have approached animism in Amazonia and elsewhere as literal accounts of other worlds. In accepting that nonhuman and even abiotic components of human environments may be considered *persons*, such ethnographies could be adduced in support of the increasingly serious political and legal deliberations on the 'rights of nature.' Luc Ferry's ([1992] 1995) book *The New Ecological Order* is a reminder that such deliberations have been conducted by parts of the environmental movement since its inception in the 1960s, but it also reminds us of their fundamental incompatibility with the worldview consolidated during the Enlightenment and what Sahlins has called the 'Second Axial Age.'[3] As Ferry asks,

> [D]oesn't claiming [that there are 'interests' held by] trees, rocks, or the biosphere as a whole lean toward an animism comparable to that which informed the medieval trials of grasshoppers or weevils?[4]

Today, more than 30 years after Ferry voiced this dismissal of deep ecology, the severity of the advancing ecological crisis at first sight appears to be eclipsing his objections. Given that *money itself is indirectly granted personhood* – through the mechanical pursuit of profits among corporations that are granted the status of 'legal persons' – it is increasingly difficult to see why the agenda of an Amazonian rainforest should have less legal support than that of capitalist enterprise. Governments in New Zealand, Ecuador, and Bolivia have famously granted legal rights to rivers and Earth itself. Do the tenets of the Enlightenment need to be abandoned in the interest of sustainability? This is a most difficult issue to digest, suggesting that we must choose between our modern ontology and survival.[5] Clearly, what we think of as historical progress does not contradict the fact that human history is inviting global disaster. It is not logically defensible to maintain faith in money and technology because they have so far been a source of benefits for the privileged. There is no contradiction in describing money as simultaneously 'devilish acid [and] as instrument and guarantor of liberty' (for some).[6] Both narratives are valid, but for different categories of people and for different species.

Let us consider the concept of 'free trade.' Neoliberal arguments for free trade suggest that it is emancipatory for everyone, but they do not consider how the artefact of money imposes restrictions and impoverishment on one part in the exchange. For instance, free flows of money imply the imposition of highly *unfree* conditions for miners and sweatshop workers in the global South. The obscenely unequal world economy was illuminated by a report from the United Nations Environment Programme which calculated that food corresponding to over a billion meals per day (19% of all food produced) was discarded in 2022 – and another 13% wasted in transport and storage – while 783 million people suffer from hunger and a third of humanity faces food insecurity.[7] Between 8% and 10% of annual emissions of greenhouse gases derive from the production of food that is wasted. The economic value of wasted food is about a trillion (a thousand billion) dollars, representing a third of all food produced globally and requiring 28% of global agricultural land. Clearly, the alleged 'efficiency' of the world market has very different implications for people depending on which household they were born into.

For a writer aiming to identify sources of social and environmental injustices, the immediate urge is to express indignation over the state of the world and to denounce its main beneficiaries. Eduardo Galeano's pioneering book *Open Veins of Latin America* is a model for such agitated narratives.[8] But on closer consideration it is difficult to derive the bulk of the suffering in the world from immoral behaviour. Most people simply make the most out of the circumstances in which they find themselves, and those circumstances tend to be generated by impersonal structural forces deriving from the social institutions and artefacts with whose logic their lives are entangled. The exoneration of individual humans from the global repercussions of money will appear to some as mystification, to others as a faith in basic human benevolence.

To trace the devastation of the world to the design of a human artefact is to reject the pervasive inclination to blame some category of people for the destruction, whether affluent consumers, capitalists, and the fossil-fuel lobby or the various implausible culprits identified by right-wing conspiracy theorists.[9] It does not seem reasonable to criticise individual humans in supermarkets or boardrooms for behaving in accordance with the injunctions inscribed in general-purpose money. To analyse the drivers of socio-ecological processes is not to moralise over wrongdoers but to identify the conditions of their existence as specified by the artefact of general-purpose money.

While there may be highly moral people who can resist the everyday avarice inscribed in money, they are unfortunately too few to make a difference. We cannot count on making the world a better place by appealing to morals, but it *is* theoretically possible to organise an economy that is more conducive to justice and sustainability than the current order. Such a reform would ultimately have to tackle the design of the money artefact. Rather than positing that nonhuman nature has legal rights, it would be more consonant with the premisses of the Enlightenment to dethrone the fetishised money god that is threatening to dismantle it. The challenge posed by the Anthropocene to modern ontology is to recognise the power of artefacts to shape human behaviour, but without attributing agency and volition to them. It is quite feasible to viably align human economies with a congenial biosphere without revitalising animism.

Global inequalities and the skewed distribution of modern technologies are clearly moral issues, but they do not derive from individual immorality. If loss of jobs, meanings, and aesthetic values were the only critiques to be launched at the advance of technocratic rationality, its progress could simply be deplored as inevitable – which indeed seems to be the majority position. But given that it is also exploitative and unjust, the logic of economic and technological expansion must ultimately be problematised as a moral and political issue, and as not at all inevitable. If techno-economic growth and monetary design are understood in this way, there is at least a chance that democratic political agency will be informed by this moral perspective.

Viewed in an evolutionary and planetary context, diversity loss and climate change are afflictions of the biosphere, like fever in an infected organism. It is insufficient to conceptualise these crises in terms of a contradiction between human society and nature. The human species is the *part* of the biosphere that is causing the crises – and simultaneously the only part that can reflect on (and perhaps mitigate) its agency. To transcend the traditional society/nature divide without relinquishing human responsibility, we must recognise that our species is the only part of the biosphere that is capable of consciously modifying its future. In that respect, pivoting on the human capacity to symbolise and imagine things otherwise, the distinction between nature and society remains warranted. If humanity will be able to avoid disaster, it will be the biosphere gaining control over itself. The lesson it/we will have learned is that the money sign was a disastrous experiment that now needs to be reconsidered.

When ancient Greeks first contemplated the stamped coins that began to circulate in the sixth century BCE, they would have been puzzled by their metaphysical properties. These little metal discs had the peculiar property of being convertible into anything at all. It is useful to remind ourselves of those original assessments. It has taken us 2,600 years to realise that money, while ultimately based only on our collective beliefs and agreements, has the power to dissolve the world.

Notes

1 This interpretation is persuasively argued by Eduardo Kohn (2015).
2 Kohn 2013.
3 Sahlins 2022.
4 Ferry [1992] 1995: 131.
5 It is not surprising to find Latour's (2024) final book not only returning to theology but also advocating a rejection of all forms of transcendentalism. Referring to Pope Francis' widely praised 2015 encyclical *Laudato Si*,' Latour writes: 'To put it bluntly, *it is transcendence that has become misleading*, not to say diabolical, and it is immanence – that immanence scorned by centuries of "spirituality" – that is becoming desirable in moral and civic terms'; Latour 2024: 52, emphasis in original. It puzzles me, however, that an ontology endorsing an immanentist version of Catholicism and emphasising the agency of artefacts should never mention Mammon or the proverbial 'root of all evil.'
6 Bloch and Parry 1989: 30.
7 United Nations Environment Programme 2024.
8 Galeano 1973.
9 While it is common to denounce the 'fossil-fuel lobby' as responsible for global warming, the extent to which humankind as a whole has become entangled in the drivers of climate change is illustrated by the fact that 'the modern world's most important – and fundamentally existential – dependence on fossil fuels is their direct and indirect use in the production of our food'; Smil 2022: 47.

References

Adas, Michael. 1989. *Machines as the measure of men: Science, technology, and ideologies of Western dominance*. Ithaca, NY: Cornell University Press.

Adelaar, Willem F.H., and Pieter C. Muysken. 2004. *The languages of the Andes*. Cambridge: Cambridge University Press.

Aikhenvald, Alexandra Y. 2002. *Language contact in Amazonia*. Oxford: Oxford University Press.

Altvater, Elmar. 2006. The social and natural environment of fossil capitalism. In *Coming to terms with nature*, edited by Leo Panitch and Colin Leys, 37–59. New York: Monthly Review Press.

Andersen, Otto. 2013. *Unintended consequences of renewable energy*. London: Springer.

Anderson, Eugene N. 1996. *Ecologies of the heart: Emotion, belief, and the environment*. Oxford: Oxford University Press.

Anderson, Will. 2006. Tribal whaling poses new threat. In *The environment in anthropology: A reader in ecology, culture, and sustainable living*, edited by Nora Haenn and Richard R. Wilk, 386–389. New York: New York University Press.

Angus, Ian. 2016a. *Facing the Anthropocene: Fossil capitalism and the crisis of the Earth system*. New York: Monthly Review Press.

Angus, Ian. 2016b. 'Anthropocene or Capitalocene?' misses the point. *Climate & Capitalism*, September 26, 2016.

Apter, Emily, and William Pietz, editors. 1993. *Fetishism as cultural discourse*. Ithaca, NY: Cornell University Press.

Århem, Kaj. 1996. The cosmic food web: Human-nature relatedness in the Northwest Amazon. In *Nature and society: Anthropological perspectives*, edited by Philippe Descola and Gísli Pálsson, 185–204. London: Routledge.

Århem, Kaj. 1998. Powers of place: Landscape, territory and local belonging in Northwest Amazonia. In *Locality and belonging*, edited by Nadia Lovell, 78–102. London: Routledge.

Århem, Kaj. 2016. Animism and the hunter's dilemma: Hunting, sacrifice and asymmetric exchange among the Katu of Vietnam. In *Animism in Southeast Asia*, edited by Kaj Århem and Guido Sprenger, 91–113. London: Routledge.

Aristotle. 1995. *Politics*. Oxford: Oxford University Press.

Asafu-Adjaye, John, Linus Blomqvist, Stewart Brand, Barry Brook, Ruth DeFries, Erle Ellis, Christopher Foreman, D. Keith, M. Lewis, M. Lynas, T. Nordhaus, R. Pielke, Jr., R. Pritzker, J. Roy, M. Sagoff, M. Shellenberger, R. Stone, and P. Teague. 2015. An ecomodernist manifesto. www.ecomodernism.org

Ayres, Robert U., and Allen V. Kneese. 1969. Production, consumption, and externalities. *The American Economic Review* 59(3): 282–297.

Balée, William. 1994. *Footprints of the forest: Ka'apor ethnobotany – The historical ecology of plant utilization by an Amazonian people*. New York: Columbia University Press.

Bar-On, Yinon M., Rob Phillips, and Ron Milo. 2018. The biomass distribution on Earth. *PNAS* 115(25): 6506–6511.

Barjamovic, Gojko. 2018. Interlocking commercial networks and the infrastructure of trade in Western Asia during the Bronze Age. In *Trade and civilization: Economic networks and cultural ties, from prehistory to the early modern era*, edited by Kristian Kristiansen, Thomas Lindkvist, and Janken Myrdal, 113–142. Cambridge: Cambridge University Press.

Barth, Fredrik, editor. [1969] 1998. *Ethnic groups and boundaries: The social organization of culture difference*. Oslo: Universitetsforlaget.

Basso, Keith. 1996. *Wisdom sits in places: Landscape and language among the Western Apache*. Albuquerque: University of New Mexico Press.

Bastani, Aaron. 2019. *Fully automated luxury communism: A manifesto*. London: Verso.

Bateson, Gregory. 1958. *Naven: A survey of the problems suggested by a composite picture of the culture of a New Guinea tribe drawn from three points of view*. Stanford, CA: Stanford University Press.

Bateson, Gregory. 1972. *Steps to an ecology of mind*. Frogmore: Paladin.

Baudrillard, Jean. [1972] 1981. *For a critique of the political economy of the sign*. St. Louis, MO: Telos.

Baudrillard, Jean. [1976] 1993. *Symbolic exchange and death*. London: Sage.

Bauer, Brian S. 2004. *Ancient Cuzco: Heartland of the Inca*. Austin: University of Texas Press.

Bauman, Zygmunt. 2012. Liquid modernity. Cambridge: Polity.

Bellah, Robert N., and Hans Joas, editors. 2012. *The Axial Age and its consequences*. Cambridge, MA: The Belknap Press of Harvard University Press.

Bellofiore, Riccardo. 2018. The multiple meanings of Marx's value theory. *Monthly Review* 69: 11.

Bennett, Jane. 2010. *Vibrant matter: A political ecology of things*. Durham, NC: Duke University Press.

Beresford-Jones, David, and Paul Heggarty. 2012. Broadening our horizons: Towards an interdisciplinary prehistory of the Andes. In *Archaeology and language in the Andes: A cross-disciplinary exploration of prehistory*, edited by Paul Heggarty and David Beresford-Jones, 57–84. Proceedings of The British Academy 173. Oxford: Oxford University Press.

Berg, Maxine. 1980. *The machinery question and the making of political economy 1815–1848*. Cambridge: Cambridge University Press.

Berkes, Fikret. 1999. *Sacred ecology: Traditional ecological knowledge and resource management*. London: Taylor & Francis.

Berman, Marshall. 1982. *All that is solid melts into air: The experience of modernity*. London: Verso.

Bijker, Wiebe E., Thomas P. Hughes, and Trevor J. Pinch, editors. 1987. *The social construction of technological systems: New directions in the sociology and history of technology*. Cambridge, MA: MIT Press.

Biolsi, Thomas, and Larry J. Zimmerman, editors. 1997. *Indians and anthropologists: Vine Deloria, Jr., and the critique of anthropology*. Tucson, AZ: The University of Arizona Press.

Bird-David, Nurit. 1999. “Animism” revisited: Personhood, environment, and relational epistemology. *Current Anthropology* 40(S): 67–91.

Bjerg, Ole. 2014. *Making money: The philosophy of crisis capitalism*. London: Verso.

Blanc, Jérôme. 2012. Thirty years of community and complementary currencies: A review of impacts, potential and challenges. *International Journal of Community Currency Research* 16: 1–4.

Bloch, Maurice, and Jonathan Parry. 1989. Introduction: Money and the morality of exchange. In *Money and the morality of exchange*, edited by Jonathan Parry and Maurice Bloch, 1–32. Cambridge: Cambridge University Press.

Bogadóttir, Ragnheidur. 2016. *Time-space appropriation in the Inka Empire: A study of imperial metabolism*. Lund Studies in Human Ecology 15. Doctoral dissertation, Lund University.

Bohannan, Paul. 1955. Some principles of exchange and investment among the Tiv. *American Anthropologist* 57: 60–70.

Bonds, Eric, and Liam Downey. 2012. ‘Green’ technology and ecologically unequal exchange: The environmental and social consequences of ecological modernization in the world-system. *Journal of World-Systems Research* 18(2): 167–186.

Bonneuil, Christophe, and Jean-Baptiste Fressoz. 2015. *The shock of the Anthropocene: The Earth, history and us*. London: Verso.

Bordewich, Fergus M. 1996. *Killing the white man’s Indian: Reinventing Native Americans at the end of the twentieth century*. New York: Doubleday.

Bouysse-Cassagne, Thérèse. 2010. Apuntes para la historia de los puquinahablantes. In *Lenguas y sociedades en el antiguo Perú: hacia un enfoque interdisciplinario*, edited by Peter Kaulicke, Rodolfo Cerrón-Palomino, Paul Heggarty, and David Beresford-Jones, 283–307. Boletín de Arqueología PUCP 14. Lima: Pontificia Universidad Católica del Perú.

Bowring, Finn. 1998. LETS: An eco-socialist initiative? *New Left Review* 232: 91–111.

Boysen, Benjamin, and Jesper Lundsfryd Rasmussen, editors. 2023. *Against new materialisms*. London: Bloomsbury.

Bramwell, Anna. 1989. *Ecology in the 20th century: A history*. New Haven, CT: Yale University Press.

Brandt, Per A. 2017. The meaning and madness of money: A semio-ecological analysis. *Cognitive Semiotics* 10(2): 141–168.

Bray, Tamara L., editor. 2015. *The archaeology of wak’as: Explorations of the sacred in the pre-Columbian Andes*. Boulder: University Press of Colorado.

Brosius, J. Peter. 2006. Endangered forest, endangered people: Environmentalist representations of indigenous knowledge. In *The environment in anthropology: A reader in ecology, culture, and sustainable living*, edited by Nora Haenn and Richard R. Wilk, 367–385. New York: New York University Press.

Bunker, Stephen G. 1985. *Underdeveloping the Amazon: Extraction, unequal exchange, and the failure of the modern state*. Chicago, IL: The University of Chicago Press.

Burger, Richard L. 2012. Central Andean language expansion and the Chavín sphere of interaction. In *Archaeology and language in the Andes: A cross-disciplinary exploration of prehistory*, edited by Paul Heggarty and David Beresford-Jones, 135–161. Proceedings of the British Academy 173. Oxford: Oxford University Press.

Burger, Richard L. 2013. In the realm of the Incas: An archaeological reconsideration of household exchange, long-distance trade, and marketplaces in the pre-Hispanic

Central Andes. In *Merchants, markets, and exchange in the pre-Columbian world*, edited by Kenneth G. Hirth and Joanne Pillsbury, 319–334. Washington, DC: Dumbarton Oaks Research Library and Collection.
Burkett, Paul. [1999] 2014. *Marx and nature: A red and green perspective*. Chicago, IL: Haymarket.
Burkett, Paul. [2005] 2009. *Marxism and ecological economics: Toward a red and green political economy*. Chicago, IL: Haymarket.
Burkett, Paul, and John Bellamy Foster. 2006. Metabolism, energy, and entropy in Marx's critique of political economy: Beyond the Podolinsky myth. *Theory and Society* 35: 109–156.
Caffentzis, George. 2013. *In letters of blood and fire: Work, machines, and the crisis of capitalism*. Oakland, CA: PM Press.
Campbell, Lyle. 1997. *American Indian languages: The historical linguistics of Native America*. Oxford: Oxford University Press.
Catton, William R., Jr. 1980. *Overshoot: The ecological basis of revolutionary change*. Urbana: University of Illinois Press.
Cerrón-Palomino, Rodolfo. 2012. Unravelling the enigma of the 'particular language' of the Incas. In *Archaeology and language in the Andes: A cross-disciplinary exploration of prehistory*, edited by Paul Heggarty and David Beresford-Jones, 265–294. Proceedings of the British Academy 173. Oxford: Oxford University Press.
Clark, Brett, and Richard York. 2005. Carbon metabolism: Global capitalism, climate change, and the biospheric rift. *Theory and Society* 34: 391–428.
Cline, Eric H. 2014. *1177 B.C.: The year civilization collapsed*. Princeton, NJ: Princeton University Press.
Commoner, Barry. 1971. *The closing circle: Nature, man and technology*. New York: Alfred A. Knopf.
Conklin, Beth A., and Laura R. Graham. 1995. The shifting middle ground: Amazonian Indians and eco-politics. *American Anthropologist* 97(4): 695–710.
Corbridge, Stuart, and Nigel Thrift. 1994. Money, power, and space: Introduction and overview. In *Money, power and space*, edited by Stuart Corbridge, Ron Martin, and Nigel Thrift, 1–25. Oxford: Blackwell.
Couldry, Nick, and Ulises A. Mejias. 2019. *The costs of connection: How data is colonizing human life and appropriating it for capitalism*. Stanford, CA: Stanford University Press.
Crawford, Kate. 2022. *Atlas of AI: Power, politics, and the planetary costs of artificial intelligence*. New Haven, CT: Yale University Press.
Cronon, William. 1983. *Changes in the land: Indians, colonists, and the ecology of New England*. New York: Hill and Wang.
Daggett, Cara N. 2019. *The birth of energy: Fossil fuels, thermodynamics, and the politics of work*. Durham, NC: Duke University Press.
Dalton, Jordan A. 2024. The use of balances in late Andean prehistory (AD 1200–1650). *Cambridge Archaeological Journal*, published online May 20, 2024. https://doi.org/10.1017/S0959774324000076
D'Altroy, Terence N. 2002. *The Incas*. Oxford: Blackwell.
D'Altroy, Terence N., and Timothy K. Earle. 1985. Staple finance, wealth finance, and storage in the Inka political economy. *Current Anthropology* 26(2): 187–206.
Davies, Glyn. 2002. *A history of money*. Cardiff: University of Wales Press.
Dawkins, Richard. 1976. *The selfish gene*. Oxford: Oxford University Press.

Deacon, Terrence. 1997. *The symbolic species: The co-evolution of language and the human brain*. London: Penguin.

De Brosses, Charles. [1760] 2017. On the worship of fetish gods: Or, a parallel of the ancient religion of Egypt with the present religion of Nigritia. In *The returns of fetishism: Charles de Brosses and the afterlives of an idea*, edited by Rosalind C. Morris and Daniel H. Leonard, 44–132. Chicago, IL: The University of Chicago Press.

De Brunhoff, Suzanne. [1973] 2015. *Marx on money*. London: Verso.

De la Cadena, Marisol. 2015. *Earth beings: Ecologies of practice across Andean worlds*. Durham, NC: Duke University Press.

Deloria, Vine, Jr. 1997. Anthros, Indians, and planetary reality. In *Indians and anthropologists: Vine Deloria, Jr., and the critique of anthropology*, edited by Thomas Biolsi and Larry J. Zimmerman, 209–221. Tucson: The University of Arizona Press.

Dennis, R.L.H., L. Dapporto, S. Fattorini, and L.M. Cook. 2011. The generalism-specialism debate: The role of generalists in the life and death of species. *Biological Journal of the Linnean Society* 104: 725–737.

Desan, Christine. 2014. *Making money: Coin, currency, and the coming of capitalism*. Oxford: Oxford University Press.

Descola, Philippe. 1994. *In the society of nature: A native ecology in Amazonia*. Cambridge: Cambridge University Press.

Descola, Philippe. 2013. *Beyond nature and culture*. Chicago, IL: The University of Chicago Press.

De Vries, Alex. 2023. The growing energy footprint of artificial intelligence. *Joule* 7(10): 2191–2194.

Dillehay, Tom D. 2013. Economic mobility, exchange, and order in the Andes. In *Merchants, markets, and exchange in the pre-Columbian world*, edited by Kenneth G. Hirth and Joanne Pillsbury, 283–308. Washington, DC: Dumbarton Oaks Research Library and Collection.

Ding, Ersu. 2016. Rethinking the Peircean trichotomy of icon, index, and symbol. *Semiotica* 213: 165–175.

Dittmer, Kristofer. 2013. Local currencies for purposive degrowth? A quality check of some proposals for changing money-as-usual. *Journal of Cleaner Production* 54: 3–13.

Dittmer, Kristofer. 2015. Community currencies. In *Degrowth: A Vocabulary for a new era*, edited by Giacomo D'Alisa, Federico Demaria, and Giorgos Kallis, 149–151. London: Routledge.

Dixon, R.M.W., and Alexandra Y. Aikhenvald, editors. 1999. *The Amazonian languages*. Cambridge: Cambridge University Press.

Dobson, Ross V.G. 1993. *Bringing the economy home from the market*. Montreal: Black Rose Books.

Dodd, Nigel. 2015. Utopianism and the future of money. In *Re-imagining economic sociology*, edited by Patrik Aspers and Nigel Dodd, 79–102. Oxford: Oxford University Press.

Domínguez-Faura, Nicanor. 2014. The *puquina* language in the early colonial Southern Andes (1548-1610): A geographical analysis. *Journal of Latin American Geography* 13(2): 181–206.

Donald, Merlin. 2012. An evolutionary approach to culture: Implications for the study of the Axial Age. In *The Axial Age and its consequences*, edited by Robert N. Bellah and Hans Joas, 47–76. Cambridge, MA: The Belknap Press of Harvard University Press.

Dorninger, Christian, and Alf Hornborg. 2015. Can EEMRIO analyses establish the occurrence of ecologically unequal exchange? *Ecological Economics* 119: 414–418.

Dorninger, Christian, Alf Hornborg, David J. Abson, Henrik von Wehrden, Anke Schaffartzik, Stefan Giljum, John-Oliver Engler, Robert L. Feller, Klaus Hubacek, and Hanspeter Wieland. 2021. Global patterns of ecologically unequal exchange: Implications for sustainability in the 21st century. *Ecological Economics* 179: 106824. https://doi.org/10.1016/j.ecolecon.2020.106824

Douglas, Mary. 1966. *Purity and danger: An analysis of concepts of pollution and taboo*. London: Routledge & Kegan Paul.

Dove, Michael R. 2006. Indigenous people and environmental politics. *Annual Review of Anthropology* 35: 191–208.

Dove, Michael R., and Carol Carpenter, editors. 2008. *Environmental anthropology: A historical reader*. Oxford: Blackwell.

Dove, Michael R., Daniel S. Smith, Marina T. Campos, Andrew S. Mathews, Anne Rademacher, Steve Rhee, and Laura M. Yoder. 2007. Globalisation and the construction of Western and non-Western knowledge. In *Local science vs. global science: Approaches to indigenous knowledge in international development*, edited by Paul Sillitoe, 129–154. Oxford: Berghahn Books.

Dryzek, John S., and Jonathan Pickering. 2019. *The politics of the Anthropocene*. Oxford: Oxford University Press.

Dumont, Louis. [1966] 1972. *Homo Hierarchicus: The caste system and its implications*. London: Paladin.

Dumont, Louis. 1977. *From Mandeville to Marx: The genesis and triumph of economic ideology*. Chicago, IL: The University of Chicago Press.

Dunlap, Alexander. 2019. *Renewing destruction: Wind energy development, conflict, and resistance in a Latin American context*. London: Rowman & Littlefield.

Earle, Timothy K. 2018. Trade-light: The political economy of Polynesian and Andean civilizations. In *Trade and civilization: Economic networks and cultural ties, from prehistory to the early modern era*, edited by Kristian Kristiansen, Thomas Lindkvist, and Janken Myrdal, 441–470. Cambridge: Cambridge University Press.

Eisenstein, Charles. 2011. *Sacred economics: Money, gift, and society in the age of transition*. Berkeley, CA: Evolver Editions.

Emmanuel, Arghiri. 1972. *Unequal exchange: A study of the imperialism of trade*. New York: Monthly Review Press.

Emmeche, Claus. 2001. Bioinvasion, globalization, and the contingency of cultural and biological diversity: Some ecosemiotic observations. *Sign Systems Studies* 29(1): 237–262.

Emmeche, Claus, Kalevi Kull, and Frederik Stjernfelt. 2002. *Reading Hoffmeyer, rethinking biology*. Tartu Semiotics Library 3. Tartu: Tartu University Press.

Epps, Patience. 2020. Amazonian linguistic diversity and its sociocultural correlates. In *Language dispersal, diversification, and contact*, edited by Mily Crevels and Pieter Muysken, 275–290. Oxford: Oxford University Press.

Eriksen, Love. 2011. *Nature and culture in prehistoric Amazonia: Using G.I.S. to reconstruct ancient ethnogenetic processes from archaeology, linguistics, geography, and ethnohistory*. Lund Studies in Human Ecology 12. PhD thesis. Lund University.

Eriksen, Thomas H. 2021. The loss of diversity in the Anthropocene: Biological and cultural dimensions. *Frontiers in Political Science*, September 6, 2021.

Eriksen, Thomas H. 2023. Threats to diversity in the shadow of Anthropocene overheating: A biosemiotic perspective. *Kritisk etnografi – Swedish Journal of Anthropology* 6(1): 9–22.

Escobar, Arturo. 2018. *Designs for the Pluriverse: Radical interdependence, autonomy, and the making of worlds*. Durham, NC: Duke University Press.
Evernden, Neil. 1985. *The natural alien: Humankind and environment*. Toronto: University of Toronto Press.
Ferguson, Charles A. 1959. Diglossia. *Word* 15: 325–344.
Ferguson, Niall. 2008. *The ascent of money: A financial history of the world*. London: Penguin.
Ferry, Luc. [1992] 1995. *The new ecological order*. Chicago, IL: The University of Chicago Press.
Fischer-Kowalski, Marina, and Helmut Haberl. 1997. Tons, Joules, and money: Modes of production and their sustainability problems. *Society & Natural Resources* 10(1): 61–85.
Foster, John B. 2000a. *Marx's ecology: Materialism and nature*. New York: Monthly Review Press.
Foster, John B. 2000b. Marx's ecological value analysis. *Monthly Review* 52(4): 39–47.
Foster, John B. 2014. Foreword. In *Marx and nature: A red and green perspective*, edited by Paul Burkett, vi–xiii. Chicago, IL: Haymarket.
Foster, John B. 2020. *The return of nature: Socialism and ecology*. New York: Monthly Review Press.
Foster, John B., and Paul Burkett. 2016. *Marx and the Earth: An anti-critique*. Leiden: Brill.
Foster, John B., Brett Clark, and Richard York. 2010. *The ecological rift: Capitalism's war on the Earth*. New York: Monthly Review Press.
Francis, Daniel. 1992. *The imaginary Indian: The image of the Indian in Canadian culture*. Vancouver, BC: Arsenal Pulp Press.
Frank, Andre G. 1993. Bronze Age world system cycles. *Current Anthropology* 34(4): 383–430.
Frank, Andre G. 1998. *ReOrient: Global economy in the Asian age*. Berkeley: University of California Press.
Franquesa, Jaume. 2018. *Power struggles: Dignity, value, and the renewable energy frontier in Spain*. Bloomington: Indiana University Press.
Frey, R. Scott, Paul K. Gellert, and Harry F. Dahms, editors. 2019. *Ecologically unequal exchange: Environmental injustice in comparative and historical perspective*. Houndmills: Palgrave Macmillan.
Galeano, Eduardo. 1973. *Open veins of Latin America: Five centuries of the pillage of a continent*. New York: Monthly Review Press.
Gare, Arran. 2020. Semiosis and information: Meeting the challenge of information science to post-reductionist biosemiotics. *Biosemiotics* 13: 327–346.
Gellner, Ernst. 1983. *Nations and nationalism*. Oxford: Blackwell.
Georgescu-Roegen, Nicholas. 1971. *The Entropy Law and the economic process*. Cambridge, MA: Harvard University Press.
Georgescu-Roegen, Nicholas. 1993. Thermodynamics and we, the humans. In Entropy and bioeconomics: Proceedings of the first international conference of the E.A.B.S., edited by Iosif C. Dragan, E.K. Seifert, and M.C. Demetrescu, 184–201. Milan: Nagard.
Giddens, Anthony. 1990. *The consequences of modernity*. Cambridge: Polity.
Givens, Jennifer E., Xiaorui Huang, and Andrew K. Jorgenson. 2019. Ecologically unequal exchange: A theory of global environmental *in*justice. *Sociology Compass* 13(5): e12693.

Godelier, Maurice. 1986. *The mental and the material.* New York: Verso.

Goldstein, Paul S. 2013. Embedded Andean economic systems and the expansive Tiwanaku state: A case for a state without market exchange. In *Merchants, markets, and exchange in the pre-Columbian world*, edited by Kenneth G. Hirth and Joanne Pillsbury, 361–387. Washington, DC: Dumbarton Oaks Research Library and Collection.

Gómez-Baggethun, Erik. 2022. Is there a future for indigenous and local knowledge? *The Journal of Peasant Studies* 49(6): 1139–1157.

Gorenflo, Larry J., Suzanne Romaine, Russell A. Mittermeier, and Kristen Walker-Painemilla. 2012. Co-occurrence of linguistic and biological diversity in biodiversity hotspots and high biodiversity wilderness areas. *PNAS* 109(21): 8032–8037.

Graeber, David. 2001. *Toward an anthropological theory of value: The false coin of our own dream.* Houndmills: Palgrave.

Graeber, David. 2005. Value: Anthropological theories of value. In *A handbook of economic anthropology*, edited by James G. Carrier, 439–454. Cheltenham: Edward Elgar.

Graeber, David. 2007. *Possibilities: Essays in hierarchy, rebellion, and desire.* Oakland, CA: AK Press.

Graeber, David. 2009. Debt, violence, and impersonal markets: Polanyian meditations. In *Market and society:* The great transformation *today*, edited by Chris Hann and Keith Hart, 106–132. Cambridge: Cambridge University Press.

Graeber, David. 2011. *Debt: The first 5,000 years.* Brooklyn, NY: Melville House.

Graeber, David, and David Wengrow. 2021. *The dawn of everything: A new history of humanity.* London: Allen Lane.

Gray, Mary, and Siddharth Suri. 2019. *Ghost work: How to stop Silicon Valley from building a new global underclass.* Boston, MA: Houghton Mifflin Harcourt.

Green, Adam S., Toby C. Wilkinson, Darryl Wilkinson, Nancy Highcock, and Thomas P. Leppard. 2024. *Cities and citadels: An archaeology of inequality and economic growth.* Abingdon: Routledge.

Greer, John M. 2008. *The long descent: A user's guide to the end of the Industrial Age.* Gabriola Island, BC: New Society Publishers.

Greer, John M. 2011. *The wealth of nature: Economics as if survival mattered.* Gabriola Island, BC: New Society Publishers.

Gren, Martin. 2009. Time geography. In *The international encyclopedia of human geography*, edited by Robert Kitchin and Nigel Thrift, 279–284. Amsterdam: Elsevier.

Gudeman, Stephen. 1986. *Economics as culture: Models and metaphors of livelihood.* London: Routledge & Kegan Paul.

Gudeman, Stephen. 2001. *The anthropology of economy: Community, market, and culture.* Malden, MA: Blackwell.

Gudeman, Stephen. 2012. Vital energy: The current of relations. *Social Analysis* 56(1): 57–73.

Gudeman, Stephen, and Alberto Rivera. 1990. *Conversations in Colombia: The domestic economy in life and text.* Cambridge: Cambridge University Press.

Haenn, Nora, and Richard R. Wilk, editors. 2006. *The environment in anthropology: A reader in ecology, culture, and sustainable living.* New York: New York University Press.

Haff, Peter K. 2013. Technology as a geological phenomenon: Implications for human well-being. In *A stratigraphical basis for the Anthropocene*, edited by Colin N.

Waters, Jan A. Zalasiewicz, Mark Williams, Michael A. Ellis, and Andrea M. Snelling, 301–309. Geological Society, London, Special Publications 395.
Haiven, Max. 2022. *Palm oil: The grease of empire*. London: Pluto.
Hall, Charles A.S., and Kent A. Klitgaard. 2011. *Energy and the wealth of nations: Understanding the biophysical economy*. New York: Springer.
Hamilton, Clive. 2010. *Requiem for a species: Why we resist the truth about climate change*. London: Earthscan.
Hao, Karen. 2022. Artificial intelligence is creating a new colonial world order. *MIT Technology Review*, April 19, 2022.
Harari, Yuval N. 2011. *Sapiens: A brief history of humankind*. London: Vintage.
Harkin, Michael E., and David R. Lewis, editors. 2007. *Native Americans and the environment: Perspectives on the ecological Indian*. Lincoln: University of Nebraska Press.
Harris, Marvin. 1980. *Cultural materialism: The struggle for a science of culture*. New York: Vintage Books.
Harrod, Howard L. 2000. *The animals came dancing: Native American sacred ecology and animal kinship*. Tucson: The University of Arizona Press.
Hart, Keith. 1986. Heads or tails? Two sides of the coin. *Man: The Journal of the Royal Anthropological Institute* (n.s.) 21(4): 637–656.
Hart, Keith. 2005. Money: One anthropologist's view. In *A handbook of economic anthropology*, edited by James G. Carrier, 160–175. Cheltenham: Edward Elgar.
Hart, Keith. 2009. Money in the making of world society. In *Market and society:* The great transformation *today*, edited by Chris Hann and Keith Hart, 91–105. Cambridge: Cambridge University Press.
Hart, Keith, and Horacio Ortiz. 2014. The anthropology of money and finance: Between ethnography and world history. *Annual Review of Anthropology* 43: 465–482.
Harvey, David. 2018. *Marx, capital, and the madness of economic reason*. Oxford: Oxford University Press.
Headrick, Daniel R. 1981. *The tools of empire: Technology and European imperialism in the nineteenth century*. Oxford: Oxford University Press.
Heggarty, Paul, and David Beresford-Jones, editors. 2012 *Archaeology and language in the Andes: A cross-disciplinary exploration of prehistory*. Proceedings of the British Academy 173. Oxford: Oxford University Press.
Heidegger, Martin. [1954] 1977. *The question concerning technology and other essays*. New York: Harper & Row.
Heinberg, Richard. 2004. *Power down: Options and actions for a post-carbon world*. Gabriola Island, BC: New Society Publishers.
Heinberg, Richard. 2005. *The party's over: Oil, war and the fate of industrial societies*. Gabriola Island, BC: New Society Publishers.
Heinberg, Richard. 2007. *Peak everything: Waking up to the century of declines*. Gabriola Island, BC: New Society Publishers.
Heinrich, Michael. 2014. Value, fetishism, and impersonal domination. *Lecture*, March 13, 2014, downloaded from YouTube.
Hickel, Jason, Christian Dorninger, Hanspeter Wieland, and Intan Suwandi. 2022. Imperialist appropriation in the world economy: Drain from the global South through unequal exchange, 1990–2015. *Global Environmental Change* 73: 102467. https://doi.org/10.1016/j.gloenvcha.2022.102467
Hill, Jonathan D., editor. 1996. *History, power, and identity: Ethnogenesis in the Americas, 1492–1992*. Iowa City, IA: University of Iowa Press.

Hill, Jonathan D. 2002. Shamanism, colonialism, and the wild woman: Fertility cultism and historical dynamics in the Upper Río Negro region. In *Comparative Arawakan histories: Rethinking language family and culture area in Amazonia*, edited by Jonathan D. Hill and Fernando Santos-Granero, 223–247. Urbana: University of Illinois Press.

Hill, Jonathan D., and Fernando Santos-Granero, editors. 2002. *Comparative Arawakan histories: Rethinking language family and culture area in Amazonia*. Urbana: University of Illinois Press.

Hine, Dougald, and Paul Kingsnorth. 2009. Uncivilisation: The Dark Mountain manifesto. The Dark Mountain Project. https://dark-mountain.net/about/manifesto/

Hirsch, Eric. 1995. Introduction. Landscape: Between place and space. In *The anthropology of landscape: Perspectives on place and space*, edited by Eric Hirsch and Michael O'Hanlon, 1–30. Oxford: Clarendon Press.

Hirsch, Eric, and Michael O'Hanlon, editors. 1995. *The anthropology of landscape: Perspectives on place and space*. Oxford: Clarendon Press.

Hirth, Kenneth G., and Joanne Pillsbury. 2013. Merchants, markets, and exchange in the pre-Columbian world. In *Merchants, markets, and exchange in the pre-Columbian world*, edited by Kenneth G. Hirth and Joanne Pillsbury, 1–22. Washington, DC: Dumbarton Oaks Research Library and Collection.

Hoffmeyer, Jesper. 1996. *Signs of meaning in the universe*. Bloomington: Indiana University Press.

Hoffmeyer, Jesper. 1998. Semiosis and biohistory: A reply. *Semiotica* 120(3/4): 455–482.

Hoffmeyer, Jesper. 2005. *Biosemiotik: En afhandling om livets tegn og tegnenes liv*. Charlottenlund, DK: Ries.

Homer-Dixon, Thomas. 2006. *The upside of down: Catastrophe, creativity, and the renewal of civilization*. Washington, DC: Island Press.

Horkheimer, Max, and Adorno, Theodor W. [1947] 1972. *Dialectic of enlightenment*. New York: Herder and Herder.

Hornborg, Alf. 1992. Machine fetishism, value, and the image of unlimited good: Toward a thermodynamics of imperialism. *Man* (n.s.) 27: 1–18.

Hornborg, Alf. 1994a. Environmentalism, ethnicity, and sacred places: Reflections on modernity, discourse and power. *Canadian Review of Sociology and Anthropology* 31(3): 245–267.

Hornborg, Alf. 1994b. Encompassing encompassment: Anthropology and the U-turn of modernity. *Ethnos* 59(3–4): 232–247.

Hornborg, Alf. 1996. Ecology as semiotics: Outlines of a contextualist paradigm for human ecology. In *Nature and society: Anthropological perspectives*, edited by Philippe Descola and Gísli Pálsson, 45–62. London: Routledge.

Hornborg, Alf. 1998. Towards an ecological theory of unequal exchange: Articulating world system theory and ecological economics. *Ecological Economics* 25(1): 127–136.

Hornborg, Alf. 1999. Money and the semiotics of ecosystem dissolution. *Journal of Material Culture* 4(2): 143–162.

Hornborg, Alf. 2001a. *The power of the machine: Global inequalities of economy, technology, and environment*. Walnut Creek, CA: AltaMira.

Hornborg, Alf. 2001b. Vital signs: An ecosemiotic perspective on the human ecology of Amazonia. *Sign Systems Studies* 29(1): 121–152.

Hornborg, Alf. 2005. Ethnogenesis, regional integration, and ecology in prehistoric Amazonia: Toward a system perspective. *Current Anthropology* 46(4): 589–620.
Hornborg, Alf. 2006. Knowledge of persons, knowledge of things: Animism, fetishism, and objectivism as strategies for knowing (or not knowing) the world. *Ethnos* 71(1): 1–12.
Hornborg, Alf. 2011. *Global ecology and unequal exchange: Fetishism in a zero-sum world.* London: Routledge.
Hornborg, Alf. 2013. *Global ecology and unequal exchange: Fetishism in a zero-sum world.* Revised paperback version. London: Routledge.
Hornborg, Alf. 2014. Political economy, ethnogenesis, and language dispersals in the prehispanic Andes: A world-system perspective. *American Anthropologist* 116(4): 810–823.
Hornborg, Alf. 2016. *Global magic: Technologies of appropriation from ancient Rome to Wall Street.* Houndmills: Palgrave Macmillan.
Hornborg, Alf. 2018. Long-distance exchange and ritual technologies of power in the pre-Hispanic Andes. In *Trade and civilization: Economic networks and cultural ties, from prehistory to the early modern era*, edited by Kristian Kristiansen, Thomas Lindkvist, and Janken Myrdal, 471–493. Cambridge: Cambridge University Press.
Hornborg, Alf. 2021. Objects don't have desires: Toward an anthropology of technology beyond anthropomorphism. *American Anthropologist* 123(4): 753–766.
Hornborg, Alf. 2023. *The magic of technology: The machine as a transformation of slavery.* London: Routledge.
Hornborg, Alf, and Jonathan D. Hill, editors. 2011. *Ethnicity in ancient Amazonia: Reconstructing past identities from archaeology, linguistics, and ethnohistory.* Boulder: University Press of Colorado.
Hornborg, Alf, and Joan Martinez-Alier, editors. 2016. Ecologically unequal exchange and ecological debt. *Journal of Political Ecology* 23: 328–491.
Hornborg, Alf, John R. McNeill, and Joan Martinez-Alier, editors. 2007. *Rethinking environmental history: World-system history and global environmental change.* Lanham, MD: AltaMira.
Hornborg, Anne-Christine. 2008. *Mi'kmaq landscapes: From animism to sacred ecology.* Aldershot: Ashgate.
Hosler, Dorothy, Heather Lechtman, and Olaf Holm. 1990. Axe-monies and their relatives. Washington, DC: Dumbarton Oaks Research Library and Collection.
Huber, Matthew T. 2008. Energizing historical materialism: Fossil fuels, space, and the capitalist mode of production. *Geoforum* 40: 105–115.
Huber, Matthew T. 2017. Value, nature and labor: A defense of Marx. *Capitalism, Nature, Socialism* 28(1): 39–52.
Huesemann, Michael, and Joyce Huesemann. 2011. *Techno-fix: Why technology won't save us or the environment.* Gabriola Island, BC: New Society Publishers.
Hughes, J. Donald. [1983] 1996. *North American Indian ecology.* El Paso: Texas Western Press.
Hultkrantz, Åke. 1979. *The religions of the American Indians.* Berkeley: University of California Press.
Iacono, Alfonso M. 2016. *The history and theory of fetishism.* Houndmills: Palgrave Macmillan.
Ihde, Don. 1993. *Philosophy of technology: An introduction.* New York: Paragon.

Illich, Ivan. 1973. *Tools for conviviality*. London: Calder and Boyars.

Illich, Ivan. [1973] 2013. The energy crisis. In *Beyond economics and ecology: The radical thought of Ivan Illich*, edited by Sajay Samuel, 73–104. London: Marion Boyars.

Illich, Ivan. [1983] 2013. The social construction of energy. In *Beyond economics and ecology: The radical thought of Ivan Illich*, edited by Sajay Samuel, 105–123. London: Marion Boyars.

Infante-Amate, Juan, and Fridolin Krausmann. 2019. Trade, ecologically unequal exchange and colonial legacy: The case of France and its former colonies (1962–2015). *Ecological Economics* 156: 98–109.

Ingham, Geoffrey. 2004. *The nature of money*. Cambridge: Polity.

Ingold, Tim. 2000. *The perception of the environment: Essays in livelihood, dwelling and skill*. London: Routledge.

Isaac, Barry L. 2005. Karl Polanyi. In *A handbook of economic anthropology*, edited by James G. Carrier, 14–25. Cheltenham: Edward Elgar.

Isaac, Barry L. 2013. Discussion. In *Merchants, markets, and exchange in the pre-Columbian world*, edited by Kenneth G. Hirth and Joanne Pillsbury, 435–448. Washington, DC: Dumbarton Oaks Research Library and Collection.

Jacob, Francois. 1974. *The logic of living systems: A history of heredity*. London: Allen Lane.

Jackson, Michael. 1995. *At home in the world*. Durham, NC: Duke University Press.

Jaspers, Karl. [1949] 2021. *The origin and goal of history*. London: Routledge.

Jensen, Cheryl. 1999. Tupí-Guaraní. In *The Amazonian Languages*, edited by R.M.W. Dixon and A.Y. Aikhenvald, 125–163. Cambridge: Cambridge University Press.

Jessen, Tyler D., Natalie C. Ban, Nicholas X. Claxton, and Chris T. Darimont. 2022. Contributions of indigenous knowledge to ecological and evolutionary understanding. *Frontiers in Ecology and the Environment* 20(2): 93–101.

Joas, Hans. 2012. The Axial Age debate as religious discourse. In *The Axial Age and its consequences*, edited by Robert N. Bellah and Hans Joas, 9–29. Cambridge, MA: The Belknap Press of Harvard University Press.

Johnson, Jim. 1988. Mixing humans and nonhumans together: The sociology of a door-closer. *Social Problems* 35(3): 298–310.

Johnson, Walter. 2004. The pedestal and the veil: Rethinking the capitalism/slavery question. *Journal of the Early Republic* 24(2): 299–308.

Jorgenson, Andrew K. 2003. Consumption and environmental degradation: A cross-national analysis of the ecological footprint. *Social Problems* 50: 374–394.

Jorgenson, Andrew K. 2012. The sociology of ecologically unequal exchange and carbon dioxide emissions, 1960–2005. *Social Science Research* 41(2): 242–252.

Jorgenson, Andrew K., and Brett Clark, editors. 2009. Ecologically unequal exchange in comparative perspective. Special issue of *International Journal of Comparative Sociology* 50(3–4): 1–409.

Jorgenson, Andrew K., and James Rice. 2007. Uneven ecological exchange and consumption-based environmental impacts: A cross-national investigation. In *Rethinking environmental history: World-system history and global environmental change*, edited by Alf Hornborg, John R. McNeill, and Joan Martinez-Alier, 273–288. Lanham, MD: AltaMira.

Jung, Matthias. 2012. Embodiment, transcendence, and contingency: Anthropological features of the Axial Age. In *The Axial Age and its consequences*, edited by

Robert N. Bellah and Hans Joas, 77–101. Cambridge, MA: The Belknap Press of Harvard University Press.

Kåberger, Tomas, and Bengt Månsson. 2001. Entropy and economic processes: Physics perspectives. *Ecological Economics* 36: 165–179.

Kaczynski, Theodore. 2016. *Anti-tech revolution: Why and how*. Scottsdale, AZ: Fitch & Madison.

Kallis, Giorgos, and Erik Swyngedouw. 2018. Do bees produce value? A conversation between an ecological economist and a Marxist geographer. *Capitalism, Nature, Socialism* 29(3): 36–50.

Kapp, K. William. 1950. *The social costs of private enterprise*. Cambridge, MA: Harvard University Press.

Klein, Naomi. 2014. *This changes everything: Capitalism vs. the climate*. London: Allen Lane.

Kohn, Eduardo. 2013. *How forests think: Toward an anthropology beyond the human*. Berkeley: University of California Press.

Kohn, Eduardo. 2015. Anthropology of ontologies. *Annual Review of Anthropology* 44: 311–327.

Kolbert, Elizabeth. 2014. *The sixth extinction: An unnatural history*. New York: Picador.

Kovel, Joel. [2002] 2007. *The enemy of nature: The end of capitalism or the end of the world?* London: Zed Books.

Krausmann, Fridolin, Dominik Wiedenhofer, Christian Lauk, Willi Haas, Hiroki Tanikawa, Tomer Fishman, Alessio Miatto, Heinz Schandl, and Helmut Haberl. 2017. Global socioeconomic material stocks rise 23-fold over the 20th century and require half of annual resource use. *PNAS* 114(8): 1880–1885.

Krech, Shepard, III. 1987. *Indians, animals and the fur trade: A critique of* Keepers of the game. Athens: University of Georgia Press.

Krech, Shepard, III. 1999. *The ecological Indian: Myth and history*. New York: W.W. Norton & Co.

Krech, Shepard, III. 2007a. Beyond *The ecological Indian*. In *Native Americans and the environment: Perspectives on the ecological Indian*, edited by Michael E. Harkin and David Rich Lewis, 3–31. Lincoln: University of Nebraska Press.

Krech, Shepard, III. 2007b. Afterword. In *Native Americans and the environment: Perspectives on the ecological Indian*, edited by Michael E. Harkin and David Rich Lewis, 343–353. Lincoln: University of Nebraska Press.

Krugman, Paul, and Robin Wells. 2018. *Economics*. Fifth edition. New York: Macmillan Education.

Kull, Kalevi. 1998. Semiotic ecology: Different natures in the semiosphere. *Sign Systems Studies* 26: 344–371.

Kull, Kalevi. 2019. Steps toward the natural meronomy and taxonomy of semiosis: Emon between index and symbol? *Sign Systems Studies* 47(1–2): 88–104.

Kunstler, James H. 2005. *The long emergency: Surviving the end of oil, climate change, and other converging catastrophes of the twenty-first century*. New York: Grove Press.

Kuper, Adam. 2003. The return of the native. *Current Anthropology* 44(3): 389–402.

Landes, David S. 1969. *The unbound prometheus: Technological change and industrial development in Western Europe from 1750 to the present*. Cambridge: Cambridge University Press.

Lane, Kevin, and Erik J. Marsh. 2023. Absolute chronology revisited: Integrating precise Bayesian models from Machu Picchu with Inca ethnohistoric praise narratives. *Quaternary International* 703: 21–31.

Lathrap, Donald W. 1970. *The upper Amazon*. London: Thames and Hudson.

Latour, Bruno. 1993. *We have never been modern*. Cambridge, MA: Harvard University Press.

Latour, Bruno. 2004. Why has critique run out of steam? From matters of fact to matters of concern. *Critical Inquiry* 30: 225–248.

Latour, Bruno. 2005. *Reassembling the social: An introduction to actor-network-theory*. Oxford: Oxford University Press.

Latour, Bruno. 2010. *On the modern cult of the factish gods*. Durham, NC: Duke University Press.

Latour, Bruno. 2017. *Facing Gaia: Eight lectures on the new climatic regime*. Cambridge: Polity.

Latour, Bruno. 2024. *If we lose the Earth, we lose our souls*. Cambridge: Polity.

Law, John. 2015. What's wrong with a one-world world? *Distinktion: Journal of Social Theory* 16(1): 126–139.

Le Goff, Jacques. 2012. *Money and the middle ages: An essay in historical anthropology*. Cambridge: Polity.

Lenzen, Manfred, Keiichiro Kanemoto, Daniel Moran, and Arne Geschke. 2012a. Mapping the structure of the world economy. *Environmental Science & Technology* 46(15): 8374–8381.

Lenzen, Manfred, Daniel Moran, Keiichiro Kanemoto, Barney Foran, Leonarda Lobefaro, and Arne Geschke. 2012b. International trade drives biodiversity threats in developing nations. *Nature* 486: 109–112.

Lenzen, Manfred, Daniel Moran, Keiichiro Kanemoto, and Arne Geschke. 2013. Building EORA: A global multi-regional input-output database at high country and sector resolution. *Economic Systems Research* 25(1): 20–49.

Leonard, Daniel H. 2017. Introduction: Fetishism, figurism, and myths of Enlightenment. In *The returns of fetishism: Charles de Brosses and the afterlives of an idea*, edited by Rosalind C. Morris and Daniel H. Leonard, 1–39. Chicago, IL: The University of Chicago Press.

Lev, Michael. 2021. The classification of South American languages. *Annual Review of Linguistics* 7: 329–349.

Lévi-Strauss, Claude. [1949] 1969. *The elementary structures of kinship*. London: Eyre & Spottiswoode.

Lévi-Strauss, Claude. [1962] 2021. Wild thought. Chicago, IL: The University of Chicago Press.

Lévi-Strauss, Claude. 1963a. Structural analysis in linguistics and in anthropology. In *Structural anthropology*, 31–54. London: Allen Lane.

Lévi-Strauss, Claude. 1963b. The structural study of myth. In *Structural anthropology*, 206–231. London: Allen Lane.

Lévi-Strauss, Claude. 1963c. Social structures of Central and Eastern Brazil. In *Structural anthropology*, 120–131. London: Allen Lane.

Lévi-Strauss, Claude. 1968. The concept of primitiveness. In *Man the hunter*, edited by Richard B. Lee and Irven DeVore, 349–352. Chicago, IL: Aldine.

Lévi-Strauss, Claude. 1994. Anthropology, race, and politics. In *Assessing cultural anthropology*, edited by Robert Borofsky, 420–429. New York: McGraw-Hill.

Lewis, Simon L., and Mark Maslin. 2015. Defining the Anthropocene. *Nature* 519: 171–180.

Lockyer, Joshua, and James R. Veteto, editors. 2013. *Environmental anthropology engaging ecotopia: Bioregionalism, permaculture, and ecovillages.* Oxford: Berghahn Books.

Lohmann, Larry. 2020. Interpretation machines: Contradictions of 'Artificial Intelligence' in 21st-century capitalism. In *Beyond digital capitalism: New ways of living*, edited by Leo Panitch and Greg Albo, 50–77. New York: Monthly Review Press.

Lonergan, Stephen C. 1988. Theory and measurement of unequal exchange: A comparison between a Marxist approach and an energy theory of value. *Ecological Modeling* 41: 127–145.

Lukács, Georg. [1923] 1971. *History and class consciousness.* Cambridge, MA: MIT Press.

Macfarlane, Alan. 1985. The root of all evil. In *The anthropology of evil*, edited by David Parkin, 57–76. Oxford: Blackwell.

Maffi, Luisa, editor. 2001. *On biocultural diversity: Linking language, knowledge, and the environment.* Washington, DC: Smithsonian Institution Press.

Maffi, Luisa. 2005. Linguistic, cultural, and biological diversity. *Annual Review of Anthropology* 29: 599–617.

Magalhães, Nelo, Jean-Baptiste Fressoz, Francois Jarrige, Thomas Le Roux, Gaëtan Levillain, Margot Lyautey, Guillaume Noblet, and Christophe Bonneuil. 2019. The physical economy of France (1830–2015). The history of a parasite? *Ecological Economics* 157: 291–300.

Magdoff, Fred, and John Bellamy Foster. 2011. *What every environmentalist needs to know about capitalism.* New York: Monthly Review Press.

Maida, Carl A., editor. 2007. *Sustainability and communities of place.* Oxford: Berghahn Books.

Malm, Andreas. 2016. *Fossil capital: The rise of steam power and the roots of global warming.* London: Verso.

Malm, Andreas. 2018. *The progress of this storm: Nature and society in a warming world.* London: Verso.

Malm, Andreas. 2021. *How to blow up a pipeline.* London: Verso.

Malm, Andreas, and Alf Hornborg. 2014. The geology of mankind? A critique of the Anthropocene narrative. *The Anthropocene Review* 1: 62–69.

Mander, Jerry, and Edward Goldsmith, editors. 1996. *The case against the global economy – and for a turn toward the local.* San Francisco, CA: Sierra Club Books.

Mann, Charles C. 2011. *1493: Uncovering the New World Columbus created.* New York: Vintage.

Mannheim, Bruce. 1991. *The language of the Inka since the European invasion.* Austin: University of Texas Press.

Maran, Timo. 2020. *Ecosemiotics: The study of signs in changing ecologies.* Cambridge: Cambridge University Press.

Maran, Timo, and Kalevi Kull. 2014. Ecosemiotics: Main principles and current developments. *Geografiska Annaler: Series B* 96(1): 41–50.

Marcos, Jorge G. 1977/1978. Cruising to Acapulco and back with the Thorny Oyster set: A model for a lineal exchange system. *Journal of the Steward Anthropological Society* 9(1/2): 99–132.

Marichal, Carlos. 2006. The Spanish-American silver peso: Export commodity and global money of the *ancien régime*, 1550–1800. In *From silver to cocaine: Latin American commodity chains and the building of the world economy, 1500–2000*, edited by Steven Topik, Carlos Marichal, and Zephyr Frank, 25–52. Durham, NC: Duke University Press.

Marks, Robert B. 2015. *The origins of the modern world: A global and environmental narrative from the fifteenth to the twenty-first century*. Lanham, MD: Rowman & Littlefield.

Marshall, Adam P., and Daniel W. O'Neill. 2018. The Bristol Pound: A tool for localisation? *Ecological Economics* 146: 273–281.

Martin, Calvin. 1978. *Keepers of the game: Indian-animal relationships and the fur trade*. Berkeley: University of California Press.

Martinez-Alier, Joan. 1987. *Ecological economics: Energy, environment and society*. Oxford: Blackwell.

Martinez-Alier, Joan. 1994. Ecological economics and ecosocialism. In *Is capitalism sustainable? Political economy and the politics of ecology*, edited by Martin O'Connor, 23–36. New York: Guilford.

Martinez-Alier, Joan. 2006. Social metabolism and environmental conflicts. In *Coming to terms with nature*, edited by Leo Panitch and Colin Leys, 273–293. New York: Monthly Review Press.

Martinez-Alier, Joan, and José M. Naredo. 1982. A Marxist precursor of energy economics: Podolinsky. *The Journal of Peasant Studies* 9(2): 207–224.

Marx, Karl. [1939] 1973. *Grundrisse: Foundations of the critique of political economy*. London: Penguin.

Marx, Karl. [1876] 1976. *Capital: A critique of political economy*. Volume 1. Harmondsworth: Penguin.

Masuda, Shozo, Izumi Shimada, and Craig Morris, editors. 1985. *Andean ecology and civilization: An interdisciplinary perspective on Andean ecological complementarity*. Tokyo: University of Tokyo Press.

Matthewman, Steve. 2011. *Technology and social theory*. Houndmills: Palgrave Macmillan.

Maturana, Humberto R., and Francisco J. Varela. 1987. *The tree of knowledge: The biological roots of human understanding*. Boulder, CO: Shambhala.

Maurer, Bill. 2006. The anthropology of money. *Annual Review of Anthropology* 35: 15–36.

Mauss, Marcel. 1925. *The gift: The form and reason for exchange in archaic societies*. London: Routledge.

Mawson, C.O. Sylvester. [1923] 1946. *Roget's pocket thesaurus: A treasury of synonyms and antonyms*. Montreal: Thomas Y. Crowell.

Maybury-Lewis, David. 2006. On the importance of being tribal: Tribal wisdom. In *The environment in anthropology: A reader in ecology, culture, and sustainable living*, edited by Nora Haenn and Richard R. Wilk, 390–399. New York: New York University Press.

Mayer, Enrique. 2013. In the realm of the Incas. In *Merchants, markets, and exchange in the pre-Columbian world*, edited by Kenneth G. Hirth and Joanne Pillsbury, 309–317. Washington, DC: Dumbarton Oaks Research Library and Collection.

McEwan, Colin, and Florencio Degado-Espinoza. 2008. Late pre-hispanic polities of coastal Ecuador. In *Handbook of South American archaeology*, edited by Helaine Silverman and William H. Isbell, 505–525. New York: Springer.

McKibben, Bill. [1989] 1990. *The end of nature*. London: Penguin.

McKibben, Bill. 2007. *Deep economy: The wealth of communities and the durable future*. New York: St. Martin's Griffin.

McNally, David. 2020. *Blood and money: War, slavery, finance, and empire*. Chicago, IL: Haymarket.

McNeill, Desmond. 2020. *Fetishism and the theory of value: Reassessing Marx in the 21st century*. Houndmills: Palgrave Macmillan.

Meadows, Donella H., Dennis L. Meadows, Jorgen Randers, and William W. Behrens III. 1972. *Limits to growth*. New York: New American Library.

Menzies, Charles R., editor. 2006. *Traditional ecological knowledge and natural resource management*. Lincoln: University of Nebraska Press.

Merchant, Carolyn. 1980. *The death of nature: Women, ecology and the scientific revolution*. New York: Harper & Row.

Merchant, Carolyn. 1989. *Ecological revolutions: Nature, gender, and science in New England*. Chapel Hill: The University of North Carolina Press.

Merchant, Carolyn. 1992. *Radical ecology: The search for a livable world*. London: Routledge.

Merriam-Webster.com Dictionary. 2021. Value.

Milton, Kay. 2002. *Loving nature: Towards an ecology of emotion*. London: Routledge.

Mirowski, Philip. 1989. *More heat than light: Economics as social physics, physics as nature's economics*. New York: Cambridge University Press.

Mitcham, Carl. 1994. *Thinking through technology: The path between engineering and philosophy*. Chicago, IL: The University of Chicago Press.

Monbiot, George. 2007. *Heat: How we can stop the planet burning*. London: Penguin.

Monbiot, George. 2016. *How did we get into this mess? Politics, equality, nature*. London: Verso.

Moore, Jason W. 2015. *Capitalism in the web of life: Ecology and the accumulation of capital*. London: Verso.

Moore, Jason W., editor. 2016. *Anthropocene or capitalocene? Nature, history, and the crisis of capitalism*. Oakland, CA: PM Press.

Moore, John H. 1994. Putting anthropology back together again: The ethnogenetic critique of cladistic theory. *American Anthropologist* 96(4): 925–948.

Morris, Rosalind C. 2017. After de Brosses: Fetishism, translation, comparativism, critique. In *The returns of fetishism: Charles de Brosses and the afterlives of an idea*, edited by Rosalind C. Morris and Daniel H. Leonard, 133–319. Chicago, IL: The University of Chicago Press.

Morris, Rosalind C., and Daniel H. Leonard. 2017. *The returns of fetishism: Charles de Brosses and the afterlives of an idea*. Chicago, IL: The University of Chicago Press.

Moseley, Fred. 2016. *Money and totality: A macro-monetary interpretation of Marx's logic in Capital and the end of the 'transformation problem.'* Leiden: Brill.

Mulvaney, Dustin. 2019. *Solar power: Innovation, sustainability, and environmental justice*. Oakland: University of California Press.

Muradian, Roldan, Martin O'Connor, and Joan Martinez-Alier. 2002. Embodied pollution in trade: Estimating the environmental load displacement of industrialised countries. *Ecological Economics* 41(1): 51–67.

Murphy, Tom W. Jr., D.J. Murphy, T.F. Love, M.L.A. LeHew, and B.J. McCall. 2021. Modernity is incompatible with planetary limits: Developing a PLAN for the future. *Energy Research & Social Science* 81: 102239.

Murra, John V. 1955. The economic organization of the Inca state. Doctoral dissertation, University of Chicago.

Murra, John V. 1958. On Inca political structure. In *Systems of political control and bureaucracy in human societies*, edited by V.F. Ray, 30–41. Washington, DC: American Ethnological Society.

Murra, John V. 1962. Cloth and its functions in the Inca state. *American Anthropologist* 64(4): 710–728.

Murra, John V. [1969] 2017. *Reciprocity and redistribution in Andean civilizations: The 1969 Lewis Henry Morgan lectures*. Prepared by Freda Yancy Wolf and Heather Lechtman. Chicago, IL: HAU Books.

Muysken, Pieter, and Mily Crevels. 2020. Patterns of dispersal and diversification in South America. In *Language dispersal, diversification, and contact*, edited by Mily Crevels and Pieter Muysken, 253–274. Oxford: Oxford University Press.

Nadasdy, Paul. 2005. Transcending the debate over the ecologically noble Indian: Indigenous peoples and environmentalism. *Ethnohistory* 52(2): 291–331.

Naess, Arne. [1976] 1989. *Ecology, community and lifestyle: Outline of an ecosophy*. Cambridge: Cambridge University Press.

Nazarea, Virginia, editor. 1998. *Ethnoecology: Situated knowledge/located lives*. Tucson: University of Arizona Press.

Nelson, Anitra. 2022. *Beyond money: A post-capitalist strategy*. London: Pluto.

Nielsen, Axel E. 2013. Circulating objects and the constitution of South Andean society (500 BC–AD 1550). In *Merchants, markets, and exchange in the pre-Columbian world*, edited by Kenneth G. Hirth and Joanne Pillsbury, 389–418. Washington, DC: Dumbarton Oaks Research Library and Collection.

North, Peter. 2007. *Money and liberation: The micropolitics of alternative currency movements*. Minneapolis: University of Minnesota Press.

Nöth, Winfried. 1998. Ecosemiotics. *Sign Systems Studies* 26: 332–343.

Oakley, Todd. 2023. Semiotics in money and finance. Bloomsbury Semiotics 2.

O'Connor, James. 1988. Capitalism, nature, socialism: A theoretical introduction. *Capitalism, Nature, Socialism* 1(1): 11–38.

O'Connor, James. 1998. *Natural causes: Essays in ecological Marxism*. New York: Guilford.

O'Connor, Martin, editor. 1994. *Is capitalism sustainable? Political economy and the politics of ecology*. New York: Guilford.

Odum, Howard T. 1971. Environment, power, and society. Hoboken, NJ: Wiley-Interscience.

Odum, Howard T. 1988. Self-organization, transformity, and information. *Science* 242: 1132–1139.

Odum, Howard T. 1996. *Environmental accounting: Emergy and environmental decision making*. New York: John Wiley & Sons.

Odum, Howard T., and Jan E. Arding. 1991. Emergy analysis of shrimp mariculture in Ecuador. Working paper. Narragansett, RI: Coastal Resources Center, University of Rhode Island.

Owen, Bruce. 2001. The economy of metal and shell wealth goods. In *Empire and domestic economy*, edited by Terence N. D'Altroy and Christine A. Hastorf, 265–293. New York: Kluwer Academic/Plenum.

Panitch, Leo, and Colin Leys, editors. 2006. Coming to terms with nature. Socialist Register 2007. New York: Monthly Review Press.

Parkhill, Thomas C. 1997. *Weaving ourselves into the land: Charles Godfrey Leland, 'Indians,' and the study of Native American religions*. Albany: State University of New York Press.

Parrique, Timothée, Jonathan Barth, Francois Briens, Christian Kerschner, Alejo Kraus-Polk, Anna Kuokkanen, and Joachim H. Spangenberg. 2019. *Decoupling debunked: Evidence and arguments against green growth as a sole strategy for sustainability*. Brussels: European Environmental Bureau.

Pels, Peter. 1998. The spirit of matter: On fetish, rarity, fact, and fancy. In *Border fetishisms: Material objects in unstable spaces*, edited by Patricia Spyer, 91–121. London: Routledge.

Pérez Rincón, Mario. 2006. Colombian international trade from a physical perspective: Towards an ecological 'Prebisch Thesis.' *Ecological Economics* 59: 519–529.

Peters, Glen P., Jan C. Minx, Christopher L. Weber, and Ottmar Edenhofer. 2011. Growth in emission transfers via international trade from 1990 to 2008. *PNAS* 108(21): 8903–8908.

Phillips, Leigh. 2015. *Austerity ecology and the collapse-porn addicts: A defence of growth, progress, industry and stuff*. Winchester: Zero Books.

Pietz, William. 1985. The problem of the fetish, I. *RES: Anthropology and Aesthetics* 9: 5–17.

Pietz, William. 1987. The problem of the fetish, II: The origin of the fetish. *RES: Anthropology and Aesthetics* 13: 23–45.

Pietz, William. 1988. The problem of the fetish, IIIa: Bosman's Guinea and the Enlightenment theory of fetishism. *RES: Anthropology and Aesthetics* 16: 105–124.

Pietz, William. 2021. Fetishism. In *Encyclopedia of African religions and philosophy*, edited by Valentin-Yves Mudimbe and Kasereka Kavwahirehi, 266–267. New York: Springer.

Plumwood, Val. 2002. *Environmental culture: The ecological crisis of reason*. London: Routledge.

Polanyi, Karl. [1944] 1957. *The great transformation: The political and economic origins of our time*. Boston, MA: Beacon.

Pomeranz, Kenneth. 2000. *The great divergence: China, Europe, and the making of the modern world economy*. Princeton, NJ: Princeton University Press.

Pomeranz, Kenneth, and Steven Topik. 1999. *The world that trade created: Society, culture, and the world economy, 1400 to the present*. Armonk, NY: M.E. Sharpe.

Posey, Darrell A., and William Balée, editors. 1989. Resource management in Amazonia: Indigenous and folk strategies. Advances in Economic Botany 7: 1–287.

Prieto, Pedro A., and Charles A. S. Hall 2013. *Spain's photovoltaic revolution: The energy return on investment*. New York: Springer.

Rabinbach, Anson. 1990. *The human motor: Energy, fatigue, and the origins of modernity*. New York: Basic Books.

Ramos, Alcida R. 2003. Comment on Adam Kuper, 'The return of the native.' *Current Anthropology* 44(3): 397–398.

Rappaport, Roy A. 1979. Ecology, meaning, and religion. Berkeley, CA: North Atlantic Books.

Rappaport, Roy A. 1994. Humanity's evolution and anthropology's future. In *Assessing cultural anthropology*, edited by Robert Borofsky, 152–166. New York: McGraw-Hill.

Relph, Edward. 1976. *Place and placelessness*. London: Pion.

Rice, James. 2007. Ecological unequal exchange: International trade and uneven utilization of environmental space in the world-system. *Social Forces* 85(3): 1369–1392.

Ritzer, George. 1993. *The McDonaldization of society: An investigation into the changing character of contemporary social life*. Newbury Park, CA: Pine Forge Press.

Roberts, J. Timmons, and Bradley C. Parks. 2009. Ecologically unequal exchange, ecological debt, and climate justice: The history and implications of three related ideas for a new social movement. *International Journal of Comparative Sociology* 50(3–4): 385–409.

Rogers, Heather. 2010. *Green gone wrong: Dispatches from the front lines of eco-capitalism.* London: Verso.

Roos, Andreas. 2023. *Solar technology and global environmental justice: The vision and the reality.* London: Routledge.

Rosenswig, Robert M. 2023. Understanding money; or, why social and financial accounting should not be conflated. *Economic Anthropology* 11: 71–86.

Rosenswig, Robert M. 2024. Money, currency, and heterodox macroeconomics for archaeology. *Current Anthropology* 65(2): 235–266.

Rostworowski de Diez Canseco, María. 1977. Coastal fishermen, merchants, and artisans in pre-Hispanic Peru. In *The sea in the pre-Columbian world*, edited by Elizabeth P. Benson, 167–186. Washington, DC: Dumbarton Oaks Research Library and Collection.

Rowe, John H. 1946. Inca culture at the time of the Spanish conquest. In *Handbook of South American Indians*, bulletin 143, vol. 2, *The Andean civilizations*, edited by Julian Steward, 183–330. Washington, DC: Bureau of American Ethnology.

Sahlins, Marshall. 1972. *Stone Age economics.* Chicago, IL: Aldine.

Sahlins, Marshall. 1976. *Culture and practical reason.* Chicago, IL: The University of Chicago Press.

Sahlins, Marshall. 1999. Two or three things that I know about culture. *MAN: Journal of the Royal Anthropological Institute* (n.s.) 5: 399–421.

Sahlins, Marshall. 2014. On the ontological scheme of *Beyond nature and culture. HAU: Journal of Ethnographic Theory* 4(1): 281–290.

Sahlins, Marshall. 2022. *The new science of the enchanted universe: An anthropology of most of humanity.* Princeton, NJ: Princeton University Press.

Saito, Kohei. 2022. *Marx in the Anthropocene: Towards the idea of degrowth communism.* Cambridge: Cambridge University Press.

Salleh, Ariel. [1997] 2017. *Ecofeminism as politics: Nature, Marx and the postmodern.* Ebook edition. London: Zed Books.

Sallnow, Mike J. 1989. Precious metals in the Andean moral economy. In *Money and the morality of exchange*, edited by Jonathan Parry and Maurice Bloch, 209–231. Cambridge: Cambridge University Press.

Salomon, Frank. 1977/1978. *Pochteca* and *mindalá*: A comparison of long-distance traders in Ecuador and Mesoamerica. *Journal of the Steward Anthropological Society* 9(1/2): 231–248.

Salomon, Frank. 1986a. *Native lords of Quito in the age of the Incas: The political economy of North Andean chiefdoms.* Cambridge: Cambridge University Press.

Salomon, Frank. 1986b. Vertical politics on the Inka frontier. In *Anthropological history of Andean polities*, edited by John V. Murra, Nathan Wachtel, and Jacques Revel, 89–117. Cambridge: Cambridge University Press.

Salomon, Frank. 1987. Ancestors, grave robbers, and the possible antecedents of Cañari "Inca-ism." In *Natives and neighbors in South America: Anthropological essays*, edited by Harald O. Skar and Frank Salomon, 207–232. Göteborgs Etnografiska Museum. Ethnological Studies 38.

Salomon, Frank. 2018. *At the mountains' altar: Anthropology of religion in an Andean community.* London: Routledge.

Samaniego, Pablo, María C. Vallejo, and Joan Martinez-Alier. 2017. Commercial and biophysical deficits in South America, 1990–2013. *Ecological Economics* 133: 62–73.

Sandweiss, Daniel H., and David A. Reid. 2016. Negotiated subjugation: Maritime trade and the incorporation of Chincha into the Inca Empire. *Journal of Island and Coastal Archaeology* 11: 311–325.

Schandl, Heinz, Marina Fischer-Kowalski, James West, Stefan Giljum, M. Dittrich, Nina Eisenmenger, Arne Geschke, M. Lieber, Hanspeter Wieland, Anke Schaffartzik, Fridolin Krausmann, S. Gierlinger, K. Hosking, Manfred Lenzen, Hiroki Tanikawa, Alessio Miatto, and Tomer Fishman. 2016. Global material flows and resource productivity: Assessment Report for the UNEP International Resource Panel. Paris: United Nations Environment Programme.

Scharff, Robert C., and Val Dusek, editors. 2014. *Philosophy of technology – the technological condition: An anthology*. Oxford: Wiley Blackwell.

Schmidt, Max. 1917. Die Aruaken: Ein beitrag zum problem der kulturverbreitung. PhD thesis, Universität Leipzig, Leipzig.

Schumacher, Ernst F. 1973. *Small is beautiful: A study of economics as if people mattered*. New York: Harper and Row.

Scott, James C. 1998. *Seeing like a state: How certain schemes to improve the human condition have failed*. New Haven, CT: Yale University Press.

Scott, James C. 2017. *Against the grain: A deep history of the earliest states*. New Haven, CT: Yale University Press.

Scranton, Roy. 2015. *Learning to die in the Anthropocene: Reflections on the end of a civilization*. San Francisco, CA: City Lights Books.

Seaford, Richard. 2004. *Money and the early Greek mind: Homer, philosophy, tragedy*. Cambridge: Cambridge University Press.

Seaford, Richard. 2020. *The origins of philosophy in ancient Greece and ancient India: A historical comparison*. Cambridge: Cambridge University Press.

Sebeok, Thomas A. 1994. *Signs: An introduction to semiotics*. Toronto: University of Toronto Press.

Servet, Jean-Michel. 2009. Toward an alternative economy: Reconsidering the market, money, and value. In *Market and society: The great transformation today*, edited by Chris Hann and Keith Hart, 72–90. Cambridge: Cambridge University Press.

Seung-Yoon Lee, Sophia, Ji-eun Lee, and Kyo-seong Kim. 2020. Evaluating basic income, basic service, and basic voucher for social and ecological sustainability. *Sustainability* 12: 8348.

Seyfang, Gill, and Noel Longhurst. 2013. Growing green money? Mapping community currencies for sustainable development. *Ecological Economics* 86: 65–77.

Shimada, Izumi, and John F. Merkel. 2021. *Naipes: Functions and significance of Middle Sicán standardized sheetmetal artifacts*. Ñawpa Pacha 41(2): 211–249.

Shweder, Richard A., and Edmund J. Bourne. 1984. Does the concept of the person vary cross-culturally? In *Culture theory: Essays on mind, self, and emotion*, edited by Richard A. Shweder and Robert A. LeVine, 159–199. Cambridge: Cambridge University Press.

Sieferle, Rolf P. 2001 [1982]. *The subterranean forest: Energy systems and the industrial revolution*. Cambridge: White Horse Press.

Sillar, Bill. 2009. The social agency of things? Animism and materiality in the Andes. *Cambridge Archaeological Journal* 19(3): 367–377.

Sillar, Bill. 2012. Accounting for the spread of Quechua and Aymara between Cuzco and Lake Titicaca. In *Archaeology and language in the Andes: A cross-disciplinary exploration of prehistory*, edited by Paul Heggarty and David Beresford-Jones, 295–319. Proceedings of the British Academy 173. Oxford: Oxford University Press.

Sillitoe, Paul, editor. 2007. *Local science vs. global science: Approaches to indigenous knowledge in international development.* Oxford: Berghahn Books.

Simas, Moana, Richard Wood, and Edgar Hertwich. 2014. Labour embodied in trade: The role of labour and energy productivity and implications for greenhouse gas emissions. *Journal of Industrial Ecology* 19(3): 343–356.

Simmel, Georg. [1900] 1990. *The philosophy of money*. London: Routledge.

Singh, Simron J., and R. Venkat Ramanujam. 2010. Exploring ecologically unequal exchange using land and labour appropriation: Trade in the Nicobar Islands, 1880–2000. In *International trade and environmental justice: Toward a global political ecology*, edited by Alf Hornborg and Andrew K. Jorgenson, 19–48. New York: Nova Science Publishers.

Skutnabb-Kangas, Tove, and David Harmon. 2017. Biological diversity and language diversity: Parallels and differences. In *The Routledge handbook of ecolinguistics*, edited by Hermine Penz and Alwin Fill, 11–25. New York: Routledge.

Skutnabb-Kangas, Tove, Luisa Maffi, and David Harmon. 2003. *Sharing a world of difference: The Earth's linguistic, cultural, and biological diversity*. Paris: UNESCO.

Smaje, Chris. 2020. *Small farm future: Making the case for a society built around local economies, self-provisioning, agricultural diversity, and a shared Earth*. London: Chelsea Green Publishing.

Smil, Vaclav. 2015. *Power density: A key to understanding energy sources and uses.* Cambridge, MA: MIT Press.

Smil, Vaclav. 2016. *Energy transitions: Global and national perspectives*. Santa Barbara, CA: Praeger.

Smil, Vaclav. 2017. *Energy and civilisation: A history*. Cambridge, MA: The MIT Press.

Smil, Vaclav. 2022. *How the world really works: A scientist's guide to our past, present and future*. London: Penguin.

Smith, Neil. [1984] 2010. *Uneven development: Nature, capital and the production of space*. London: Verso.

Sohn-Rethel, Alfred. 1978. *Intellectual and manual labour: A critique of epistemology*. Atlantic Highlands, NJ: Humanities Press.

Sokolovskii, Sergey, and Valery Tishkov. 1996. Ethnicity. In *Encyclopedia of social and cultural anthropology*, edited by Alan Barnard and Jonathan Spencer, 190–193. London: Routledge.

Soper, Kate. 1995. *What is nature? Culture, politics and the non-human*. Oxford: Blackwell.

Sovacool, Benjamin K. 2014. *Global energy justice: Problems, principles, and practices*. Cambridge: Cambridge University Press.

Sovacool, Benjamin K. 2017. Experts, theories, and electric mobility transitions: Toward an integrated conceptual framework for the adoption of electric vehicles. *Energy Research & Social Science* 27: 78–95.

Sovacool, Benjamin K. 2021a. Who are the victims of low-carbon transitions? Towards a political ecology of climate change mitigation. *Energy Research & Social Science* 73: 101916.

Sovacool, Benjamin K. 2021b. When subterranean slavery supports sustainability transitions? Power, patriarchy, and child labor in artisanal Congolese cobalt mining. *The Extractive Industries and Society* 8: 271–293.

Spyer, Patricia. 1998a. Introduction. In *Border fetishisms: Material objects in unstable spaces*, edited by Patricia Spyer, 1–11. London: Routledge.

Spyer, Patricia, editor. 1998b. *Border fetishisms: Material objects in unstable spaces.* London: Routledge.

Stanish, Charles, and Lawrence S. Coben. 2013. Barter markets in the pre-Hispanic Andes. In *Merchants, markets, and exchange in the pre-Columbian world*, edited by Kenneth G. Hirth and Joanne Pillsbury, 419–434. Washington, DC: Dumbarton Oaks Research Library and Collection.

Stark, Louisa R. 1972. Machaj-Juyai: Secret language of the Callahuayas. *Papers in Andean Linguistics* 1: 199–227.

Stiglitz, Joseph. 2021. Lecture, April 29, 2021, downloaded from Youtube.

Suzuki, David, and Peter Knudtson. 1992. *Wisdom of the elders: Sacred native stories of nature.* New York: Bantam Books.

Tainter, Joseph A. 1988. *The collapse of complex societies.* Cambridge: Cambridge University Press.

Taussig, Michael. 1980. *The devil and commodity fetishism in South America.* Chapel Hill: The University of North Carolina Press.

Taussig, Michael. 1992. *The nervous system.* London: Routledge.

Taylor, Bron. 1997. Earthen spirituality or cultural genocide? Radical environmentalism's appropriation of Native American spirituality. *Religion* 27: 183–215.

Taylor, Charles. 2012. What was the Axial revolution? In *The Axial Age and its consequences*, edited by Robert N. Bellah and Hans Joas, 30–46. Cambridge, MA: The Belknap Press of Harvard University Press.

Thoden van Velzen, Bonno. 1990. Social fetishism among the Surinamese Maroons. *Etnofoor* 3(1): 77–95.

Tom, Miye N., Elizabeth S. Huaman, and Teresa L. McCarty. 2019. Indigenous knowledges as vital contributions to sustainability. *International Review of Education* 65: 1–18.

Topic, John R. 2013. Exchange on the equatorial frontier: A comparison of Ecuador and Northern Peru. In *Merchants, markets, and exchange in the pre-Columbian world*, edited by Kenneth G. Hirth and Joanne Pillsbury, 335–360. Washington, DC: Dumbarton Oaks Research Library and Collection.

Torero, Alfredo. 1987. Lenguas y pueblos altiplánicos en torno al siglo XVI. *Revista Andina* 5(2): 329–405.

Torero, Alfredo. 2002. *Idiomas de los Andes: Lingüística e historia.* Lima: Instituto Francés de Estudios Andinos.

Trainer, Ted. 2020. *The simpler way: Collected writings of Ted Trainer*, edited by S. Alexander and J. Rutherford. Melbourne: Simplicity Institute.

Tylor, Edward B. 1871. *Primitive culture: Researches into the development of mythology, philosophy, religion, language, art, and custom.* London: John Murray.

Uexküll, Jakob v. [1940] 1982. The theory of meaning. *Semiotica* 42: 25–82.

United Nations Environment Programme (UNEP). 2024. Food waste index report 2024. New York: UNEP.

Vecsey, Christopher. 1980. American Indian environmental religions. In *American Indian environments: Ecological issues in Native American history*, edited by Christopher Vecsey and Robert W. Venables, 1–37. Syracuse, NY: Syracuse University Press.

Vilar, Pierre. 1976. *A history of gold and money 1450–1920.* London: Verso.

Viveiros de Castro, Eduardo. 1998. Cosmological deixis and Amerindian perspectivism. *Journal of the Royal Anthropological Institute* (n.s.) 4(3): 469–488.

Vogel, Steven. 1996. *Against nature: The concept of nature in critical theory*. Albany: State University of New York Press.
Wackernagel, Mathis, and William E. Rees. 1996. *Our ecological footprint: Reducing human impact on the Earth*. Gabriola Island, BC: New Society Publishers.
Wainwright, Joel, and Geoff Mann. 2018. *Climate Leviathan: A political theory of our planetary future*. London: Verso.
Wallace-Wells, David. 2019. *The uninhabitable Earth: A story of the future*. London: Allen Lane.
Wallerstein, Immanuel. 1974–1989. *The modern world-system*, 1–3. San Diego, CA: Academic Press.
Warburton, David A. 2018. Prices and values: Origins and early history in the Near East. In *Trade and civilization: Economic networks and cultural ties, from prehistory to the early modern era*, edited by Kristian Kristiansen, Thomas Lindkvist, and Janken Myrdal, 56–86. Cambridge: Cambridge University Press.
Warlenius, Rikard. 2016. Core and periphery in the early modern world system: A time-space appropriation assessment. In *Methods in world history: A critical approach*, edited by Arne Jarrick, Janken Myrdal, and Maria Wallenberg Bondesson, 185–225. Lund: Nordic Academic Press.
Wax, Murray L. 1997. Educating an anthro: The influence of Vine Deloria, Jr. In *Indians and anthropologists: Vine Deloria, Jr., and the critique of anthropology*. edited by Thomas Biolsi and Larry J. Zimmerman, 50–60. Tucson: The University of Arizona Press.
Weatherford, Jack. 1997. *The history of money: From sandstone to cyberspace*. New York: Three Rivers Press.
White, Leslie A. 1940. The symbol: The origin and basis of human behaviour. *Philosophy of Science* 7(4): 451–463.
Wiedmann, Thomas O., and Manfred Lenzen. 2018. Environmental and social footprints of international trade. *Nature Geoscience* 11: 314–321.
Wilcken, Patrick. 2010. *Claude Lévi-Strauss: The poet in the laboratory*. New York: Penguin.
Wilkinson, Darryl. 2022. Incas and Arawaks: A special relationship along the Andes-Amazonian frontier. *Andean Past* 13: Article 13.
Wilkinson, Richard G. 1973. *Poverty and progress: An ecological model of economic development*. London: Methuen.
Wilkinson, Toby C. 2018. Cloth and currency: On the ritual-economics of Eurasian textile circulation and the origins of trade, fifth to second millennia BC. In *Trade and civilization: Economic networks and cultural ties, from prehistory to the early modern era*, edited by Kristian Kristiansen, Thomas Lindkvist, and Janken Myrdal, 25–55. Cambridge: Cambridge University Press.
Wilson, Edward O. 1992. *The diversity of Life*. New York: W.W. Norton.
Winner, Langdon. 1980. Do artifacts have politics? *Daedalus* 109(1): 121–136.
Wittrock, Björn. 2012. The Axial Age in global history: Cultural crystallizations and societal transformations. In *The Axial Age and its consequences*, edited by Robert N. Bellah and Hans Joas, 102–125. Cambridge, MA: The Belknap Press of Harvard University Press.
Wolf, Eric R. 1982. *Europe and the people without history*. Berkeley: University of California Press.
World Commission on Environment and Development (WCED). 1987. *Our common future*. Oxford: Oxford University Press.

Wrigley, E. Anthony. 1988. *Continuity, chance, and change: The character of the Industrial Revolution in England*. Cambridge: Cambridge University Press.
WorldWide Fund for Nature (WWF). 2022. Living Planet Report 2022. Gland, Switzerland: WWF.
York, Richard, and Shannon E. Bell. 2019. Energy transitions or additions? Why a transition from fossil fuels requires more than the growth of renewable energy. *Energy Research & Social Science* 51: 40–43.
York, Richard, Eugene A. Rosa, and Thomas Dietz. 2003. Footprints on the Earth: The environmental consequences of modernity. *American Sociological Review* 68: 279–300.
Yu, Yang, Kuishuang Feng, and Klaus Hubacek. 2013. Tele-connecting local consumption to global land use. *Global Environmental Change* 23(5): 1178–1186.
Zalasiewicz, Jan, M. Williams, C.N. Waters, A.D. Barnosky, J. Palmesino, A-S. Rönnskog, M. Edgeworth, C. Neal, A. Cearreta, E.C. Ellis, J. Grinevald, P. Haff, J.A. Ivar do Sul, C. Jeandel, R. Leinfelder, J.R. McNeill, E. Odada, N. Oreskes, S.J. Price, A. Revkin, W. Steffen, C. Summerhayes, D. Vidas, S. Wing, and A.P. Wolfe. 2017. Scale and diversity of the physical technosphere: A geological perspective. *The Anthropocene Review* 4(1): 9–22.
Zehner, Ozzie. 2012. *Green illusions: The dirty secrets of clean energy and the future of environmentalism*. Lincoln: University of Nebraska Press.
Zerzan, John. 2002. *Running on emptiness: The pathology of civilization*. Los Angeles, CA: Feral House.
Zuboff, Shoshana. 2019. *The age of surveillance capitalism: The fight for a human future at the new frontier of power*. London: Profile Books.

Index

Note: Page numbers followed by "n" denote endnotes.